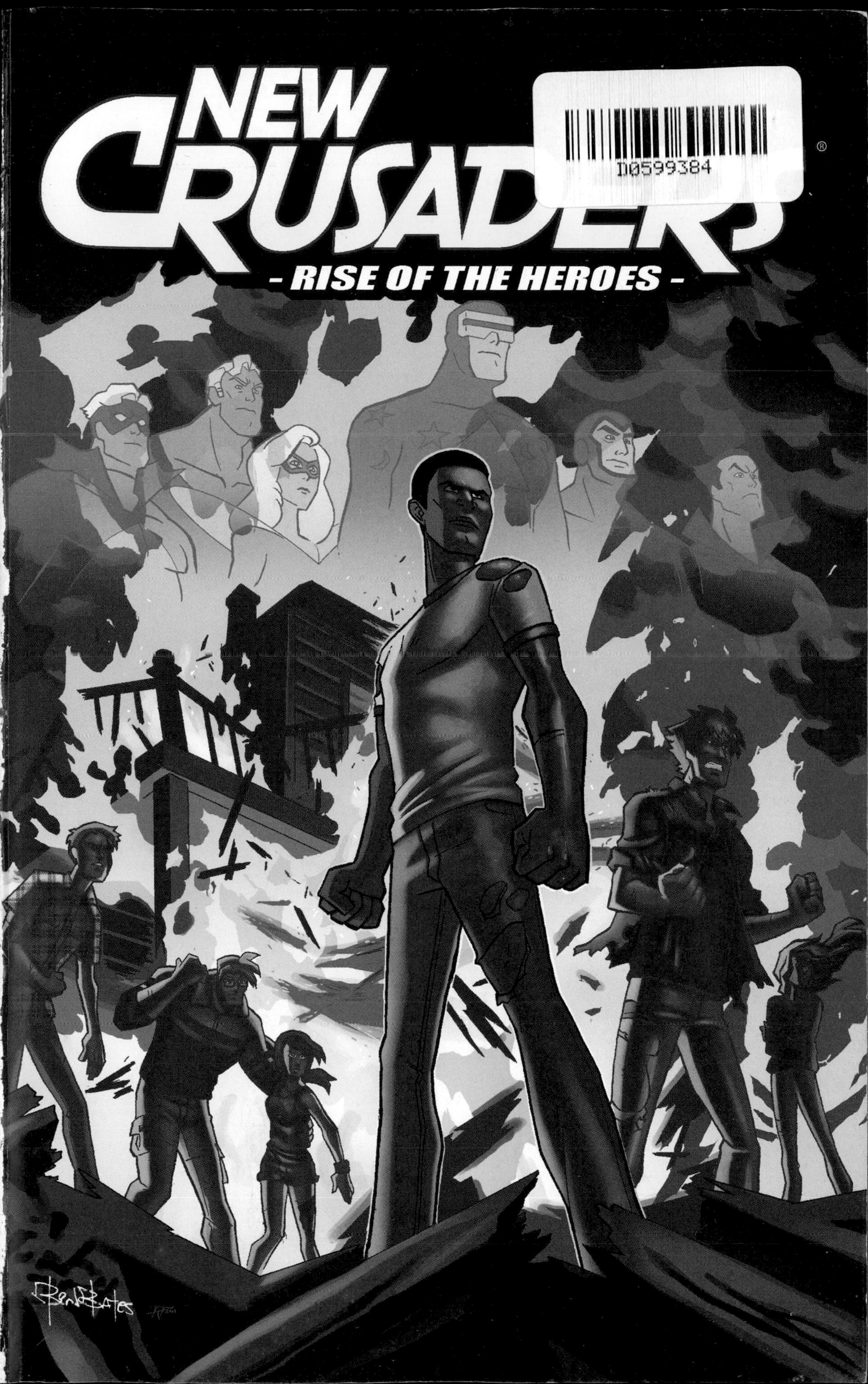
NEW CRUSADERS®
- RISE OF THE HEROES -

SHIELD™
JAGUAR™
WEB™
STEEL STERLING™
COMET™
FLY GIRL™
FIREBALL™

NEW CRUSADERS®
- RISE OF THE HEROES -

Writer: IAN FLYNN

Pencils (issues 1, 2, & 3): BEN BATES

Pencils (issues 3, 4, 5, & 6): ALITHA MARTINEZ

Inks: GARY MARTIN

Colors (issues 1-5): MATT HERMS

Colors (issue 6): STEVE DOWNER

Letters: JOHN WORKMAN

Assistant Editor: VINCENT LOVALLO

Editor/Exec. Director of Editorial: PAUL KAMINSKI

Editor-in-Chief: VICTOR GORELICK

President: MIKE PELLERITO

Publisher: JON GOLDWATER

RED CIRCLE Braintrust: IAN FLYNN, PAUL KAMINSKI, JIM SOKOLOWSKI AND MIKE PELLERITO

Special thanks to MICHAEL MURPHEY and IVERSE MEDIA

ARCHIE COMIC PUBLICATIONS, INC.

JONATHAN GOLDWATER, publisher/co-ceo
NANCY SILBERKLEIT, co-ceo
MIKE PELLERITO, president
VICTOR GORELICK, co-president/e-i-c
JIM SOKOLOWSKI, senior vice president sales/business development
HAROLD BUCHHOLZ, senior vice president publishing/operations
WILLIAM MOOAR, CFO
STEVE MOOAR, vice president of special projects
PAUL KAMINSKI, exec. director of editorial/compilation editor
VINCENT LOVALLO, assistant editor
STEVEN SCOTT, director of publicity & marketing
STEPHEN OSWALD, production manager
JAMIE LEE ROTANTE, proofreader/editorial assistant
ELIZABETH BORGATTI, design intern

NEW CRUSADERS, Book 1: Rise of the Heroes, 2013. Printed in Canada. Published by Archie Comic Publications, Inc., 325 Fayette Avenue, Mamaroneck, NY 10543-2318. Originally published in single magazine form in New Crusaders - Rise of the Heroes # 1-6. NEW CRUSADERS and RED CIRCLE COMICS ® ACP, Inc. The individual characters' names and likenesses are the exclusive trademarks of Archie Comic Publications, Inc.
ISBN: 978-1-936975-31-0

- RISE OF THE HEROES -

CHAPTER 1

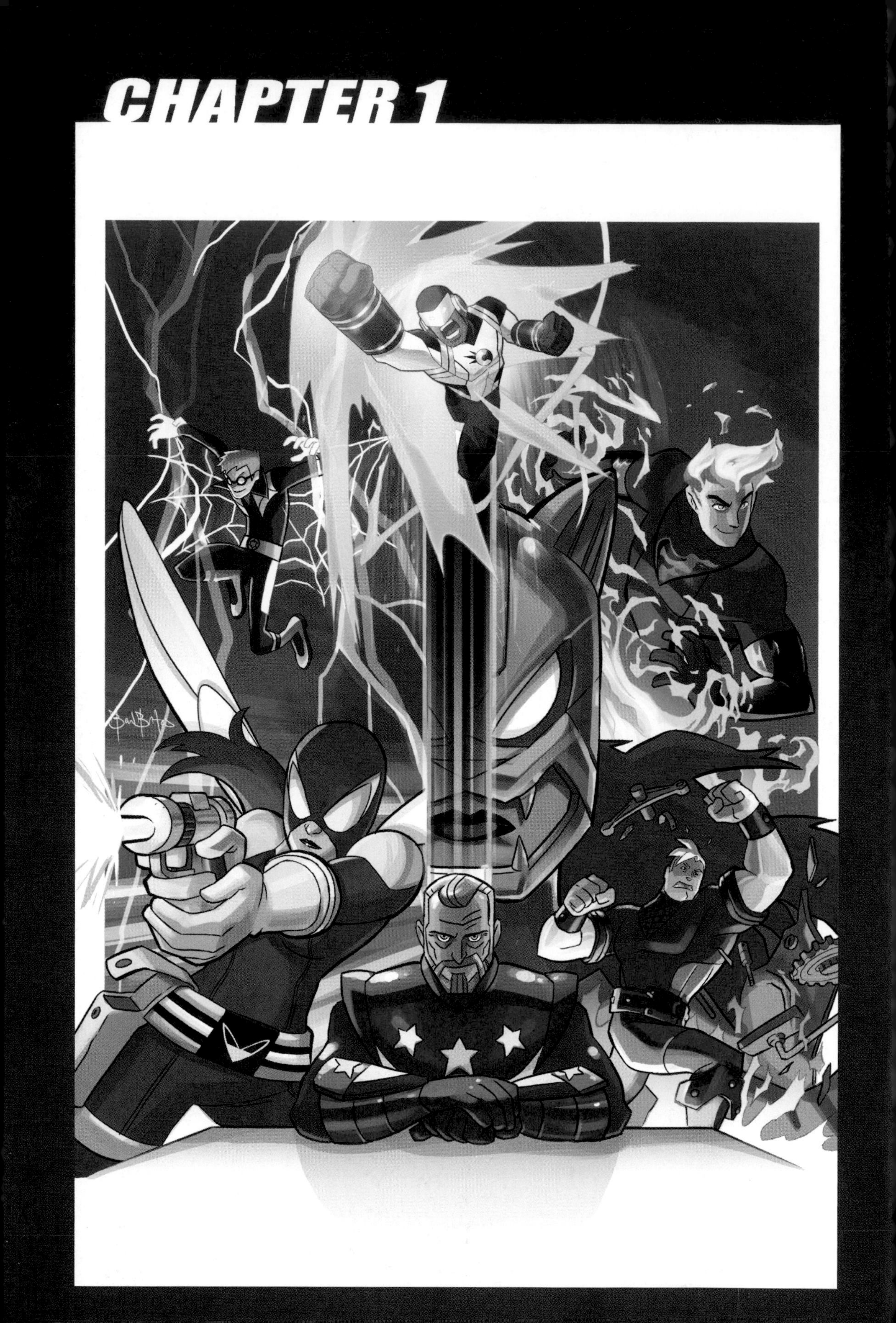

NEW CRUSADERS - RISE OF THE HEROES - ISSUE 1 COVER BY: BEN BATES

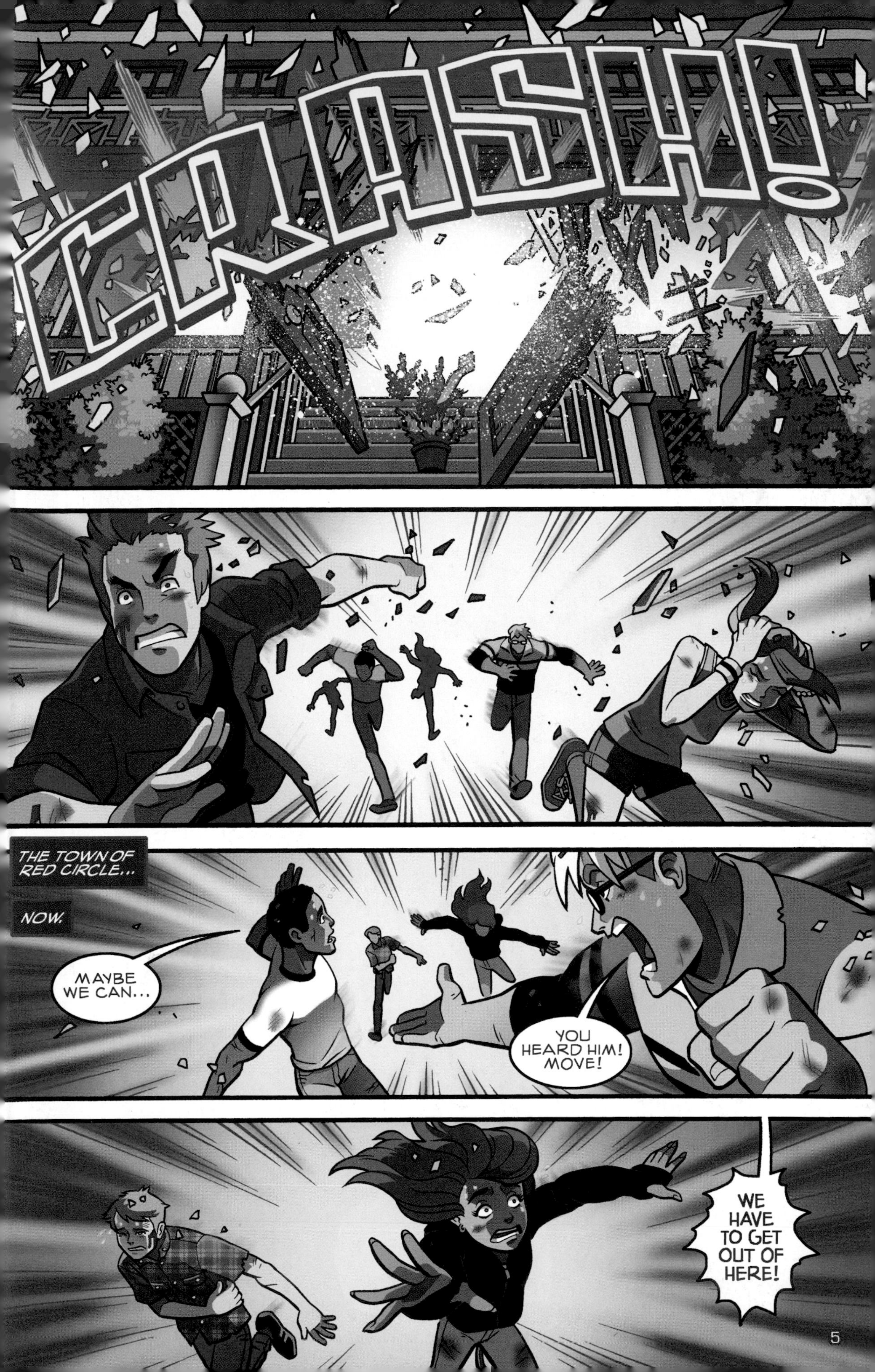
CRASH!
THE TOWN OF RED CIRCLE...
NOW.
MAYBE WE CAN...
YOU HEARD HIM! MOVE!
WE HAVE TO GET OUT OF HERE!

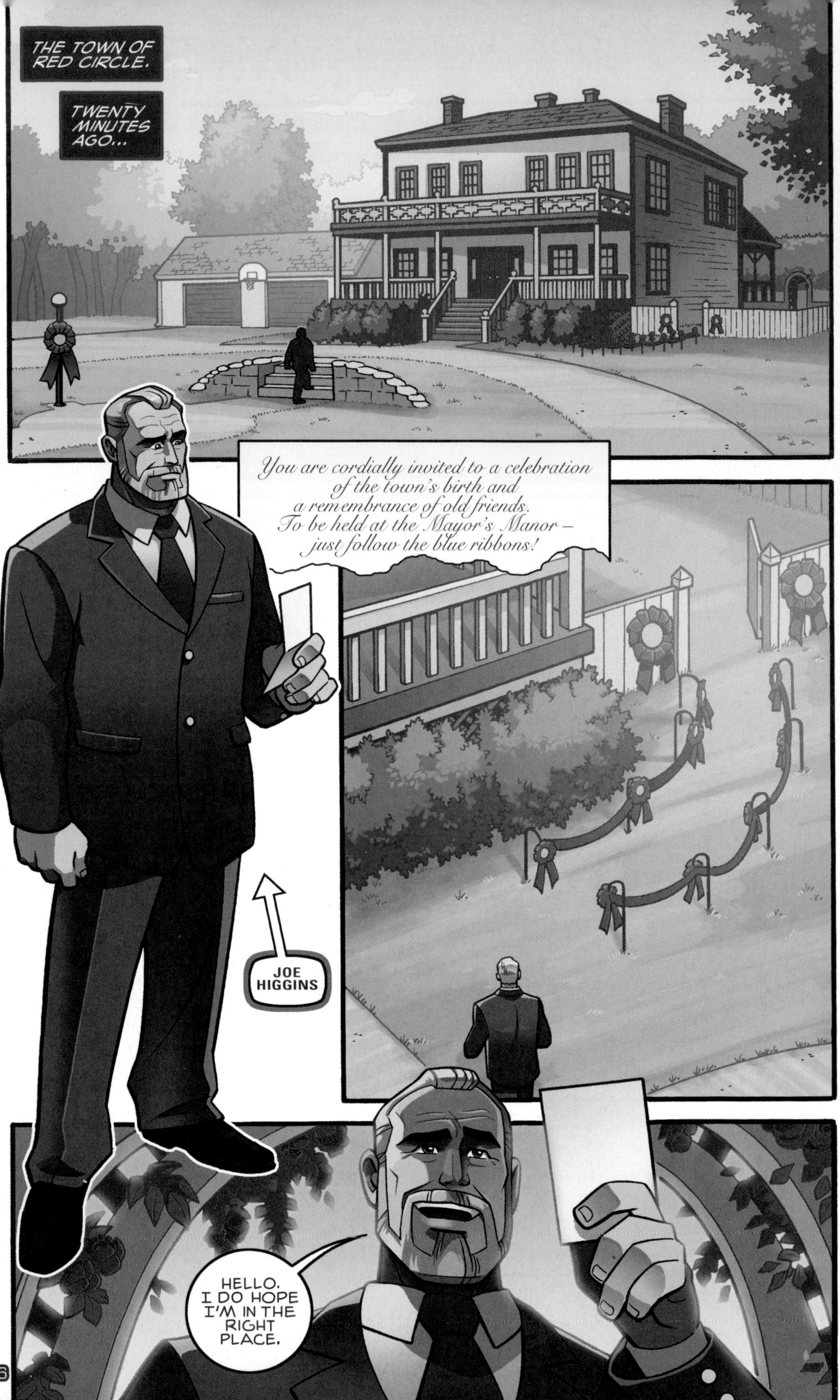
THE TOWN OF RED CIRCLE.
TWENTY MINUTES AGO...
You are cordially invited to a celebration of the town's birth and a remembrance of old friends. To be held at the Mayor's Manor – just follow the blue ribbons!
JOE HIGGINS
HELLO. I DO HOPE I'M IN THE RIGHT PLACE.

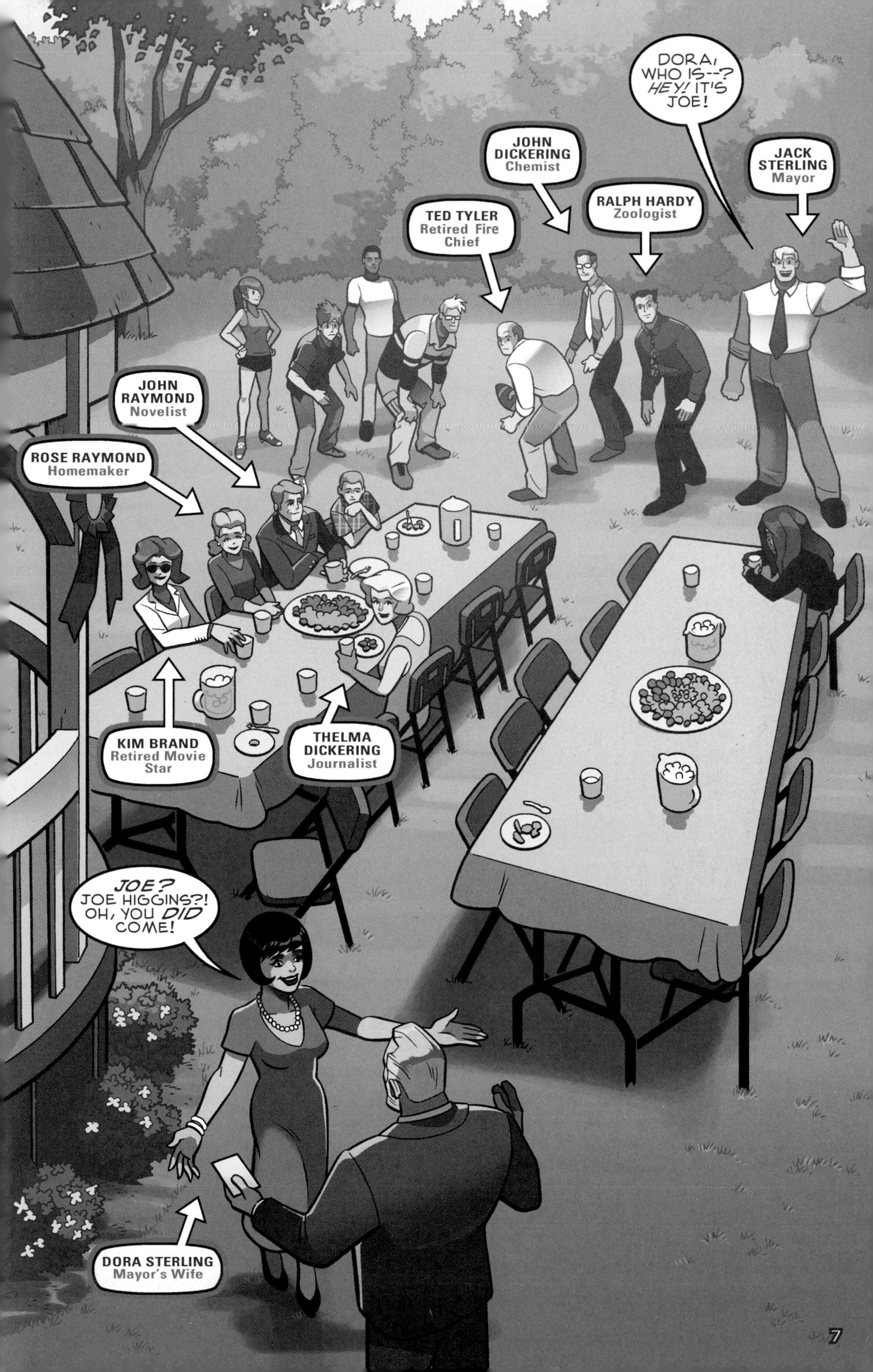

DORA, WHO IS--? HEY! IT'S JOE!
JOHN DICKERING Chemist
JACK STERLING Mayor
RALPH HARDY Zoologist
TED TYLER Retired Fire Chief
JOHN RAYMOND Novelist
ROSE RAYMOND Homemaker
KIM BRAND Retired Movie Star
THELMA DICKERING Journalist
JOE? JOE HIGGINS?! OH, YOU DID COME!
DORA STERLING Mayor's Wife

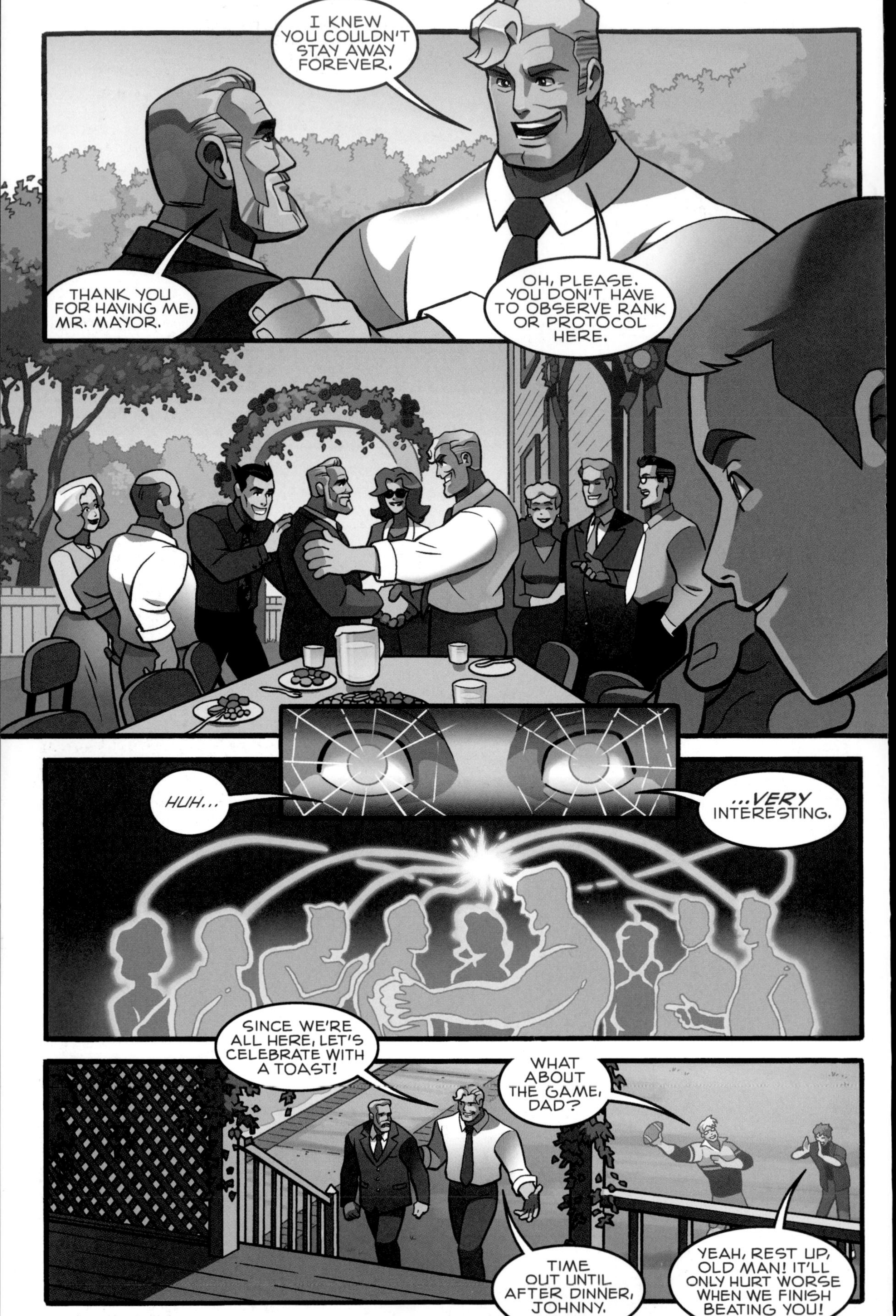
I KNEW YOU COULDN'T STAY AWAY FOREVER.
THANK YOU FOR HAVING ME, MR. MAYOR.
OH, PLEASE. YOU DON'T HAVE TO OBSERVE RANK OR PROTOCOL HERE.
HUH...
...VERY INTERESTING.
SINCE WE'RE ALL HERE, LET'S CELEBRATE WITH A TOAST!
WHAT ABOUT THE GAME, DAD?
TIME OUT UNTIL AFTER DINNER, JOHNNY.
YEAH, REST UP, OLD MAN! IT'LL ONLY HURT WORSE WHEN WE FINISH BEATING YOU!

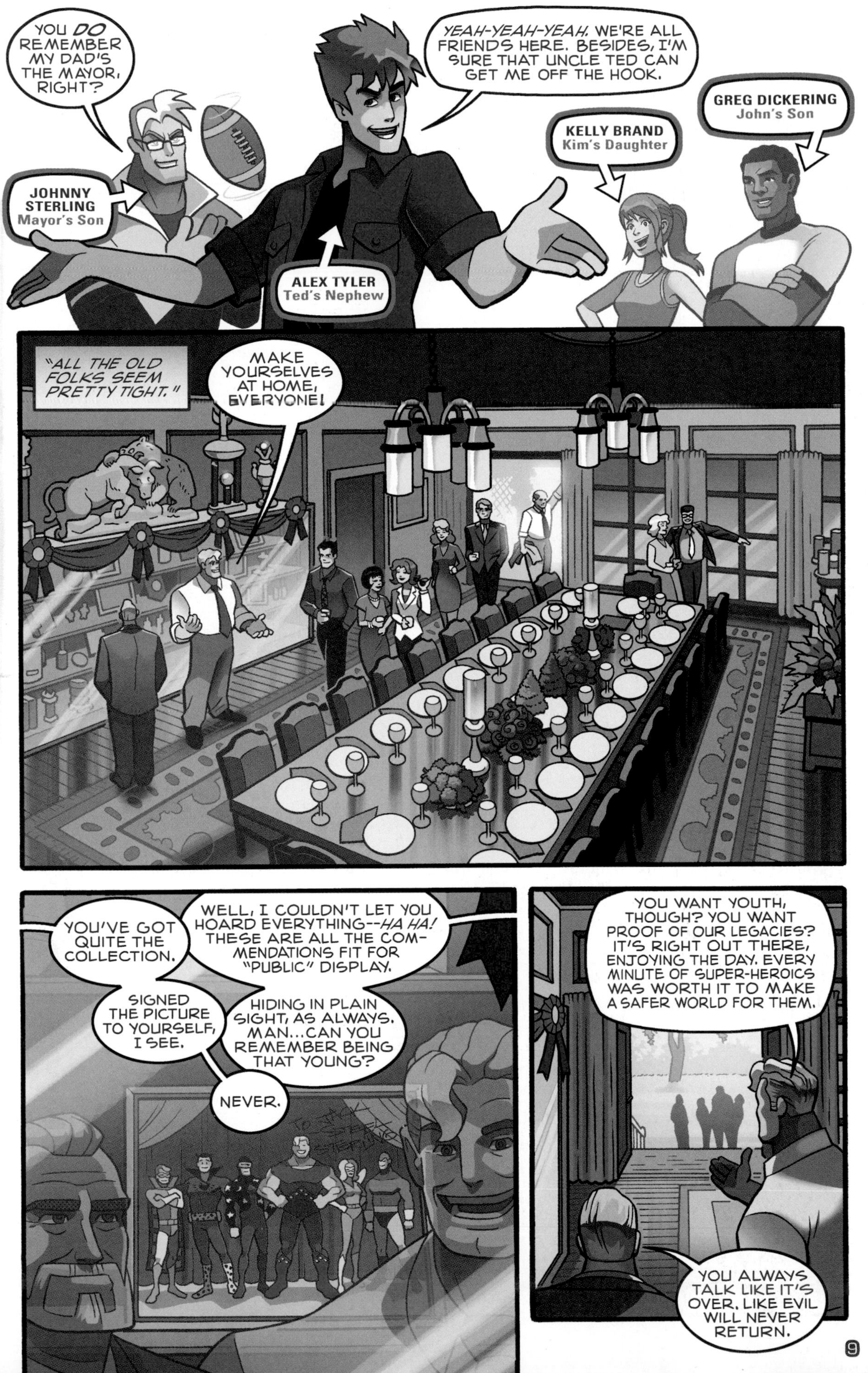

YOU *DO* REMEMBER MY DAD'S THE MAYOR, RIGHT?
YEAH-YEAH-YEAH. WE'RE ALL FRIENDS HERE. BESIDES, I'M SURE THAT UNCLE TED CAN GET ME OFF THE HOOK.
JOHNNY STERLING Mayor's Son
ALEX TYLER Ted's Nephew
KELLY BRAND Kim's Daughter
GREG DICKERING John's Son
"ALL THE OLD FOLKS SEEM PRETTY TIGHT."
MAKE YOURSELVES AT HOME, EVERYONE!
YOU'VE GOT QUITE THE COLLECTION.
WELL, I COULDN'T LET YOU HOARD EVERYTHING--*HA HA!* THESE ARE ALL THE COM-MENDATIONS FIT FOR "PUBLIC" DISPLAY.
SIGNED THE PICTURE TO YOURSELF, I SEE.
HIDING IN PLAIN SIGHT, AS ALWAYS. MAN...CAN YOU REMEMBER BEING THAT YOUNG?
NEVER.
YOU WANT YOUTH, THOUGH? YOU WANT PROOF OF OUR LEGACIES? IT'S RIGHT OUT THERE, ENJOYING THE DAY. EVERY MINUTE OF SUPER-HEROICS WAS WORTH IT TO MAKE A SAFER WORLD FOR THEM.
YOU ALWAYS TALK LIKE IT'S OVER, LIKE EVIL WILL NEVER RETURN.

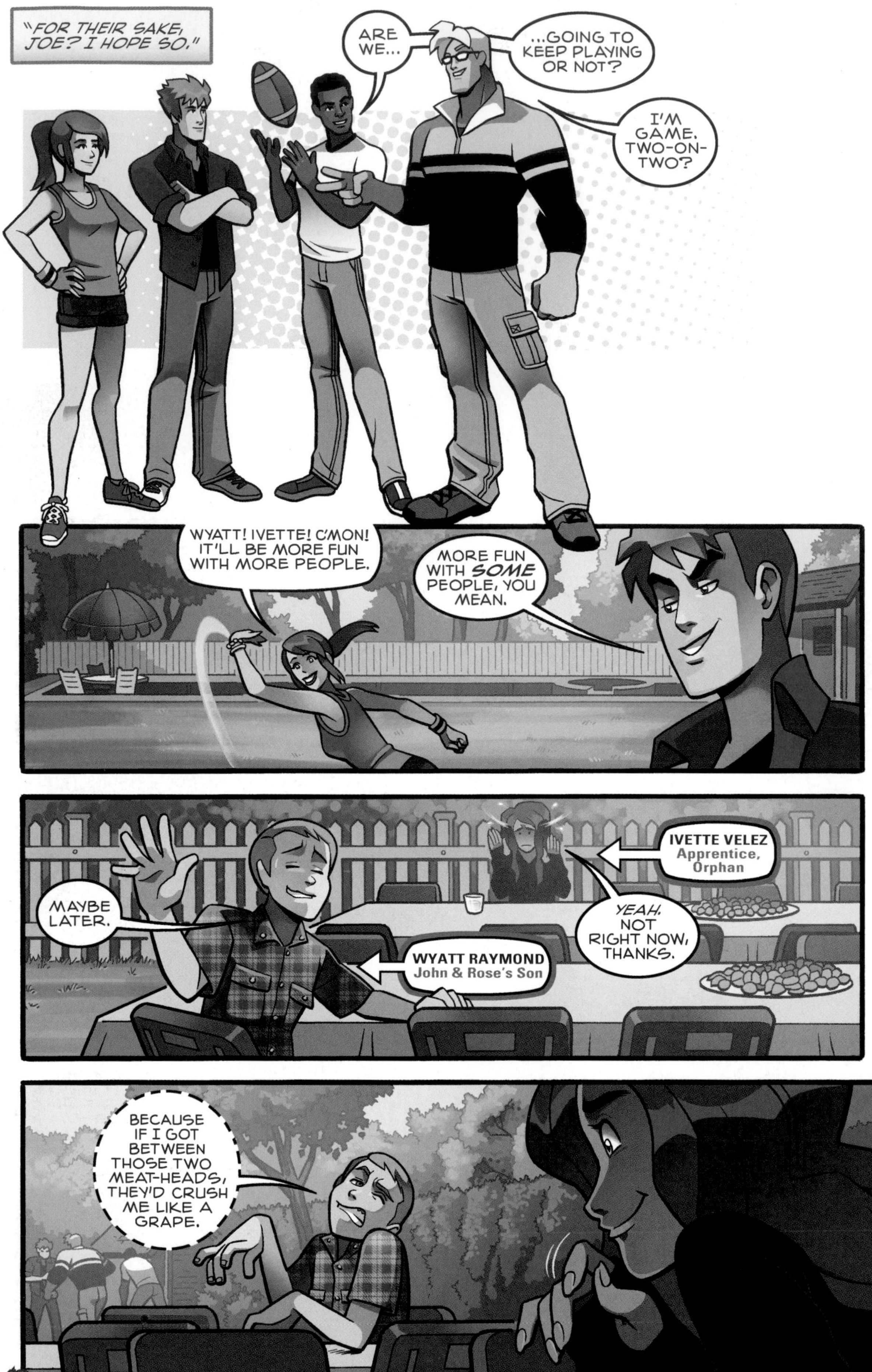
"FOR THEIR SAKE, JOE? I HOPE SO."
ARE WE...
...GOING TO KEEP PLAYING OR NOT?
I'M GAME. TWO-ON-TWO?
WYATT! IVETTE! C'MON! IT'LL BE MORE FUN WITH MORE PEOPLE.
MORE FUN WITH SOME PEOPLE, YOU MEAN.
IVETTE VELEZ Apprentice, Orphan
MAYBE LATER.
YEAH. NOT RIGHT NOW, THANKS.
WYATT RAYMOND John & Rose's Son
BECAUSE IF I GOT BETWEEN THOSE TWO MEAT-HEADS, THEY'D CRUSH ME LIKE A GRAPE.

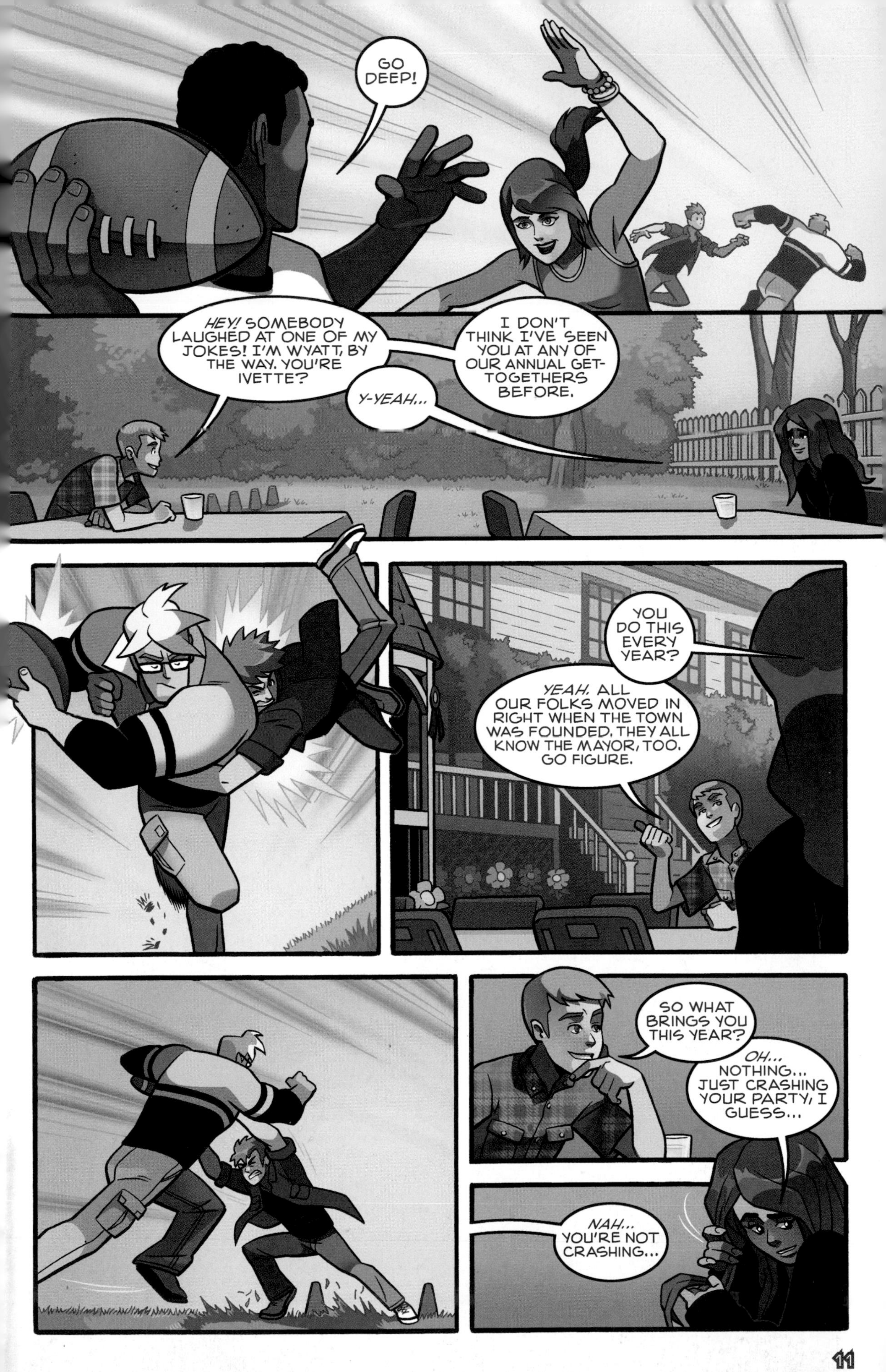
GO DEEP!
HEY! SOMEBODY LAUGHED AT ONE OF MY JOKES! I'M WYATT, BY THE WAY. YOU'RE IVETTE?
Y-YEAH...
I DON'T THINK I'VE SEEN YOU AT ANY OF OUR ANNUAL GET-TOGETHERS BEFORE.
YOU DO THIS EVERY YEAR?
YEAH. ALL OUR FOLKS MOVED IN RIGHT WHEN THE TOWN WAS FOUNDED. THEY ALL KNOW THE MAYOR, TOO. GO FIGURE.
SO WHAT BRINGS YOU THIS YEAR?
OH... NOTHING... JUST CRASHING YOUR PARTY, I GUESS...
NAH... YOU'RE NOT CRASHING...

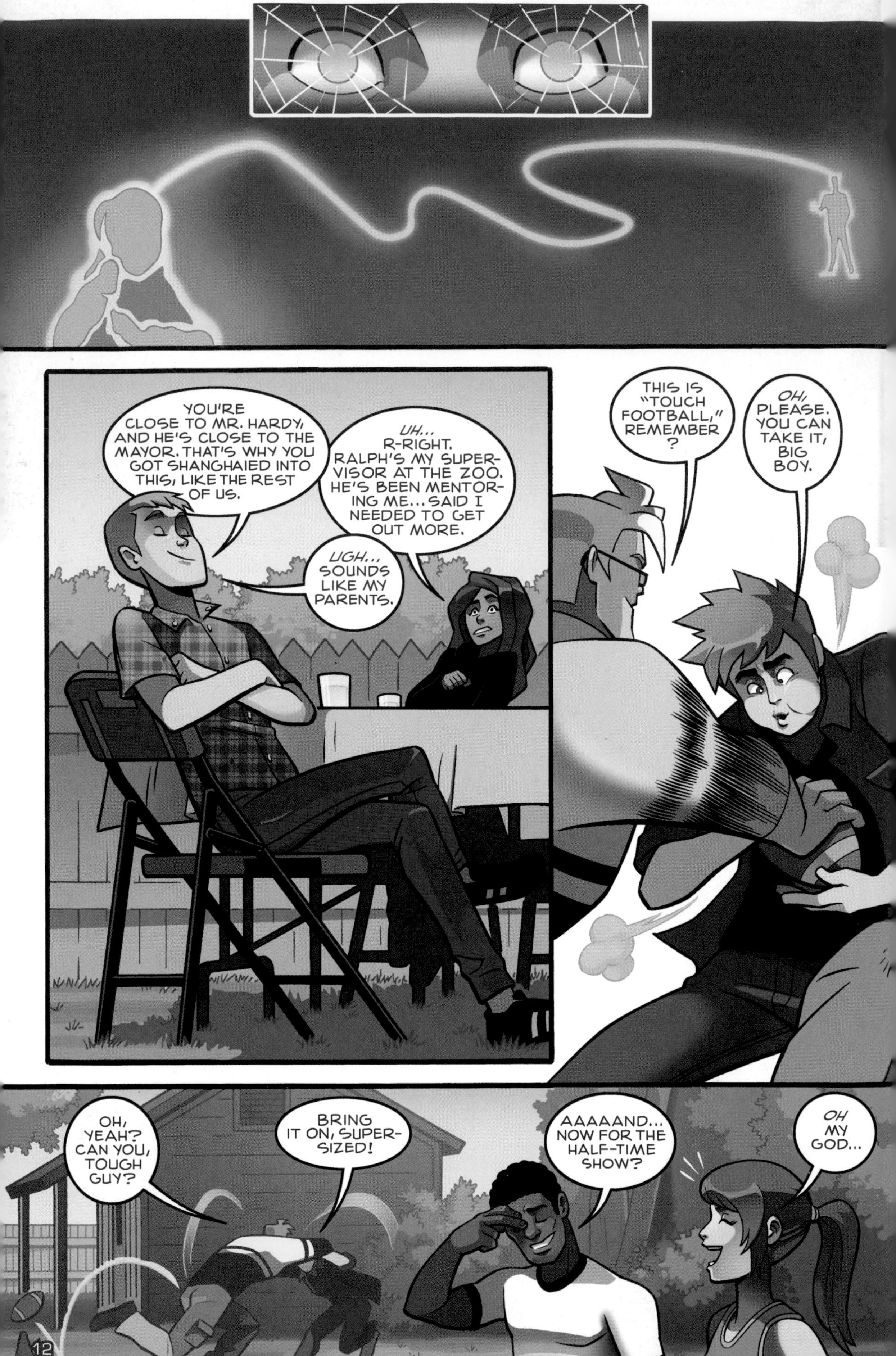
YOU'RE CLOSE TO MR. HARDY, AND HE'S CLOSE TO THE MAYOR. THAT'S WHY YOU GOT SHANGHAIED INTO THIS, LIKE THE REST OF US.
UH... R-RIGHT. RALPH'S MY SUPERVISOR AT THE ZOO. HE'S BEEN MENTORING ME... SAID I NEEDED TO GET OUT MORE.
UGH... SOUNDS LIKE MY PARENTS.
THIS IS "TOUCH FOOTBALL," REMEMBER?
OH, PLEASE. YOU CAN TAKE IT, BIG BOY.
OH, YEAH? CAN YOU, TOUGH GUY?
BRING IT ON, SUPER-SIZED!
AAAAAND... NOW FOR THE HALF-TIME SHOW?
OH MY GOD...

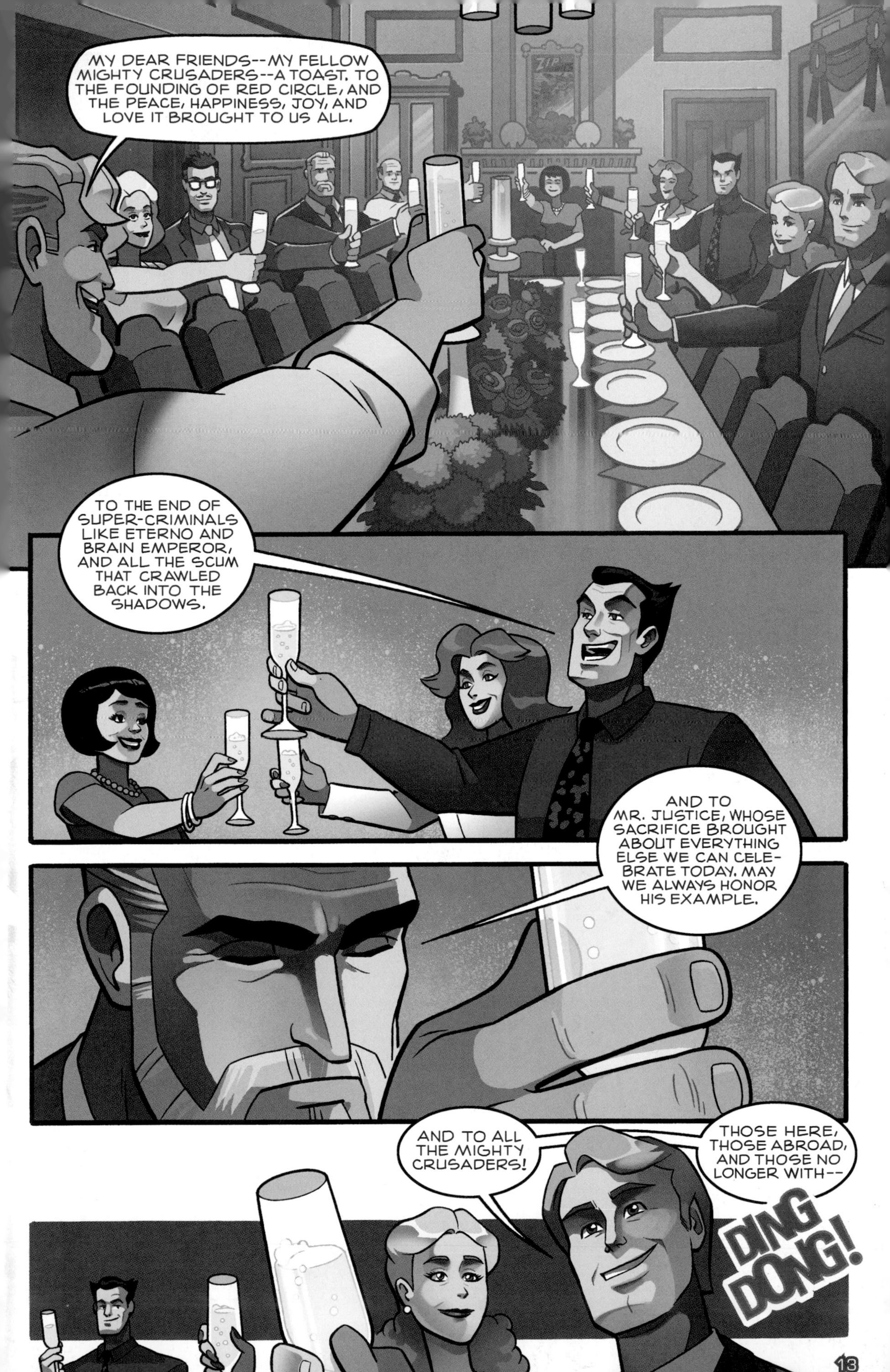
MY DEAR FRIENDS--MY FELLOW MIGHTY CRUSADERS--A TOAST. TO THE FOUNDING OF RED CIRCLE, AND THE PEACE, HAPPINESS, JOY, AND LOVE IT BROUGHT TO US ALL.
TO THE END OF SUPER-CRIMINALS LIKE ETERNO AND BRAIN EMPEROR, AND ALL THE SCUM THAT CRAWLED BACK INTO THE SHADOWS.
AND TO MR. JUSTICE, WHOSE SACRIFICE BROUGHT ABOUT EVERYTHING ELSE WE CAN CELE-BRATE TODAY. MAY WE ALWAYS HONOR HIS EXAMPLE.
AND TO ALL THE MIGHTY CRUSADERS!
THOSE HERE, THOSE ABROAD, AND THOSE NO LONGER WITH--
DING DONG!

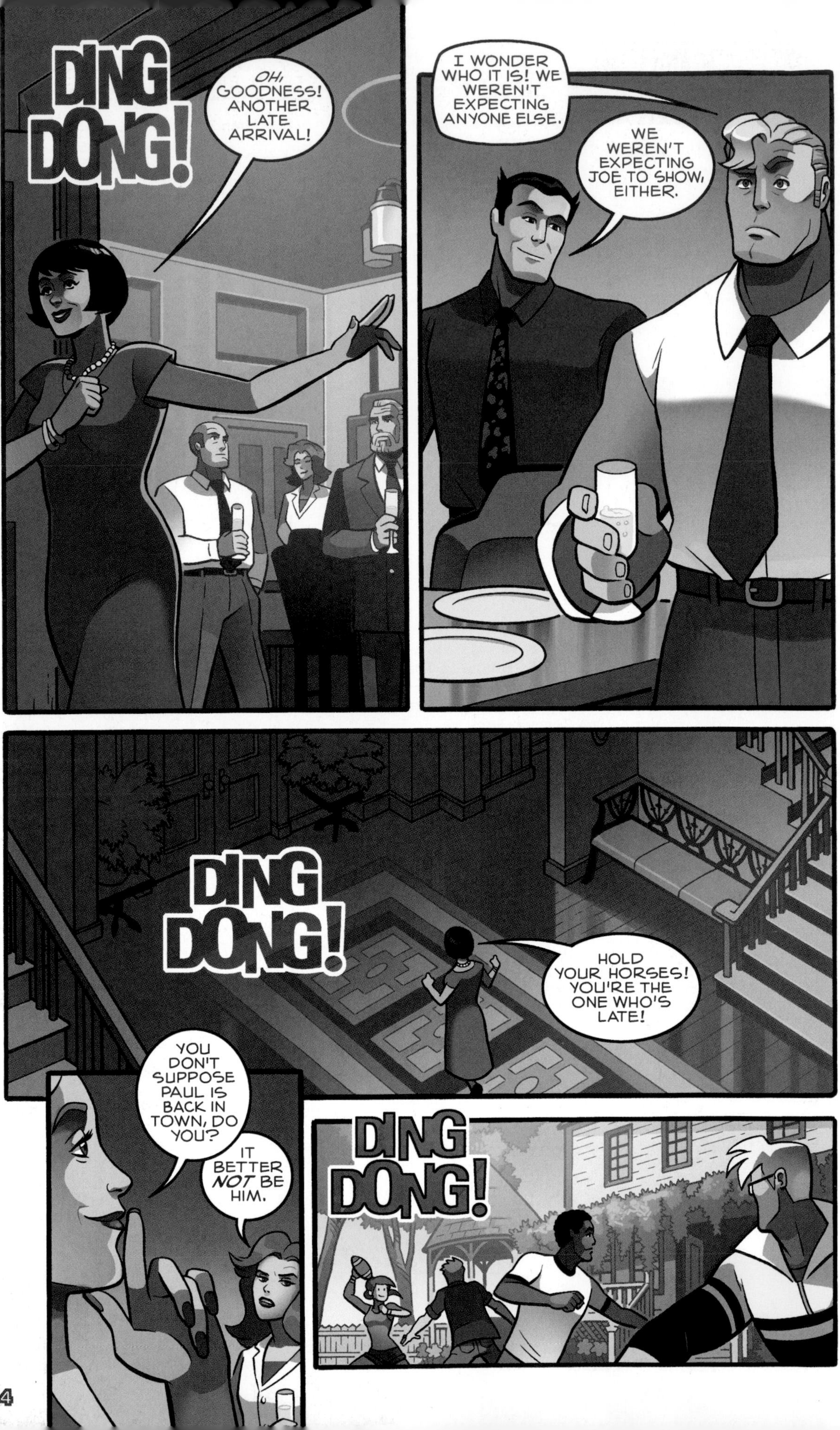
DING DONG!
OH, GOODNESS! ANOTHER LATE ARRIVAL!
I WONDER WHO IT IS! WE WEREN'T EXPECTING ANYONE ELSE.
WE WEREN'T EXPECTING JOE TO SHOW, EITHER.
DING DONG!
HOLD YOUR HORSES! YOU'RE THE ONE WHO'S LATE!
YOU DON'T SUPPOSE PAUL IS BACK IN TOWN, DO YOU?
IT BETTER NOT BE HIM.
DING DONG!

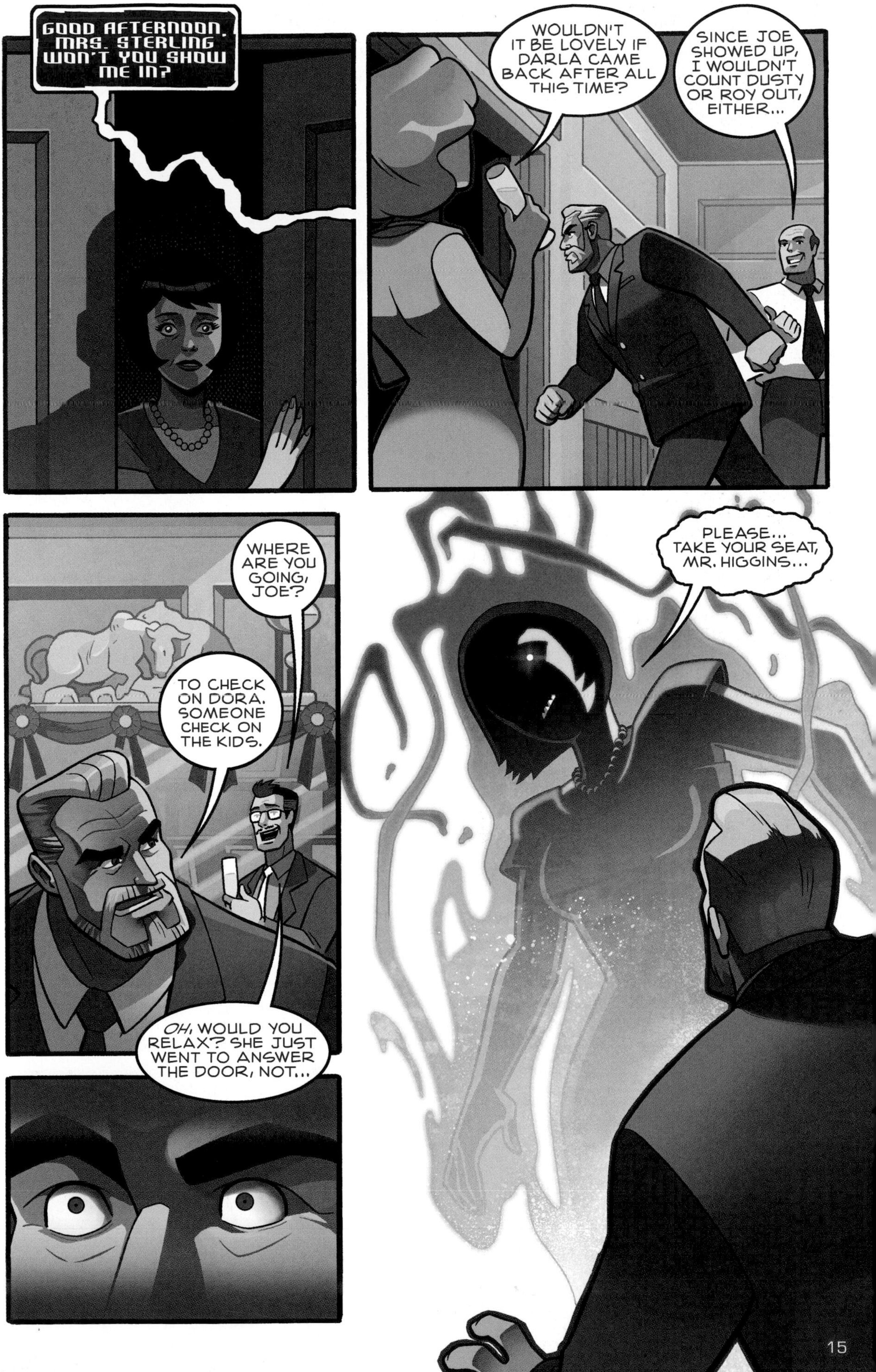
GOOD AFTERNOON, MRS. STERLING. WON'T YOU SHOW ME IN?
WOULDN'T IT BE LOVELY IF DARLA CAME BACK AFTER ALL THIS TIME?
SINCE JOE SHOWED UP, I WOULDN'T COUNT DUSTY OR ROY OUT, EITHER...
WHERE ARE YOU GOING, JOE?
TO CHECK ON DORA. SOMEONE CHECK ON THE KIDS.
OH, WOULD YOU RELAX? SHE JUST WENT TO ANSWER THE DOOR, NOT...
PLEASE... TAKE YOUR SEAT, MR. HIGGINS...

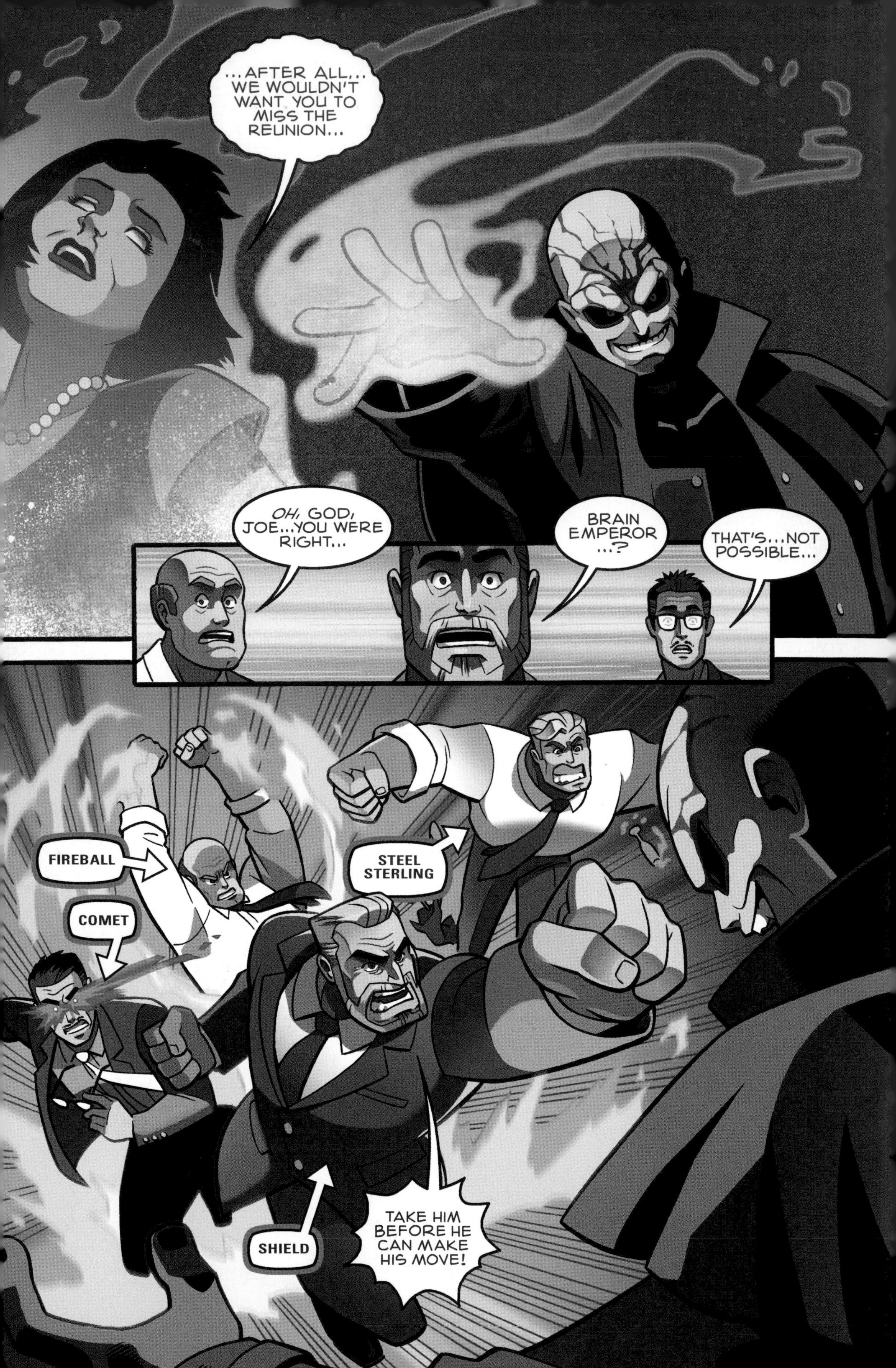
...AFTER ALL,... WE WOULDN'T WANT YOU TO MISS THE REUNION...
OH, GOD, JOE...YOU WERE RIGHT...
BRAIN EMPEROR ...?
THAT'S...NOT POSSIBLE...
FIREBALL
STEEL STERLING
COMET
SHIELD
TAKE HIM BEFORE HE CAN MAKE HIS MOVE!

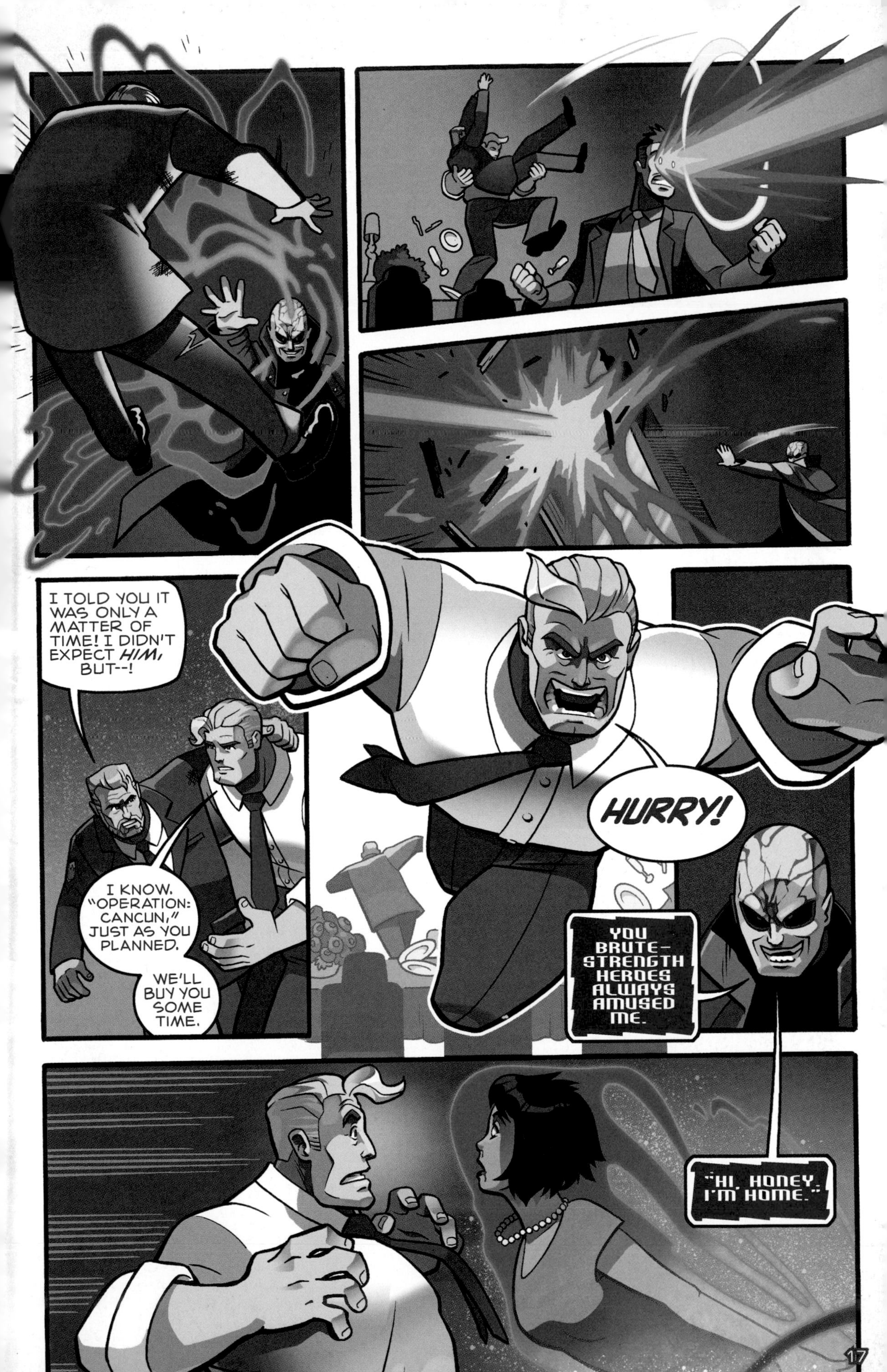
I TOLD YOU IT WAS ONLY A MATTER OF TIME! I DIDN'T EXPECT *HIM,* BUT--!
I KNOW. "OPERATION: CANCUN," JUST AS YOU PLANNED.
WE'LL BUY YOU SOME TIME.
HURRY!
YOU BRUTE-STRENGTH HEROES ALWAYS AMUSED ME.
"HI, HONEY. I'M HOME."

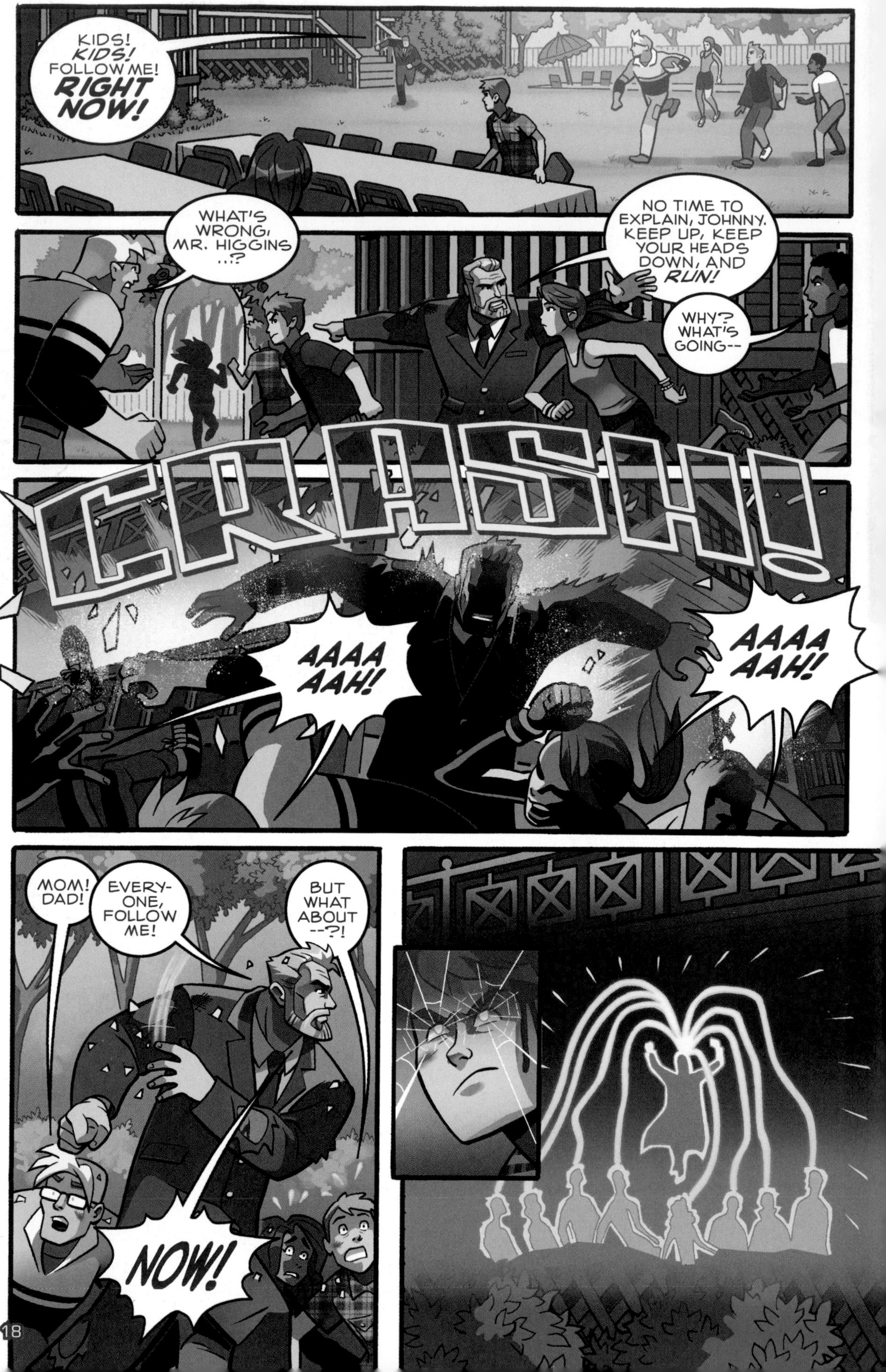
KIDS! KIDS! FOLLOW ME! RIGHT NOW!
WHAT'S WRONG, MR. HIGGINS ...?
NO TIME TO EXPLAIN, JOHNNY. KEEP UP, KEEP YOUR HEADS DOWN, AND RUN!
WHY? WHAT'S GOING--
CRASH!
AAAA AAH!
AAAA AAH!
MOM! DAD!
EVERY- ONE, FOLLOW ME!
BUT WHAT ABOUT --?!
NOW!

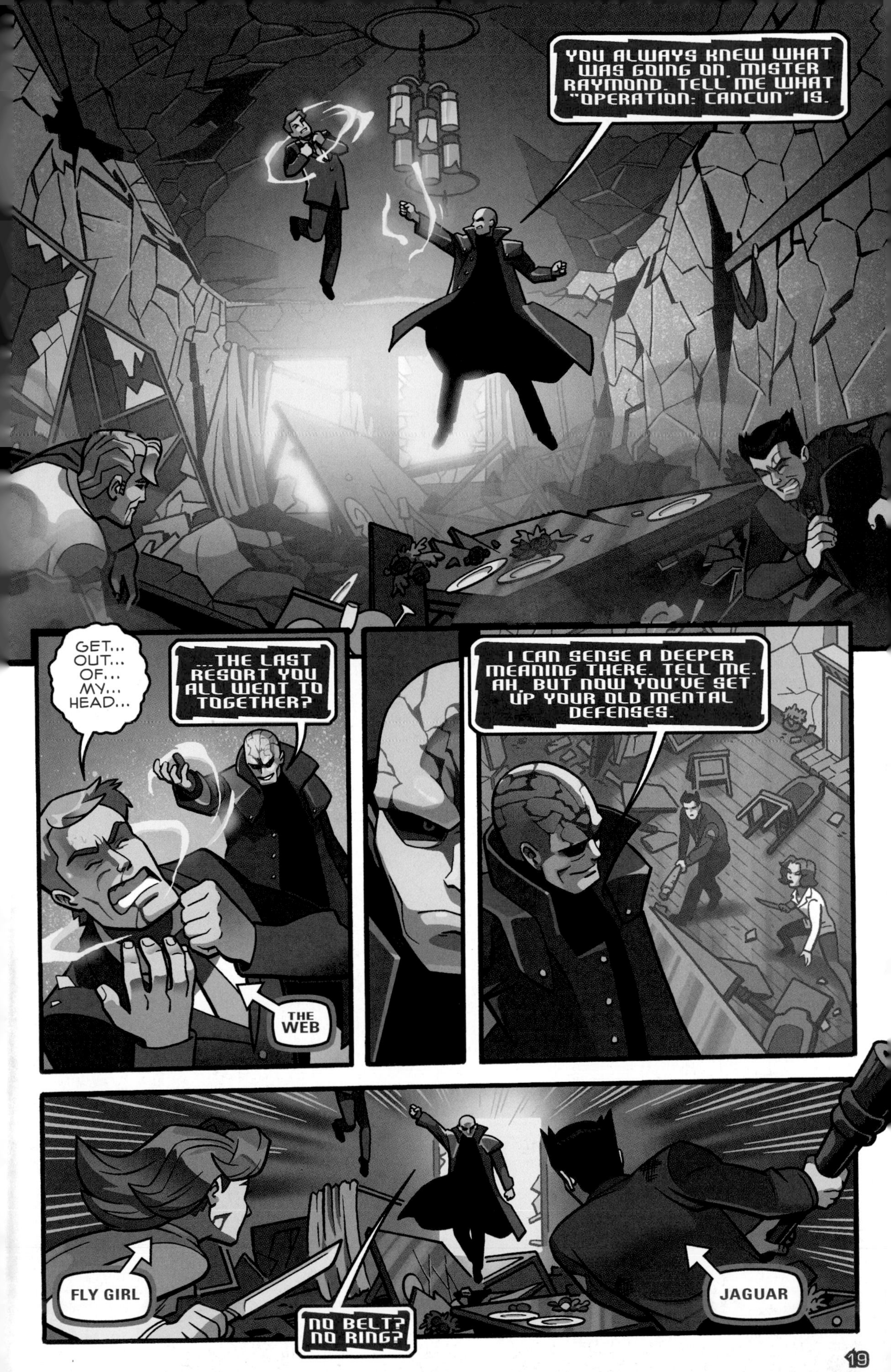

YOU ALWAYS KNEW WHAT WAS GOING ON, MISTER RAYMOND. TELL ME WHAT "OPERATION: CANCUN" IS.
GET... OUT... OF... MY... HEAD...
...THE LAST RESORT YOU ALL WENT TO TOGETHER?
THE WEB
I CAN SENSE A DEEPER MEANING THERE. TELL ME. AH, BUT NOW YOU'VE SET UP YOUR OLD MENTAL DEFENSES.
FLY GIRL
NO BELT? NO RING?
JAGUAR

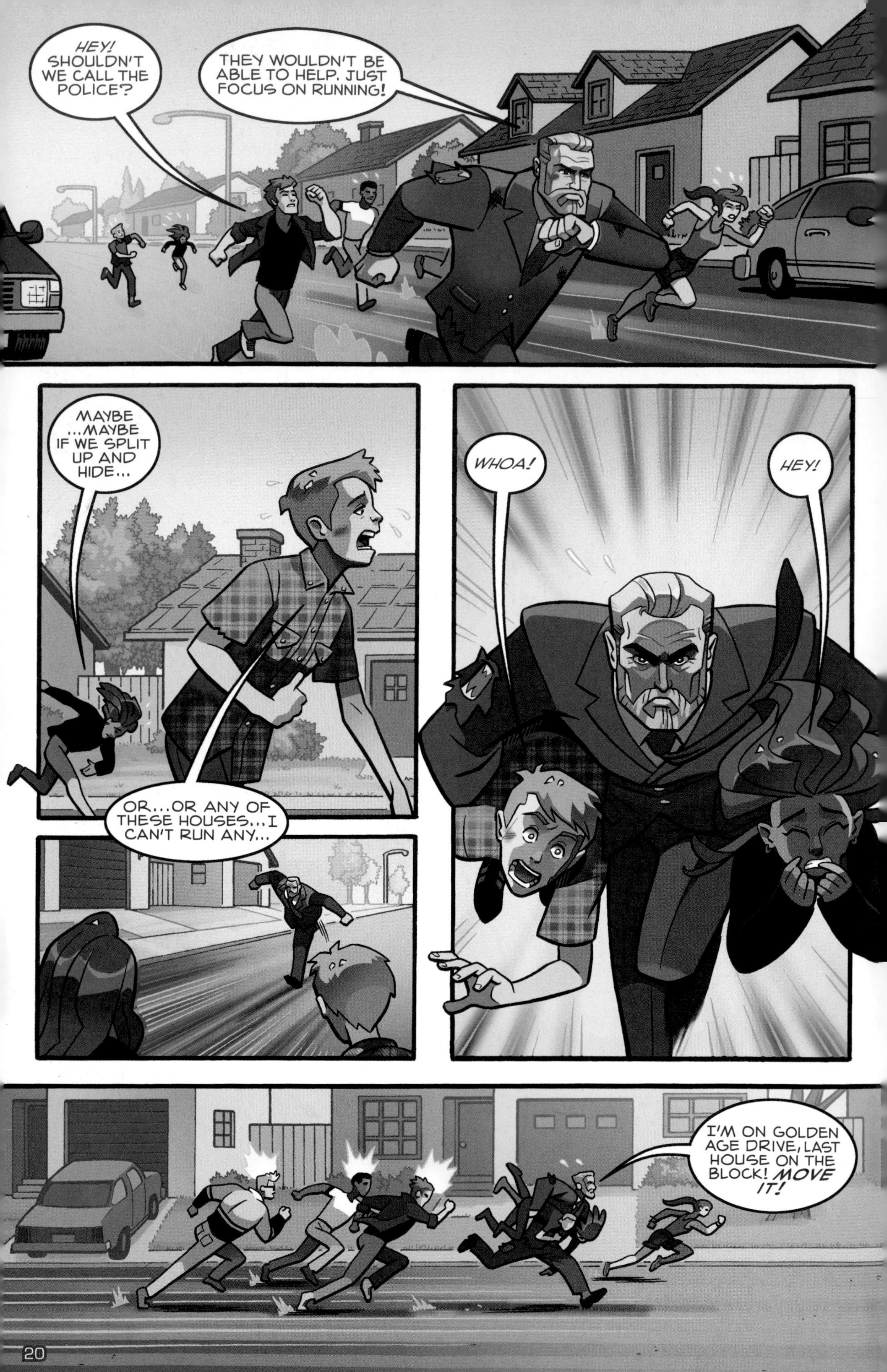
HEY! SHOULDN'T WE CALL THE POLICE?
THEY WOULDN'T BE ABLE TO HELP. JUST FOCUS ON RUNNING!
MAYBE ...MAYBE IF WE SPLIT UP AND HIDE...
OR...OR ANY OF THESE HOUSES...I CAN'T RUN ANY...
WHOA!
HEY!
I'M ON GOLDEN AGE DRIVE, LAST HOUSE ON THE BLOCK! MOVE IT!

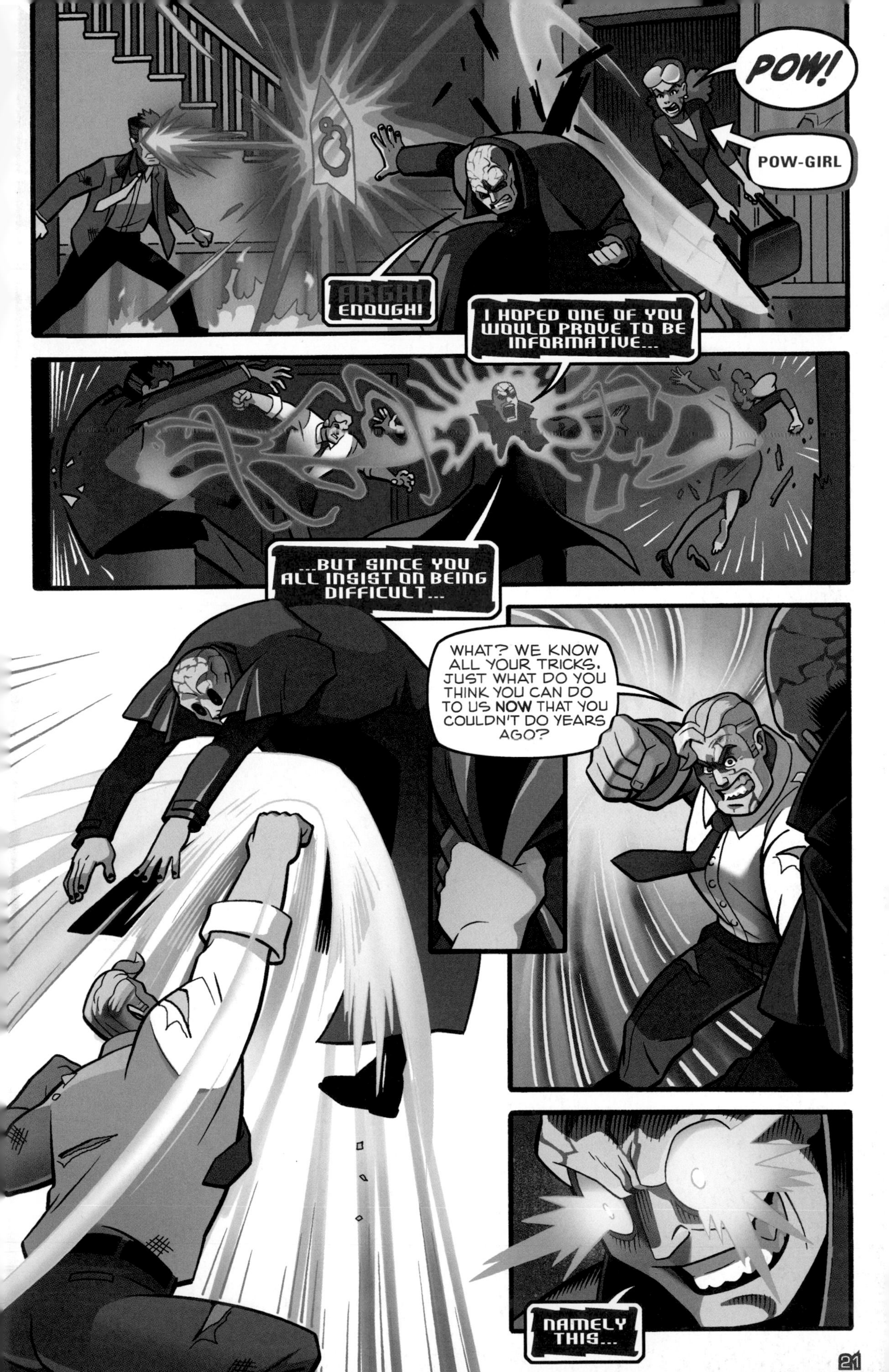
POW!
POW-GIRL
ARGH! ENOUGH!
I HOPED ONE OF YOU WOULD PROVE TO BE INFORMATIVE...
...BUT SINCE YOU ALL INSIST ON BEING DIFFICULT...
WHAT? WE KNOW ALL YOUR TRICKS. JUST WHAT DO YOU THINK YOU CAN DO TO US NOW THAT YOU COULDN'T DO YEARS AGO?
NAMELY THIS...

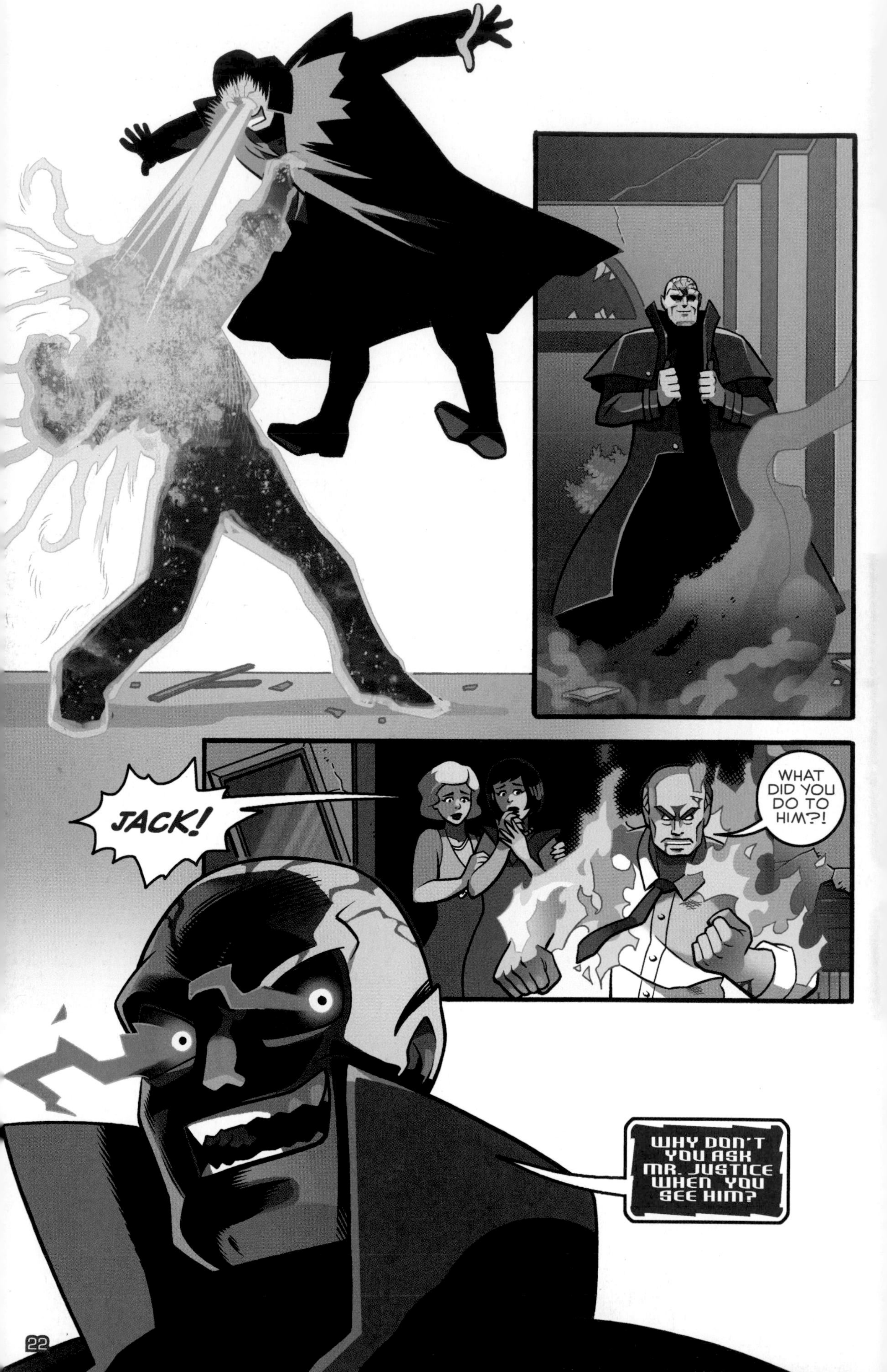
JACK!
WHAT DID YOU DO TO HIM?!
WHY DON'T YOU ASK MR. JUSTICE WHEN YOU SEE HIM?

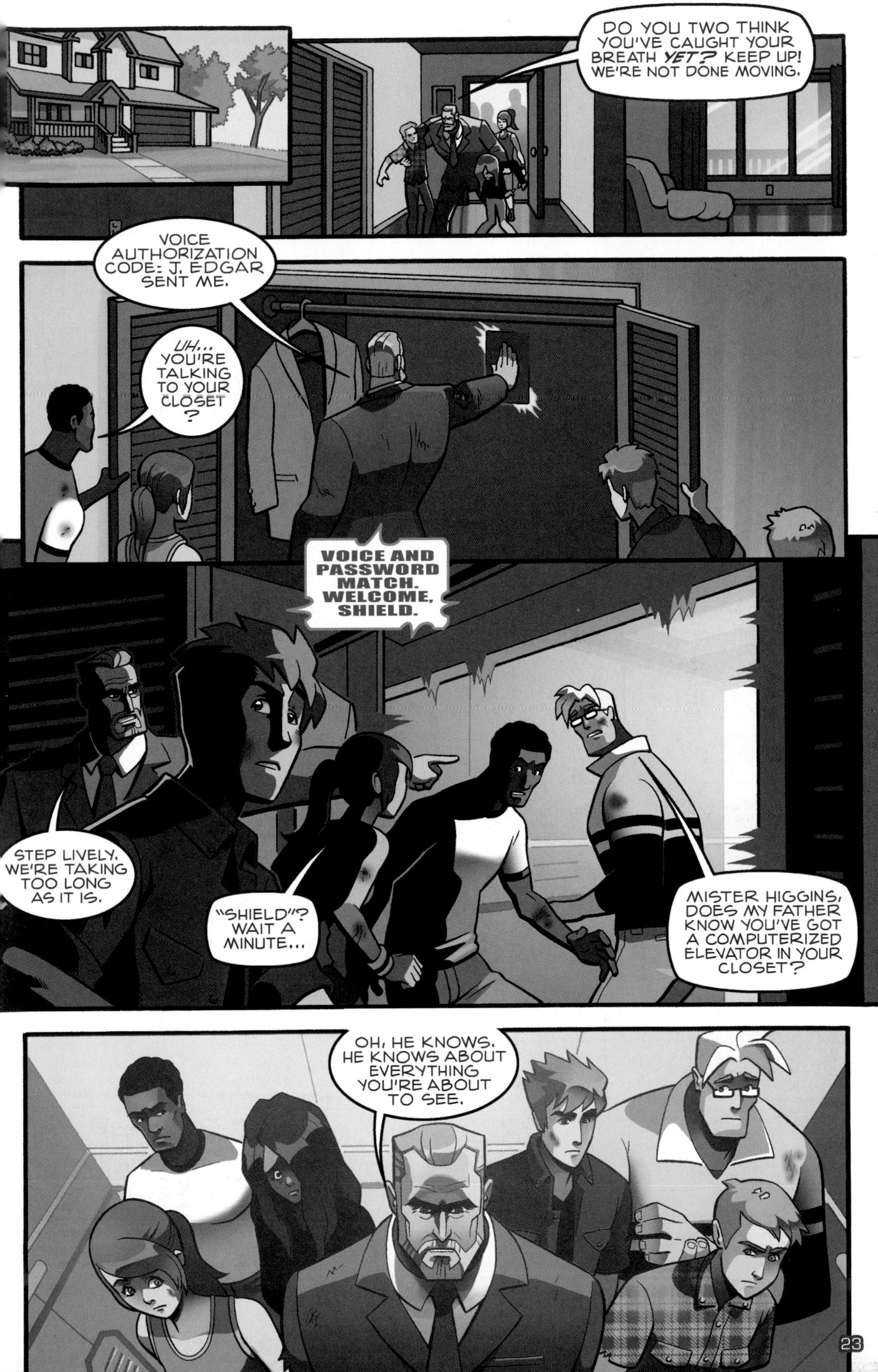

DO YOU TWO THINK YOU'VE CAUGHT YOUR BREATH *YET?* KEEP UP! WE'RE NOT DONE MOVING.
VOICE AUTHORIZATION CODE: J. EDGAR SENT ME.
UH... YOU'RE TALKING TO YOUR CLOSET?
VOICE AND PASSWORD MATCH. WELCOME, SHIELD.
STEP LIVELY. WE'RE TAKING TOO LONG AS IT IS.
"SHIELD"? WAIT A MINUTE...
MISTER HIGGINS, DOES MY FATHER KNOW YOU'VE GOT A COMPUTERIZED ELEVATOR IN YOUR CLOSET?
OH, HE KNOWS. HE KNOWS ABOUT EVERYTHING YOU'RE ABOUT TO SEE.

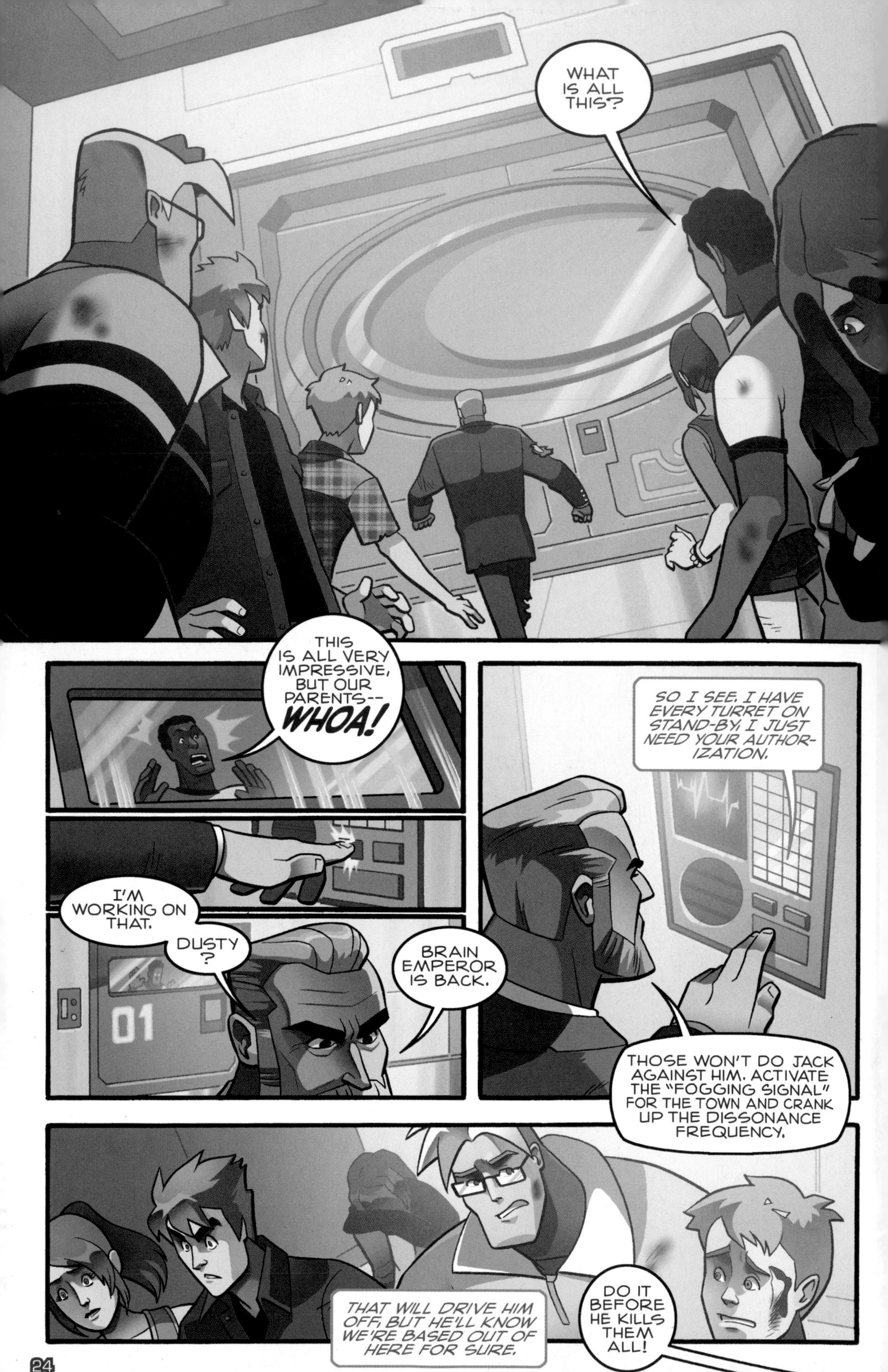
WHAT IS ALL THIS?
THIS IS ALL VERY IMPRESSIVE, BUT OUR PARENTS-- WHOA!
I'M WORKING ON THAT.
DUSTY?
BRAIN EMPEROR IS BACK.
SO I SEE. I HAVE EVERY TURRET ON STAND-BY. I JUST NEED YOUR AUTHORIZATION.
THOSE WON'T DO JACK AGAINST HIM. ACTIVATE THE "FOGGING SIGNAL" FOR THE TOWN AND CRANK UP THE DISSONANCE FREQUENCY.
01
THAT WILL DRIVE HIM OFF, BUT HE'LL KNOW WE'RE BASED OUT OF HERE FOR SURE.
DO IT BEFORE HE KILLS THEM ALL!

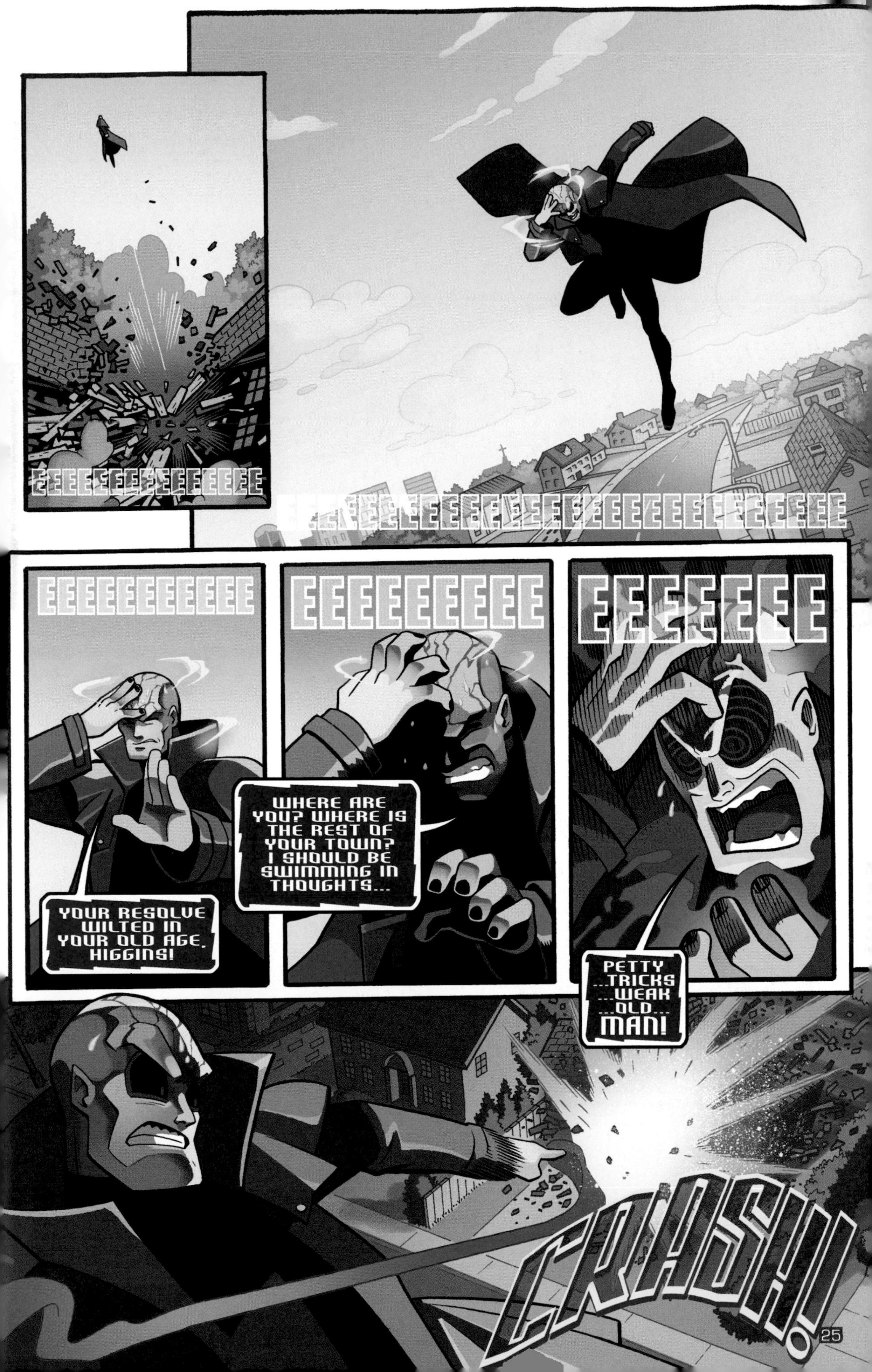
EEEEEEEEEEEEEE
EEEEEEEEEEEEEEEEEEEEEEEEEEEEE
EEEEEEEEEEE
YOUR RESOLVE WILTED IN YOUR OLD AGE, HIGGINS!
EEEEEEEEE
WHERE ARE YOU? WHERE IS THE REST OF YOUR TOWN? I SHOULD BE SWIMMING IN THOUGHTS...
EEEEEEE
PETTY ...TRICKS ...WEAK ...OLD... MAN!
CRASH!

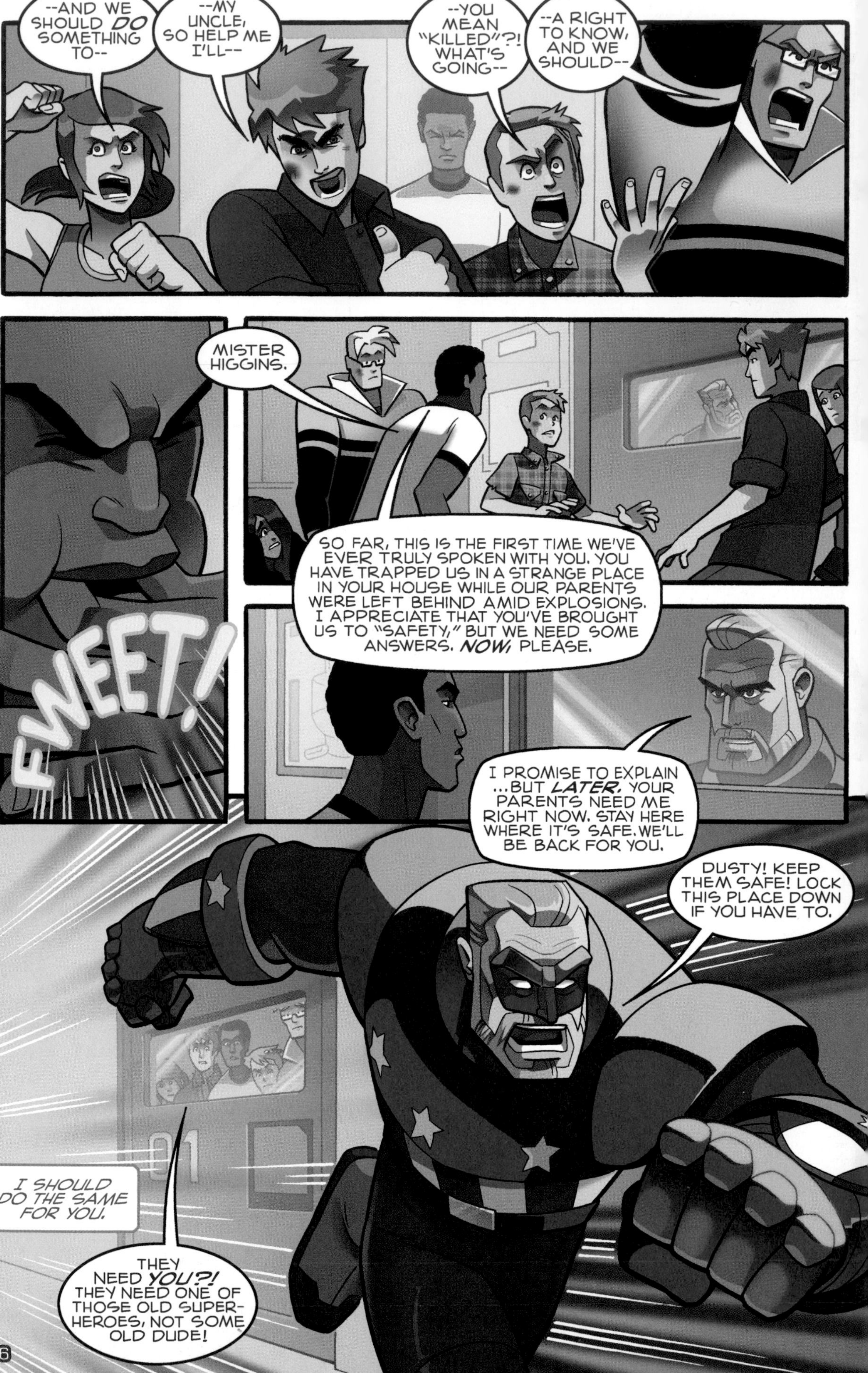
--AND WE SHOULD *DO* SOMETHING TO--
--MY UNCLE, SO HELP ME I'LL--
--YOU MEAN "KILLED"?! WHAT'S GOING--
--A RIGHT TO KNOW, AND WE SHOULD--
FWEET!
MISTER HIGGINS.
SO FAR, THIS IS THE FIRST TIME WE'VE EVER TRULY SPOKEN WITH YOU. YOU HAVE TRAPPED US IN A STRANGE PLACE IN YOUR HOUSE WHILE OUR PARENTS WERE LEFT BEHIND AMID EXPLOSIONS. I APPRECIATE THAT YOU'VE BROUGHT US TO "SAFETY," BUT WE NEED SOME ANSWERS. *NOW,* PLEASE.
I PROMISE TO EXPLAIN ...BUT *LATER.* YOUR PARENTS NEED ME RIGHT NOW. STAY HERE WHERE IT'S SAFE. WE'LL BE BACK FOR YOU.
DUSTY! KEEP THEM SAFE! LOCK THIS PLACE DOWN IF YOU HAVE TO.
I SHOULD DO THE SAME FOR YOU.
THEY NEED *YOU?!* THEY NEED ONE OF THOSE OLD SUPER-HEROES, NOT SOME OLD DUDE!

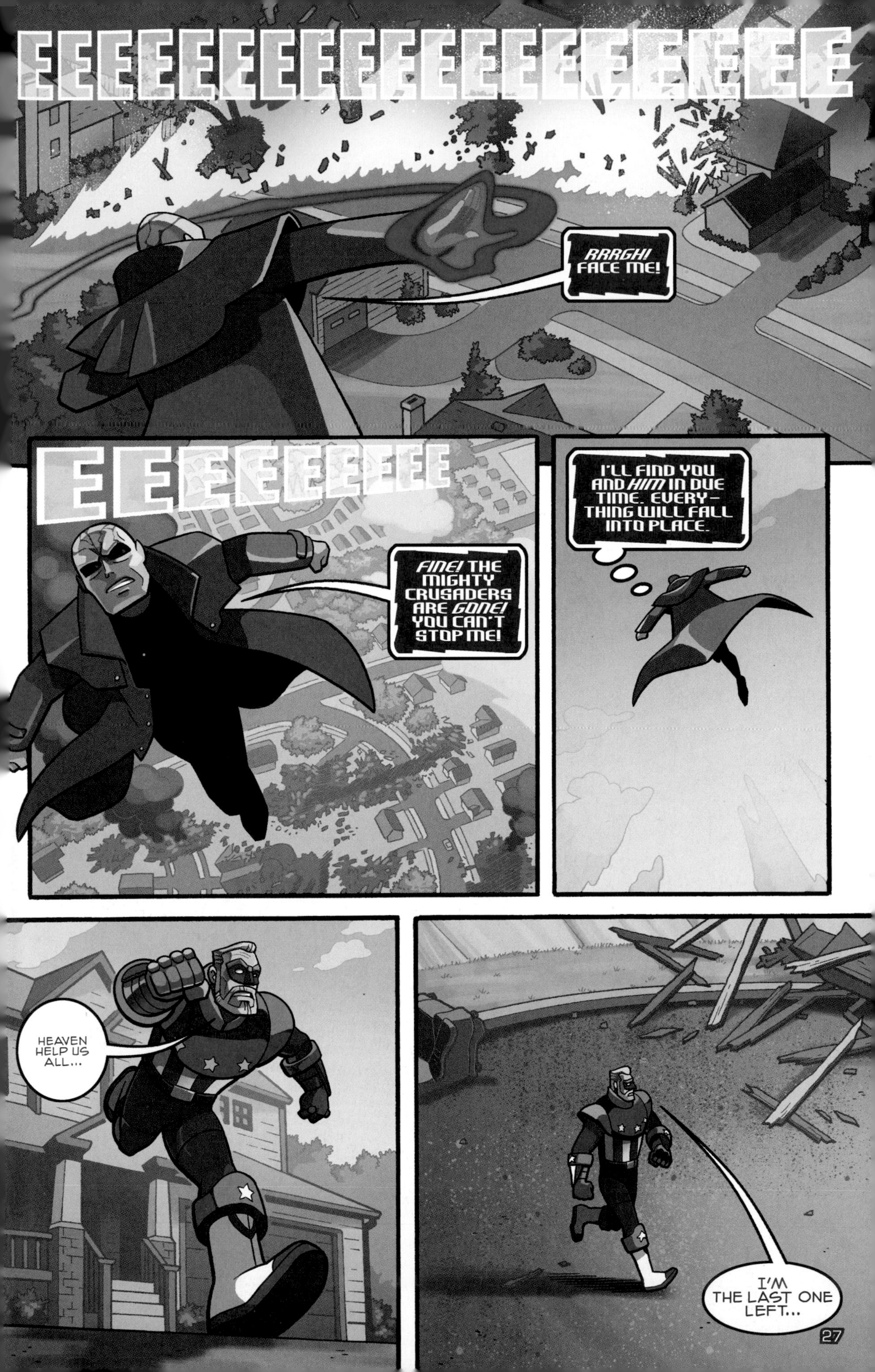

EEEEEEEEEEEEEEEEEE
RRRGH! FACE ME!
EEEEEEEEE
FINE! THE MIGHTY CRUSADERS ARE GONE! YOU CAN'T STOP ME!
I'LL FIND YOU AND HIM IN DUE TIME. EVERY-THING WILL FALL INTO PLACE.
HEAVEN HELP US ALL...
I'M THE LAST ONE LEFT...

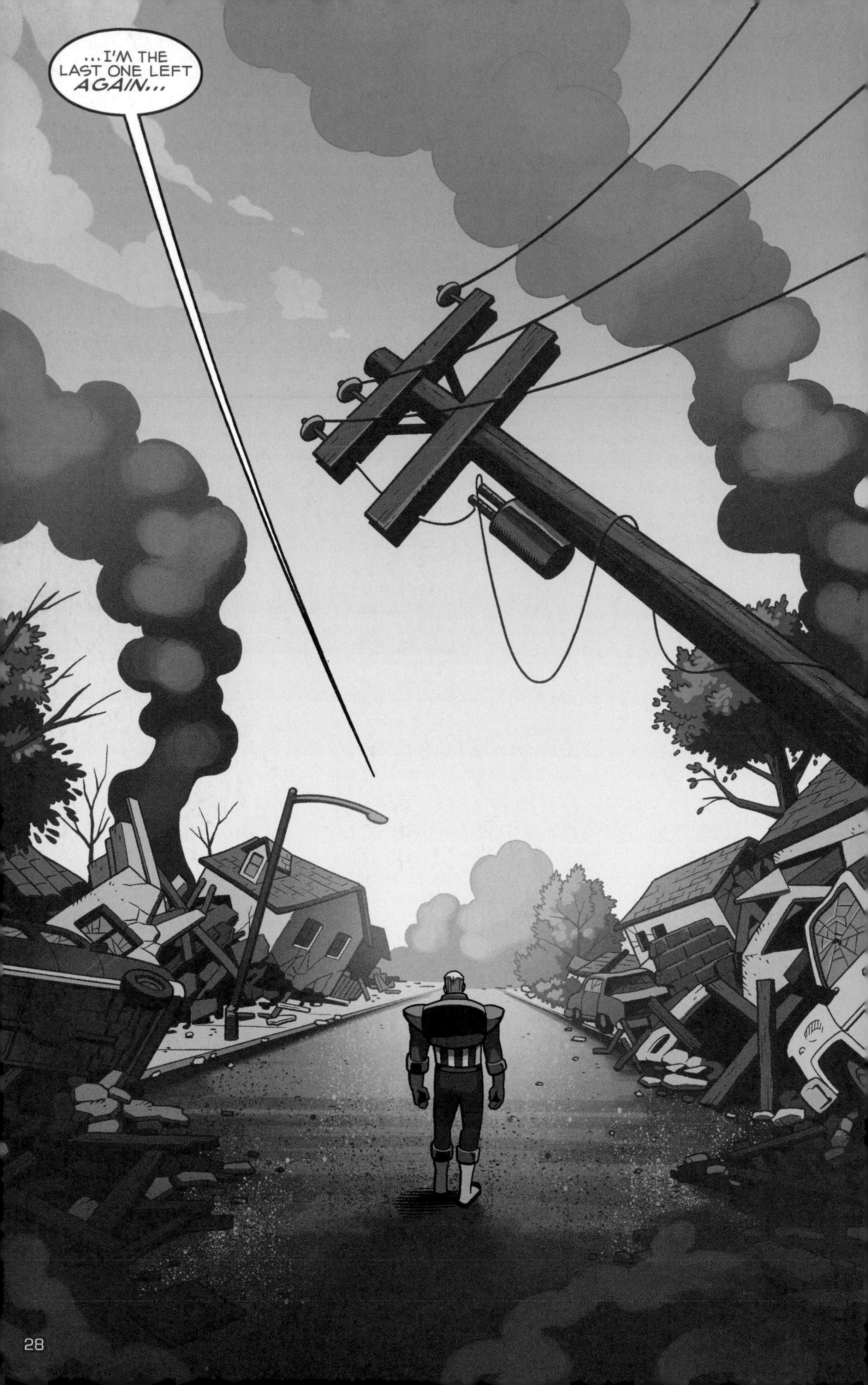
...I'M THE LAST ONE LEFT AGAIN...

CHAPTER 2

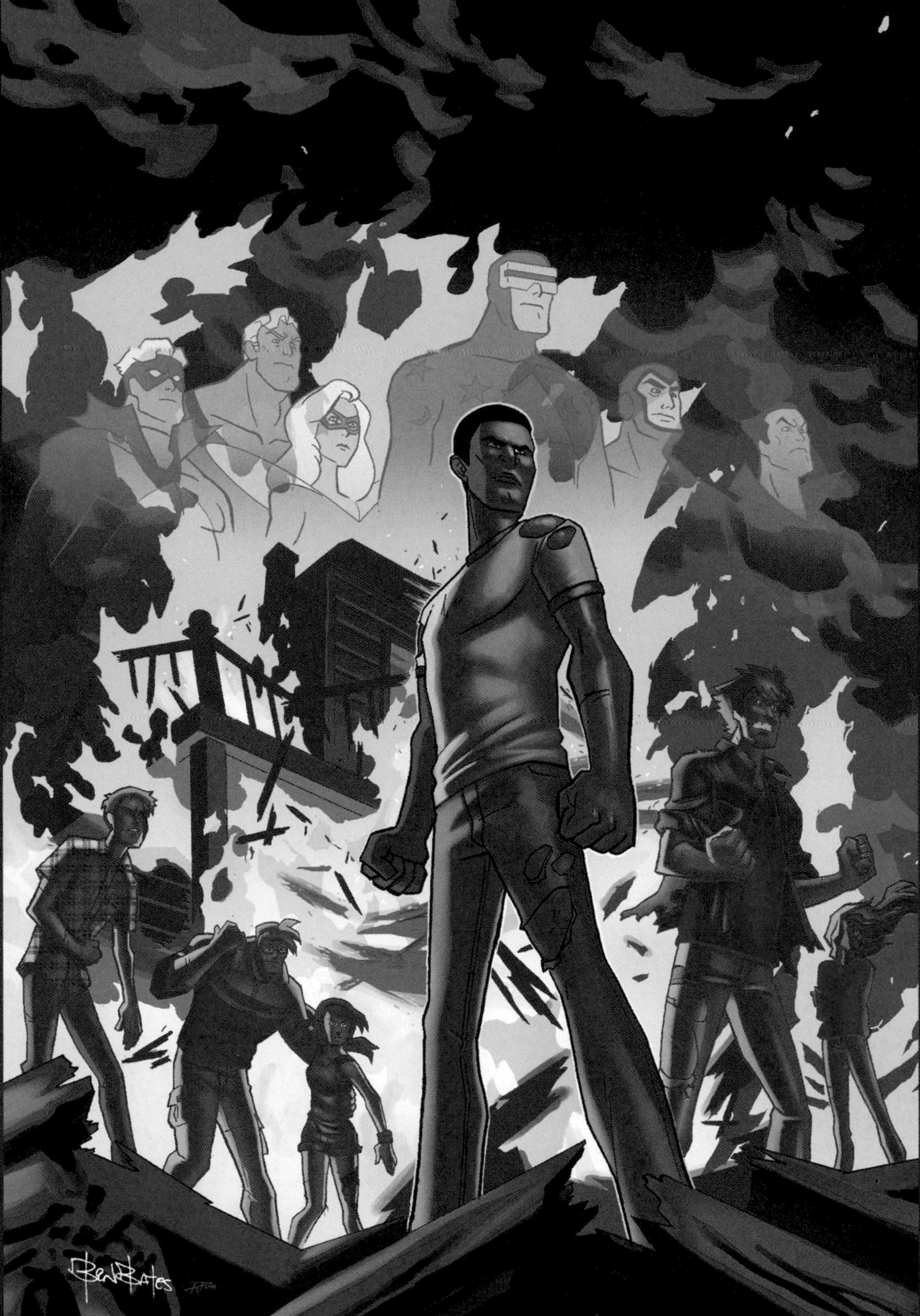
BEN BATES

NEW CRUSADERS - RISE OF THE HEROES - ISSUE 2

COVER BY: BEN BATES

CRUSADER CIRCLE --THE HIGH-TECH SECRET BASE...
...HIDDEN UNDER OLD MAN HIGGINS' HOUSE.
AND NOW CASSIE O'NEAL WITH IMPACT CITY NEWS'S CONTINUING COVERAGE OF THE TRAGEDY IN RED CIRCLE.

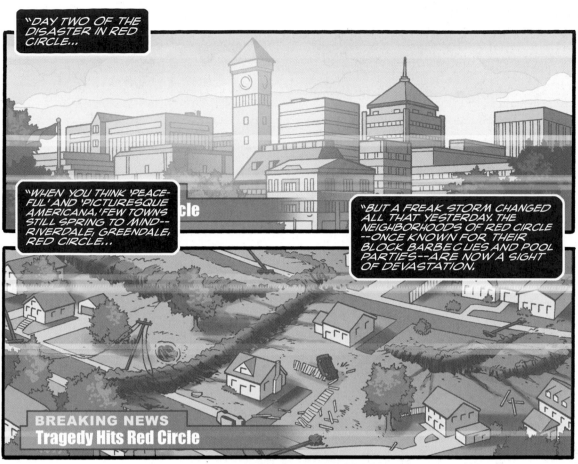

"DAY TWO OF THE DISASTER IN RED CIRCLE...

"WHEN YOU THINK 'PEACE-FUL' AND 'PICTURESQUE AMERICANA,' FEW TOWNS STILL SPRING TO MIND--RIVERDALE, GREENDALE, RED CIRCLE...

"BUT A FREAK STORM CHANGED ALL THAT YESTERDAY. THE NEIGHBORHOODS OF RED CIRCLE --ONCE KNOWN FOR THEIR BLOCK BARBECUES AND POOL PARTIES--ARE NOW A SIGHT OF DEVASTATION.

BREAKING NEWS
Tragedy Hits Red Circle

"HARDEST HIT WAS THE MAYOR'S HOME, WHICH SEEMED TO CLAIM THE LIVES OF THE TOWN'S BELOVED COMMUNITY LEADER JACK STERLING AND HIS FAMILY.

BREAKING NEWS
Tragedy Hits Red Circle

"GOVERNMENT RESPONSE HAS BEEN SURPRISINGLY QUICK, WITH THE MILITARY LOGISTICS AND JURIS-DICTION BUREAU HAVING ALREADY SET UP TEMPORARY SHELTERS AND FIRST AID FACILITIES. PERHAPS THE M.L.J.'S EFFORTS ARE TO PRE-SERVE THIS PLACE--THIS FOND MEMORY OF A SIMPLER, NICER TIME."

BREAKING NEWS
Tragedy Hits Red Circle

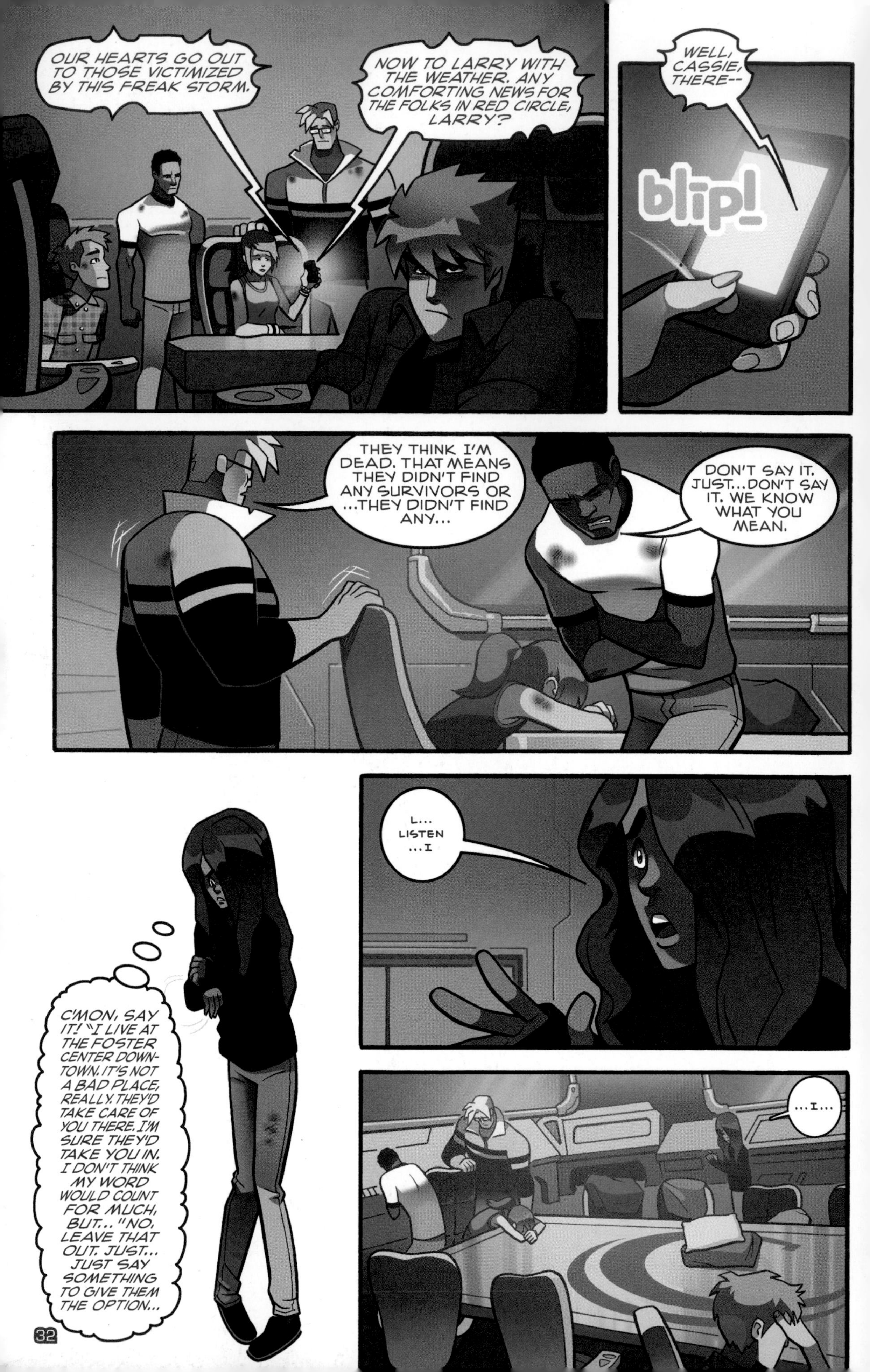
OUR HEARTS GO OUT TO THOSE VICTIMIZED BY THIS FREAK STORM.
NOW TO LARRY WITH THE WEATHER. ANY COMFORTING NEWS FOR THE FOLKS IN RED CIRCLE, LARRY?
WELL, CASSIE, THERE--
blip!
THEY THINK I'M DEAD. THAT MEANS THEY DIDN'T FIND ANY SURVIVORS OR ...THEY DIDN'T FIND ANY...
DON'T SAY IT. JUST...DON'T SAY IT. WE KNOW WHAT YOU MEAN.
C'MON, SAY IT! "I LIVE AT THE FOSTER CENTER DOWN-TOWN. IT'S NOT A BAD PLACE, REALLY. THEY'D TAKE CARE OF YOU THERE. I'M SURE THEY'D TAKE YOU IN. I DON'T THINK MY WORD WOULD COUNT FOR MUCH, BUT..." NO, LEAVE THAT OUT. JUST... JUST SAY SOMETHING TO GIVE THEM THE OPTION...
L... LISTEN ...I
...I...

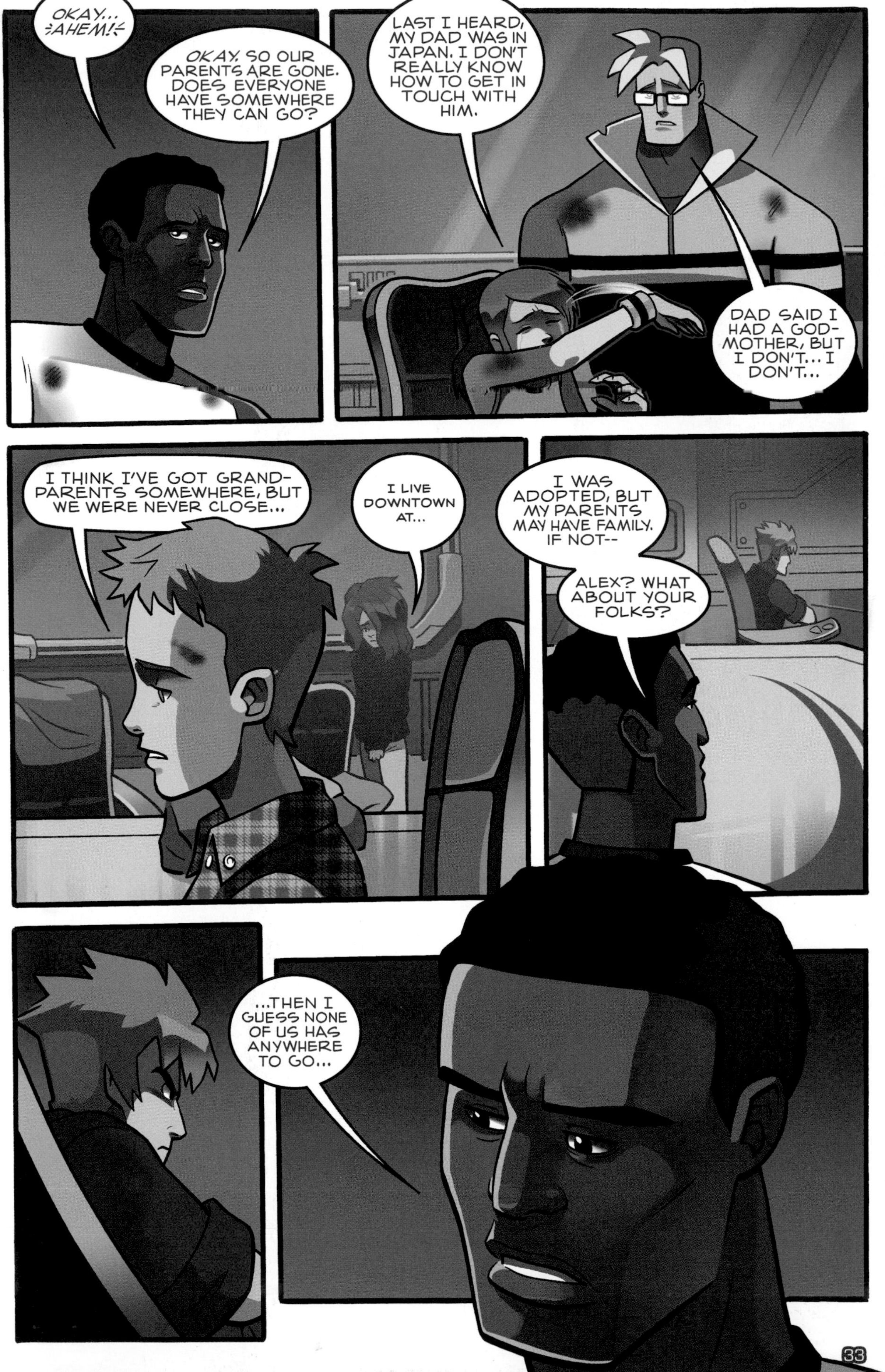
OKAY... ≈AHEM!≈
OKAY. SO OUR PARENTS ARE GONE. DOES EVERYONE HAVE SOMEWHERE THEY CAN GO?
LAST I HEARD, MY DAD WAS IN JAPAN. I DON'T REALLY KNOW HOW TO GET IN TOUCH WITH HIM.
DAD SAID I HAD A GOD-MOTHER, BUT I DON'T... I DON'T...
I THINK I'VE GOT GRAND-PARENTS SOMEWHERE, BUT WE WERE NEVER CLOSE...
I LIVE DOWNTOWN AT...
I WAS ADOPTED, BUT MY PARENTS MAY HAVE FAMILY. IF NOT--
ALEX? WHAT ABOUT YOUR FOLKS?
...THEN I GUESS NONE OF US HAS ANYWHERE TO GO...

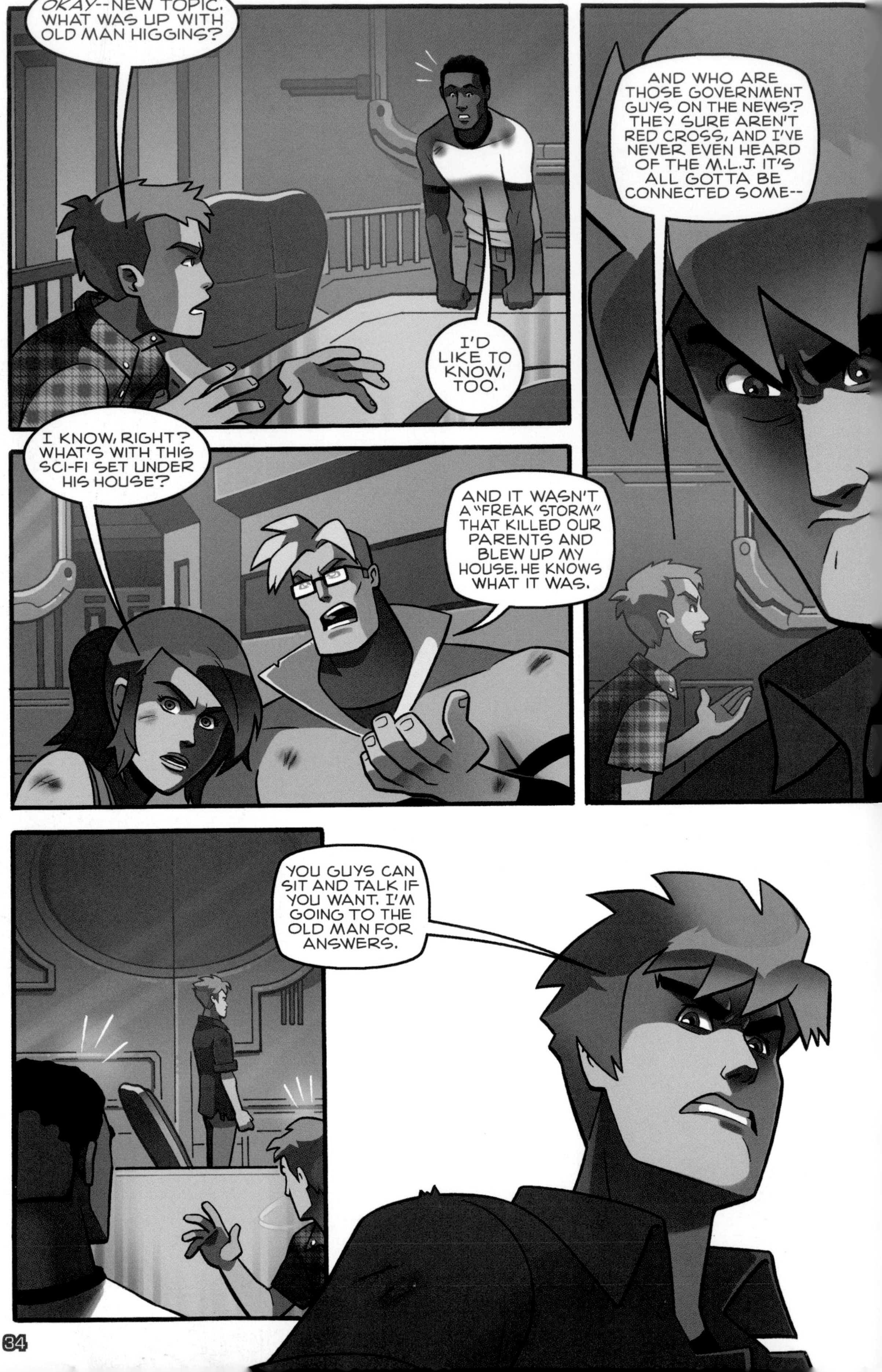
OKAY--NEW TOPIC. WHAT WAS UP WITH OLD MAN HIGGINS?
I'D LIKE TO KNOW, TOO.
AND WHO ARE THOSE GOVERNMENT GUYS ON THE NEWS? THEY SURE AREN'T RED CROSS, AND I'VE NEVER EVEN HEARD OF THE M.L.J. IT'S ALL GOTTA BE CONNECTED SOME--
I KNOW, RIGHT? WHAT'S WITH THIS SCI-FI SET UNDER HIS HOUSE?
AND IT WASN'T A "FREAK STORM" THAT KILLED OUR PARENTS AND BLEW UP MY HOUSE. HE KNOWS WHAT IT WAS.
YOU GUYS CAN SIT AND TALK IF YOU WANT. I'M GOING TO THE OLD MAN FOR ANSWERS.

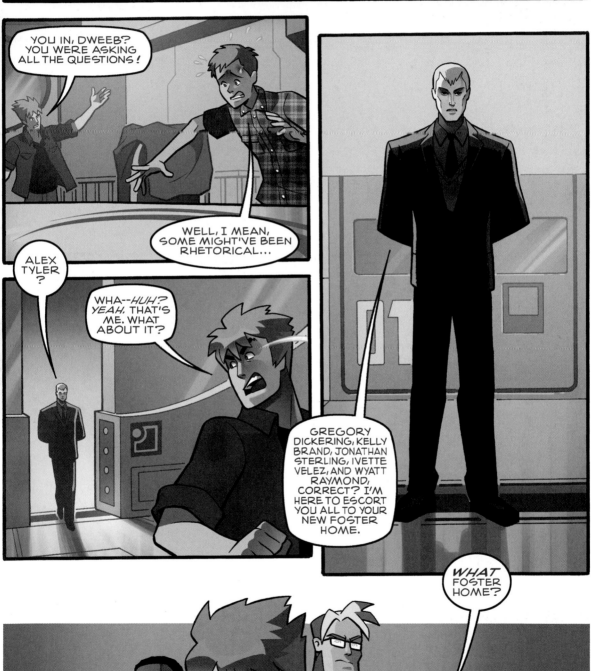

YOU IN, DWEEB? YOU WERE ASKING ALL THE QUESTIONS!

WELL, I MEAN, SOME MIGHT'VE BEEN RHETORICAL...

ALEX TYLER?

WHA--HUH? YEAH, THAT'S ME. WHAT ABOUT IT?

GREGORY DICKERING, KELLY BRAND, JONATHAN STERLING, IVETTE VELEZ, AND WYATT RAYMOND, CORRECT? I'M HERE TO ESCORT YOU ALL TO YOUR NEW FOSTER HOME.

WHAT FOSTER HOME?

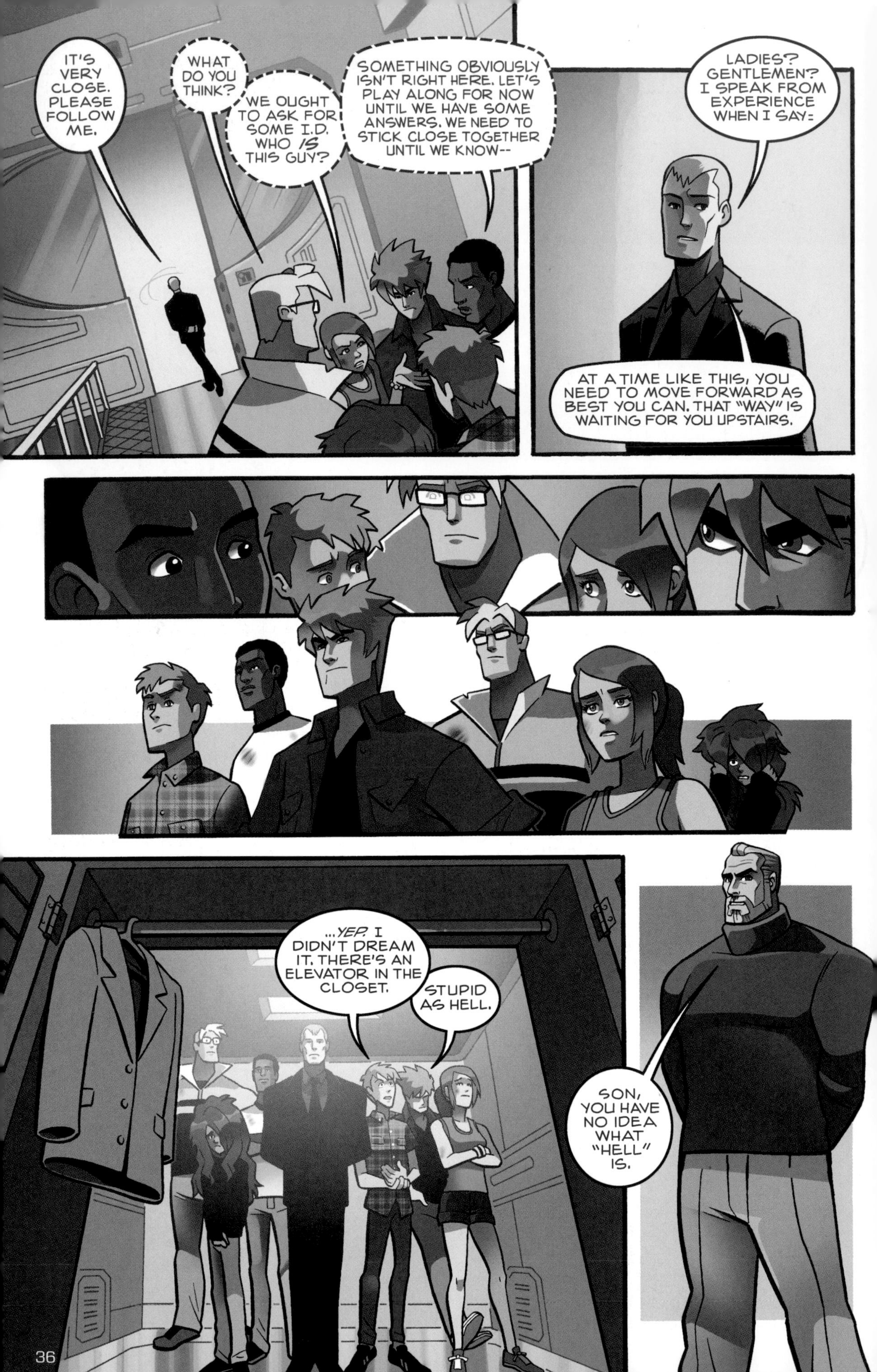
IT'S VERY CLOSE. PLEASE FOLLOW ME.
WHAT DO YOU THINK?
WE OUGHT TO ASK FOR SOME I.D. WHO *IS* THIS GUY?
SOMETHING OBVIOUSLY ISN'T RIGHT HERE. LET'S PLAY ALONG FOR NOW UNTIL WE HAVE SOME ANSWERS. WE NEED TO STICK CLOSE TOGETHER UNTIL WE KNOW--
LADIES? GENTLEMEN? I SPEAK FROM EXPERIENCE WHEN I SAY:
AT A TIME LIKE THIS, YOU NEED TO MOVE FORWARD AS BEST YOU CAN. THAT "WAY" IS WAITING FOR YOU UPSTAIRS.
...*YEP.* I DIDN'T DREAM IT. THERE'S AN ELEVATOR IN THE CLOSET.
STUPID AS HELL.
SON, YOU HAVE NO IDEA WHAT "HELL" IS.

WHAT ARE YOU GOING TO TELL THEM?

WHAT THEY NEED TO KNOW.

CONSIDERING THE CIRCUMSTANCES, I BELIEVE RE-INTRODUCTIONS ARE IN ORDER. I AM JOE HIGGINS, AND THE SIX OF YOU HAVE BEEN ENTRUSTED TO MY CARE. THIS IS MY HOME--AND NOW IT'S YOUR HOME, TOO.

YOU'LL EACH HAVE YOUR OWN ROOM. GENTLEMEN, THAT HALL BELONGS TO YOU.

LADIES, YOU ARE ON THE OTHER SIDE OF THE HOUSE.

THE KITCHEN IS HERE AT THE CENTER, AND THERE'S A REC ROOM OUT BACK.

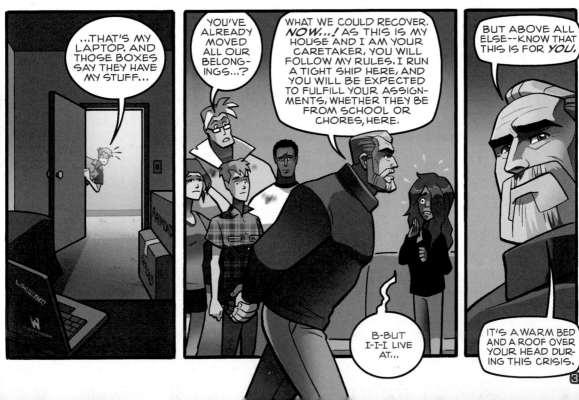

...THAT'S MY LAPTOP. AND THOSE BOXES SAY THEY HAVE MY STUFF...

YOU'VE ALREADY MOVED ALL OUR BELONG-INGS...?

WHAT WE COULD RECOVER, NOW...! AS THIS IS MY HOUSE AND I AM YOUR CARETAKER, YOU WILL FOLLOW MY RULES. I RUN A TIGHT SHIP HERE, AND YOU WILL BE EXPECTED TO FULFILL YOUR ASSIGN-MENTS, WHETHER THEY BE FROM SCHOOL OR CHORES, HERE.

BUT ABOVE ALL ELSE--KNOW THAT THIS IS FOR YOU.

B-BUT I-I-I LIVE AT...

IT'S A WARM BED AND A ROOF OVER YOUR HEAD DUR-ING THIS CRISIS.

37

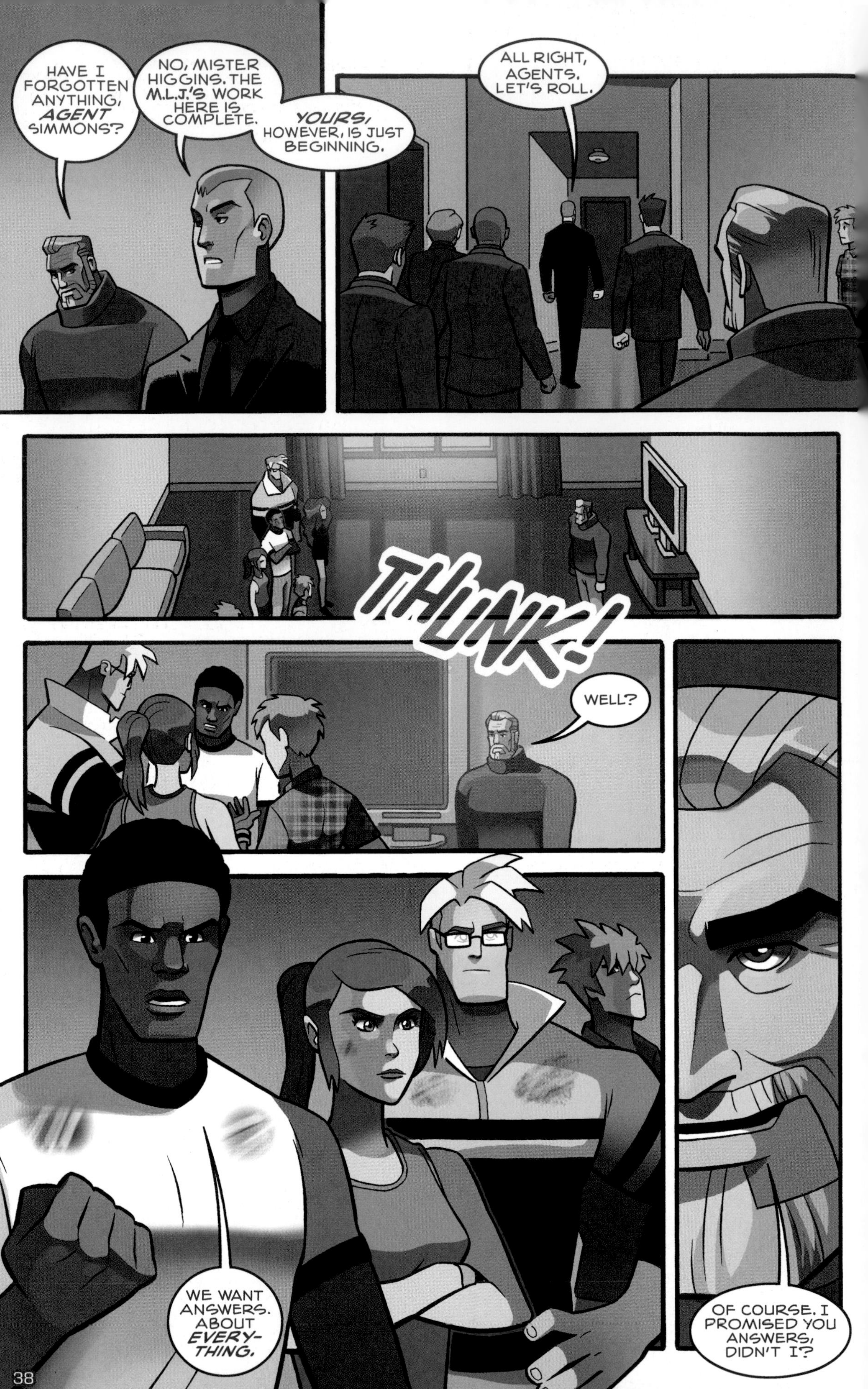
HAVE I FORGOTTEN ANYTHING, AGENT SIMMONS?
NO, MISTER HIGGINS. THE M.L.J.'S WORK HERE IS COMPLETE.
YOURS, HOWEVER, IS JUST BEGINNING.
ALL RIGHT, AGENTS. LET'S ROLL.
THUNK!
WELL?
WE WANT ANSWERS. ABOUT EVERYTHING.
OF COURSE. I PROMISED YOU ANSWERS, DIDN'T I?

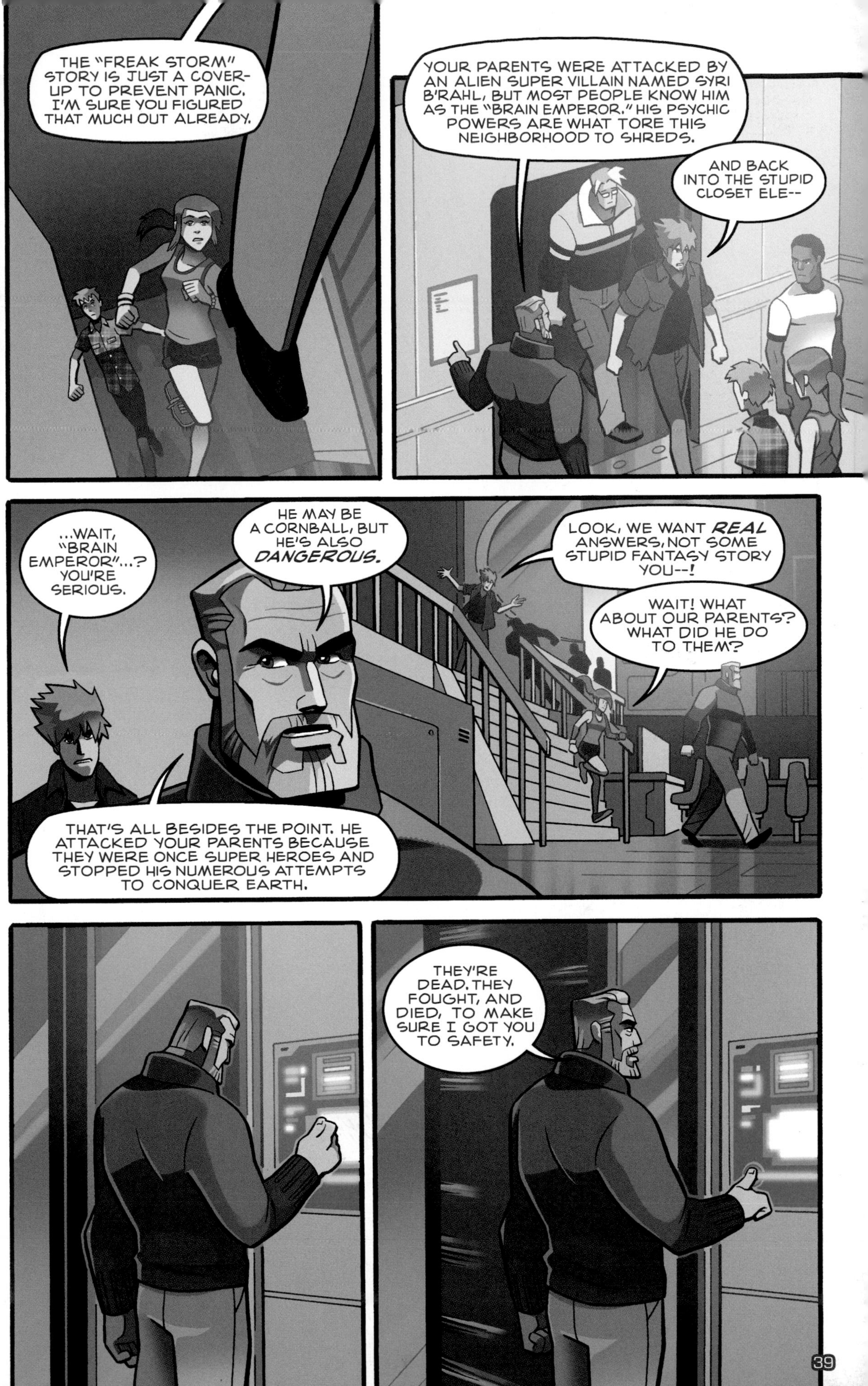
THE "FREAK STORM" STORY IS JUST A COVER-UP TO PREVENT PANIC. I'M SURE YOU FIGURED THAT MUCH OUT ALREADY.
YOUR PARENTS WERE ATTACKED BY AN ALIEN SUPER VILLAIN NAMED SYRI B'RAHL, BUT MOST PEOPLE KNOW HIM AS THE "BRAIN EMPEROR." HIS PSYCHIC POWERS ARE WHAT TORE THIS NEIGHBORHOOD TO SHREDS.
AND BACK INTO THE STUPID CLOSET ELE--
...WAIT, "BRAIN EMPEROR"...? YOU'RE SERIOUS.
HE MAY BE A CORNBALL, BUT HE'S ALSO *DANGEROUS.*
LOOK, WE WANT *REAL* ANSWERS, NOT SOME STUPID FANTASY STORY YOU--!
WAIT! WHAT ABOUT OUR PARENTS? WHAT DID HE DO TO THEM?
THAT'S ALL BESIDES THE POINT. HE ATTACKED YOUR PARENTS BECAUSE THEY WERE ONCE SUPER HEROES AND STOPPED HIS NUMEROUS ATTEMPTS TO CONQUER EARTH.
THEY'RE DEAD. THEY FOUGHT, AND DIED, TO MAKE SURE I GOT YOU TO SAFETY.

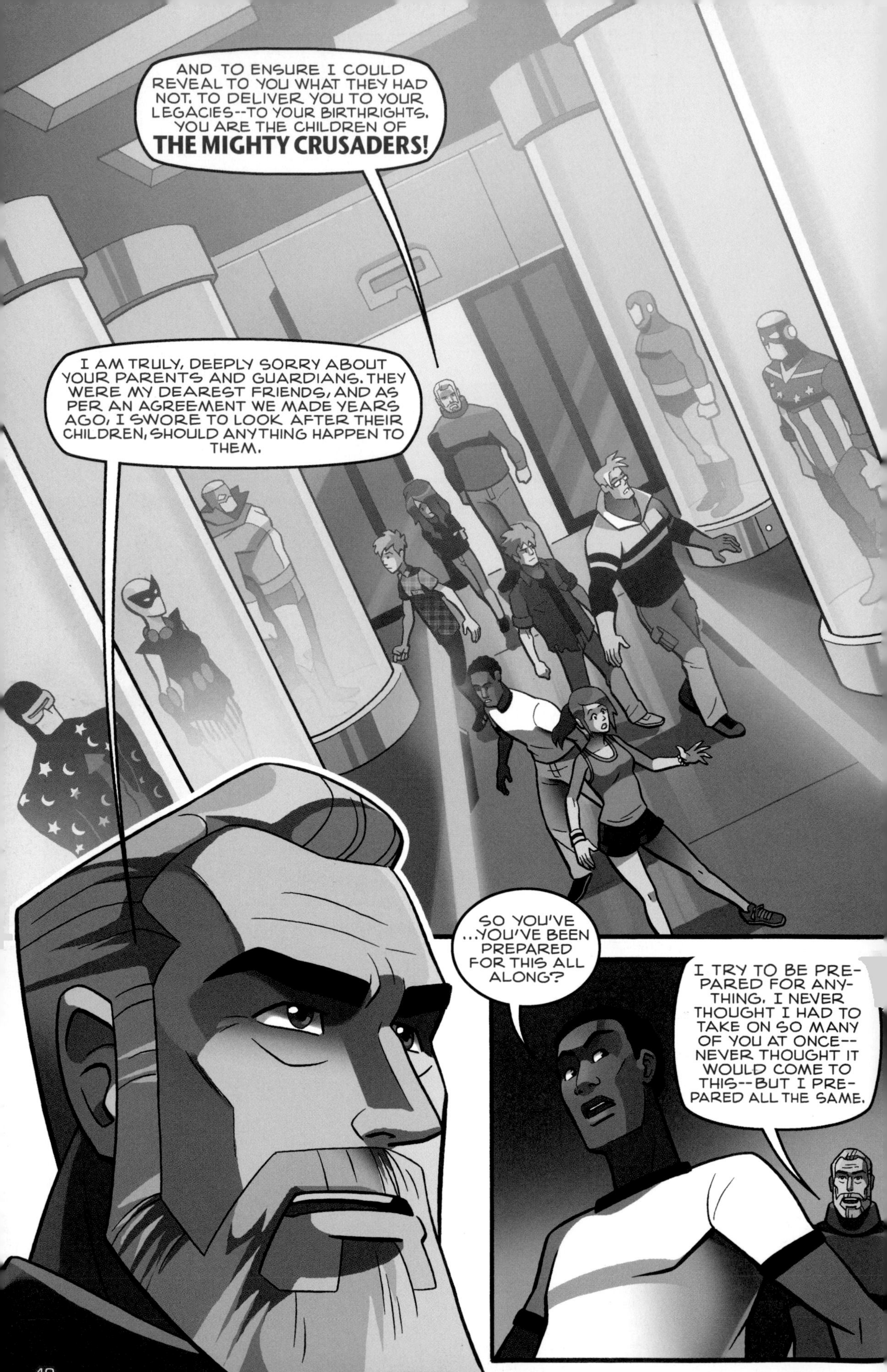

AND TO ENSURE I COULD REVEAL TO YOU WHAT THEY HAD NOT. TO DELIVER YOU TO YOUR LEGACIES--TO YOUR BIRTHRIGHTS. YOU ARE THE CHILDREN OF THE MIGHTY CRUSADERS!
I AM TRULY, DEEPLY SORRY ABOUT YOUR PARENTS AND GUARDIANS. THEY WERE MY DEAREST FRIENDS, AND AS PER AN AGREEMENT WE MADE YEARS AGO, I SWORE TO LOOK AFTER THEIR CHILDREN, SHOULD ANYTHING HAPPEN TO THEM.
SO YOU'VE ...YOU'VE BEEN PREPARED FOR THIS ALL ALONG?
I TRY TO BE PRE-PARED FOR ANY-THING. I NEVER THOUGHT I HAD TO TAKE ON SO MANY OF YOU AT ONCE--NEVER THOUGHT IT WOULD COME TO THIS--BUT I PRE-PARED ALL THE SAME.

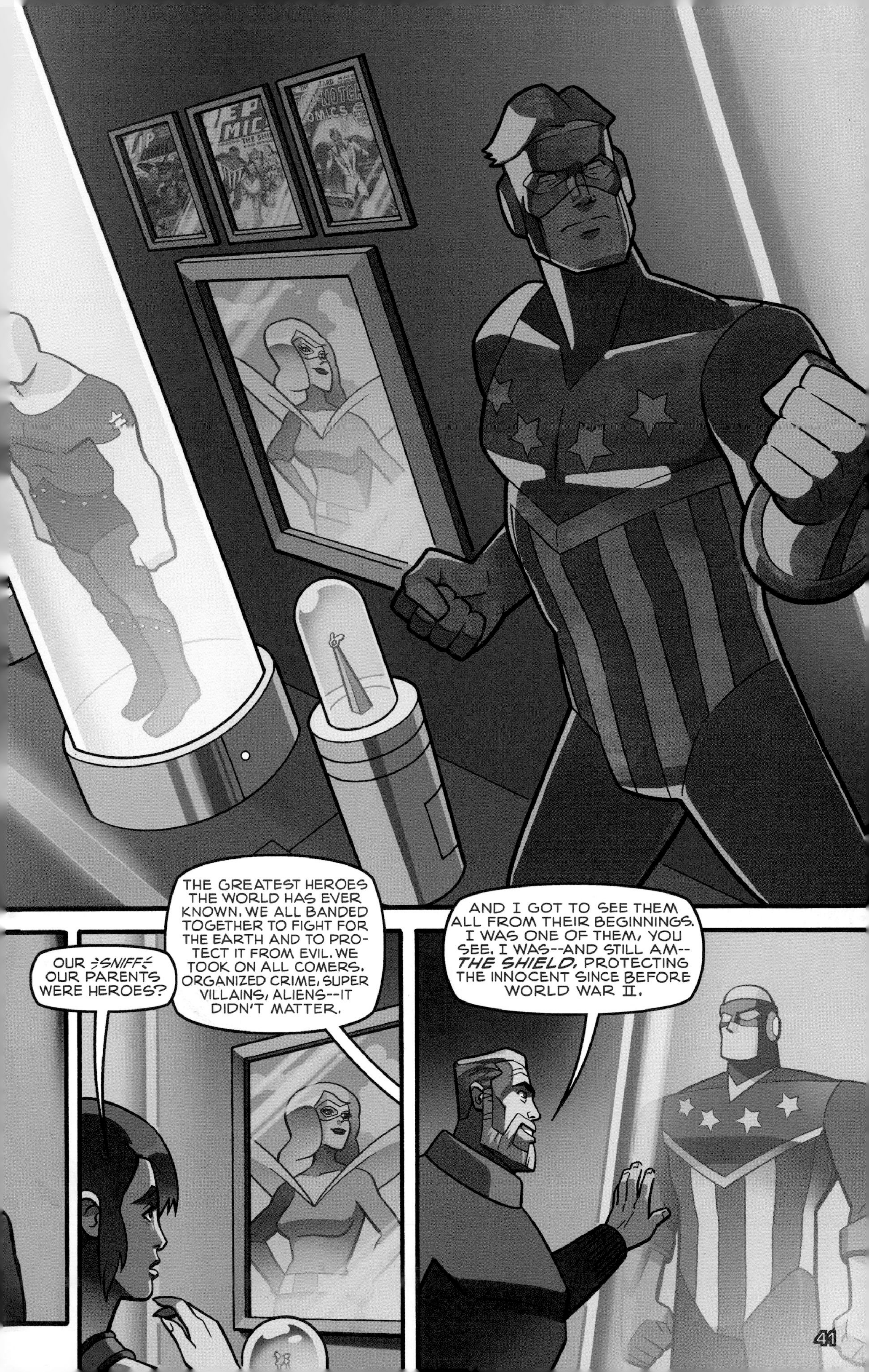
OUR ⚡SNIFF⚡ OUR PARENTS WERE HEROES?
THE GREATEST HEROES THE WORLD HAS EVER KNOWN. WE ALL BANDED TOGETHER TO FIGHT FOR THE EARTH AND TO PROTECT IT FROM EVIL. WE TOOK ON ALL COMERS. ORGANIZED CRIME, SUPER VILLAINS, ALIENS--IT DIDN'T MATTER.
AND I GOT TO SEE THEM ALL FROM THEIR BEGINNINGS. I WAS ONE OF THEM, YOU SEE. I WAS--AND STILL AM--*THE SHIELD*, PROTECTING THE INNOCENT SINCE BEFORE WORLD WAR II.

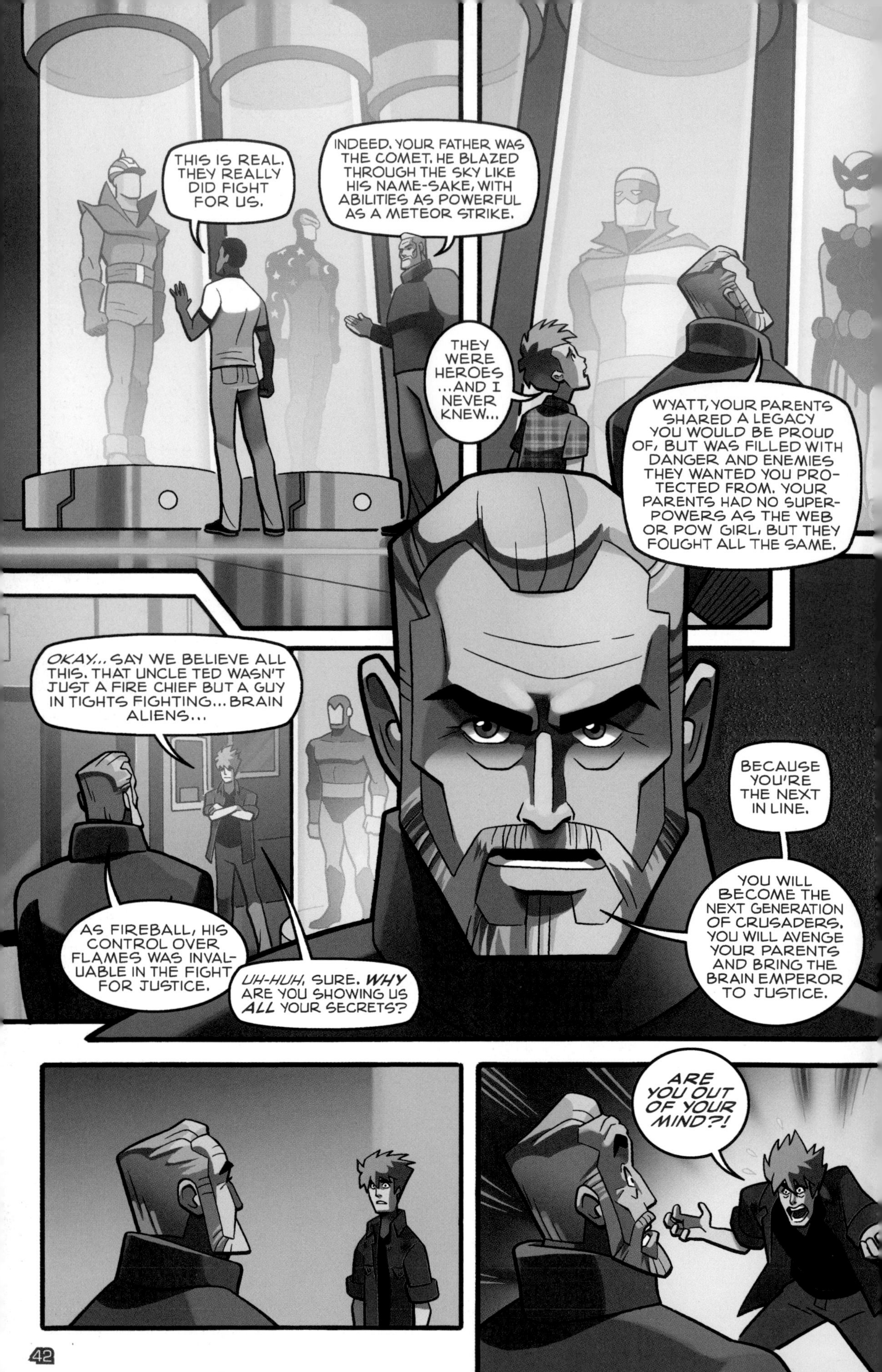
THIS IS REAL. THEY REALLY DID FIGHT FOR US.
INDEED. YOUR FATHER WAS THE COMET. HE BLAZED THROUGH THE SKY LIKE HIS NAME-SAKE, WITH ABILITIES AS POWERFUL AS A METEOR STRIKE.
THEY WERE HEROES ...AND I NEVER KNEW...
WYATT, YOUR PARENTS SHARED A LEGACY YOU WOULD BE PROUD OF, BUT WAS FILLED WITH DANGER AND ENEMIES THEY WANTED YOU PROTECTED FROM. YOUR PARENTS HAD NO SUPER-POWERS AS THE WEB OR POW GIRL, BUT THEY FOUGHT ALL THE SAME.
OKAY... SAY WE BELIEVE ALL THIS. THAT UNCLE TED WASN'T JUST A FIRE CHIEF BUT A GUY IN TIGHTS FIGHTING... BRAIN ALIENS...
AS FIREBALL, HIS CONTROL OVER FLAMES WAS INVALUABLE IN THE FIGHT FOR JUSTICE.
UH-HUH, SURE. ***WHY*** ARE YOU SHOWING US ***ALL*** YOUR SECRETS?
BECAUSE YOU'RE THE NEXT IN LINE.
YOU WILL BECOME THE NEXT GENERATION OF CRUSADERS. YOU WILL AVENGE YOUR PARENTS AND BRING THE BRAIN EMPEROR TO JUSTICE.
ARE YOU OUT OF YOUR MIND?!

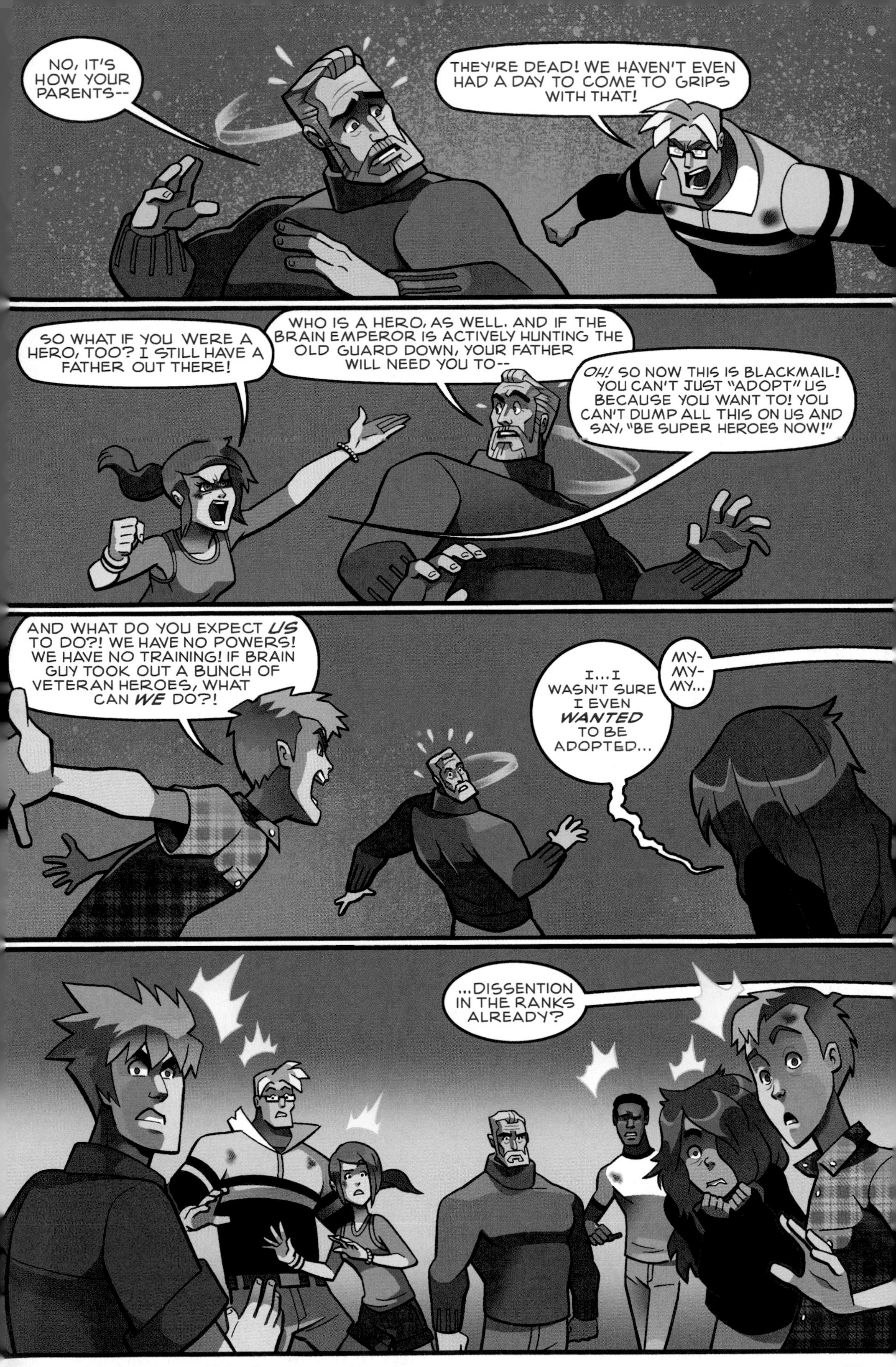
NO, IT'S HOW YOUR PARENTS--
THEY'RE DEAD! WE HAVEN'T EVEN HAD A DAY TO COME TO GRIPS WITH THAT!
SO WHAT IF YOU WERE A HERO, TOO? I STILL HAVE A FATHER OUT THERE!
WHO IS A HERO, AS WELL. AND IF THE BRAIN EMPEROR IS ACTIVELY HUNTING THE OLD GUARD DOWN, YOUR FATHER WILL NEED YOU TO--
OH! SO NOW THIS IS BLACKMAIL! YOU CAN'T JUST "ADOPT" US BECAUSE YOU WANT TO! YOU CAN'T DUMP ALL THIS ON US AND SAY, "BE SUPER HEROES NOW!"
AND WHAT DO YOU EXPECT US TO DO?! WE HAVE NO POWERS! WE HAVE NO TRAINING! IF BRAIN GUY TOOK OUT A BUNCH OF VETERAN HEROES, WHAT CAN WE DO?!
I...I WASN'T SURE I EVEN WANTED TO BE ADOPTED...
MY-MY-MY...
...DISSENTION IN THE RANKS ALREADY?

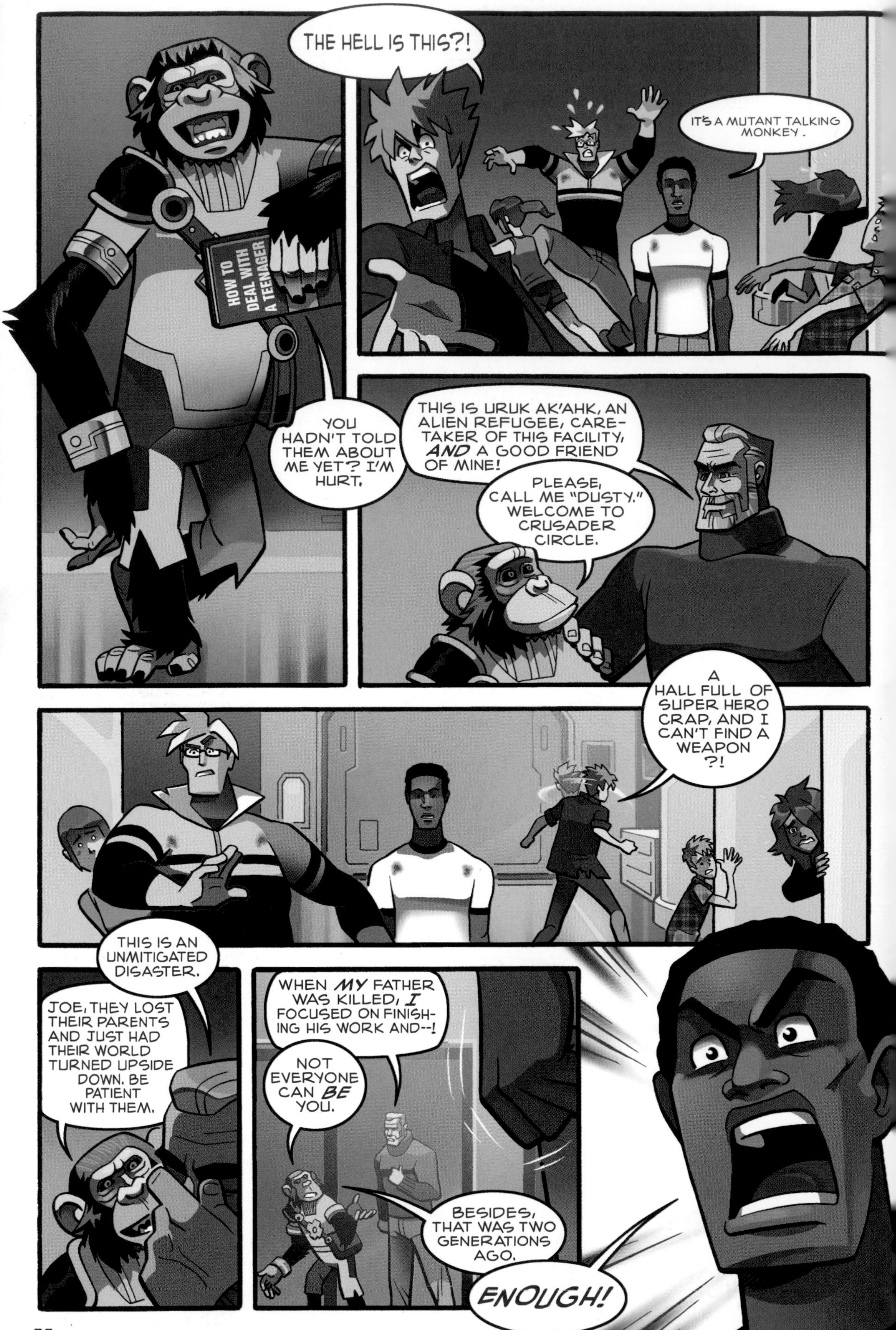
THE HELL IS THIS?!
IT'S A MUTANT TALKING MONKEY.
HOW TO DEAL WITH A TEENAGER
YOU HADN'T TOLD THEM ABOUT ME YET? I'M HURT.
THIS IS URUK AK'AHK, AN ALIEN REFUGEE, CARETAKER OF THIS FACILITY, AND A GOOD FRIEND OF MINE!
PLEASE, CALL ME "DUSTY." WELCOME TO CRUSADER CIRCLE.
A HALL FULL OF SUPER HERO CRAP, AND I CAN'T FIND A WEAPON?!
THIS IS AN UNMITIGATED DISASTER.
JOE, THEY LOST THEIR PARENTS AND JUST HAD THEIR WORLD TURNED UPSIDE DOWN. BE PATIENT WITH THEM.
WHEN MY FATHER WAS KILLED, I FOCUSED ON FINISHING HIS WORK AND--!
NOT EVERYONE CAN BE YOU.
BESIDES, THAT WAS TWO GENERATIONS AGO.
ENOUGH!

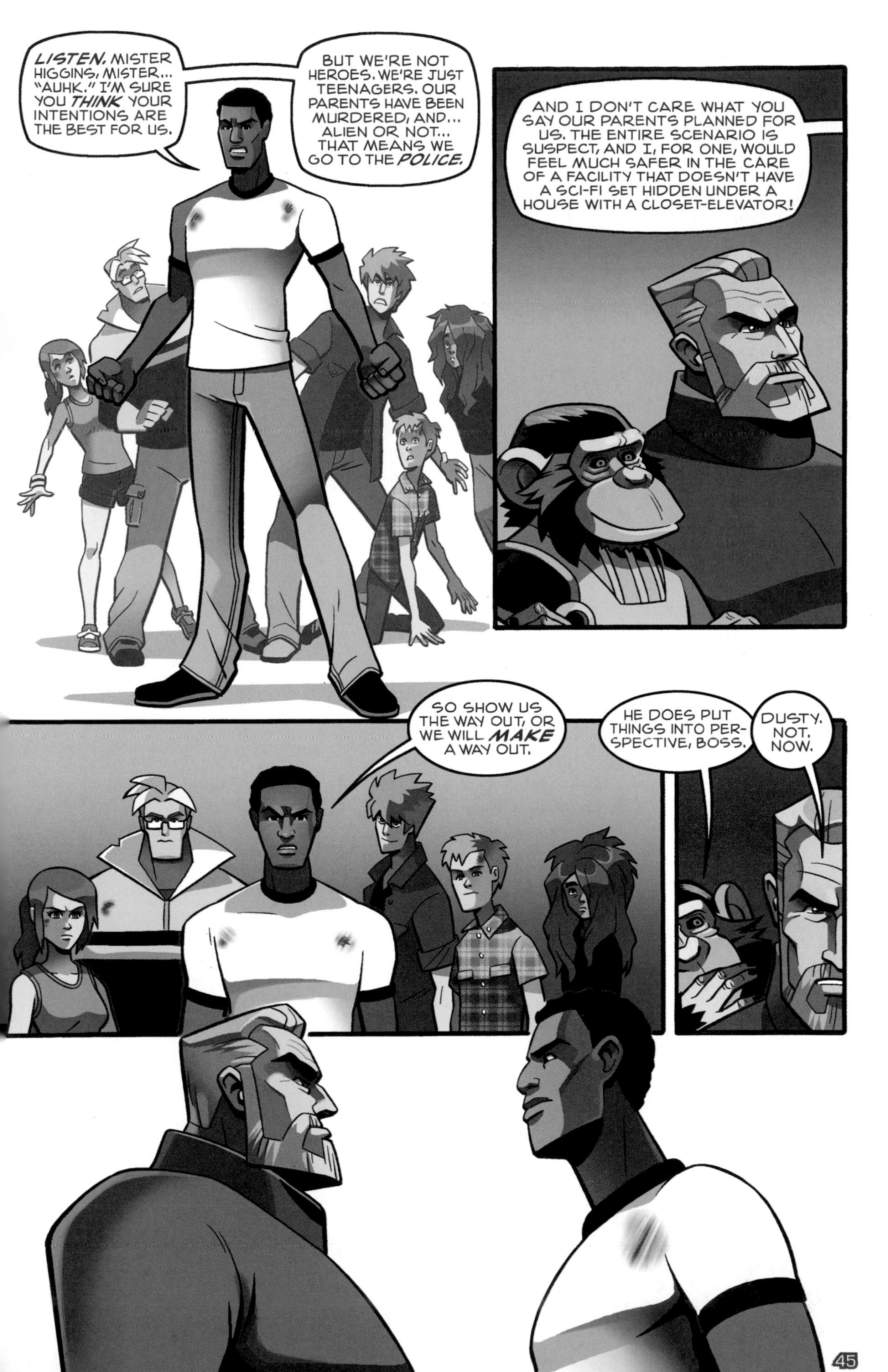
LISTEN. MISTER HIGGINS, MISTER... "AUHK." I'M SURE YOU THINK YOUR INTENTIONS ARE THE BEST FOR US.
BUT WE'RE NOT HEROES. WE'RE JUST TEENAGERS. OUR PARENTS HAVE BEEN MURDERED, AND... ALIEN OR NOT... THAT MEANS WE GO TO THE POLICE.
AND I DON'T CARE WHAT YOU SAY OUR PARENTS PLANNED FOR US. THE ENTIRE SCENARIO IS SUSPECT, AND I, FOR ONE, WOULD FEEL MUCH SAFER IN THE CARE OF A FACILITY THAT DOESN'T HAVE A SCI-FI SET HIDDEN UNDER A HOUSE WITH A CLOSET-ELEVATOR!
SO SHOW US THE WAY OUT, OR WE WILL MAKE A WAY OUT.
HE DOES PUT THINGS INTO PER-SPECTIVE, BOSS.
DUSTY. NOT. NOW.

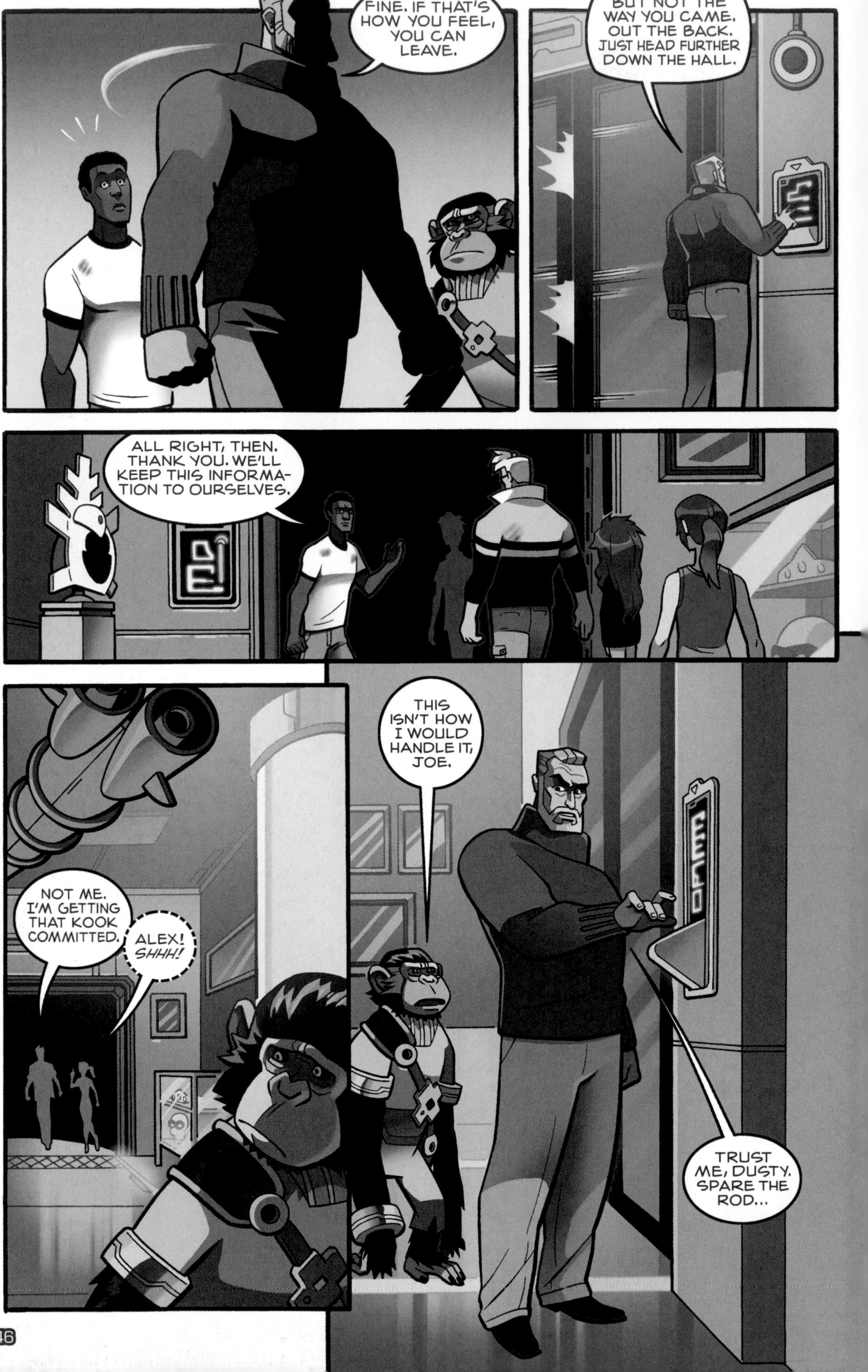
FINE. IF THAT'S HOW YOU FEEL, YOU CAN LEAVE.
BUT NOT THE WAY YOU CAME. OUT THE BACK. JUST HEAD FURTHER DOWN THE HALL.
ALL RIGHT, THEN. THANK YOU. WE'LL KEEP THIS INFORMATION TO OURSELVES.
THIS ISN'T HOW I WOULD HANDLE IT, JOE.
NOT ME. I'M GETTING THAT KOOK COMMITTED.
ALEX! SHHH!
TRUST ME, DUSTY. SPARE THE ROD...

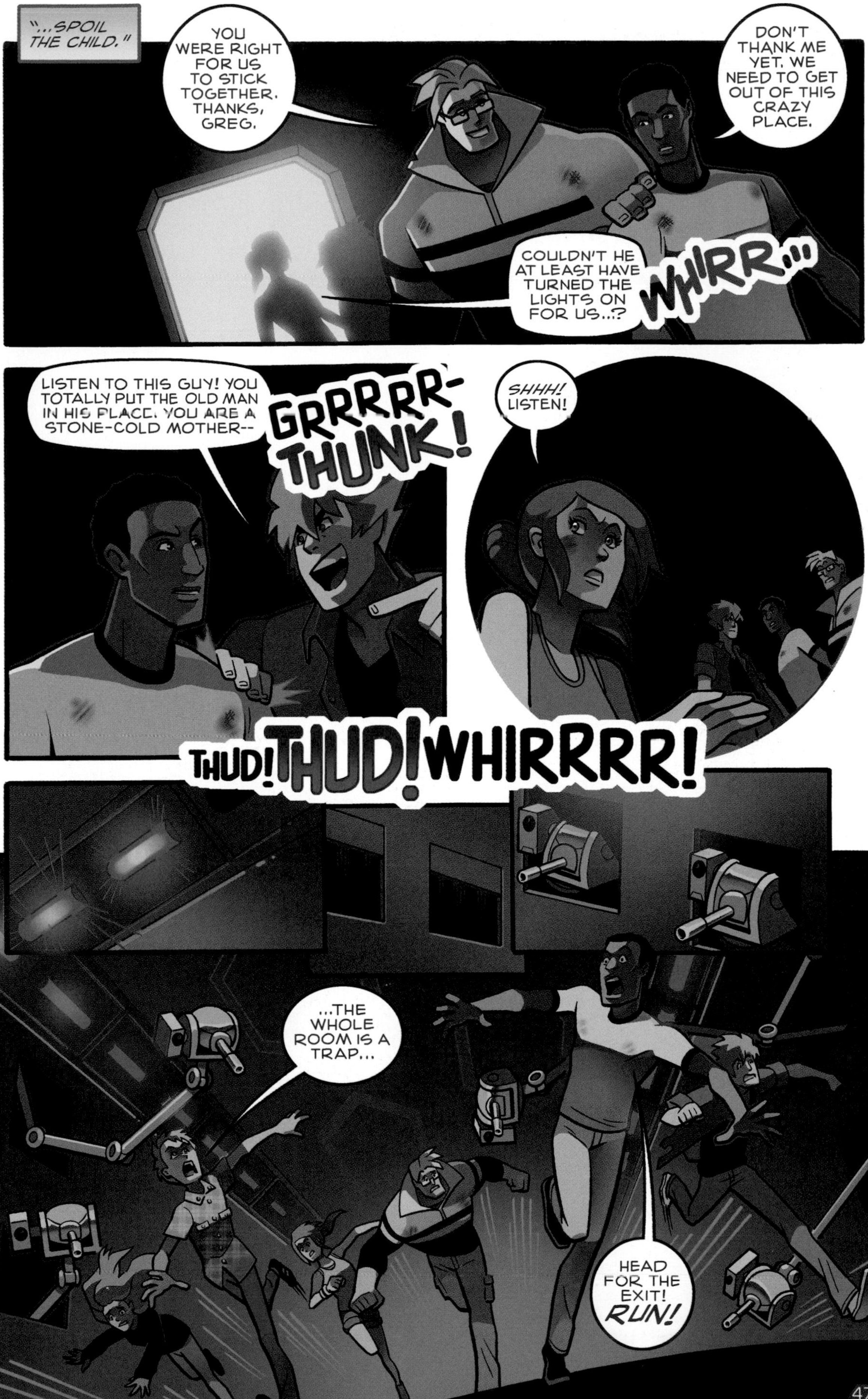
"...SPOIL THE CHILD."
YOU WERE RIGHT FOR US TO STICK TOGETHER. THANKS, GREG.
DON'T THANK ME YET. WE NEED TO GET OUT OF THIS CRAZY PLACE.
COULDN'T HE AT LEAST HAVE TURNED THE LIGHTS ON FOR US...?
WHIRR...
LISTEN TO THIS GUY! YOU TOTALLY PUT THE OLD MAN IN HIS PLACE. YOU ARE A STONE-COLD MOTHER--
GRRRRR-THUNK!
SHHH! LISTEN!
THUD! THUD! WHIRRRR!
...THE WHOLE ROOM IS A TRAP...
HEAD FOR THE EXIT! RUN!

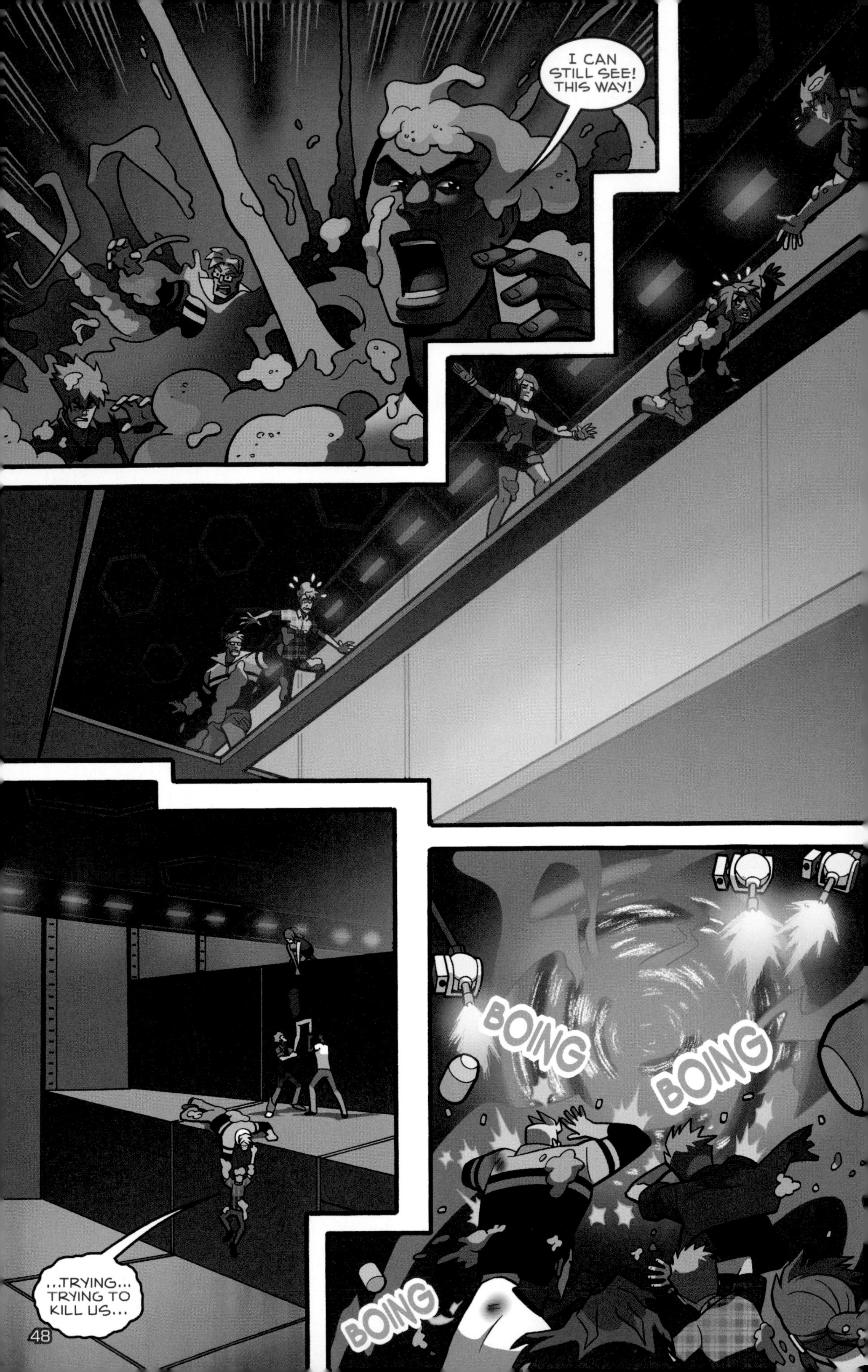

I CAN STILL SEE! THIS WAY!
BOING
BOING
...TRYING... TRYING TO KILL US...
BOING

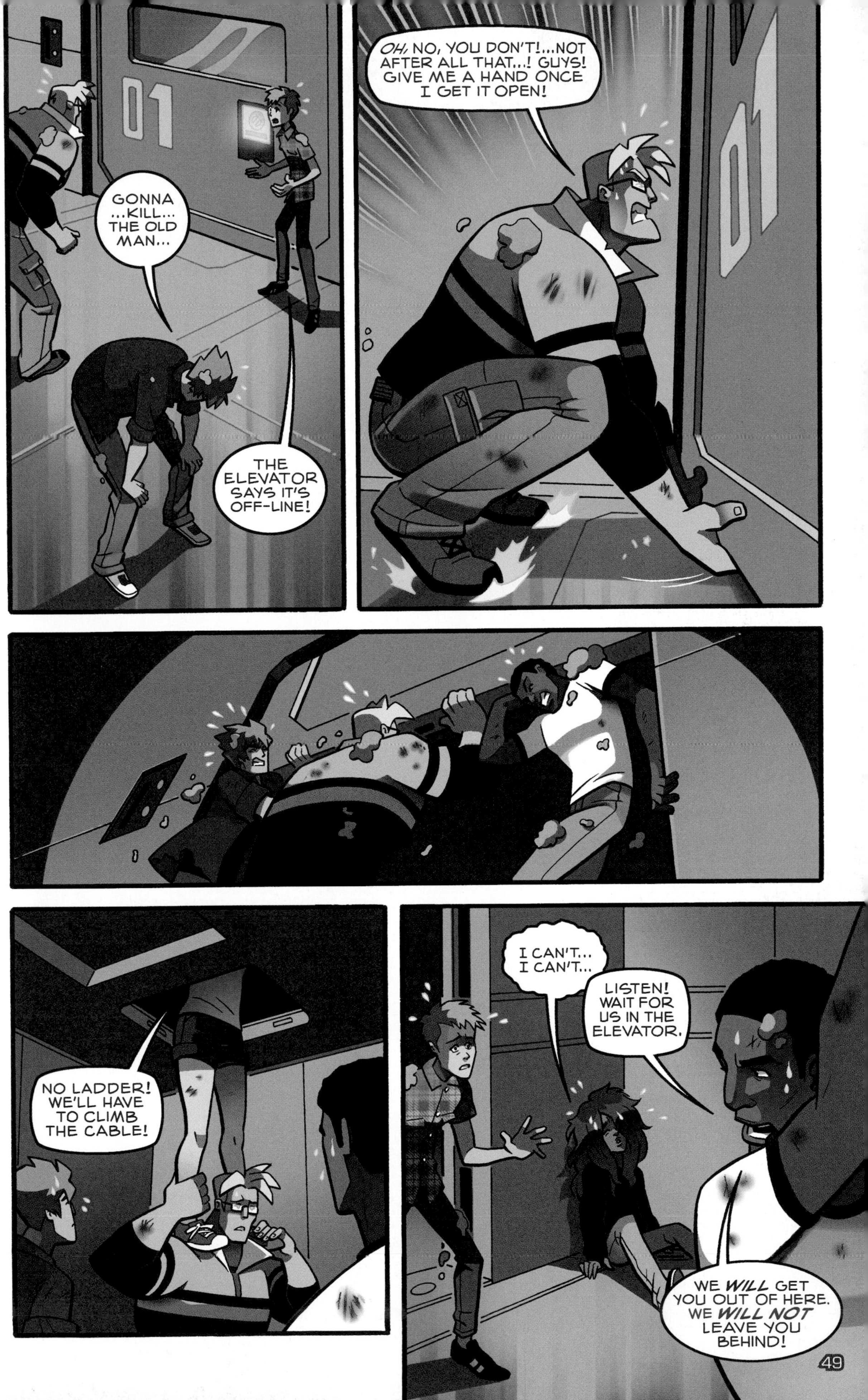
GONNA ...KILL... THE OLD MAN...
THE ELEVATOR SAYS IT'S OFF-LINE!
OH, NO, YOU DON'T!...NOT AFTER ALL THAT...! GUYS! GIVE ME A HAND ONCE I GET IT OPEN!
NO LADDER! WE'LL HAVE TO CLIMB THE CABLE!
I CAN'T... I CAN'T...
LISTEN! WAIT FOR US IN THE ELEVATOR.
WE *WILL* GET YOU OUT OF HERE. WE *WILL NOT* LEAVE YOU BEHIND!

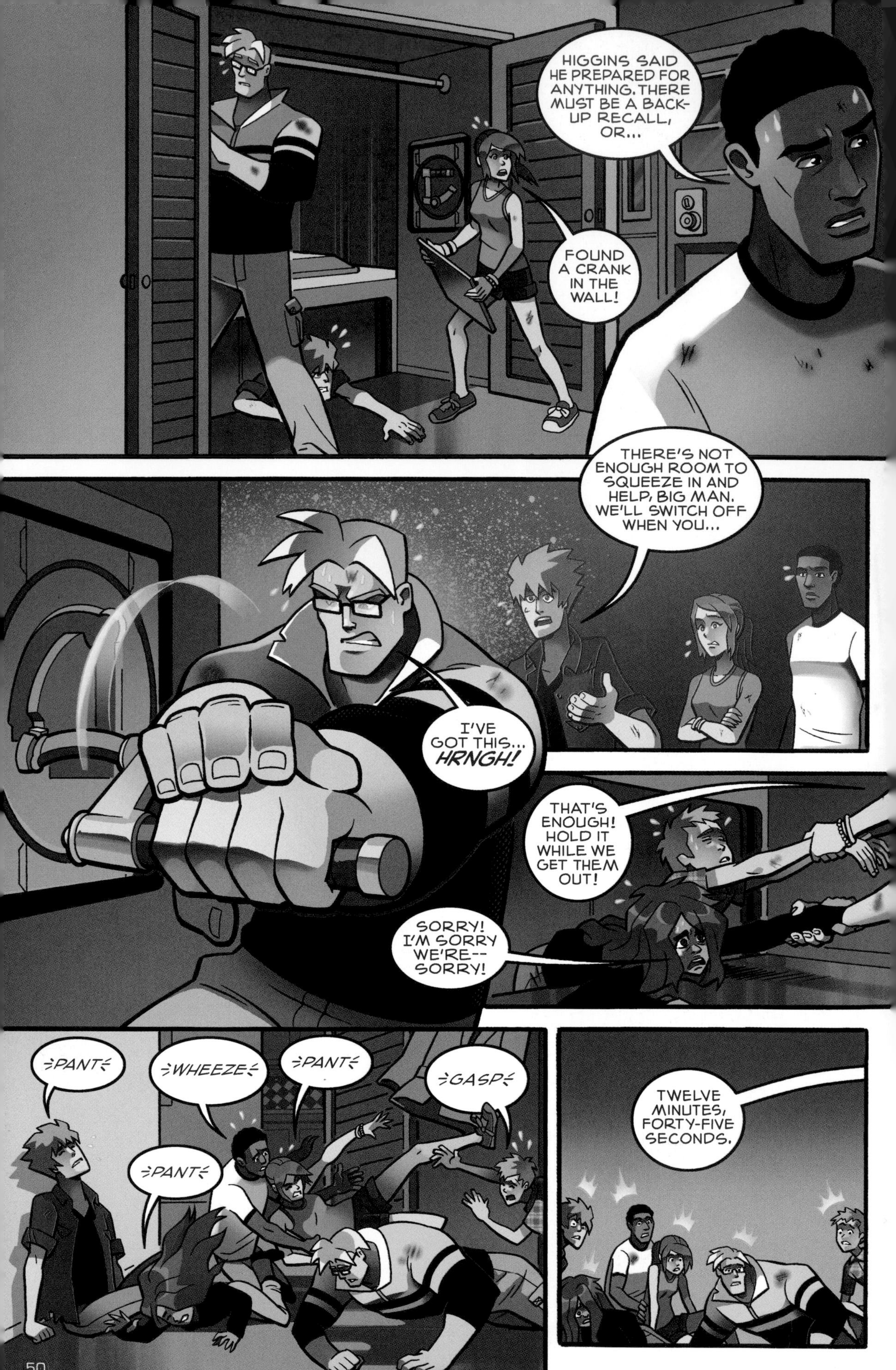

HIGGINS SAID HE PREPARED FOR ANYTHING. THERE MUST BE A BACK-UP RECALL, OR...
FOUND A CRANK IN THE WALL!
THERE'S NOT ENOUGH ROOM TO SQUEEZE IN AND HELP, BIG MAN. WE'LL SWITCH OFF WHEN YOU...
I'VE GOT THIS... *HRNGH!*
THAT'S ENOUGH! HOLD IT WHILE WE GET THEM OUT!
SORRY! I'M SORRY WE'RE-- SORRY!
PANT
WHEEZE
PANT
GASP
PANT
TWELVE MINUTES, FORTY-FIVE SECONDS.

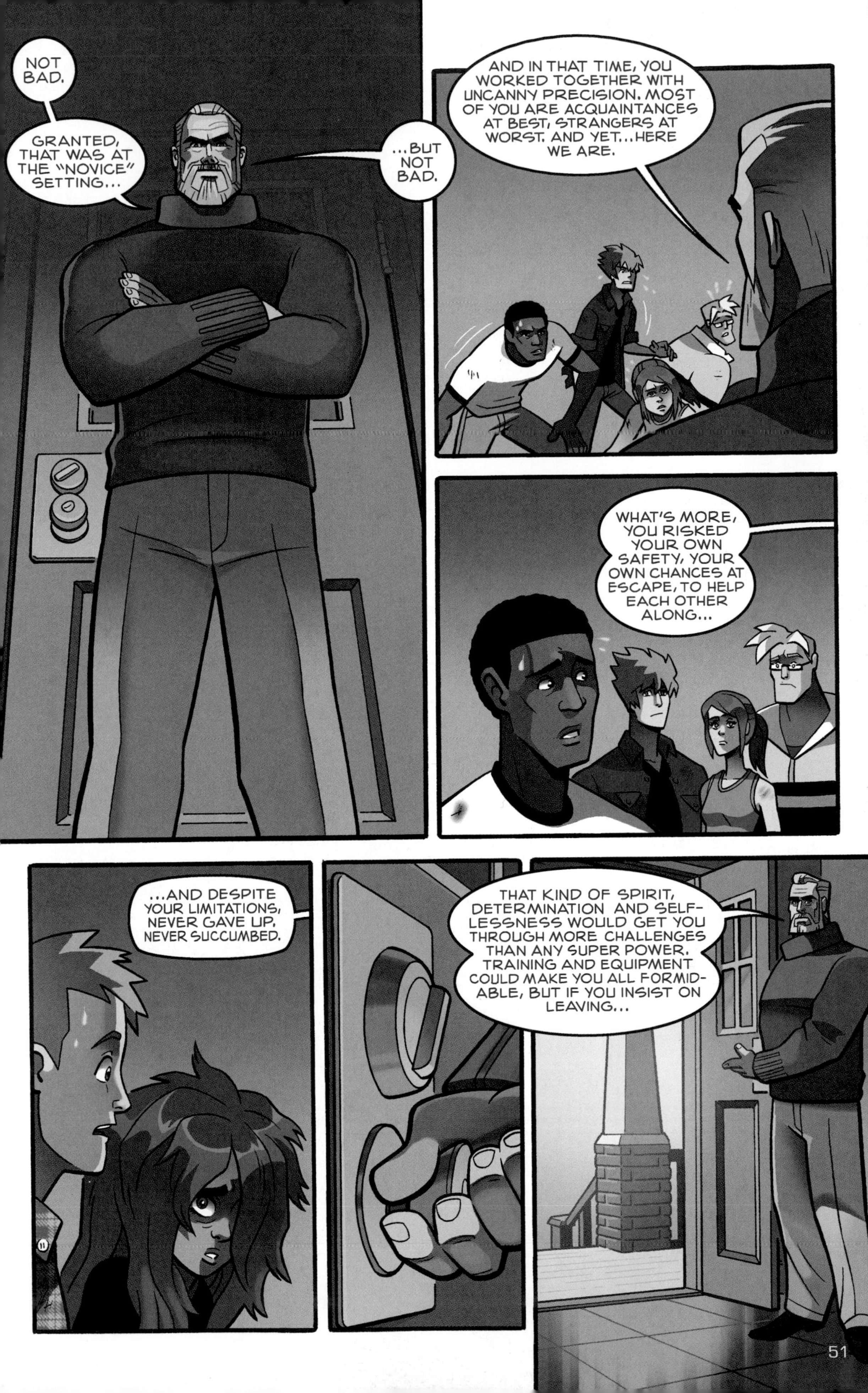
NOT BAD.
GRANTED, THAT WAS AT THE "NOVICE" SETTING...
...BUT NOT BAD.
AND IN THAT TIME, YOU WORKED TOGETHER WITH UNCANNY PRECISION. MOST OF YOU ARE ACQUAINTANCES AT BEST, STRANGERS AT WORST. AND YET...HERE WE ARE.
WHAT'S MORE, YOU RISKED YOUR OWN SAFETY, YOUR OWN CHANCES AT ESCAPE, TO HELP EACH OTHER ALONG...
...AND DESPITE YOUR LIMITATIONS, NEVER GAVE UP. NEVER SUCCUMBED.
THAT KIND OF SPIRIT, DETERMINATION AND SELF-LESSNESS WOULD GET YOU THROUGH MORE CHALLENGES THAN ANY SUPER POWER. TRAINING AND EQUIPMENT COULD MAKE YOU ALL FORMID-ABLE, BUT IF YOU INSIST ON LEAVING...

THE FINEST HEROES IN THE WORLD, YOUR PARENTS AND GUARDIANS, COULDN'T STAND AGAINST THE BRAIN EMPEROR. REMEMBER THAT WHEN YOU ASK THE "PROPER AUTHORITIES" TO STEP IN.

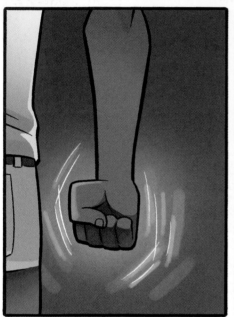

YOU REALLY THINK YOU CAN MAKE US SUPER HEROES?

BETWEEN YOUR COLLECTIVE LEGACIES AND MY LEADERSHIP?

I DON'T THINK--I *KNOW* I CAN.

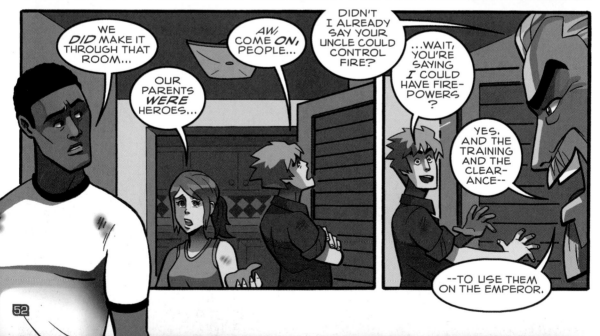

WE *DID* MAKE IT THROUGH THAT ROOM...

OUR PARENTS *WERE* HEROES...

AW, COME *ON,* PEOPLE...

DIDN'T I ALREADY SAY YOUR UNCLE COULD CONTROL FIRE?

...WAIT, YOU'RE SAYING *I* COULD HAVE FIRE-POWERS?

YES. AND THE TRAINING AND THE CLEAR-ANCE--

--TO USE THEM ON THE EMPEROR.

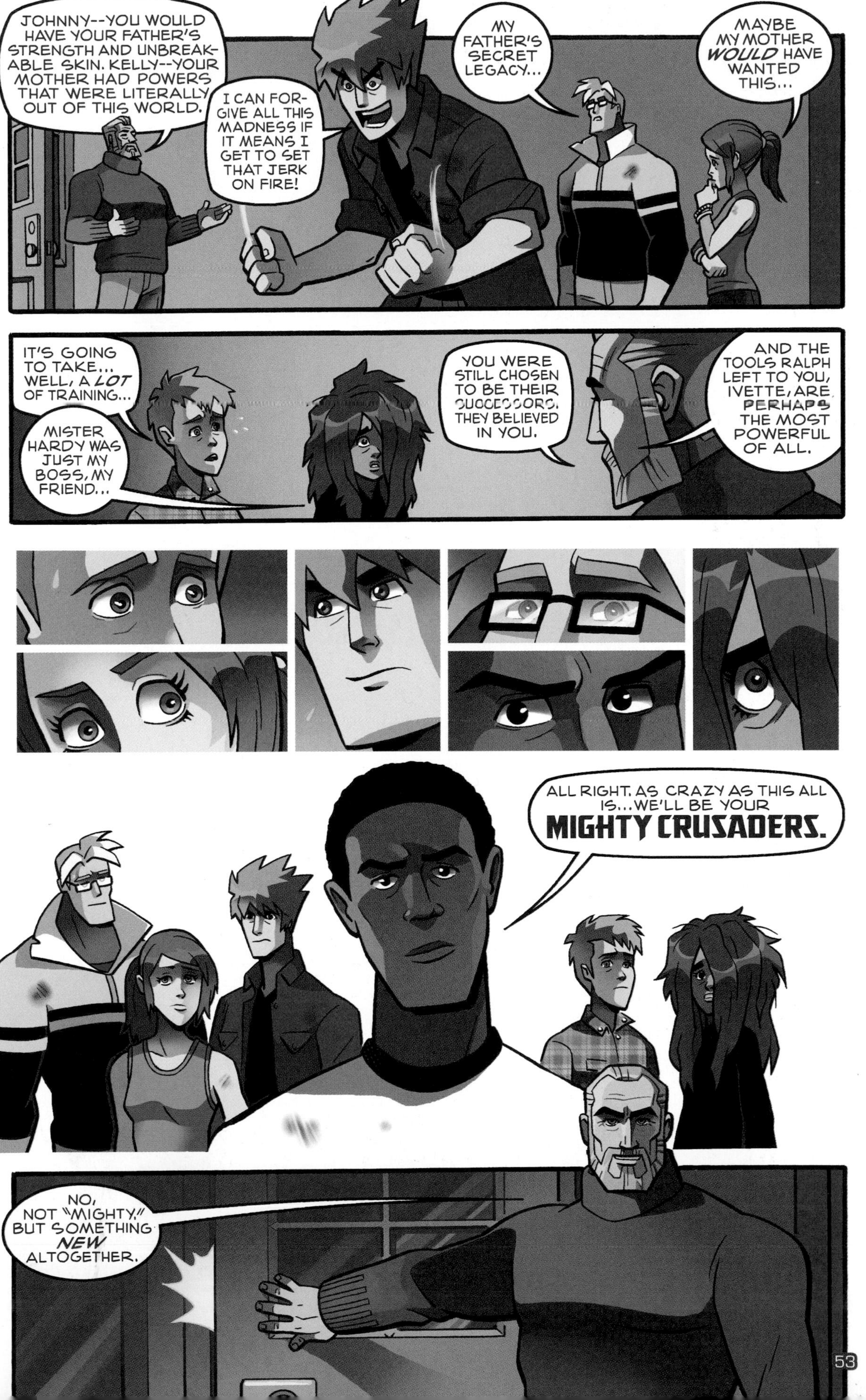
JOHNNY--YOU WOULD HAVE YOUR FATHER'S STRENGTH AND UNBREAKABLE SKIN. KELLY--YOUR MOTHER HAD POWERS THAT WERE LITERALLY OUT OF THIS WORLD.
I CAN FORGIVE ALL THIS MADNESS IF IT MEANS I GET TO SET THAT JERK ON FIRE!
MY FATHER'S SECRET LEGACY...
MAYBE MY MOTHER *WOULD* HAVE WANTED THIS...
IT'S GOING TO TAKE... WELL, A *LOT* OF TRAINING...
MISTER HARDY WAS JUST MY BOSS, MY FRIEND...
YOU WERE STILL CHOSEN TO BE THEIR SUCCESSORS. THEY BELIEVED IN YOU.
AND THE TOOLS RALPH LEFT TO YOU, IVETTE, ARE PERHAPS THE MOST POWERFUL OF ALL.
ALL RIGHT. AS CRAZY AS THIS ALL IS...WE'LL BE YOUR MIGHTY CRUSADERS.
NO, NOT "MIGHTY," BUT SOMETHING *NEW* ALTOGETHER.

CHAPTER 3

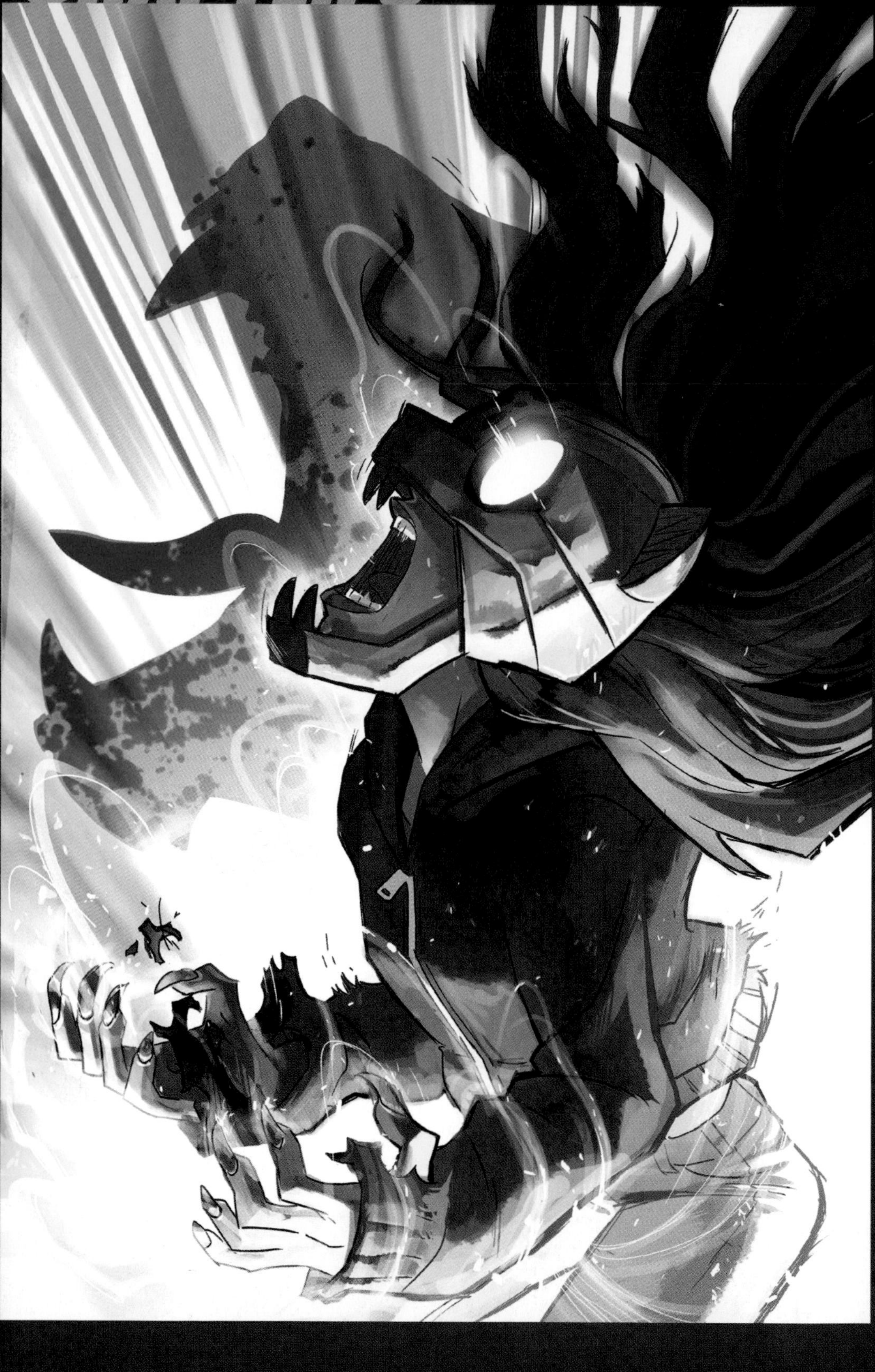

NEW CRUSADERS - RISE OF THE HEROES - ISSUE 3

COVER BY: BEN BATES

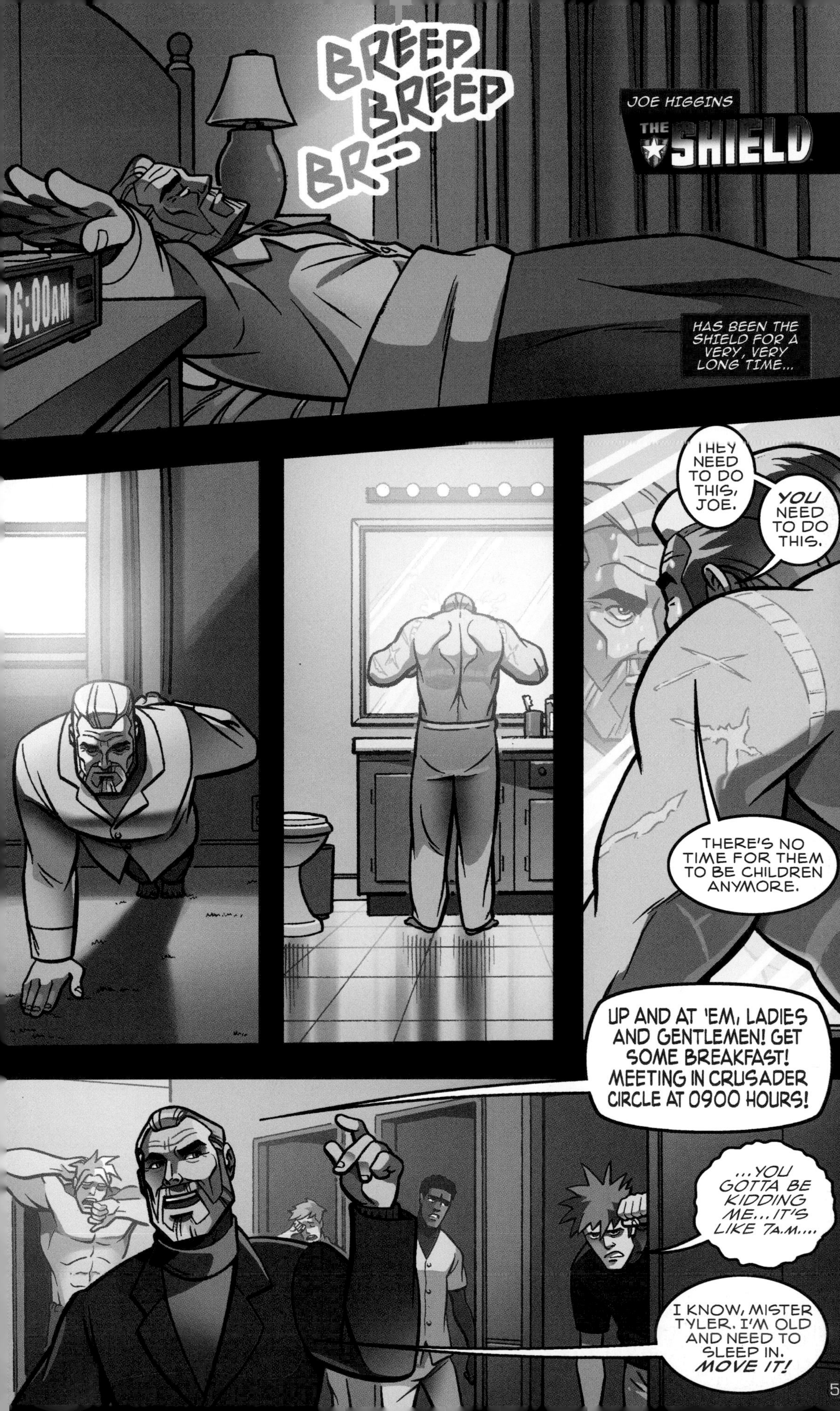
BREEP
BREEP
BR--
06:00AM
JOE HIGGINS
THE SHIELD
HAS BEEN THE SHIELD FOR A VERY, VERY LONG TIME...
THEY NEED TO DO THIS, JOE.
YOU NEED TO DO THIS.
THERE'S NO TIME FOR THEM TO BE CHILDREN ANYMORE.
UP AND AT 'EM, LADIES AND GENTLEMEN! GET SOME BREAKFAST! MEETING IN CRUSADER CIRCLE AT 0900 HOURS!
...YOU GOTTA BE KIDDING ME...IT'S LIKE 7A.M....
I KNOW, MISTER TYLER. I'M OLD AND NEED TO SLEEP IN. MOVE IT!

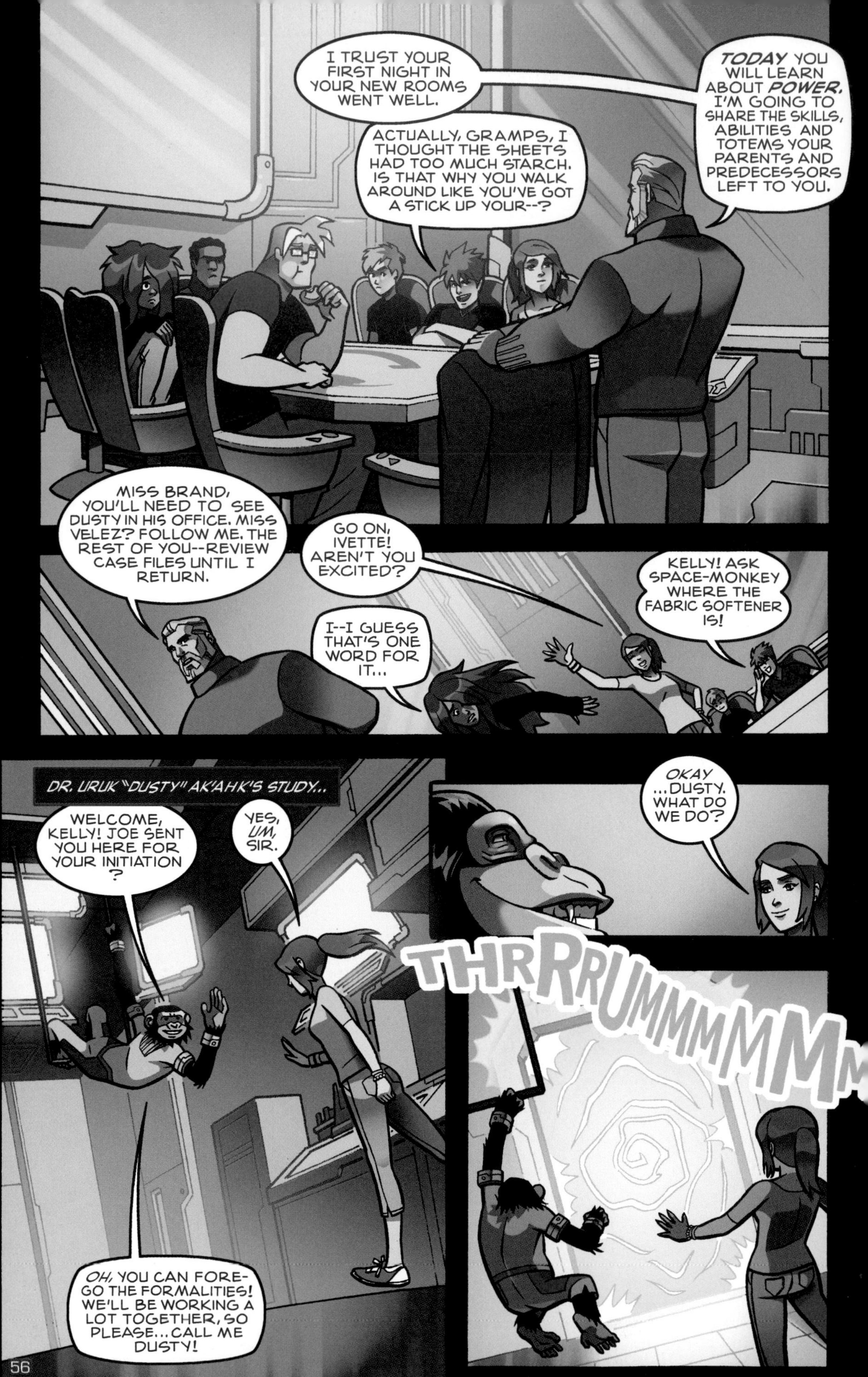
I TRUST YOUR FIRST NIGHT IN YOUR NEW ROOMS WENT WELL.
ACTUALLY, GRAMPS, I THOUGHT THE SHEETS HAD TOO MUCH STARCH. IS THAT WHY YOU WALK AROUND LIKE YOU'VE GOT A STICK UP YOUR--?
TODAY YOU WILL LEARN ABOUT POWER. I'M GOING TO SHARE THE SKILLS, ABILITIES AND TOTEMS YOUR PARENTS AND PREDECESSORS LEFT TO YOU.
MISS BRAND, YOU'LL NEED TO SEE DUSTY IN HIS OFFICE. MISS VELEZ? FOLLOW ME. THE REST OF YOU--REVIEW CASE FILES UNTIL I RETURN.
GO ON, IVETTE! AREN'T YOU EXCITED?
I--I GUESS THAT'S ONE WORD FOR IT...
KELLY! ASK SPACE-MONKEY WHERE THE FABRIC SOFTENER IS!
DR. URUK "DUSTY" AK'AHK'S STUDY...
WELCOME, KELLY! JOE SENT YOU HERE FOR YOUR INITIATION?
YES, UM, SIR.
OH, YOU CAN FORE-GO THE FORMALITIES! WE'LL BE WORKING A LOT TOGETHER, SO PLEASE...CALL ME DUSTY!
OKAY ...DUSTY. WHAT DO WE DO?
THRRRUMMMMMMM

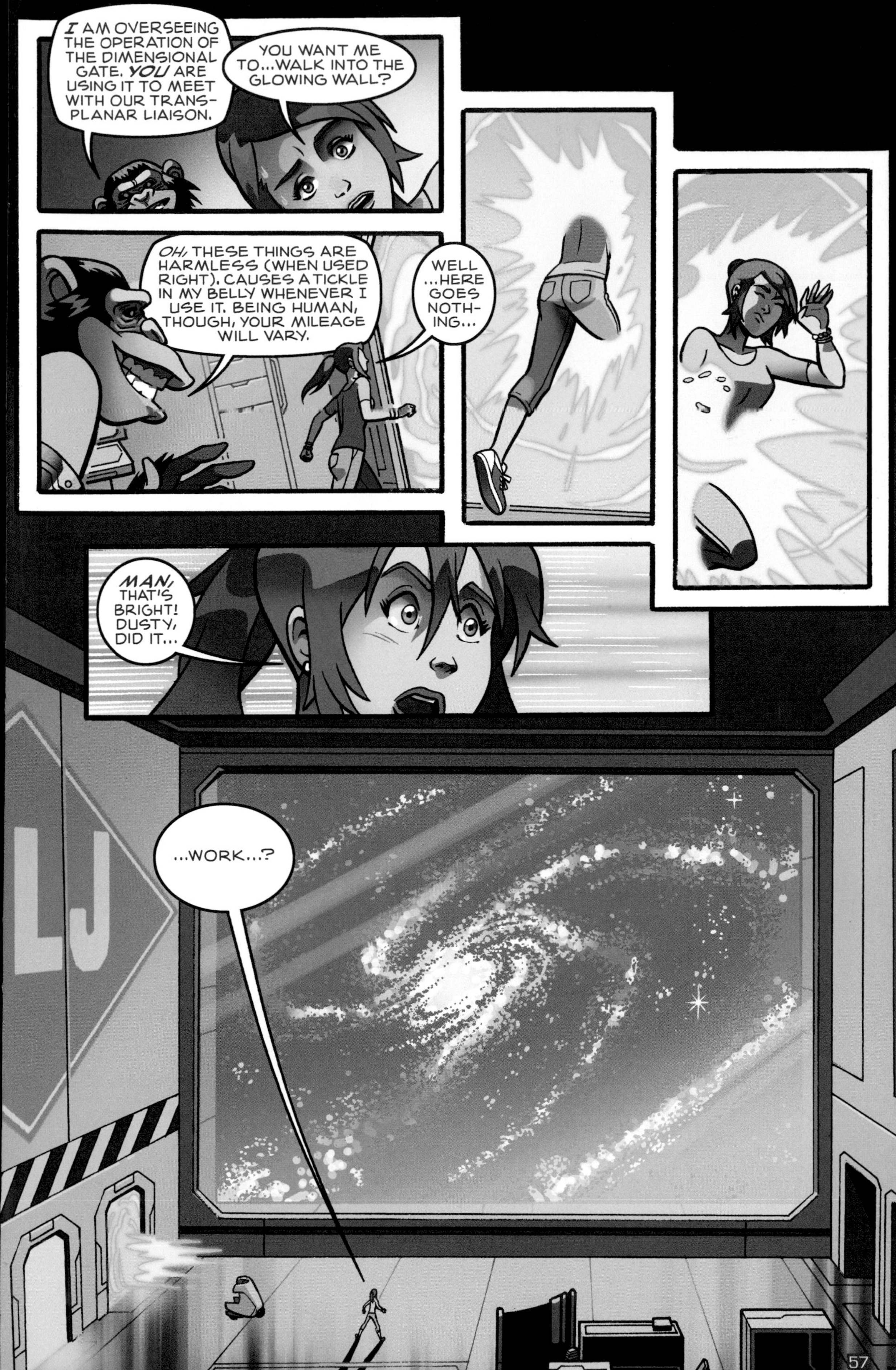
I AM OVERSEEING THE OPERATION OF THE DIMENSIONAL GATE. YOU ARE USING IT TO MEET WITH OUR TRANS-PLANAR LIAISON.
YOU WANT ME TO...WALK INTO THE GLOWING WALL?
OH, THESE THINGS ARE HARMLESS (WHEN USED RIGHT). CAUSES A TICKLE IN MY BELLY WHENEVER I USE IT. BEING HUMAN, THOUGH, YOUR MILEAGE WILL VARY.
WELL ...HERE GOES NOTHING...
MAN, THAT'S BRIGHT! DUSTY, DID IT...
LJ
...WORK...?

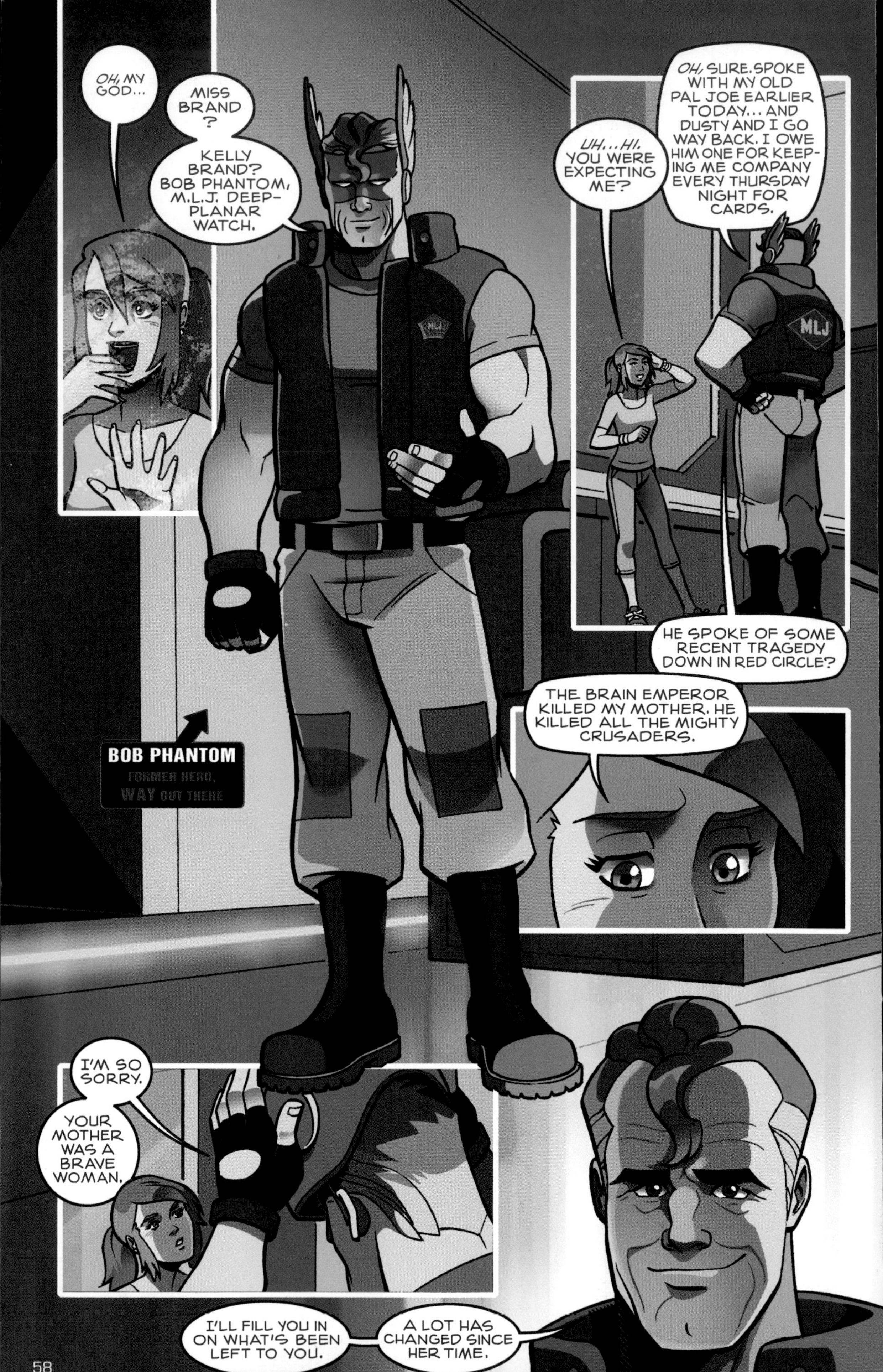
OH, MY GOD...
MISS BRAND?
KELLY BRAND? BOB PHANTOM, M.L.J. DEEP-PLANAR WATCH.
MLJ
BOB PHANTOM
FORMER HERO, WAY OUT THERE
UH...HI. YOU WERE EXPECTING ME?
OH, SURE. SPOKE WITH MY OLD PAL JOE EARLIER TODAY... AND DUSTY AND I GO WAY BACK. I OWE HIM ONE FOR KEEPING ME COMPANY EVERY THURSDAY NIGHT FOR CARDS.
MLJ
HE SPOKE OF SOME RECENT TRAGEDY DOWN IN RED CIRCLE?
THE BRAIN EMPEROR KILLED MY MOTHER. HE KILLED ALL THE MIGHTY CRUSADERS.
I'M SO SORRY.
YOUR MOTHER WAS A BRAVE WOMAN.
A LOT HAS CHANGED SINCE HER TIME.
I'LL FILL YOU IN ON WHAT'S BEEN LEFT TO YOU.

THE NATURE OF YOUR ABILITIES WILL BE BASED ON MYSTICAL POWER.

Y-YOU MEAN MAGIC?

THAT'S A BROAD TERM, BUT ACCURATE ENOUGH.

...THAT ALLOWS THE WEARER TO CHANNEL THE ABILITIES OF WHAT SOME ANCIENT CIVILIZATIONS DUBBED AS "GODS."

YOU'LL RECEIVE ONE OF THESE JAGUAR ARTIFACTS.

THE ARTIFACTS YOU SEE HERE EACH REPRESENT A UNIQUE POWER, A LIVING FORCE...

THE ...UM... BELT?

NO, THE BELT OF VARIGON BELONGED TO RALPH. OVER THE YEARS, HE LEARNED IT WAS A PIECE TO A SET OF ARMOR. HE RECOVERED ONLY THE HELMET OF AI APAEC...

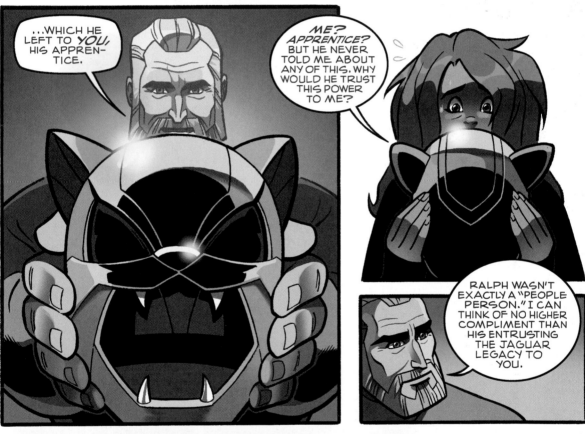

...WHICH HE LEFT TO YOU, HIS APPRENTICE.

ME? APPRENTICE? BUT HE NEVER TOLD ME ABOUT ANY OF THIS. WHY WOULD HE TRUST THIS POWER TO ME?

RALPH WASN'T EXACTLY A "PEOPLE PERSON." I CAN THINK OF NO HIGHER COMPLIMENT THAN HIS ENTRUSTING THE JAGUAR LEGACY TO YOU.

IT'S WHAT HE WANTED.

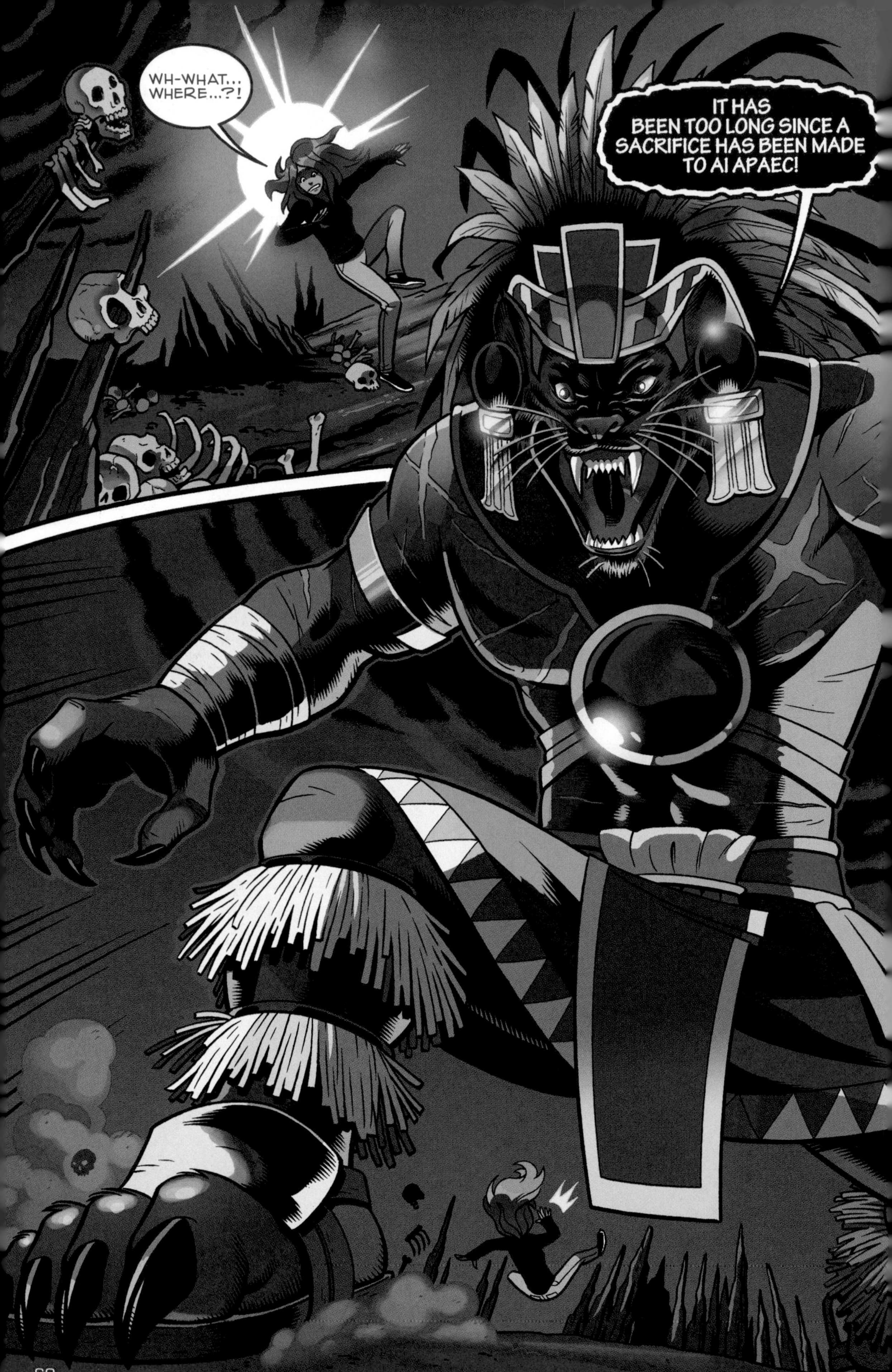
WH-WHAT... WHERE...?!
IT HAS BEEN TOO LONG SINCE A SACRIFICE HAS BEEN MADE TO AI APAEC!

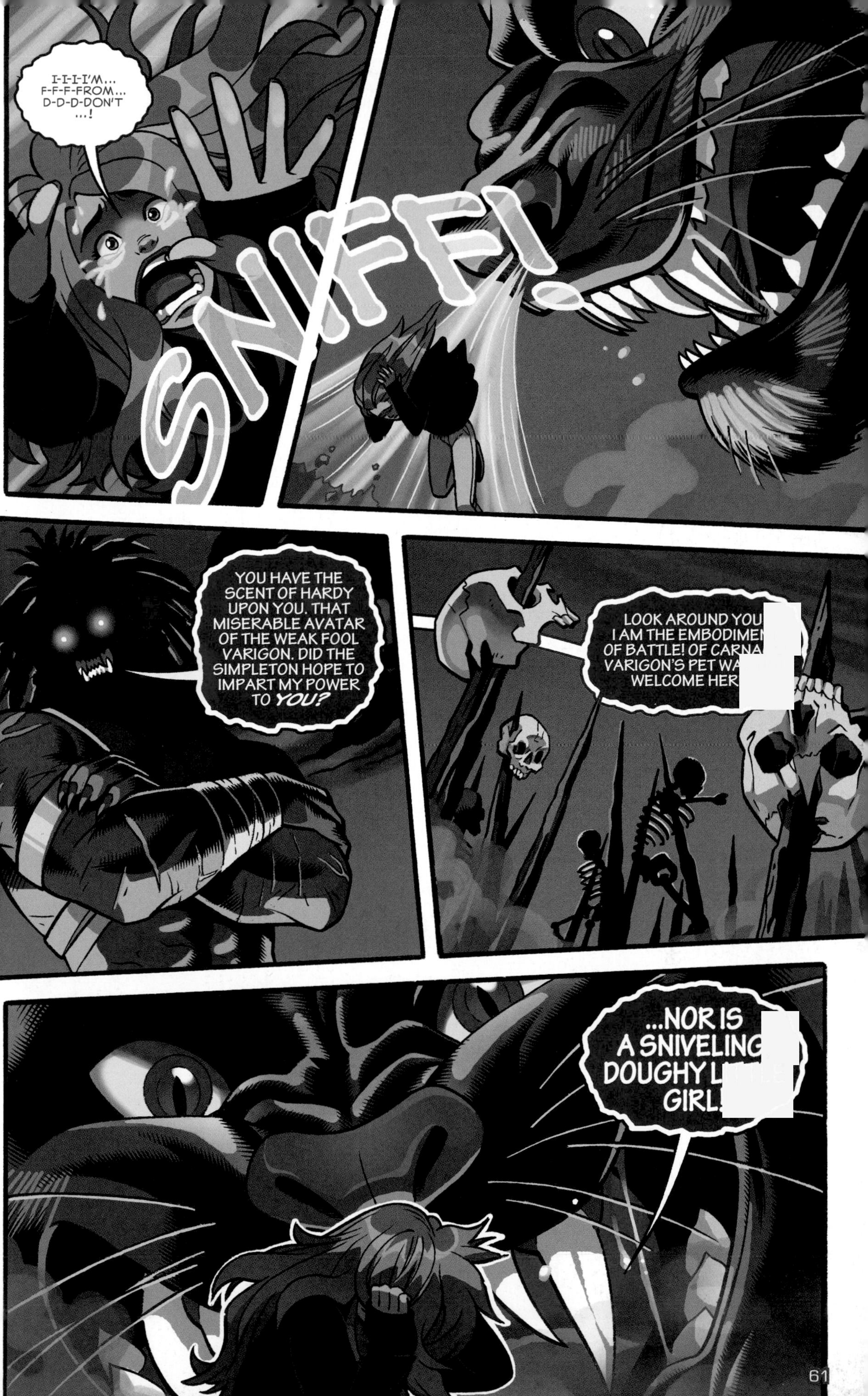

I-I-I-I'M... F-F-F-FROM... D-D-D-DON'T ...!
SNIFF!
YOU HAVE THE SCENT OF HARDY UPON YOU. THAT MISERABLE AVATAR OF THE WEAK FOOL VARIGON. DID THE SIMPLETON HOPE TO IMPART MY POWER TO *YOU?*
LOOK AROUND YOU I AM THE EMBODIMEN OF BATTLE! OF CARNA VARIGON'S PET WA WELCOME HER
...NOR IS A SNIVELING DOUGHY L GIRL!

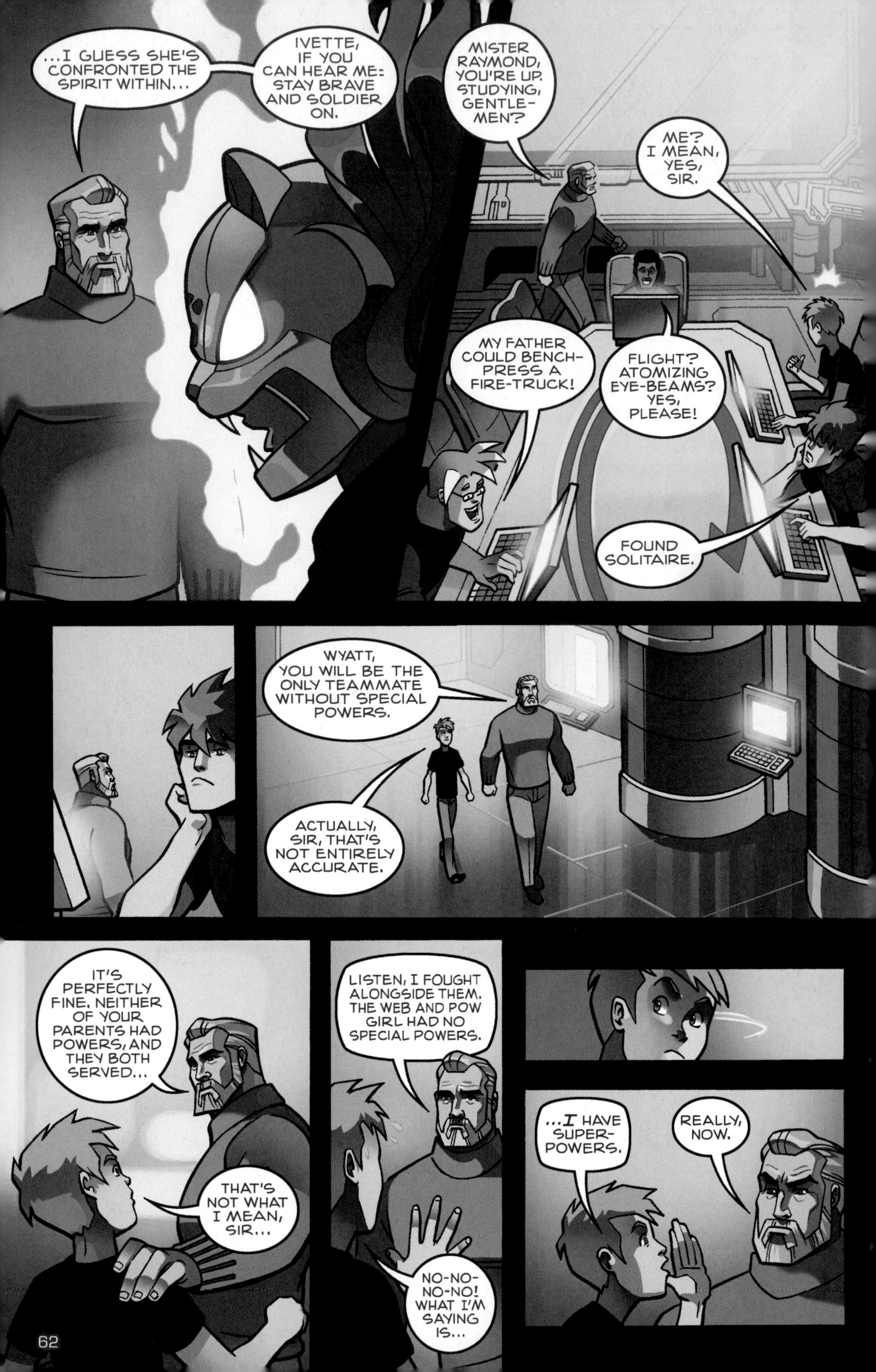
...I GUESS SHE'S CONFRONTED THE SPIRIT WITHIN...
IVETTE, IF YOU CAN HEAR ME: STAY BRAVE AND SOLDIER ON.
MISTER RAYMOND, YOU'RE UP. STUDYING, GENTLE-MEN?
ME? I MEAN, YES, SIR.
MY FATHER COULD BENCH-PRESS A FIRE-TRUCK!
FLIGHT? ATOMIZING EYE-BEAMS? YES, PLEASE!
FOUND SOLITAIRE.
WYATT, YOU WILL BE THE ONLY TEAMMATE WITHOUT SPECIAL POWERS.
ACTUALLY, SIR, THAT'S NOT ENTIRELY ACCURATE.
IT'S PERFECTLY FINE. NEITHER OF YOUR PARENTS HAD POWERS, AND THEY BOTH SERVED...
THAT'S NOT WHAT I MEAN, SIR...
LISTEN, I FOUGHT ALONGSIDE THEM. THE WEB AND POW GIRL HAD NO SPECIAL POWERS.
NO-NO-NO-NO! WHAT I'M SAYING IS...
...I HAVE SUPER-POWERS.
REALLY, NOW.

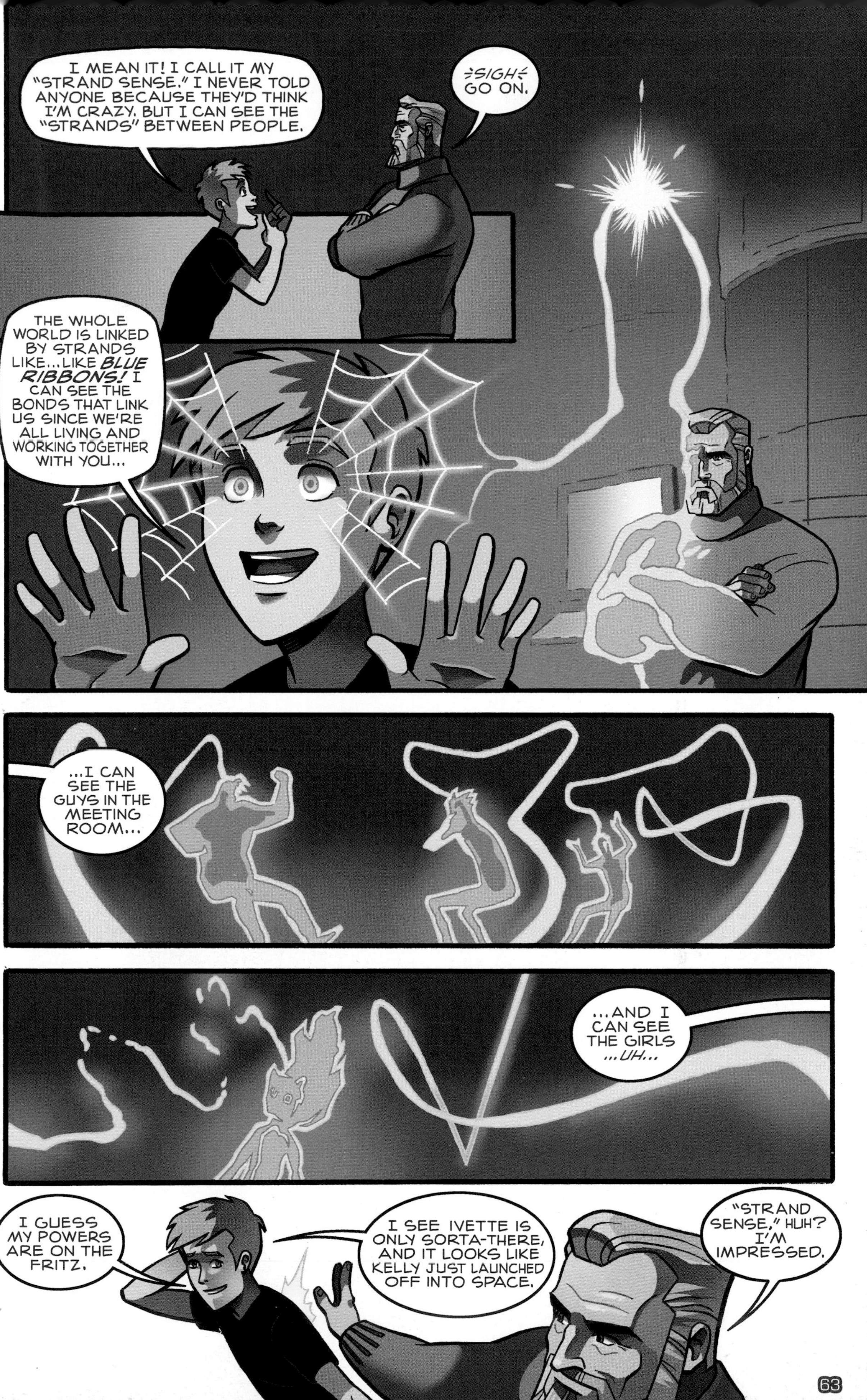
I MEAN IT! I CALL IT MY "STRAND SENSE." I NEVER TOLD ANYONE BECAUSE THEY'D THINK I'M CRAZY. BUT I CAN SEE THE "STRANDS" BETWEEN PEOPLE.
SIGH GO ON.
THE WHOLE WORLD IS LINKED BY STRANDS LIKE...LIKE *BLUE RIBBONS!* I CAN SEE THE BONDS THAT LINK US SINCE WE'RE ALL LIVING AND WORKING TOGETHER WITH YOU...
...I CAN SEE THE GUYS IN THE MEETING ROOM...
...AND I CAN SEE THE GIRLS ...UH...
I GUESS MY POWERS ARE ON THE FRITZ.
I SEE IVETTE IS ONLY SORTA-THERE, AND IT LOOKS LIKE KELLY JUST LAUNCHED OFF INTO SPACE.
"STRAND SENSE," HUH? I'M IMPRESSED.

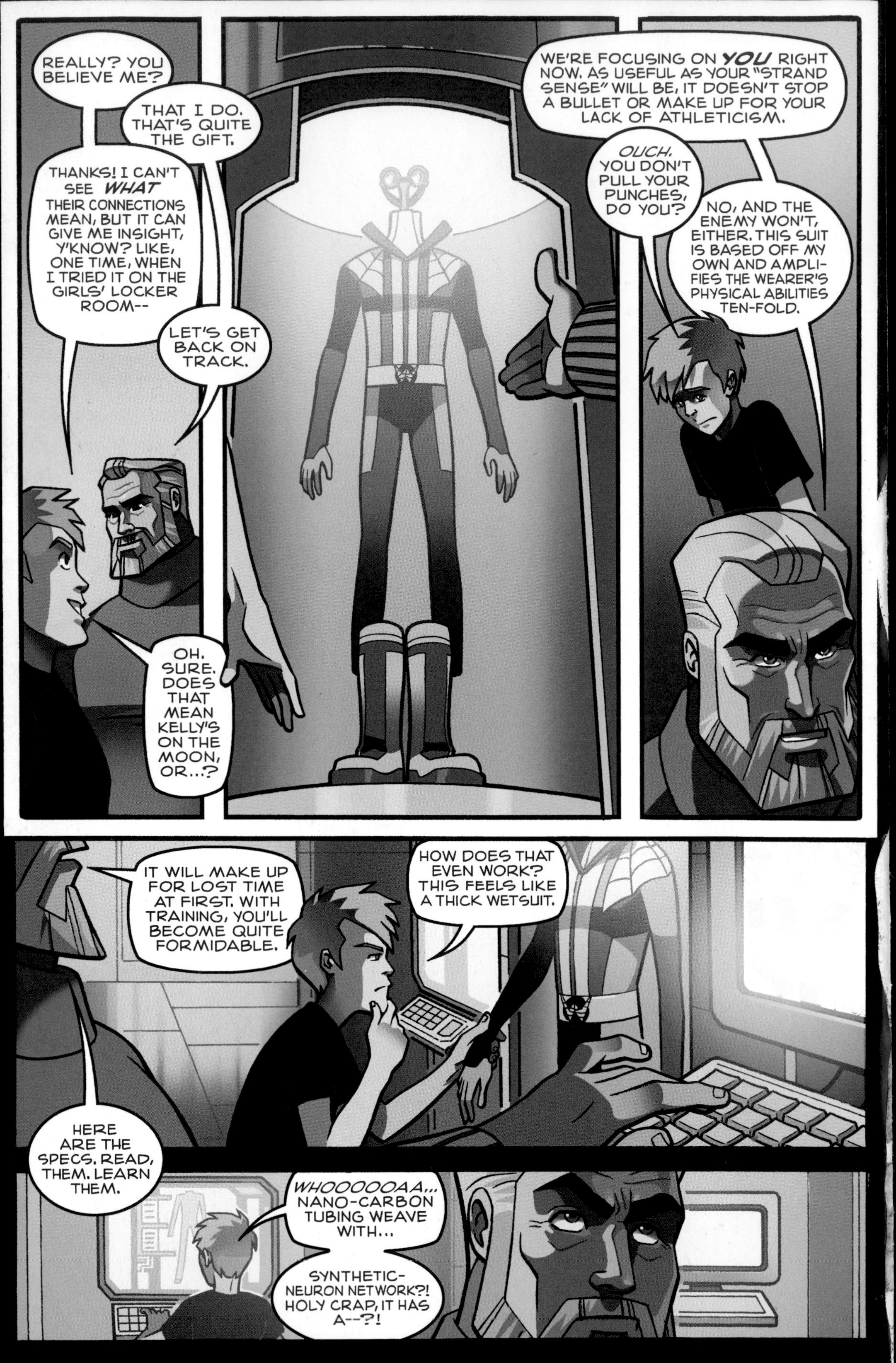
REALLY? YOU BELIEVE ME?
THAT I DO. THAT'S QUITE THE GIFT.
THANKS! I CAN'T SEE *WHAT* THEIR CONNECTIONS MEAN, BUT IT CAN GIVE ME INSIGHT, Y'KNOW? LIKE, ONE TIME, WHEN I TRIED IT ON THE GIRLS' LOCKER ROOM--
LET'S GET BACK ON TRACK.
OH. SURE. DOES THAT MEAN KELLY'S ON THE MOON, OR...?
WE'RE FOCUSING ON ***YOU*** RIGHT NOW. AS USEFUL AS YOUR "STRAND SENSE" WILL BE, IT DOESN'T STOP A BULLET OR MAKE UP FOR YOUR LACK OF ATHLETICISM.
OUCH. YOU DON'T PULL YOUR PUNCHES, DO YOU?
NO, AND THE ENEMY WON'T, EITHER. THIS SUIT IS BASED OFF MY OWN AND AMPLIFIES THE WEARER'S PHYSICAL ABILITIES TEN-FOLD.
IT WILL MAKE UP FOR LOST TIME AT FIRST. WITH TRAINING, YOU'LL BECOME QUITE FORMIDABLE.
HOW DOES THAT EVEN WORK? THIS FEELS LIKE A THICK WETSUIT.
HERE ARE THE SPECS. READ. THEM. LEARN THEM.
WHOOOOOAA... NANO-CARBON TUBING WEAVE WITH...
SYNTHETIC-NEURON NETWORK?! HOLY CRAP, IT HAS A--?!

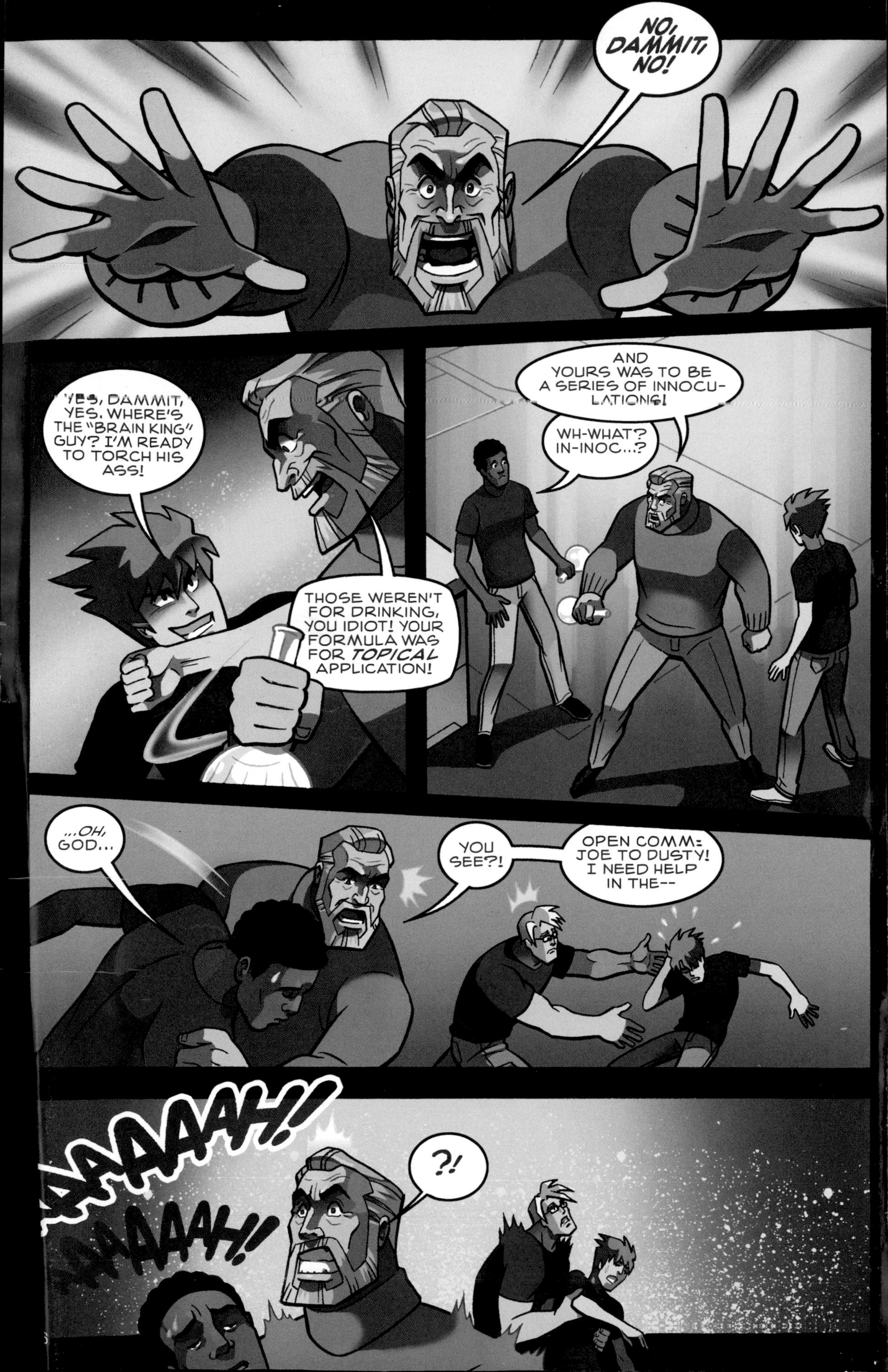
NO, DAMMIT, NO!
YES, DAMMIT, YES. WHERE'S THE "BRAIN KING" GUY? I'M READY TO TORCH HIS ASS!
THOSE WEREN'T FOR DRINKING, YOU IDIOT! YOUR FORMULA WAS FOR TOPICAL APPLICATION!
AND YOURS WAS TO BE A SERIES OF INNOCU-LATIONS!
WH-WHAT? IN-INOC...?
...OH, GOD...
YOU SEE?!
OPEN COMM: JOE TO DUSTY! I NEED HELP IN THE--
AAAAAAH!!
AAAAAH!!
?!

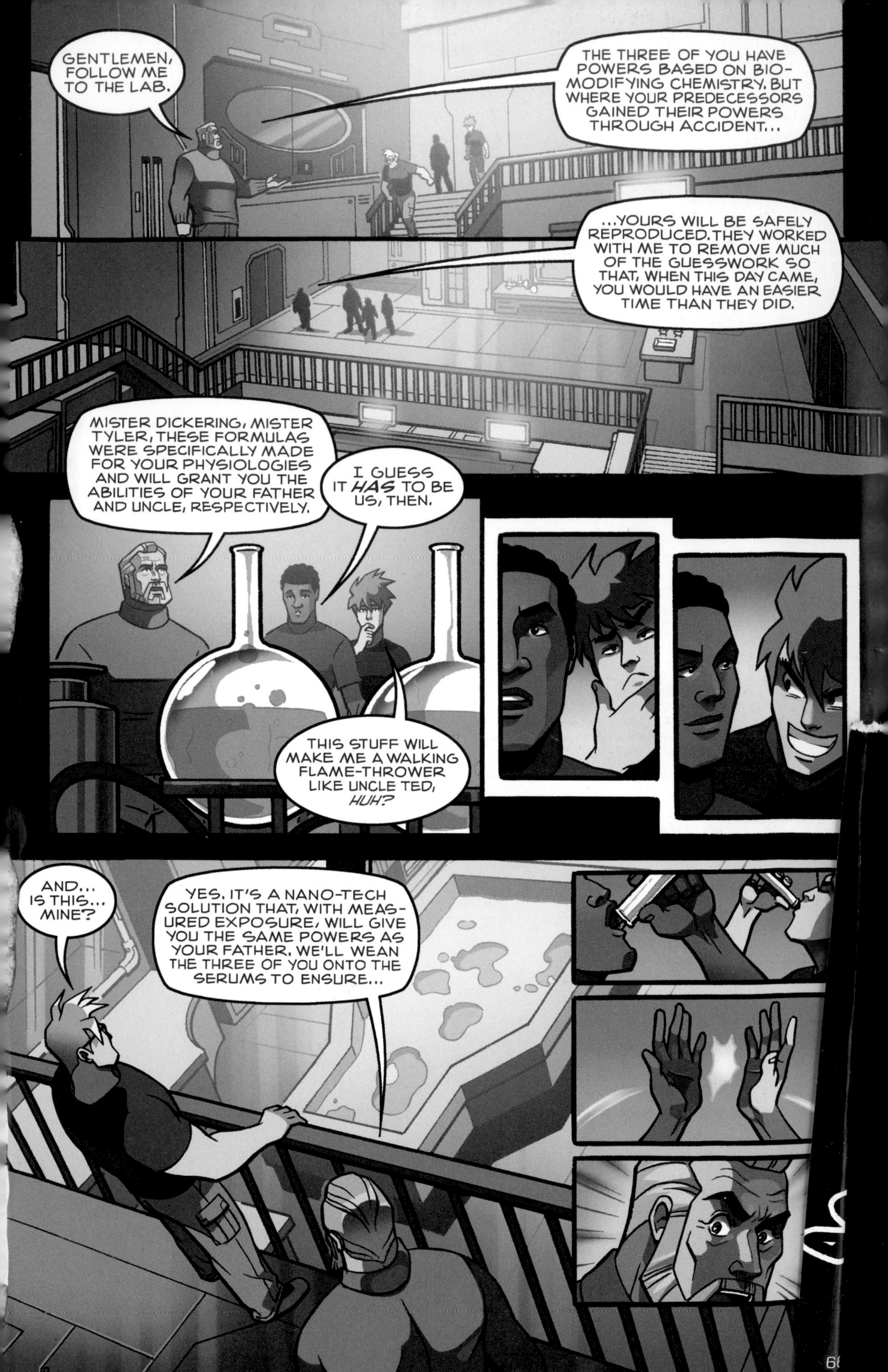

GENTLEMEN, FOLLOW ME TO THE LAB.
THE THREE OF YOU HAVE POWERS BASED ON BIO-MODIFYING CHEMISTRY. BUT WHERE YOUR PREDECESSORS GAINED THEIR POWERS THROUGH ACCIDENT...
...YOURS WILL BE SAFELY REPRODUCED. THEY WORKED WITH ME TO REMOVE MUCH OF THE GUESSWORK SO THAT, WHEN THIS DAY CAME, YOU WOULD HAVE AN EASIER TIME THAN THEY DID.
MISTER DICKERING, MISTER TYLER, THESE FORMULAS WERE SPECIFICALLY MADE FOR YOUR PHYSIOLOGIES AND WILL GRANT YOU THE ABILITIES OF YOUR FATHER AND UNCLE, RESPECTIVELY.
I GUESS IT *HAS* TO BE US, THEN.
THIS STUFF WILL MAKE ME A WALKING FLAME-THROWER LIKE UNCLE TED, *HUH?*
AND... IS THIS... MINE?
YES. IT'S A NANO-TECH SOLUTION THAT, WITH MEASURED EXPOSURE, WILL GIVE YOU THE SAME POWERS AS YOUR FATHER. WE'LL WEAN THE THREE OF YOU ONTO THE SERUMS TO ENSURE...

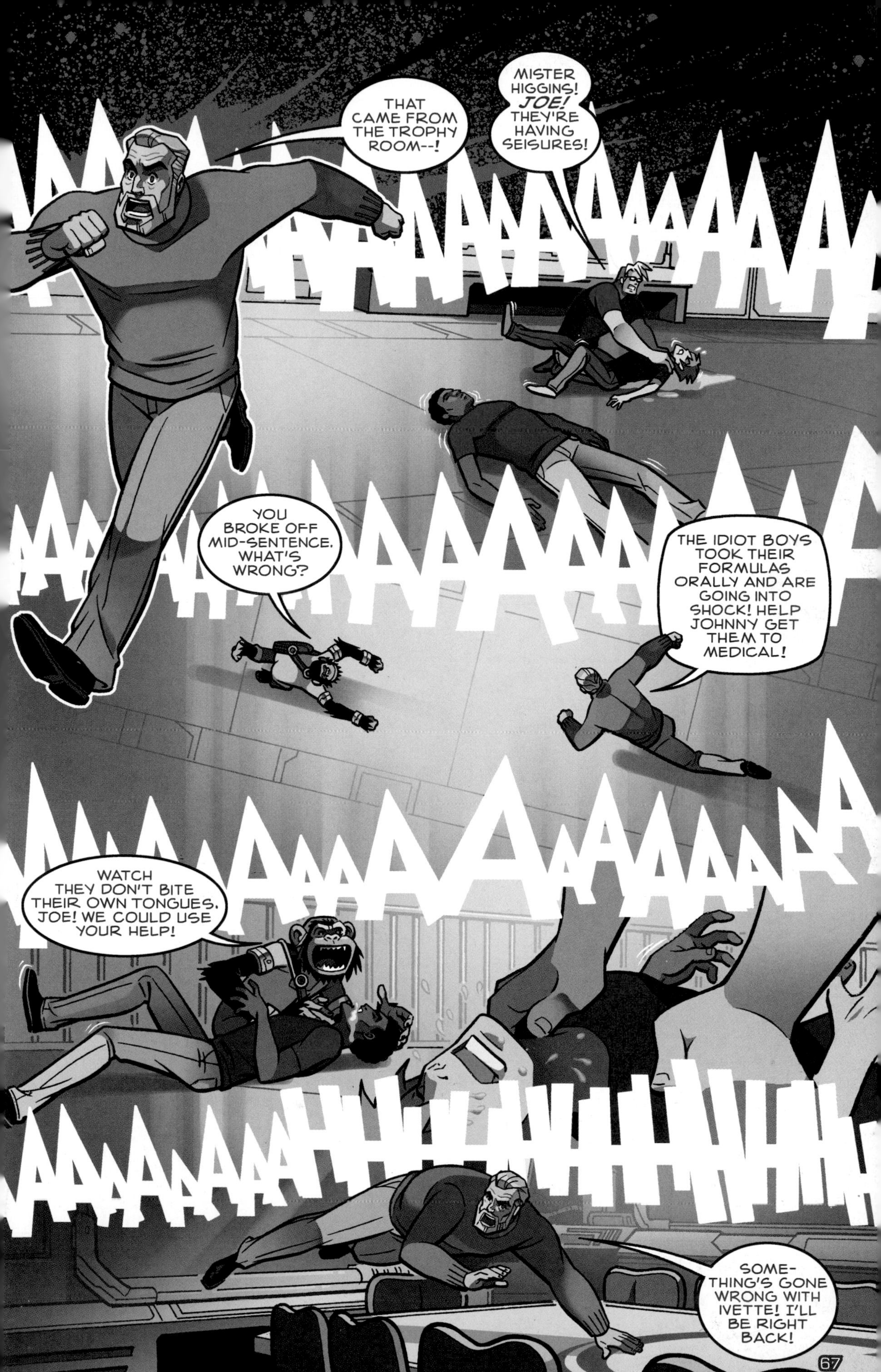
THAT CAME FROM THE TROPHY ROOM--!
MISTER HIGGINS! JOE! THEY'RE HAVING SEISURES!
YOU BROKE OFF MID-SENTENCE. WHAT'S WRONG?
THE IDIOT BOYS TOOK THEIR FORMULAS ORALLY AND ARE GOING INTO SHOCK! HELP JOHNNY GET THEM TO MEDICAL!
WATCH THEY DON'T BITE THEIR OWN TONGUES. JOE! WE COULD USE YOUR HELP!
SOME-THING'S GONE WRONG WITH IVETTE! I'LL BE RIGHT BACK!

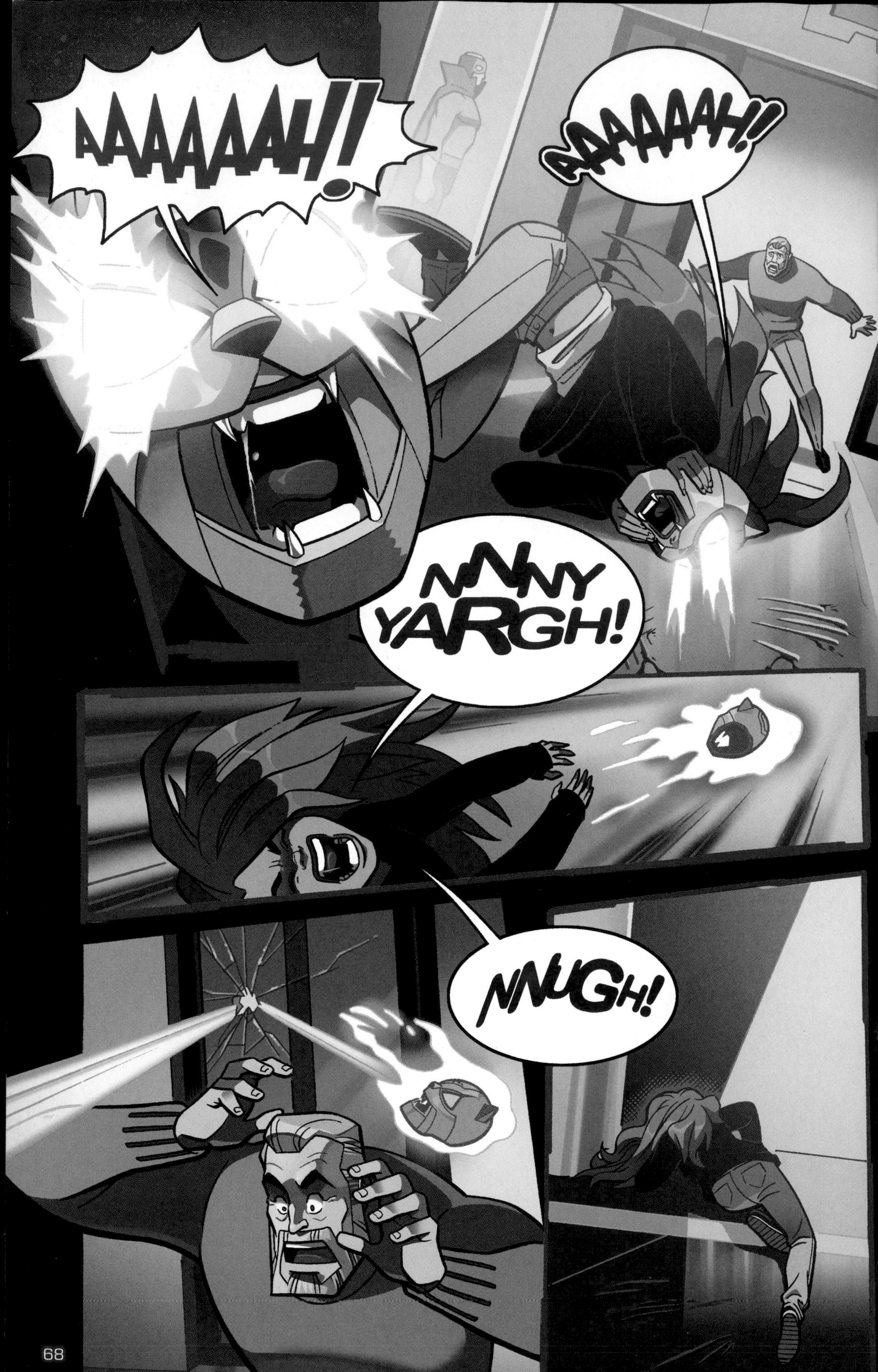
AAAAAAH!!
AAAAAAH!!
NNNY YARGH!
NNUGH!

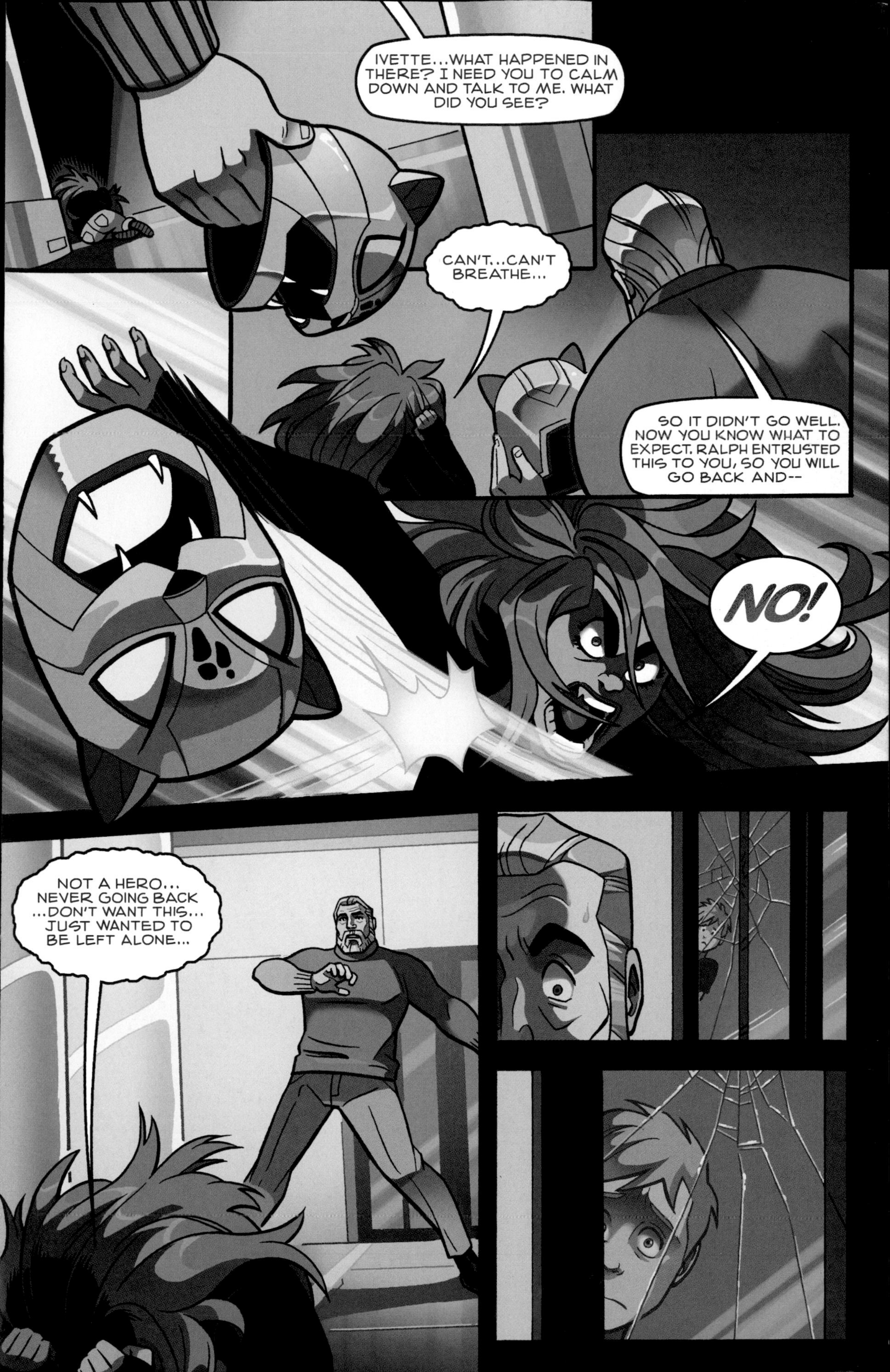
IVETTE...WHAT HAPPENED IN THERE? I NEED YOU TO CALM DOWN AND TALK TO ME. WHAT DID YOU SEE?
CAN'T...CAN'T BREATHE...
SO IT DIDN'T GO WELL. NOW YOU KNOW WHAT TO EXPECT. RALPH ENTRUSTED THIS TO YOU, SO YOU WILL GO BACK AND--
NO!
NOT A HERO... NEVER GOING BACK ...DON'T WANT THIS... JUST WANTED TO BE LEFT ALONE...

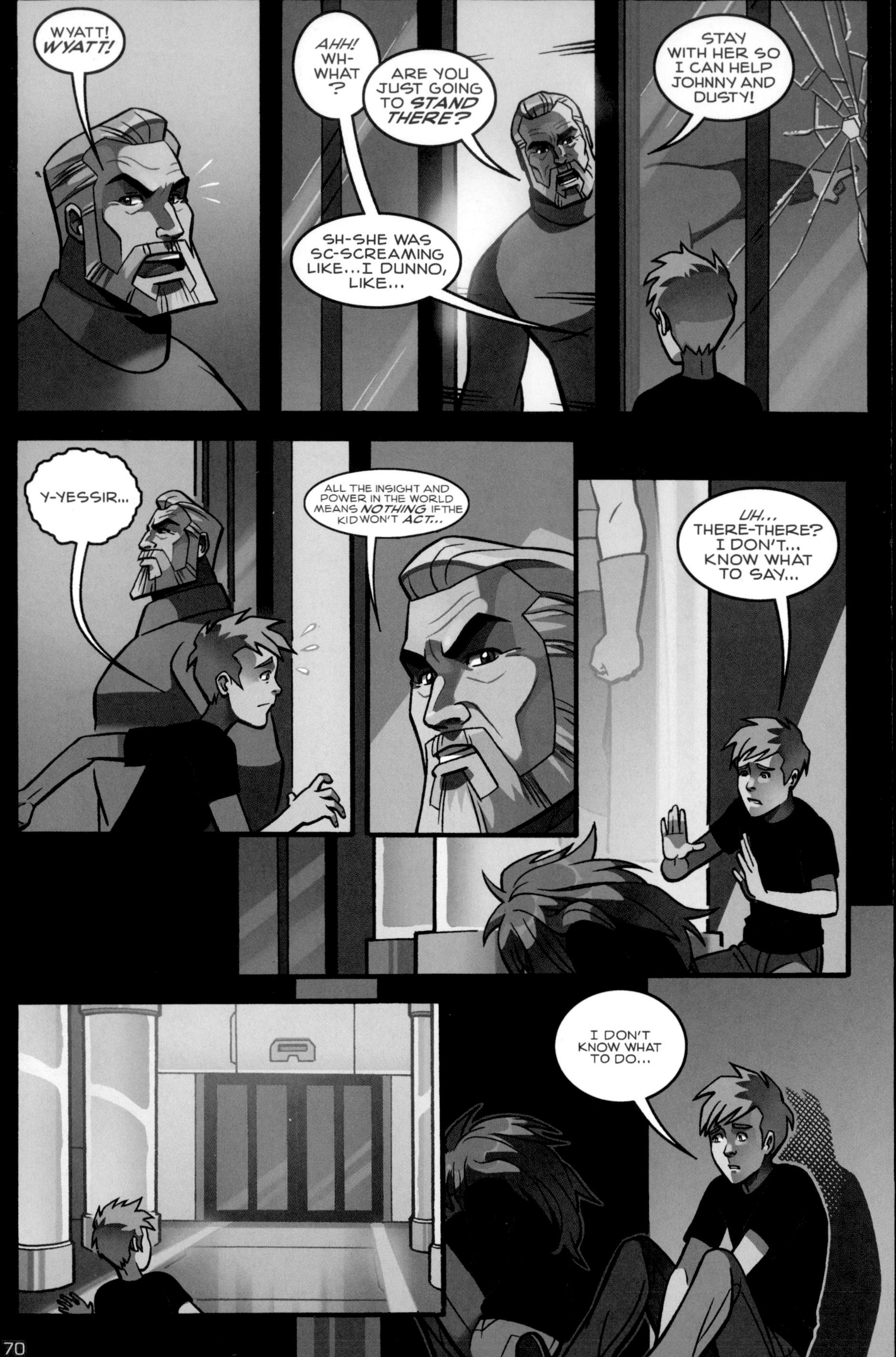
WYATT! WYATT!
AHH! WH-WHAT?
ARE YOU JUST GOING TO STAND THERE?
SH-SHE WAS SC-SCREAMING LIKE...I DUNNO, LIKE...
STAY WITH HER SO I CAN HELP JOHNNY AND DUSTY!
Y-YESSIR...
ALL THE INSIGHT AND POWER IN THE WORLD MEANS NOTHING IF THE KID WON'T ACT...
UH... THERE-THERE? I DON'T... KNOW WHAT TO SAY...
I DON'T KNOW WHAT TO DO...

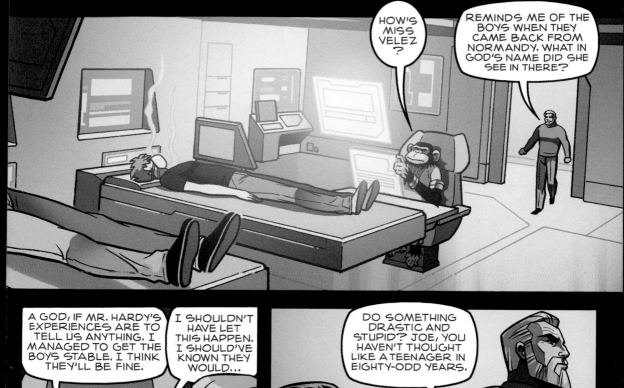

HOW'S MISS VELEZ?

REMINDS ME OF THE BOYS WHEN THEY CAME BACK FROM NORMANDY. WHAT IN GOD'S NAME DID SHE SEE IN THERE?

A GOD, IF MR. HARDY'S EXPERIENCES ARE TO TELL US ANYTHING. I MANAGED TO GET THE BOYS STABLE. I THINK THEY'LL BE FINE.

I SHOULDN'T HAVE LET THIS HAPPEN. I SHOULD'VE KNOWN THEY WOULD...

DO SOMETHING DRASTIC AND STUPID? JOE, YOU HAVEN'T THOUGHT LIKE A TEENAGER IN EIGHTY-ODD YEARS.

THEY'RE *MY* RESPONSIBILITY, DUSTY. THEIR PARENTS *TRUSTED* ME TO LOOK AFTER THEM, AND NOW THEY'RE...

STABLE, AS I'VE SAID. GO TALK TO JOHNNY. HE'S PRETTY SHAKEN. I'LL LOOK AFTER THINGS HERE.

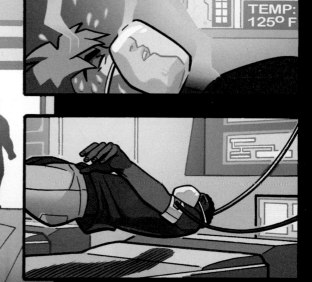

TEMP: 125° F

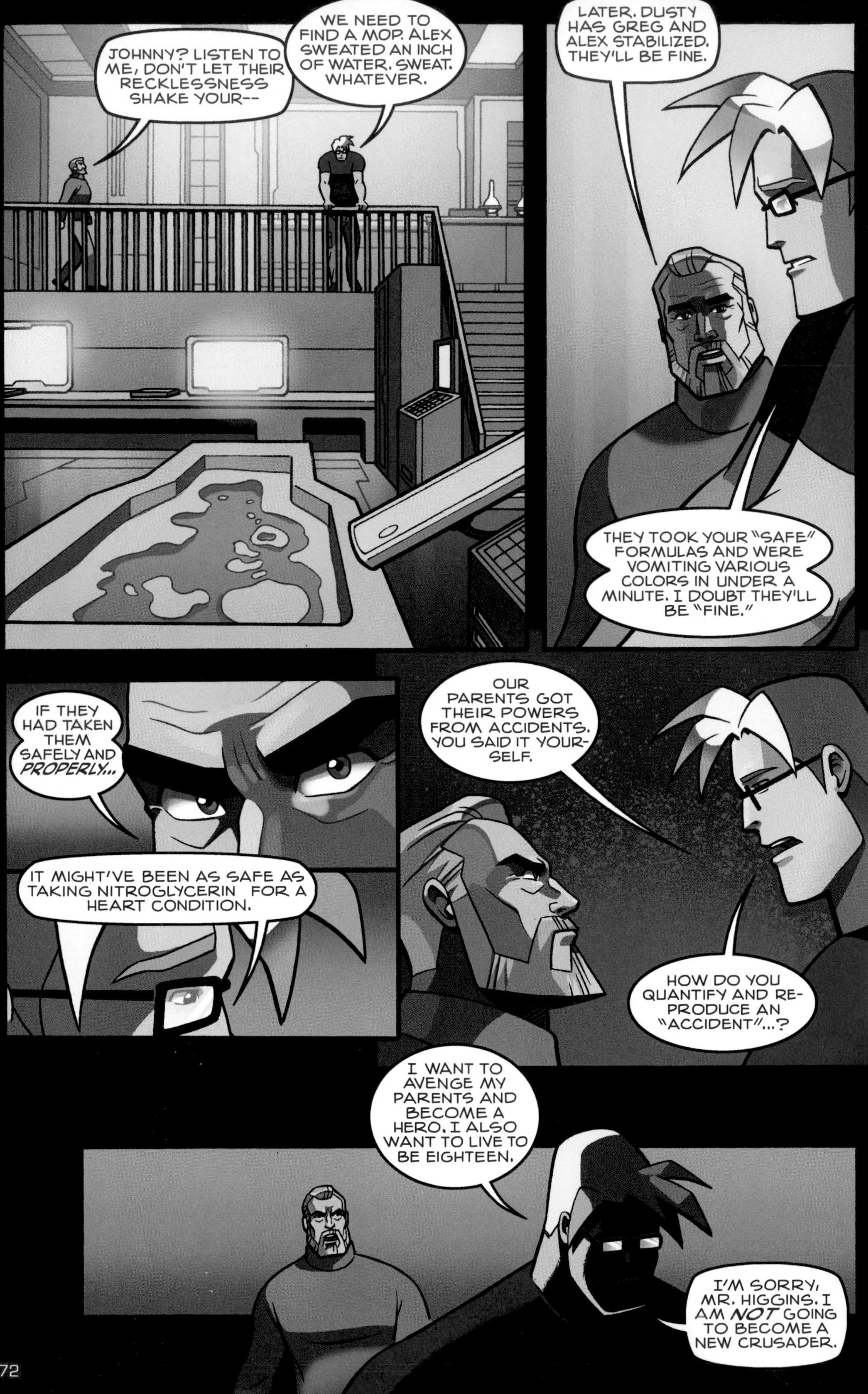
JOHNNY? LISTEN TO ME, DON'T LET THEIR RECKLESSNESS SHAKE YOUR--
WE NEED TO FIND A MOP. ALEX SWEATED AN INCH OF WATER. SWEAT. WHATEVER.
LATER. DUSTY HAS GREG AND ALEX STABILIZED. THEY'LL BE FINE.
THEY TOOK YOUR "SAFE" FORMULAS AND WERE VOMITING VARIOUS COLORS IN UNDER A MINUTE. I DOUBT THEY'LL BE "FINE."
IF THEY HAD TAKEN THEM SAFELY AND *PROPERLY*...
IT MIGHT'VE BEEN AS SAFE AS TAKING NITROGLYCERIN FOR A HEART CONDITION.
OUR PARENTS GOT THEIR POWERS FROM ACCIDENTS. YOU SAID IT YOURSELF.
HOW DO YOU QUANTIFY AND REPRODUCE AN "ACCIDENT"...?
I WANT TO AVENGE MY PARENTS AND BECOME A HERO. I ALSO WANT TO LIVE TO BE EIGHTEEN.
I'M SORRY, MR. HIGGINS. I AM ***NOT*** GOING TO BECOME A NEW CRUSADER.

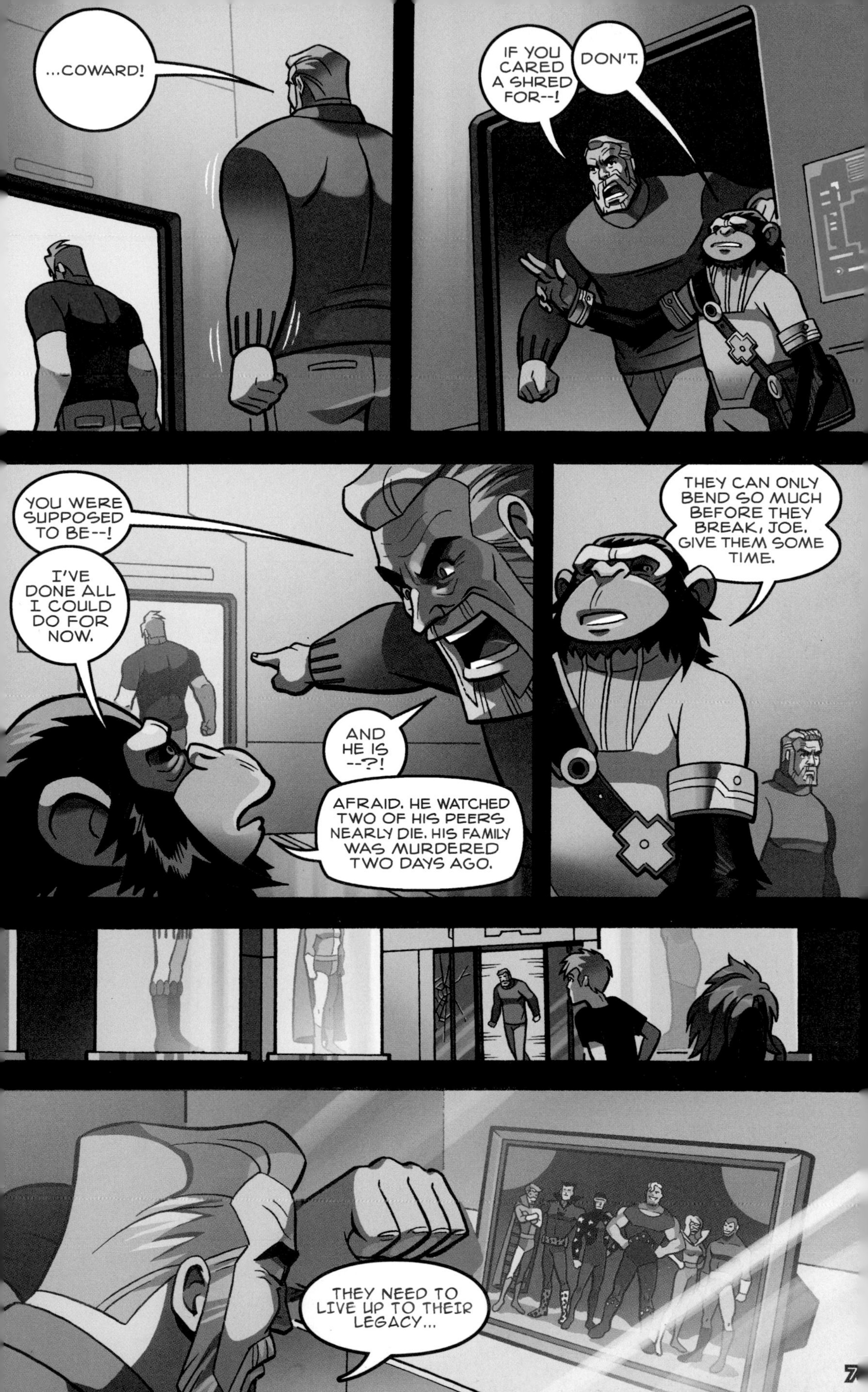
...COWARD!
IF YOU CARED A SHRED FOR--!
DON'T.
YOU WERE SUPPOSED TO BE--!
I'VE DONE ALL I COULD DO FOR NOW.
AND HE IS --?!
AFRAID. HE WATCHED TWO OF HIS PEERS NEARLY DIE. HIS FAMILY WAS MURDERED TWO DAYS AGO.
THEY CAN ONLY BEND SO MUCH BEFORE THEY BREAK, JOE. GIVE THEM SOME TIME.
THEY NEED TO LIVE UP TO THEIR LEGACY...

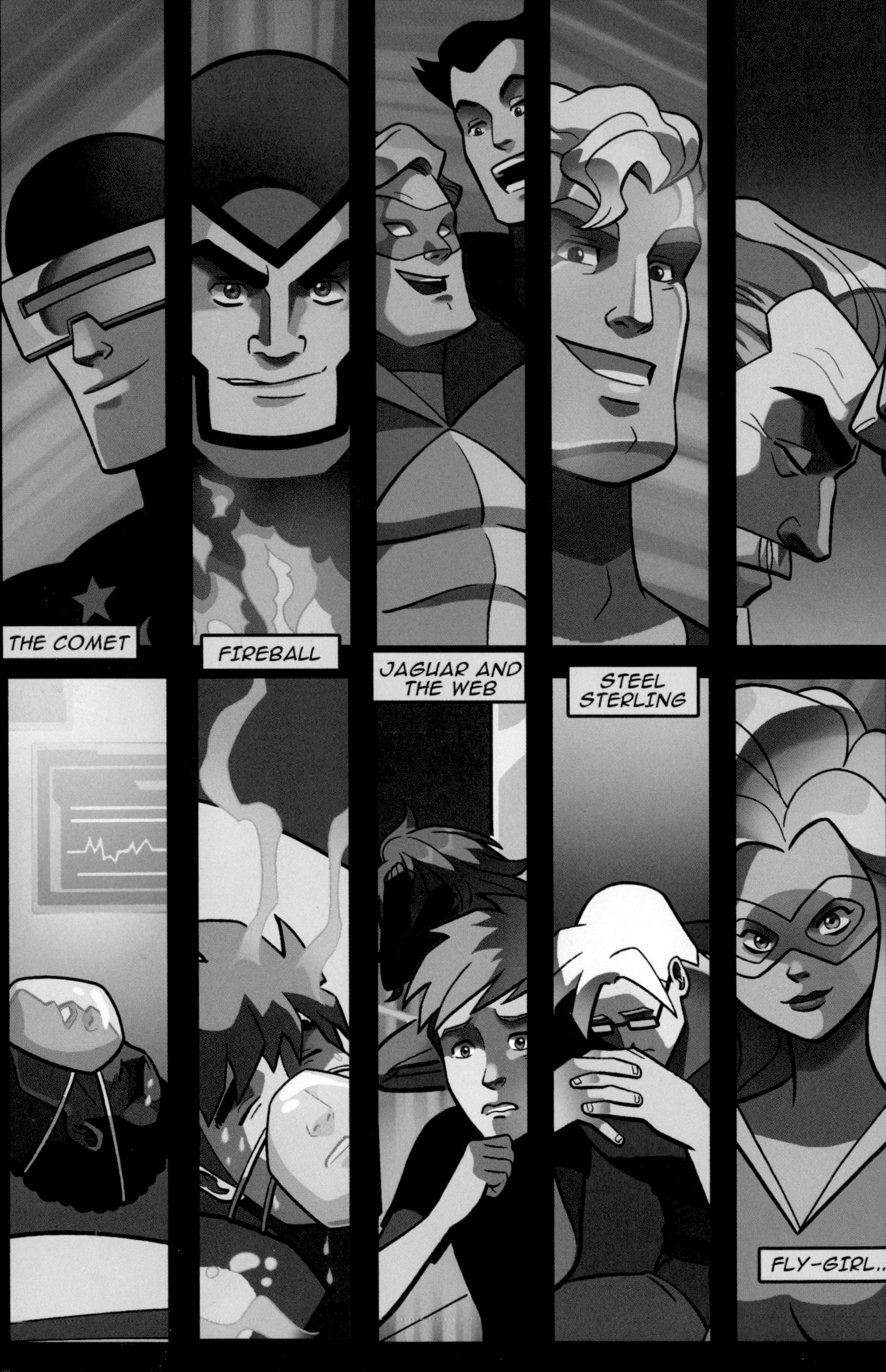
THE COMET
FIREBALL
JAGUAR AND THE WEB
STEEL STERLING
FLY-GIRL...

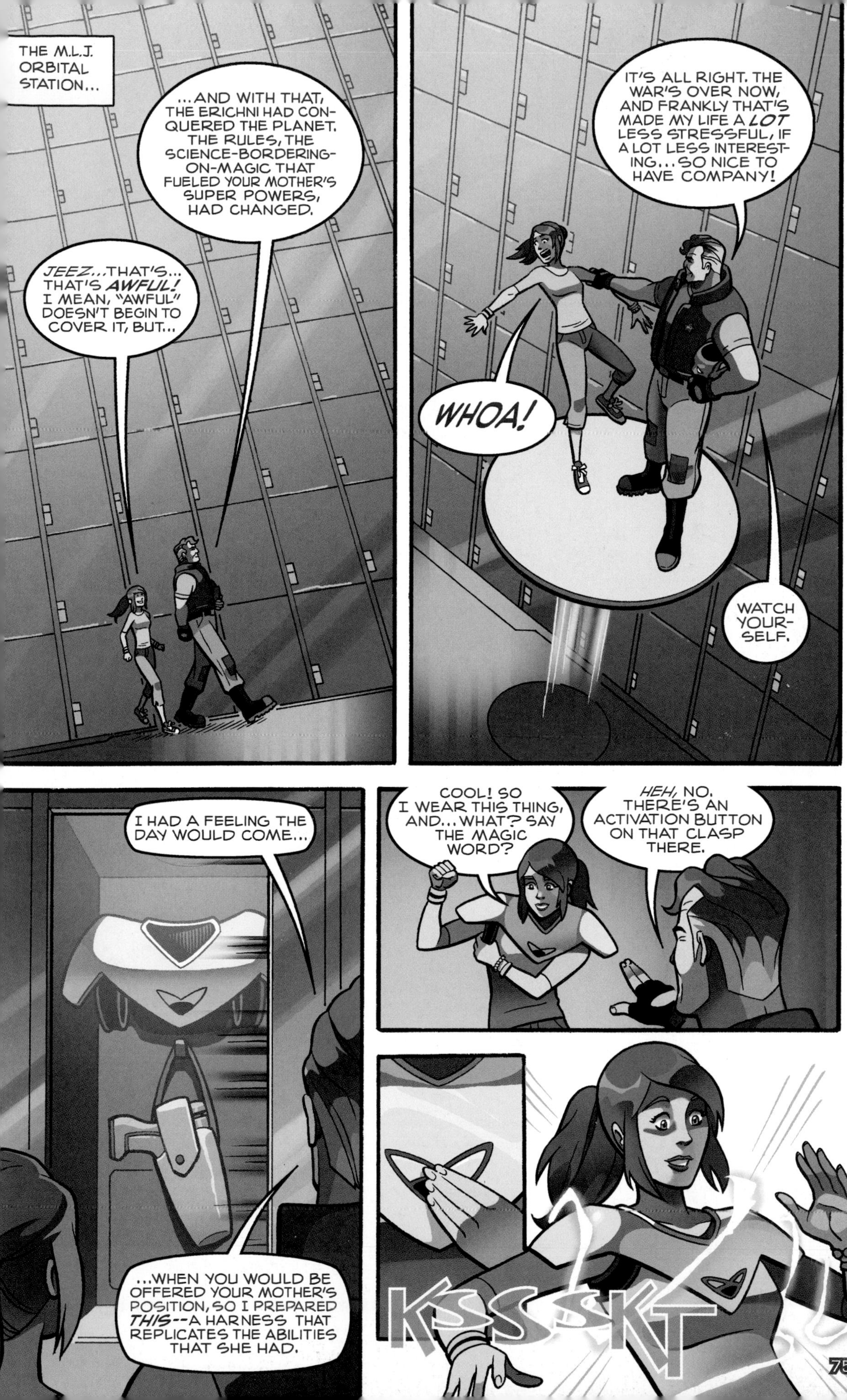
THE M.L.J. ORBITAL STATION...
...AND WITH THAT, THE ERICHNI HAD CONQUERED THE PLANET. THE RULES, THE SCIENCE-BORDERING-ON-MAGIC THAT FUELED YOUR MOTHER'S SUPER POWERS, HAD CHANGED.
JEEZ...THAT'S... THAT'S AWFUL! I MEAN, "AWFUL" DOESN'T BEGIN TO COVER IT, BUT...
IT'S ALL RIGHT. THE WAR'S OVER NOW, AND FRANKLY THAT'S MADE MY LIFE A LOT LESS STRESSFUL, IF A LOT LESS INTERESTING... SO NICE TO HAVE COMPANY!
WHOA!
WATCH YOURSELF.
I HAD A FEELING THE DAY WOULD COME...
...WHEN YOU WOULD BE OFFERED YOUR MOTHER'S POSITION, SO I PREPARED THIS--A HARNESS THAT REPLICATES THE ABILITIES THAT SHE HAD.
COOL! SO I WEAR THIS THING, AND...WHAT? SAY THE MAGIC WORD?
HEH, NO. THERE'S AN ACTIVATION BUTTON ON THAT CLASP THERE.
KSSSKT

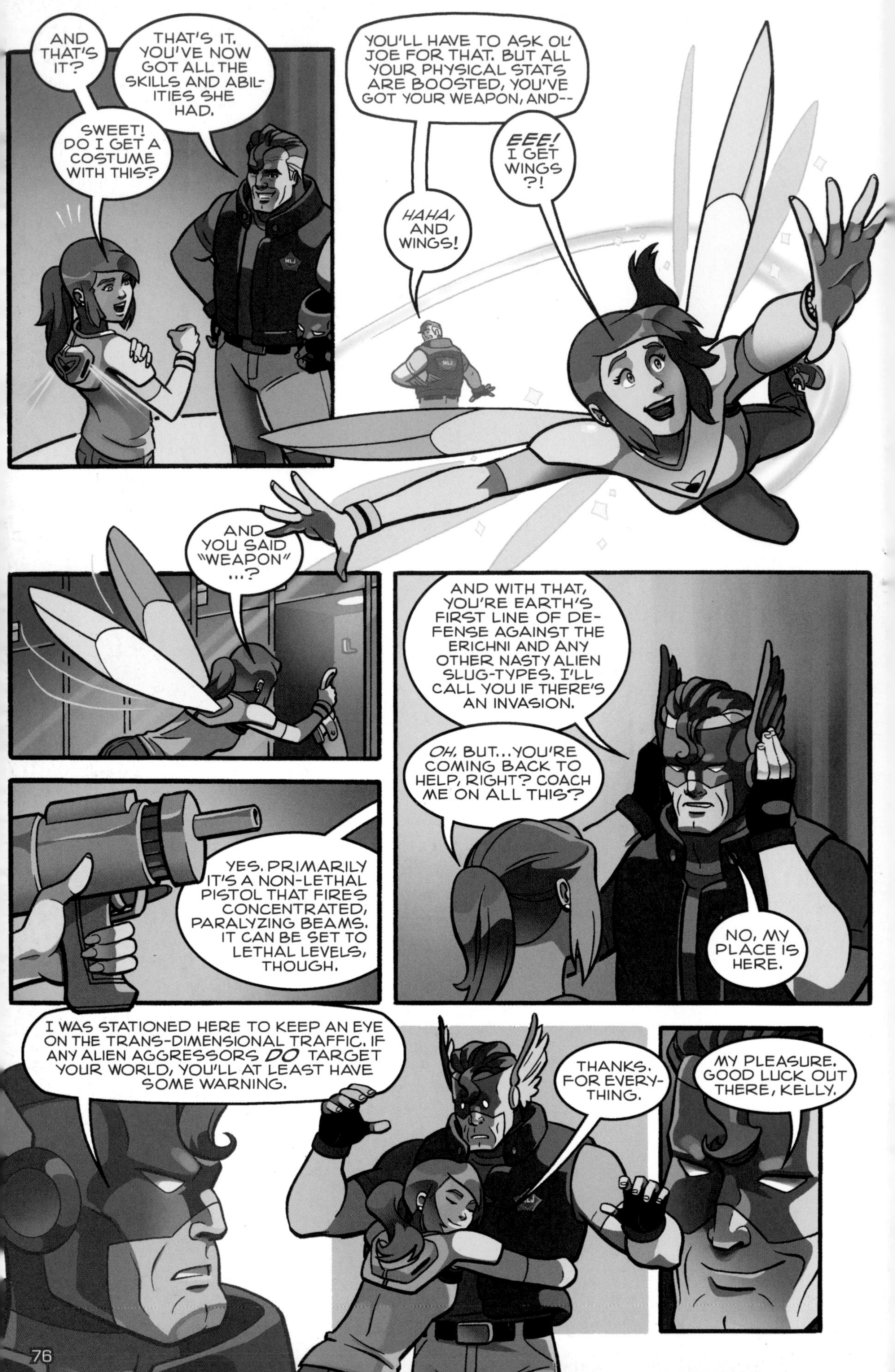
AND THAT'S IT?
THAT'S IT. YOU'VE NOW GOT ALL THE SKILLS AND ABIL-ITIES SHE HAD.
SWEET! DO I GET A COSTUME WITH THIS?
YOU'LL HAVE TO ASK OL' JOE FOR THAT. BUT ALL YOUR PHYSICAL STATS ARE BOOSTED, YOU'VE GOT YOUR WEAPON, AND--
EEE! I GET WINGS?!
HAHA, AND WINGS!
AND YOU SAID "WEAPON"...?
YES. PRIMARILY IT'S A NON-LETHAL PISTOL THAT FIRES CONCENTRATED, PARALYZING BEAMS. IT CAN BE SET TO LETHAL LEVELS, THOUGH.
AND WITH THAT, YOU'RE EARTH'S FIRST LINE OF DE-FENSE AGAINST THE ERICHNI AND ANY OTHER NASTY ALIEN SLUG-TYPES. I'LL CALL YOU IF THERE'S AN INVASION.
OH, BUT...YOU'RE COMING BACK TO HELP, RIGHT? COACH ME ON ALL THIS?
NO, MY PLACE IS HERE.
I WAS STATIONED HERE TO KEEP AN EYE ON THE TRANS-DIMENSIONAL TRAFFIC. IF ANY ALIEN AGGRESSORS DO TARGET YOUR WORLD, YOU'LL AT LEAST HAVE SOME WARNING.
THANKS. FOR EVERY-THING.
MY PLEASURE. GOOD LUCK OUT THERE, KELLY.

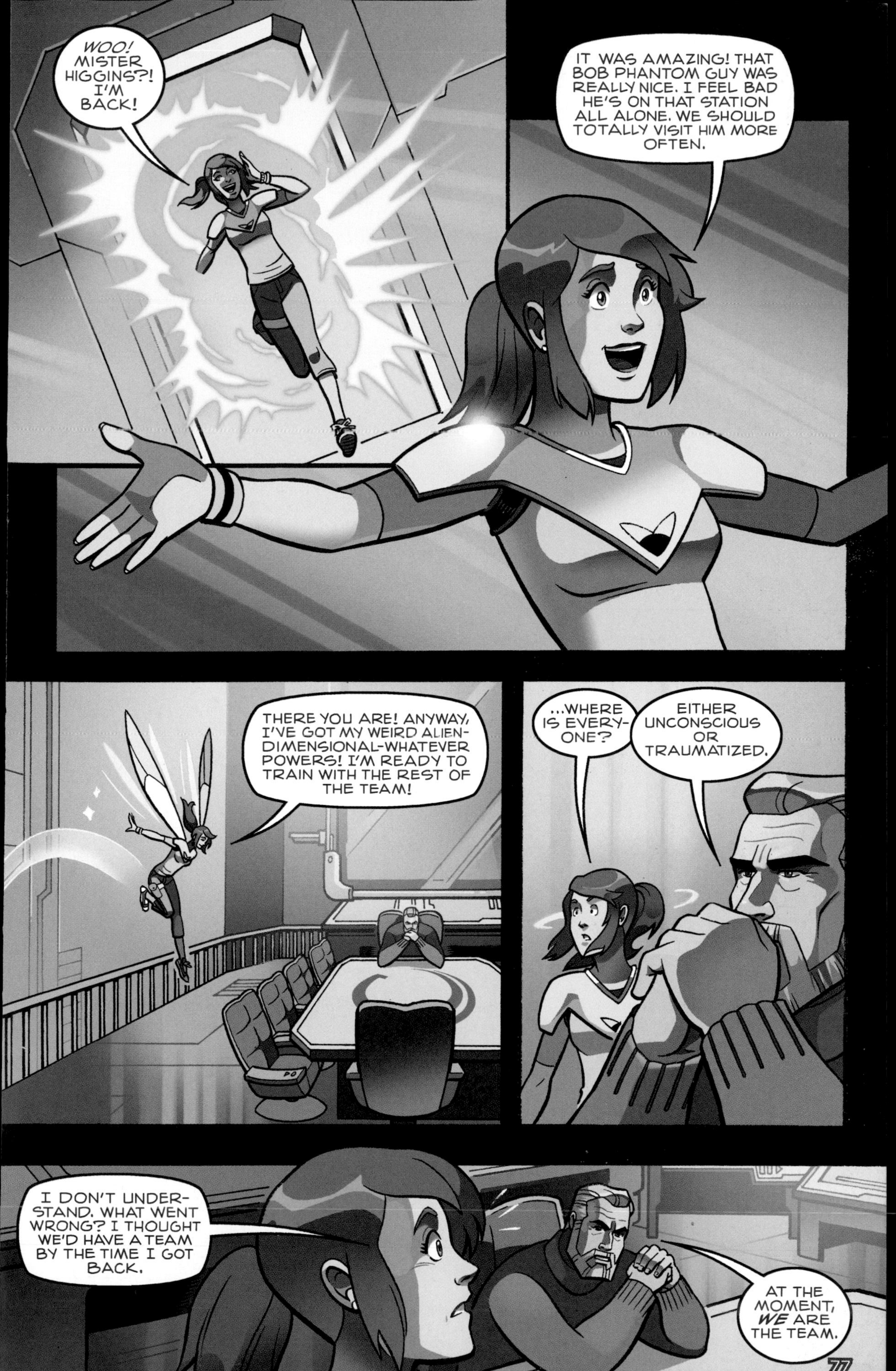
WOO! MISTER HIGGINS?! I'M BACK!
IT WAS AMAZING! THAT BOB PHANTOM GUY WAS REALLY NICE. I FEEL BAD HE'S ON THAT STATION ALL ALONE. WE SHOULD TOTALLY VISIT HIM MORE OFTEN.
THERE YOU ARE! ANYWAY, I'VE GOT MY WEIRD ALIEN-DIMENSIONAL-WHATEVER POWERS! I'M READY TO TRAIN WITH THE REST OF THE TEAM!
...WHERE IS EVERY-ONE?
EITHER UNCONSCIOUS OR TRAUMATIZED.
I DON'T UNDER-STAND. WHAT WENT WRONG? I THOUGHT WE'D HAVE A TEAM BY THE TIME I GOT BACK.
AT THE MOMENT, WE ARE THE TEAM.

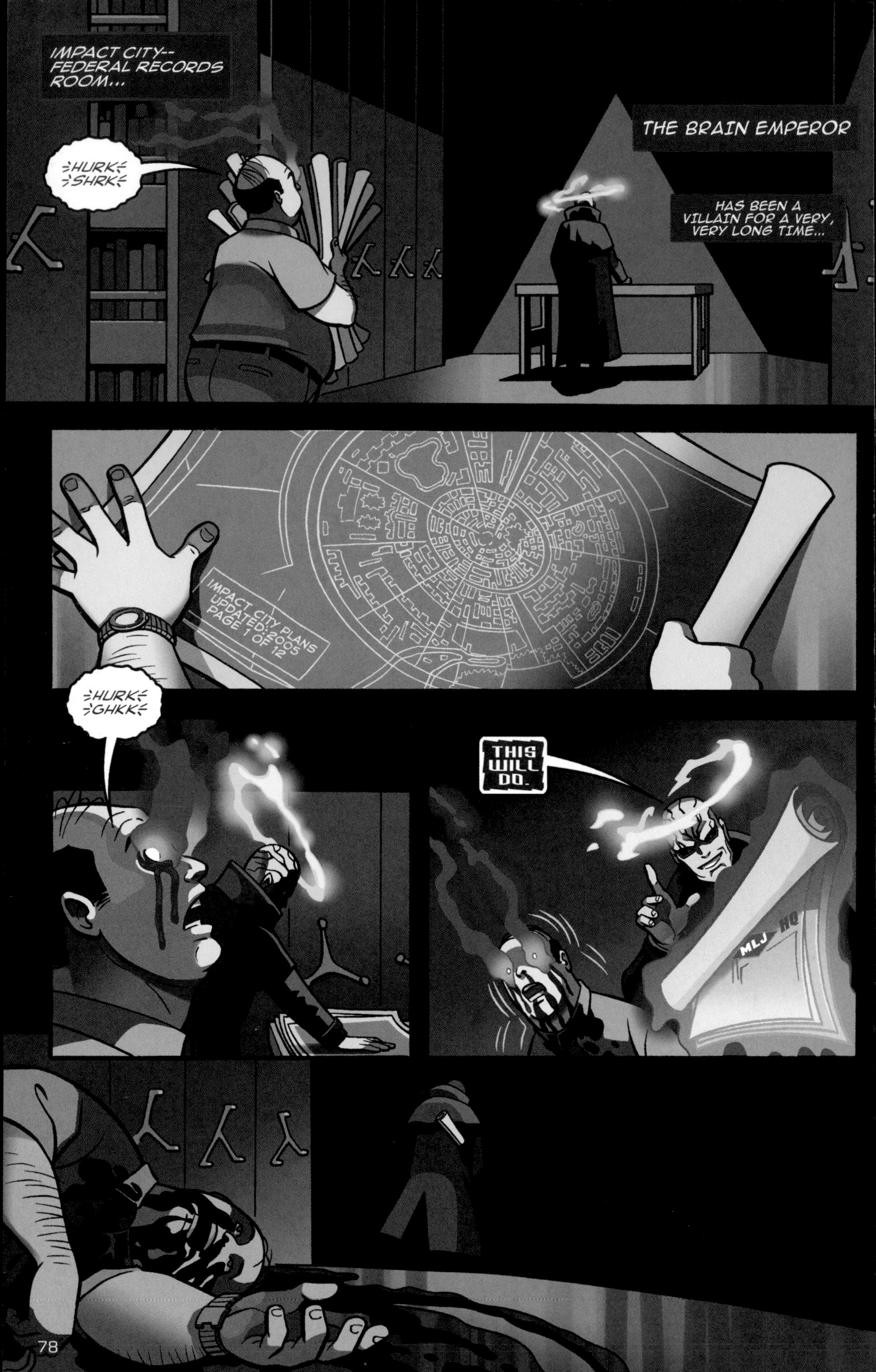
IMPACT CITY-- FEDERAL RECORDS ROOM...
THE BRAIN EMPEROR
HAS BEEN A VILLAIN FOR A VERY, VERY LONG TIME...
HURK SHRK
IMPACT CITY PLANS UPDATED: 2005 PAGE 1 OF 12
HURK GHKK
THIS WILL DO.
MLJ HQ

CHAPTER 4

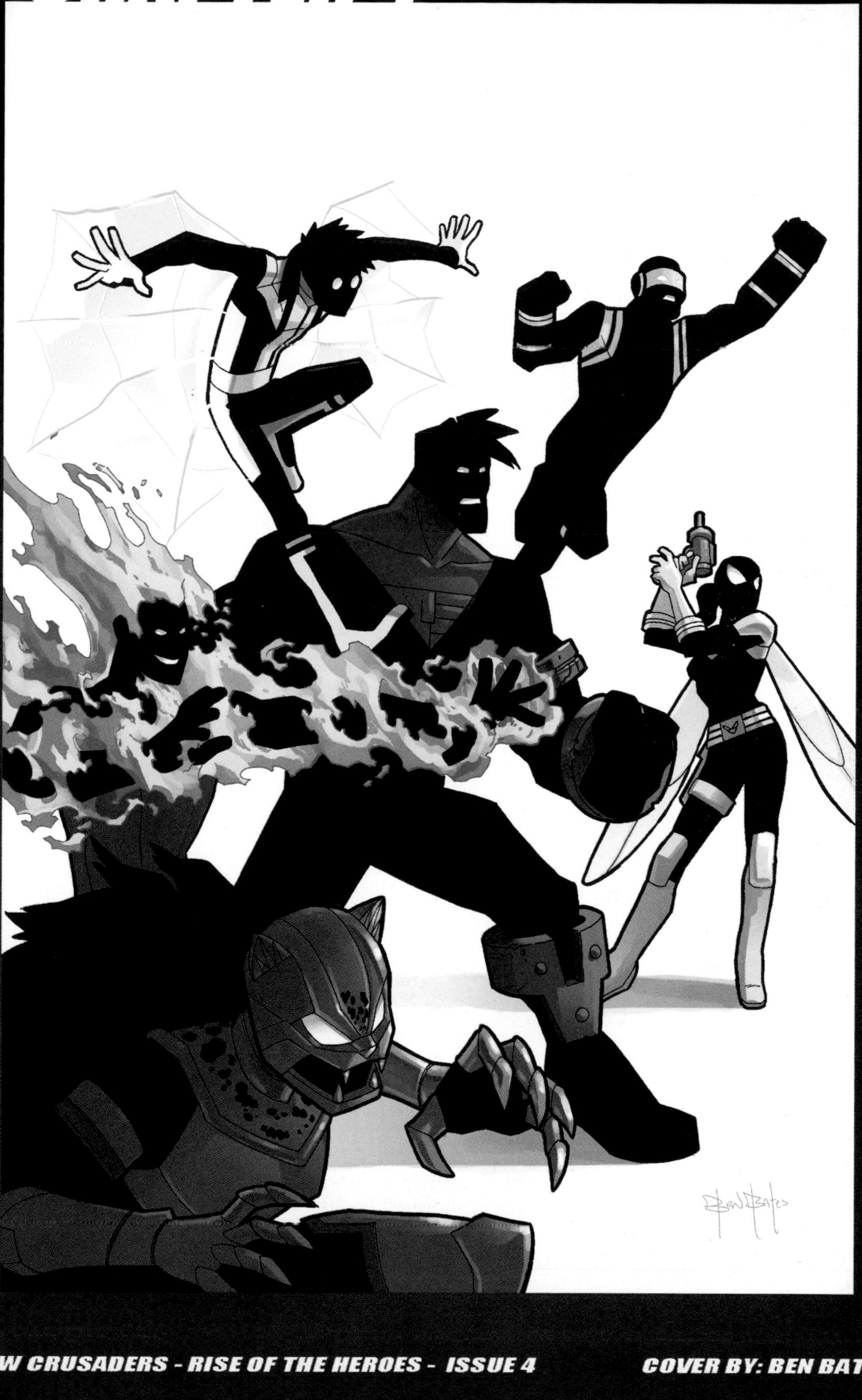
BEN BATES

NEW CRUSADERS - RISE OF THE HEROES - ISSUE 4 COVER BY: BEN BATES

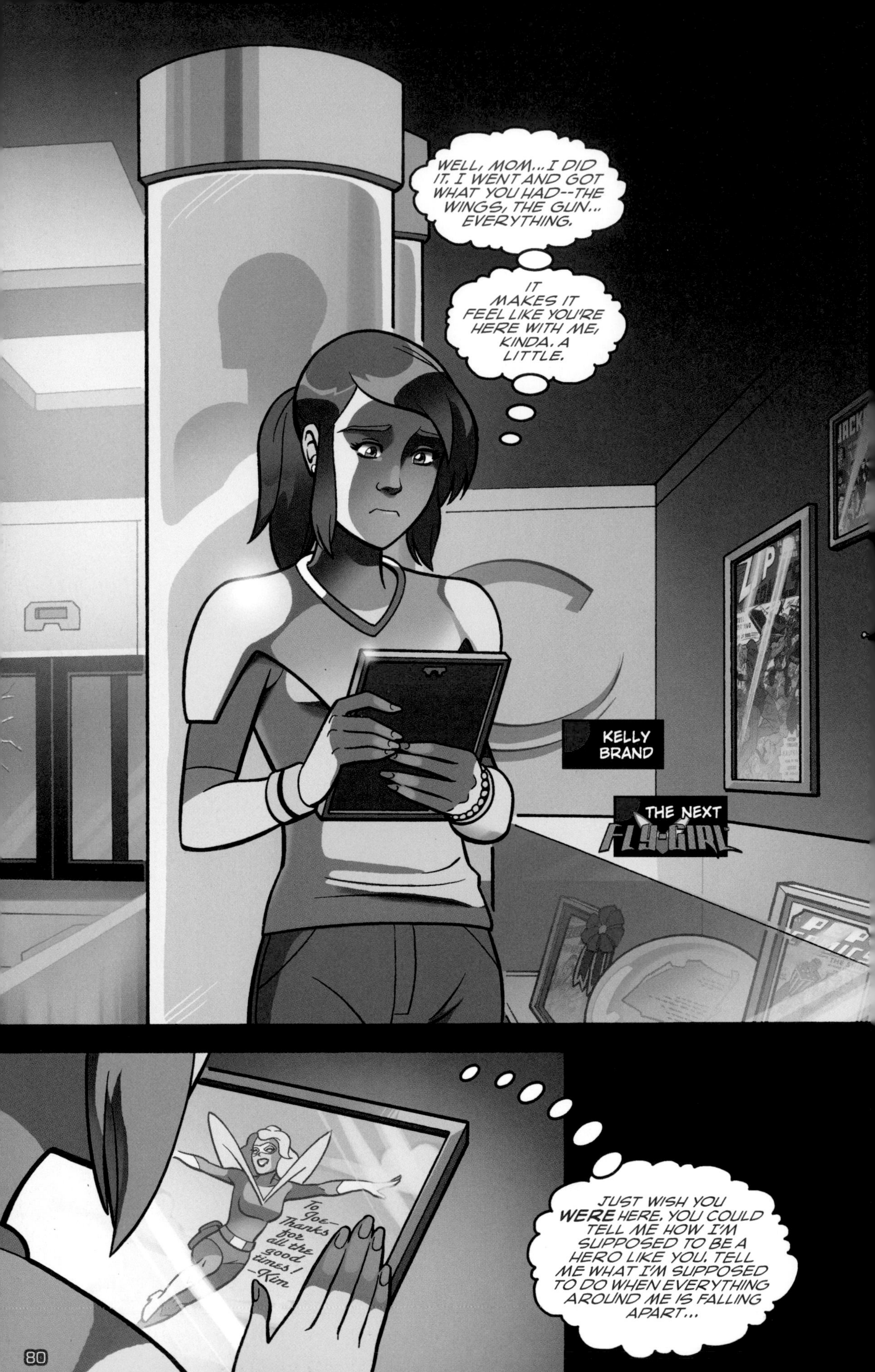
WELL, MOM... I DID IT. I WENT AND GOT WHAT YOU HAD--THE WINGS, THE GUN... EVERYTHING.
IT MAKES IT FEEL LIKE YOU'RE HERE WITH ME, KINDA. A LITTLE.
KELLY BRAND
THE NEXT FLY-GIRL
To Joe-- Thanks for all the good times! --Kim
JUST WISH YOU WERE HERE. YOU COULD TELL ME HOW I'M SUPPOSED TO BE A HERO LIKE YOU. TELL ME WHAT I'M SUPPOSED TO DO WHEN EVERYTHING AROUND ME IS FALLING APART...

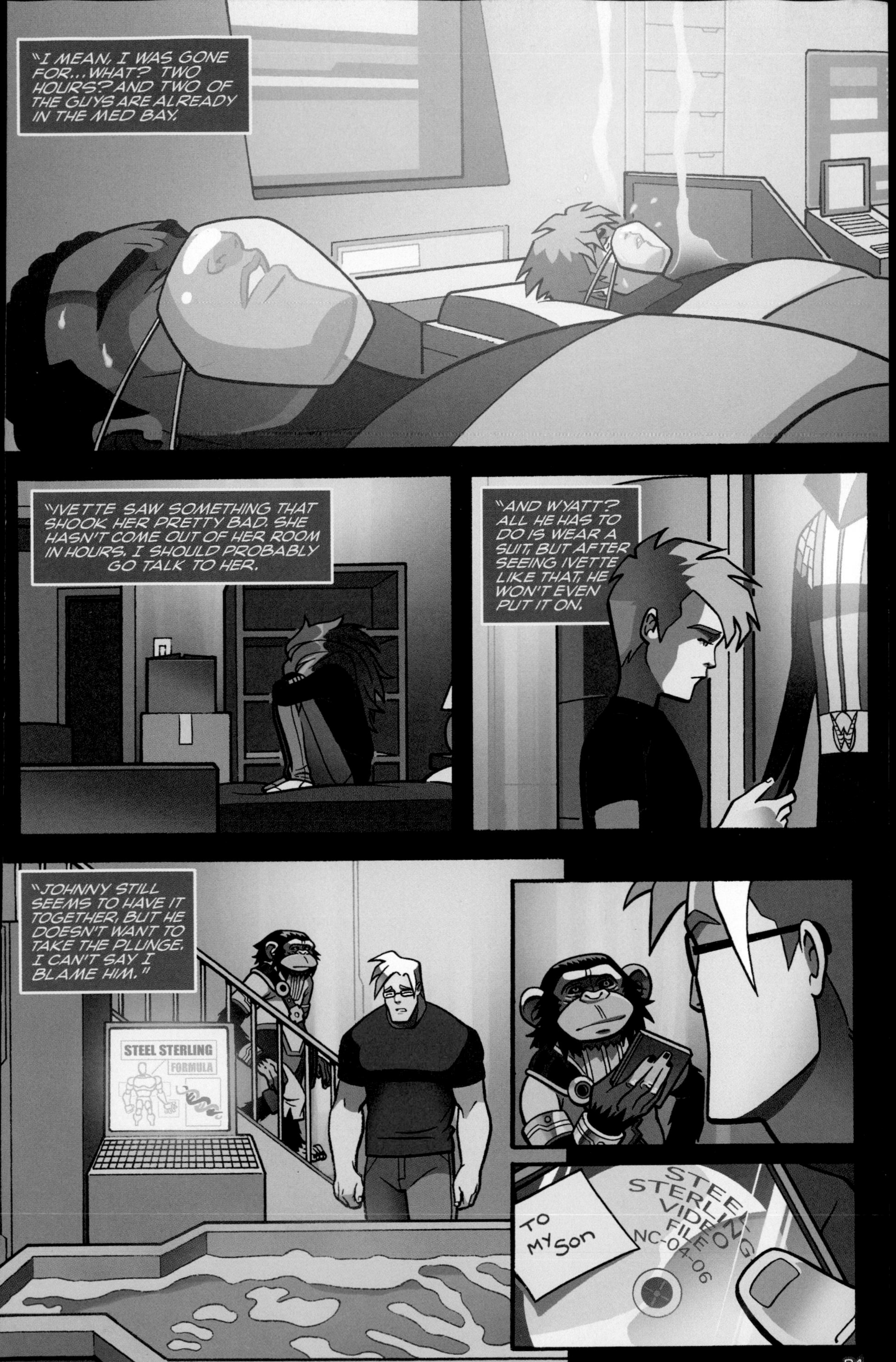
"I MEAN, I WAS GONE FOR...WHAT? TWO HOURS? AND TWO OF THE GUYS ARE ALREADY IN THE MED BAY.
"IVETTE SAW SOMETHING THAT SHOOK HER PRETTY BAD. SHE HASN'T COME OUT OF HER ROOM IN HOURS. I SHOULD PROBABLY GO TALK TO HER.
"AND WYATT? ALL HE HAS TO DO IS WEAR A SUIT, BUT AFTER SEEING IVETTE LIKE THAT, HE WON'T EVEN PUT IT ON.
"JOHNNY STILL SEEMS TO HAVE IT TOGETHER, BUT HE DOESN'T WANT TO TAKE THE PLUNGE. I CAN'T SAY I BLAME HIM."
STEEL STERLING
FORMULA
TO MY Son
STEEL STERLING VIDEO FILE
NC-04-06

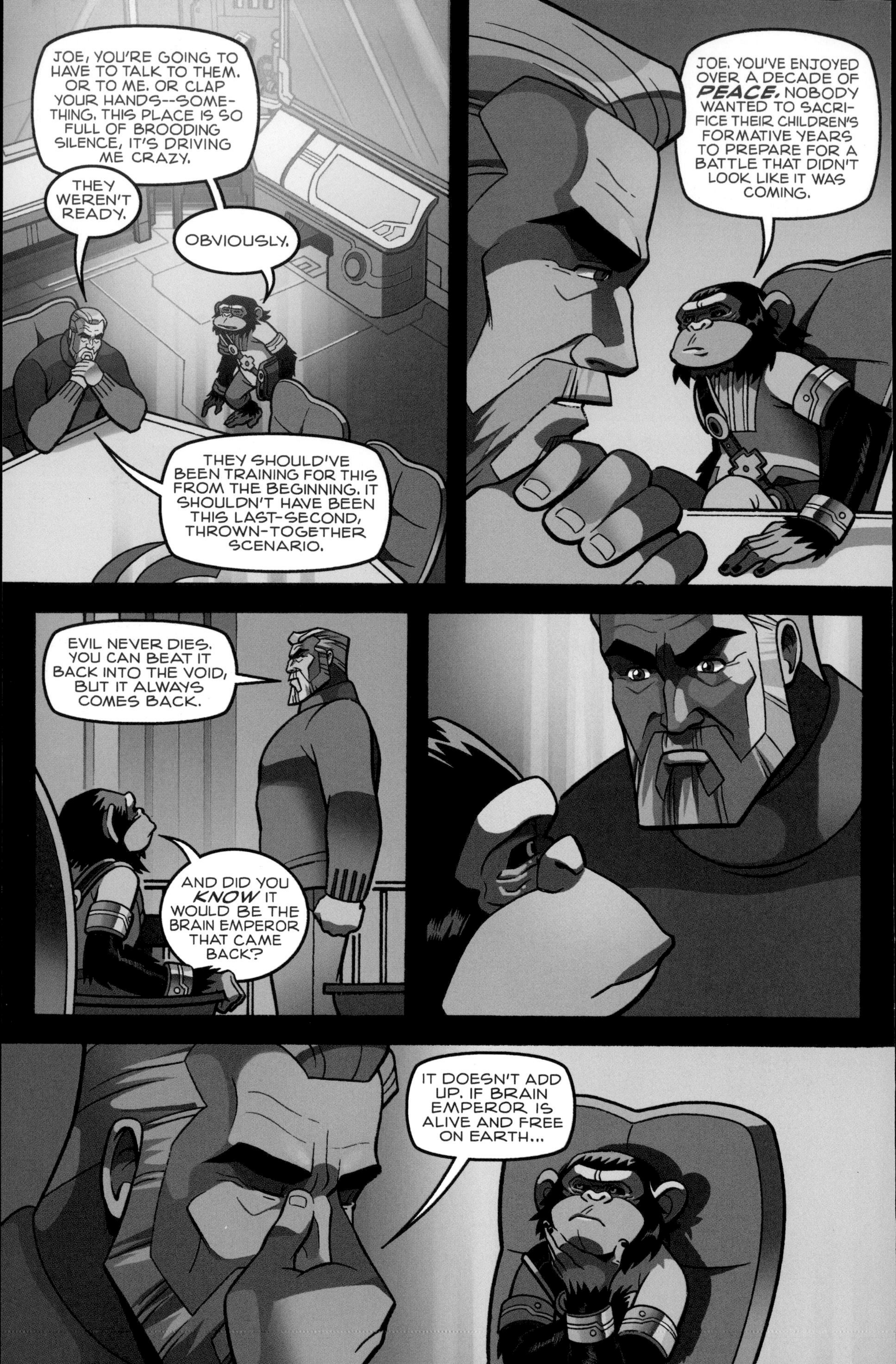
JOE, YOU'RE GOING TO HAVE TO TALK TO THEM. OR TO ME. OR CLAP YOUR HANDS--SOMETHING. THIS PLACE IS SO FULL OF BROODING SILENCE, IT'S DRIVING ME CRAZY.
THEY WEREN'T READY.
OBVIOUSLY.
THEY SHOULD'VE BEEN TRAINING FOR THIS FROM THE BEGINNING. IT SHOULDN'T HAVE BEEN THIS LAST-SECOND, THROWN-TOGETHER SCENARIO.
JOE. YOU'VE ENJOYED OVER A DECADE OF ***PEACE.*** NOBODY WANTED TO SACRIFICE THEIR CHILDREN'S FORMATIVE YEARS TO PREPARE FOR A BATTLE THAT DIDN'T LOOK LIKE IT WAS COMING.
EVIL NEVER DIES. YOU CAN BEAT IT BACK INTO THE VOID, BUT IT ALWAYS COMES BACK.
AND DID YOU ***KNOW*** IT WOULD BE THE BRAIN EMPEROR THAT CAME BACK?
IT DOESN'T ADD UP. IF BRAIN EMPEROR IS ALIVE AND FREE ON EARTH...

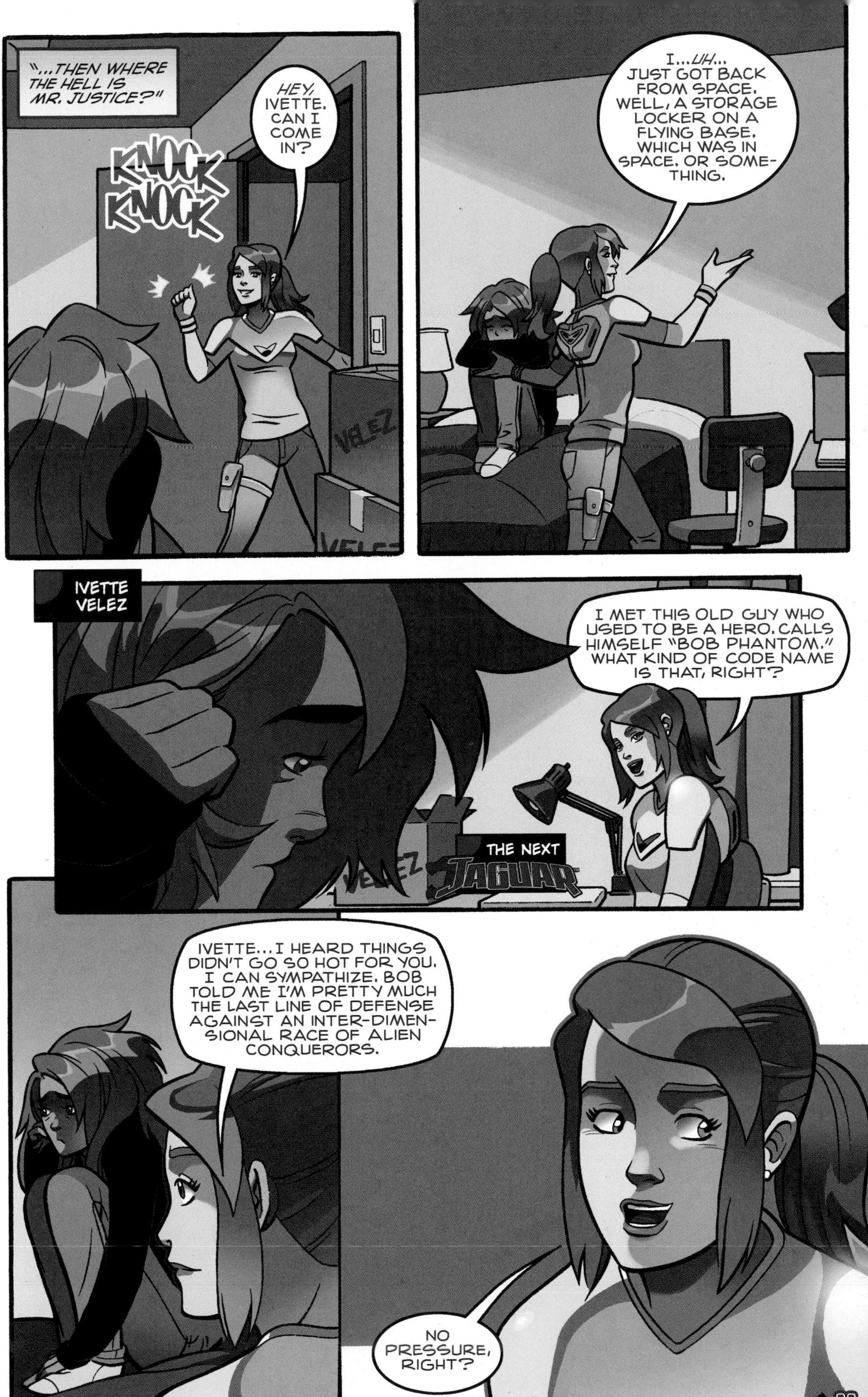
"...THEN WHERE THE HELL IS MR. JUSTICE?"
HEY, IVETTE. CAN I COME IN?
KNOCK KNOCK
VELEZ
I...UH... JUST GOT BACK FROM SPACE. WELL, A STORAGE LOCKER ON A FLYING BASE. WHICH WAS IN SPACE. OR SOMETHING.
IVETTE VELEZ
I MET THIS OLD GUY WHO USED TO BE A HERO. CALLS HIMSELF "BOB PHANTOM." WHAT KIND OF CODE NAME IS THAT, RIGHT?
THE NEXT JAGUAR
IVETTE... I HEARD THINGS DIDN'T GO SO HOT FOR YOU. I CAN SYMPATHIZE. BOB TOLD ME I'M PRETTY MUCH THE LAST LINE OF DEFENSE AGAINST AN INTER-DIMENSIONAL RACE OF ALIEN CONQUERORS.
NO PRESSURE, RIGHT?

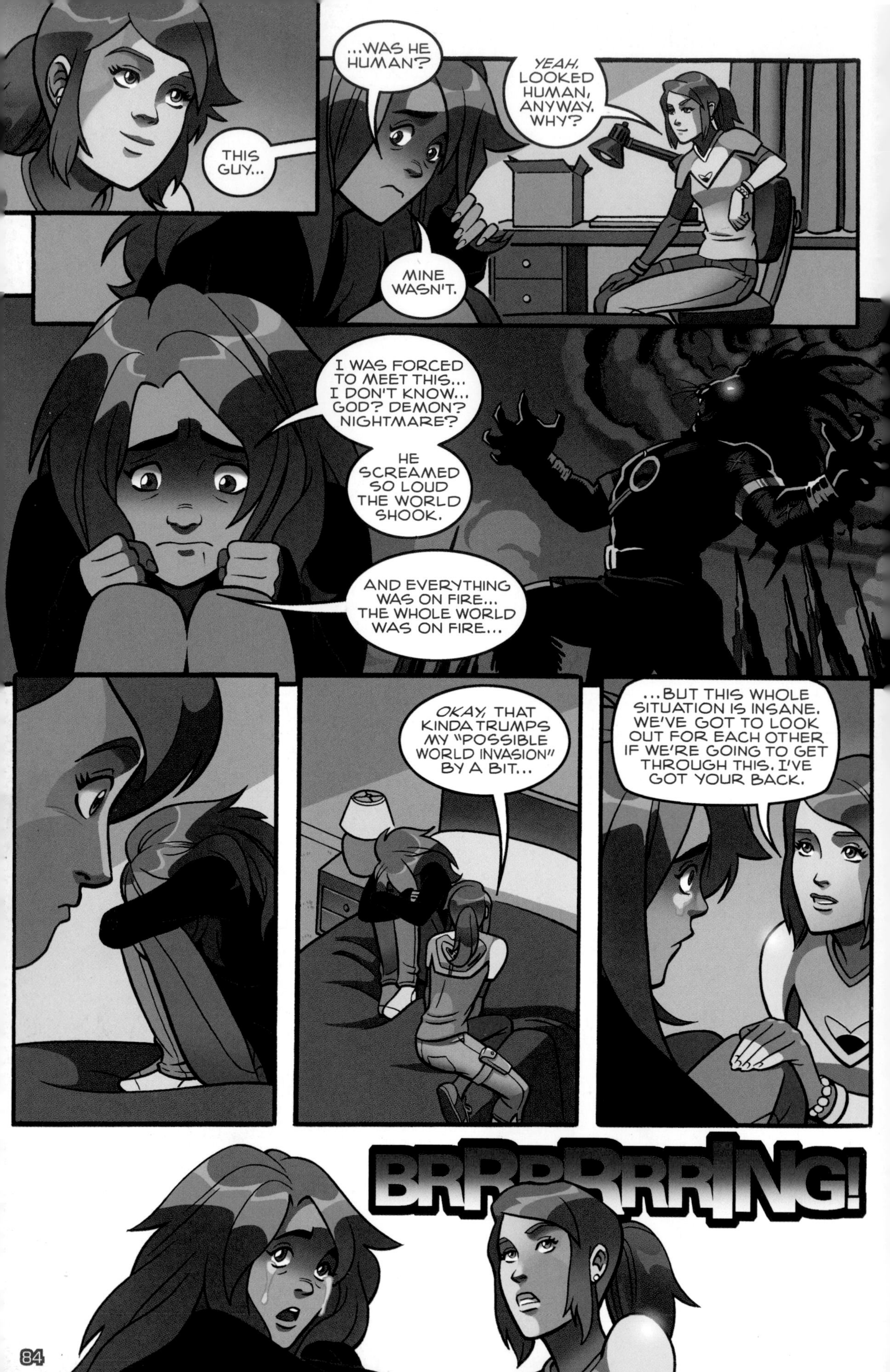
THIS GUY...
...WAS HE HUMAN?
YEAH, LOOKED HUMAN, ANYWAY. WHY?
MINE WASN'T.
I WAS FORCED TO MEET THIS... I DON'T KNOW... GOD? DEMON? NIGHTMARE?
HE SCREAMED SO LOUD THE WORLD SHOOK.
AND EVERYTHING WAS ON FIRE... THE WHOLE WORLD WAS ON FIRE...
OKAY, THAT KINDA TRUMPS MY "POSSIBLE WORLD INVASION" BY A BIT...
...BUT THIS WHOLE SITUATION IS INSANE. WE'VE GOT TO LOOK OUT FOR EACH OTHER IF WE'RE GOING TO GET THROUGH THIS. I'VE GOT YOUR BACK.
BRRRRRRRING!

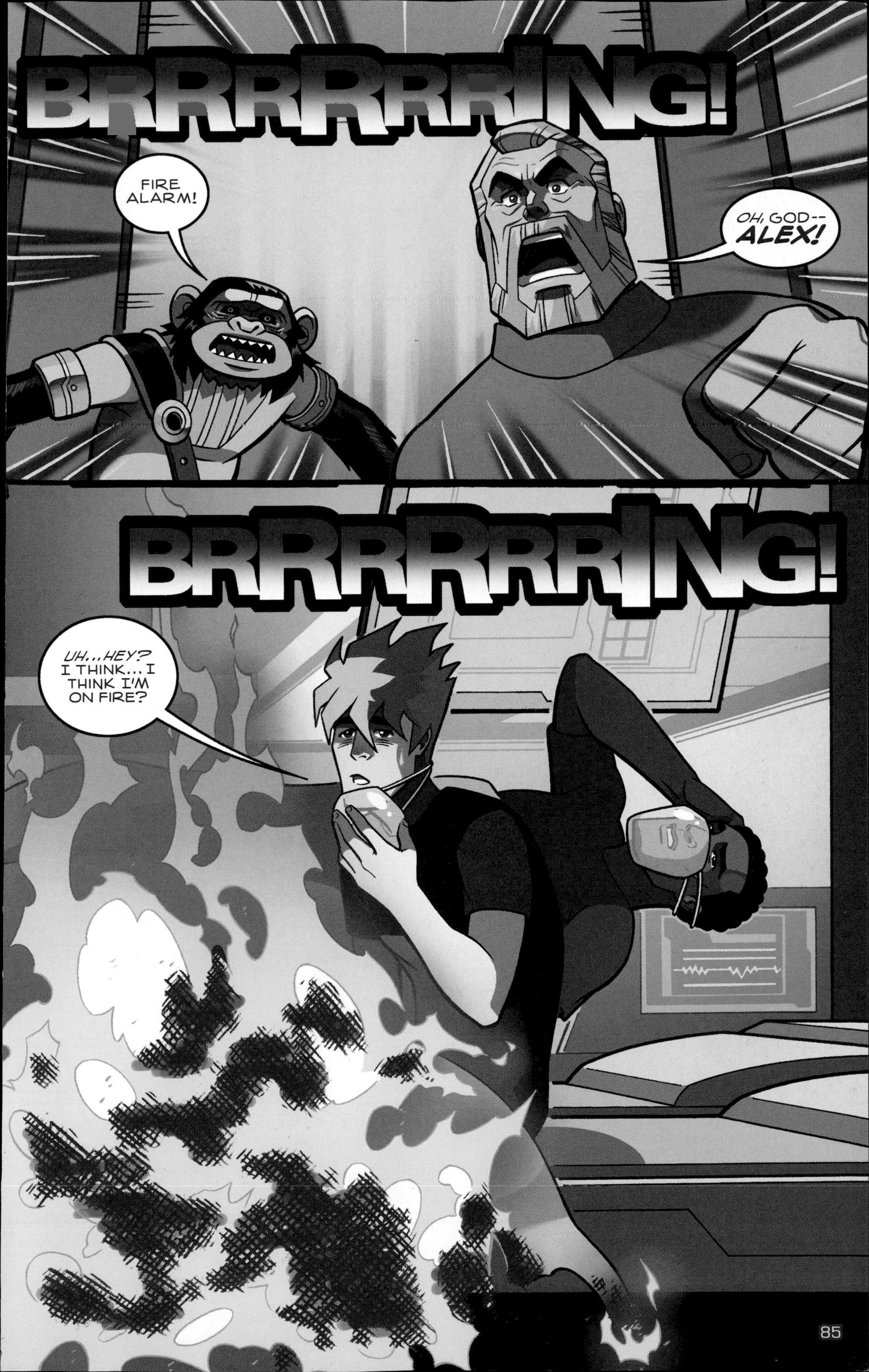
BRRRRRRRING!
FIRE ALARM!
OH, GOD-- ALEX!
BRRRRRRRING!
UH...HEY? I THINK... I THINK I'M ON FIRE?

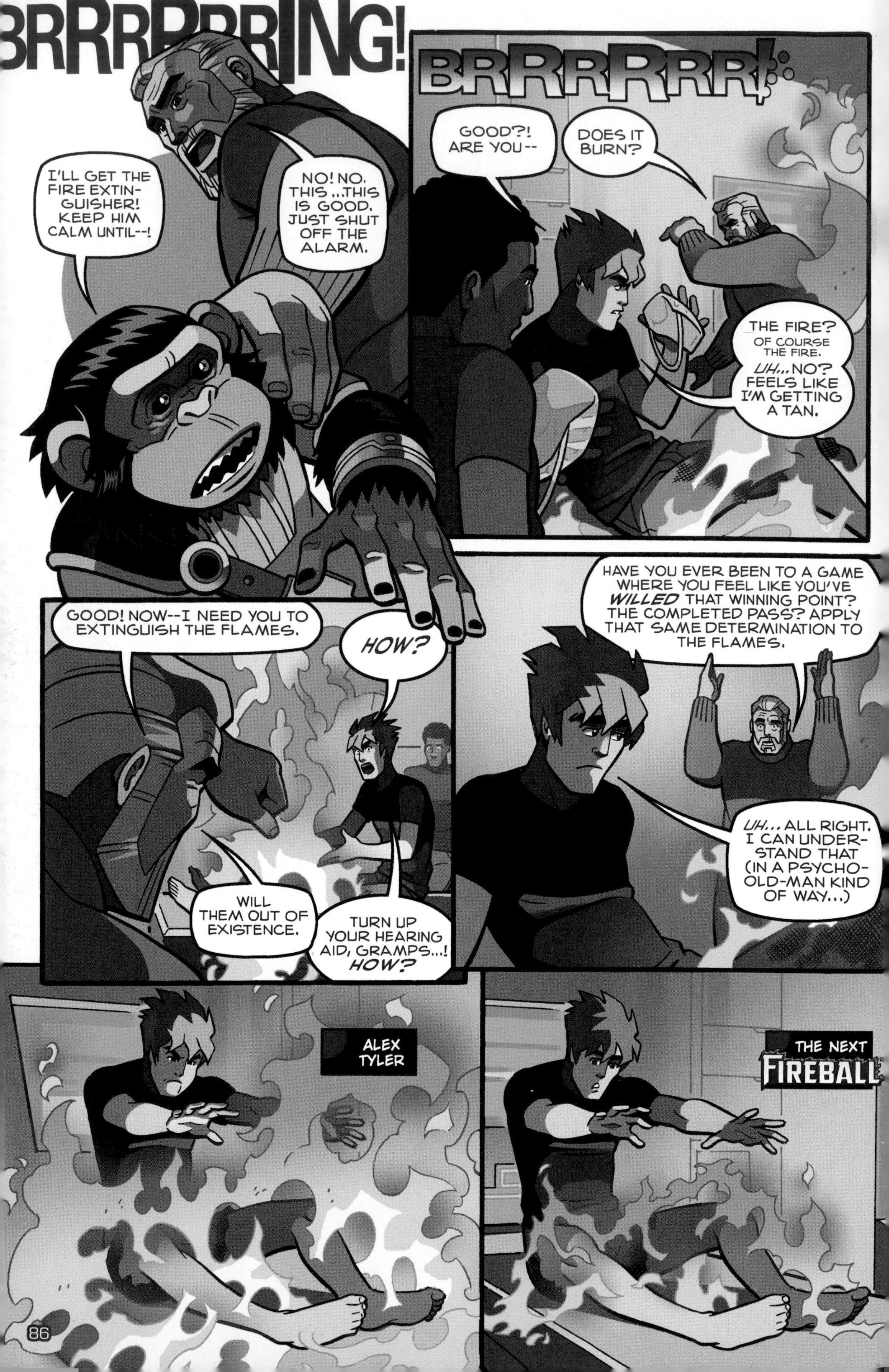

BRRRRRRING!
I'LL GET THE FIRE EXTIN-GUISHER! KEEP HIM CALM UNTIL--!
NO! NO. THIS ...THIS IS GOOD. JUST SHUT OFF THE ALARM.
BRRRRRRR!
GOOD?! ARE YOU--
DOES IT BURN?
THE FIRE? OF COURSE THE FIRE.
UH... NO? FEELS LIKE I'M GETTING A TAN.
GOOD! NOW--I NEED YOU TO EXTINGUISH THE FLAMES.
HOW?
WILL THEM OUT OF EXISTENCE.
TURN UP YOUR HEARING AID, GRAMPS...! HOW?
HAVE YOU EVER BEEN TO A GAME WHERE YOU FEEL LIKE YOU'VE WILLED THAT WINNING POINT? THE COMPLETED PASS? APPLY THAT SAME DETERMINATION TO THE FLAMES.
UH... ALL RIGHT. I CAN UNDER-STAND THAT (IN A PSYCHO-OLD-MAN KIND OF WAY...)
ALEX TYLER
THE NEXT FIREBALL

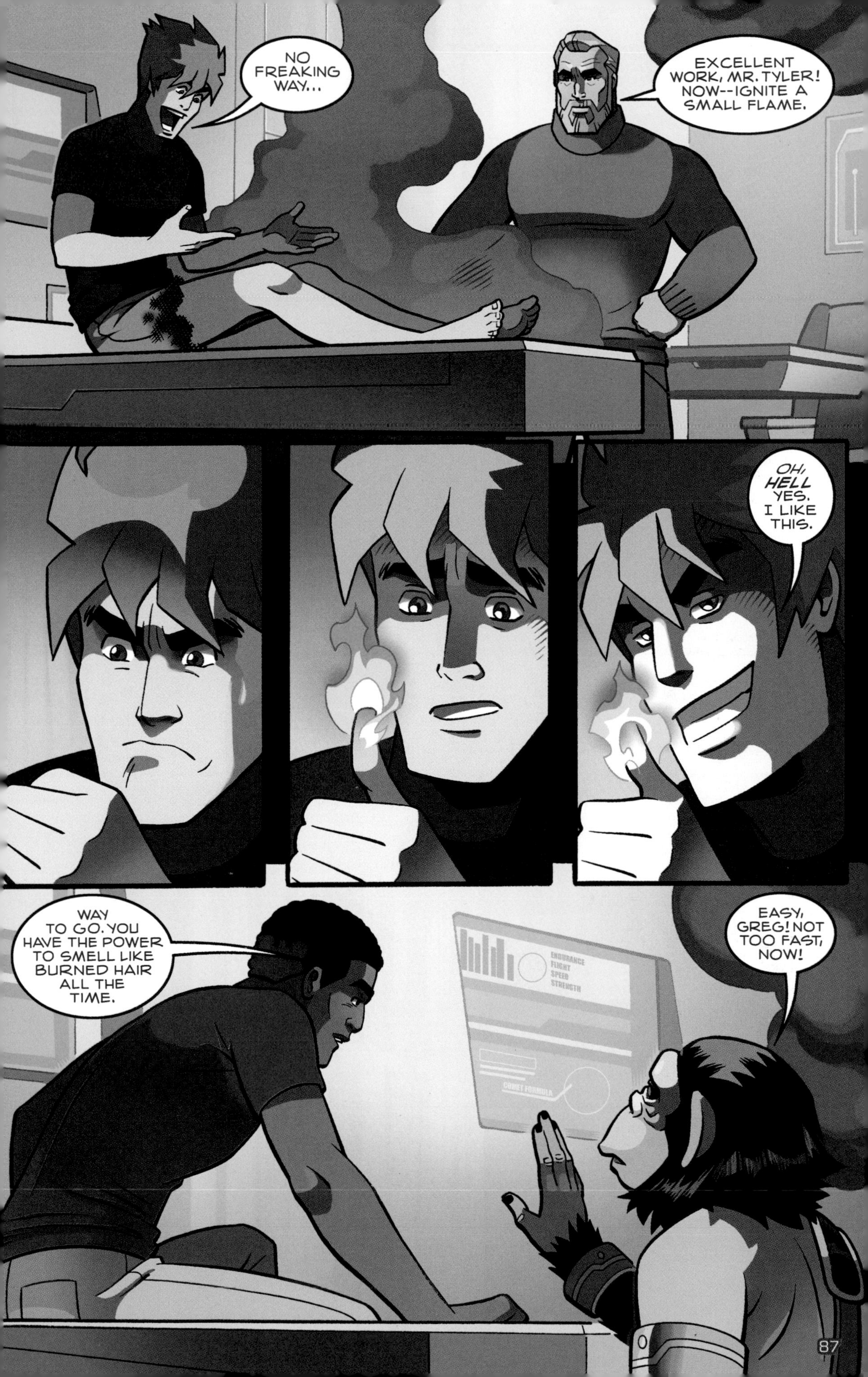
NO FREAKING WAY...
EXCELLENT WORK, MR. TYLER! NOW--IGNITE A SMALL FLAME.
OH, HELL YES. I LIKE THIS.
WAY TO GO. YOU HAVE THE POWER TO SMELL LIKE BURNED HAIR ALL THE TIME.
EASY, GREG! NOT TOO FAST, NOW!
ENDURANCE
FLIGHT
SPEED
STRENGTH
COMET FORMULA

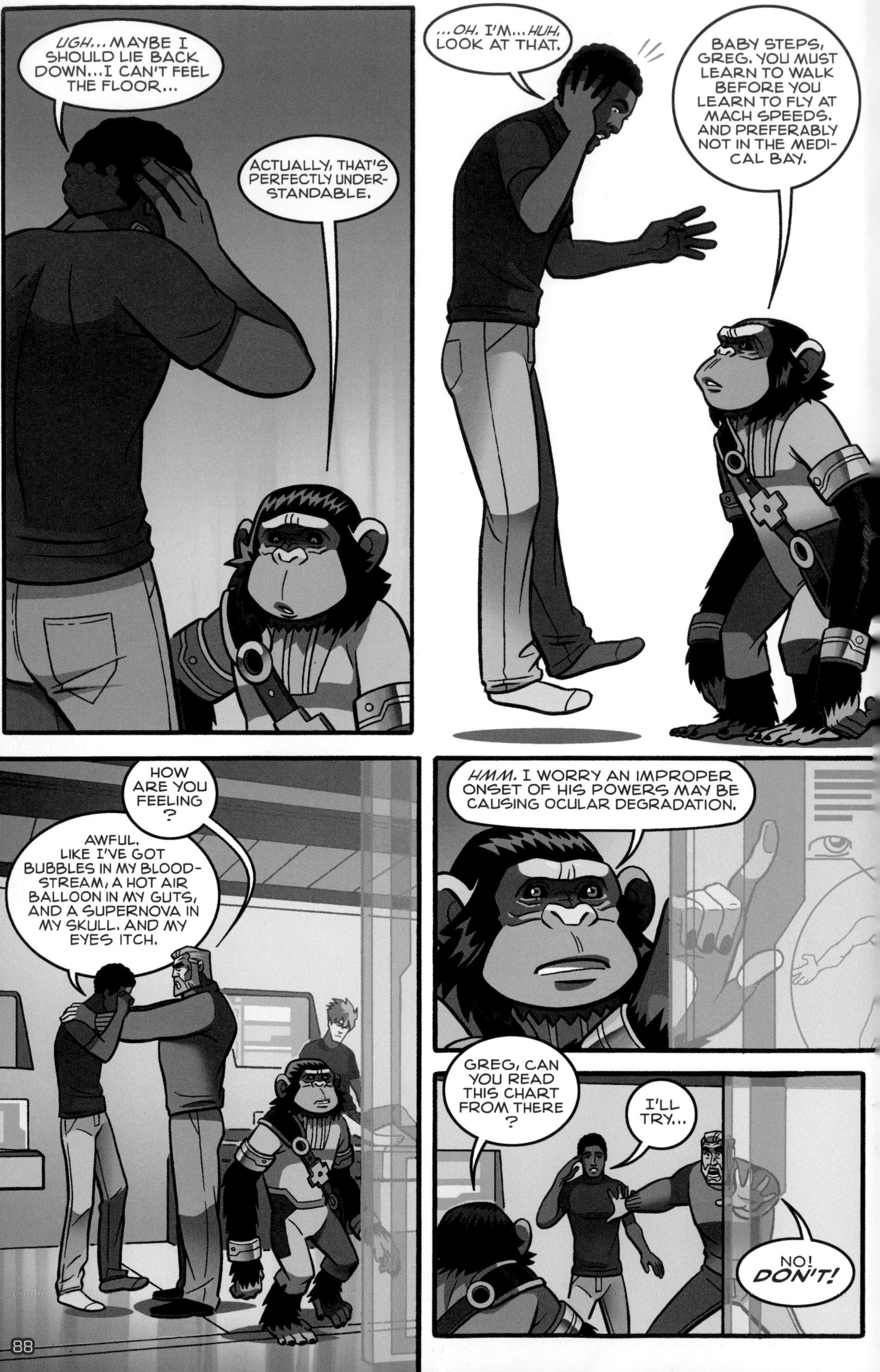
UGH... MAYBE I SHOULD LIE BACK DOWN...I CAN'T FEEL THE FLOOR...
ACTUALLY, THAT'S PERFECTLY UNDER-STANDABLE.
...OH. I'M...HUH. LOOK AT THAT.
BABY STEPS, GREG. YOU MUST LEARN TO WALK BEFORE YOU LEARN TO FLY AT MACH SPEEDS. AND PREFERABLY NOT IN THE MEDI-CAL BAY.
HOW ARE YOU FEELING?
AWFUL. LIKE I'VE GOT BUBBLES IN MY BLOOD-STREAM, A HOT AIR BALLOON IN MY GUTS, AND A SUPERNOVA IN MY SKULL. AND MY EYES ITCH.
HMM. I WORRY AN IMPROPER ONSET OF HIS POWERS MAY BE CAUSING OCULAR DEGRADATION.
GREG, CAN YOU READ THIS CHART FROM THERE?
I'LL TRY...
NO! DON'T!

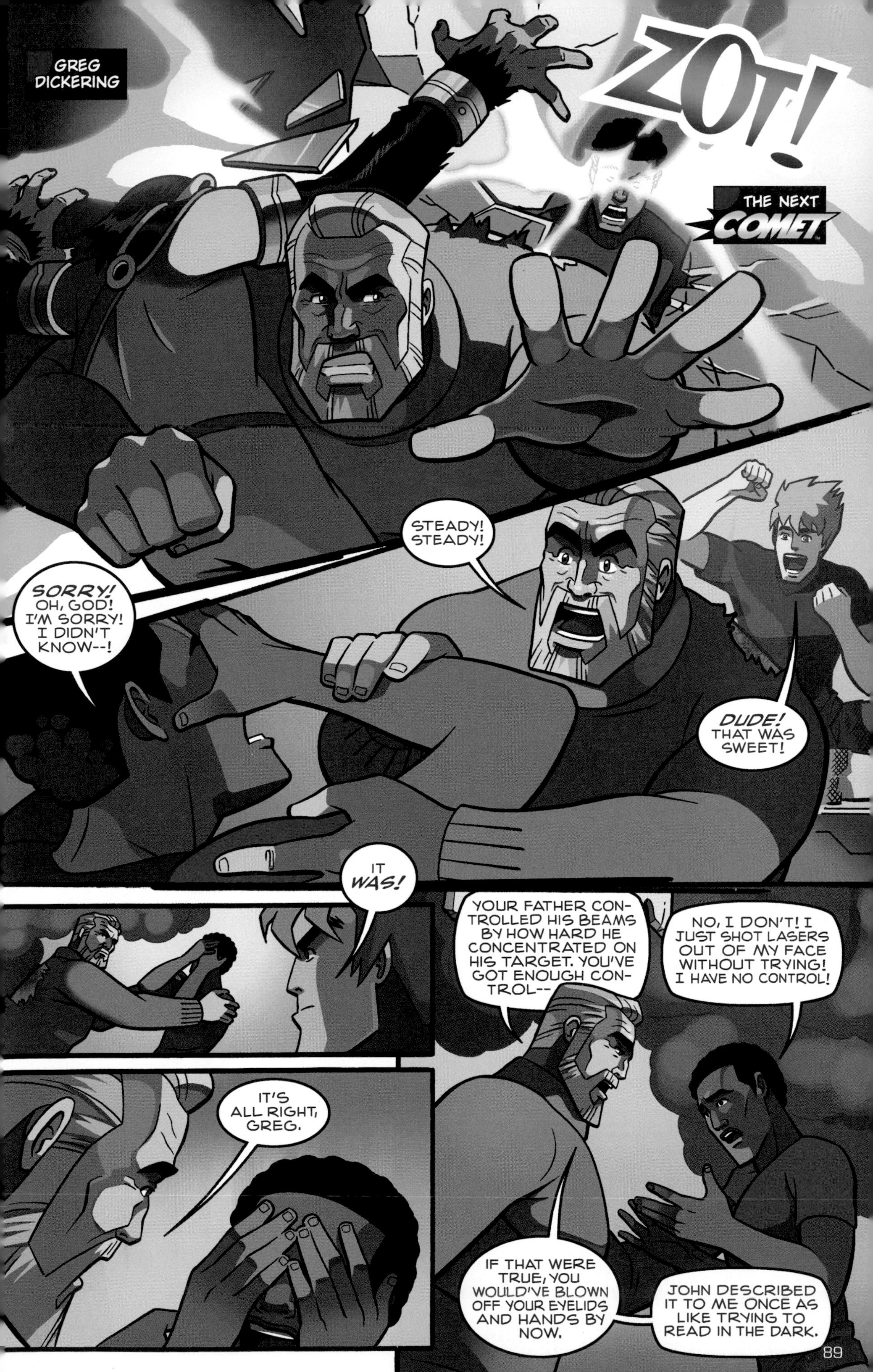
GREG DICKERING
ZOT!
THE NEXT COMET
STEADY! STEADY!
SORRY! OH, GOD! I'M SORRY! I DIDN'T KNOW--!
DUDE! THAT WAS SWEET!
IT WAS!
IT'S ALL RIGHT, GREG.
YOUR FATHER CONTROLLED HIS BEAMS BY HOW HARD HE CONCENTRATED ON HIS TARGET. YOU'VE GOT ENOUGH CONTROL--
NO, I DON'T! I JUST SHOT LASERS OUT OF MY FACE WITHOUT TRYING! I HAVE NO CONTROL!
IF THAT WERE TRUE, YOU WOULD'VE BLOWN OFF YOUR EYELIDS AND HANDS BY NOW.
JOHN DESCRIBED IT TO ME ONCE AS LIKE TRYING TO READ IN THE DARK.

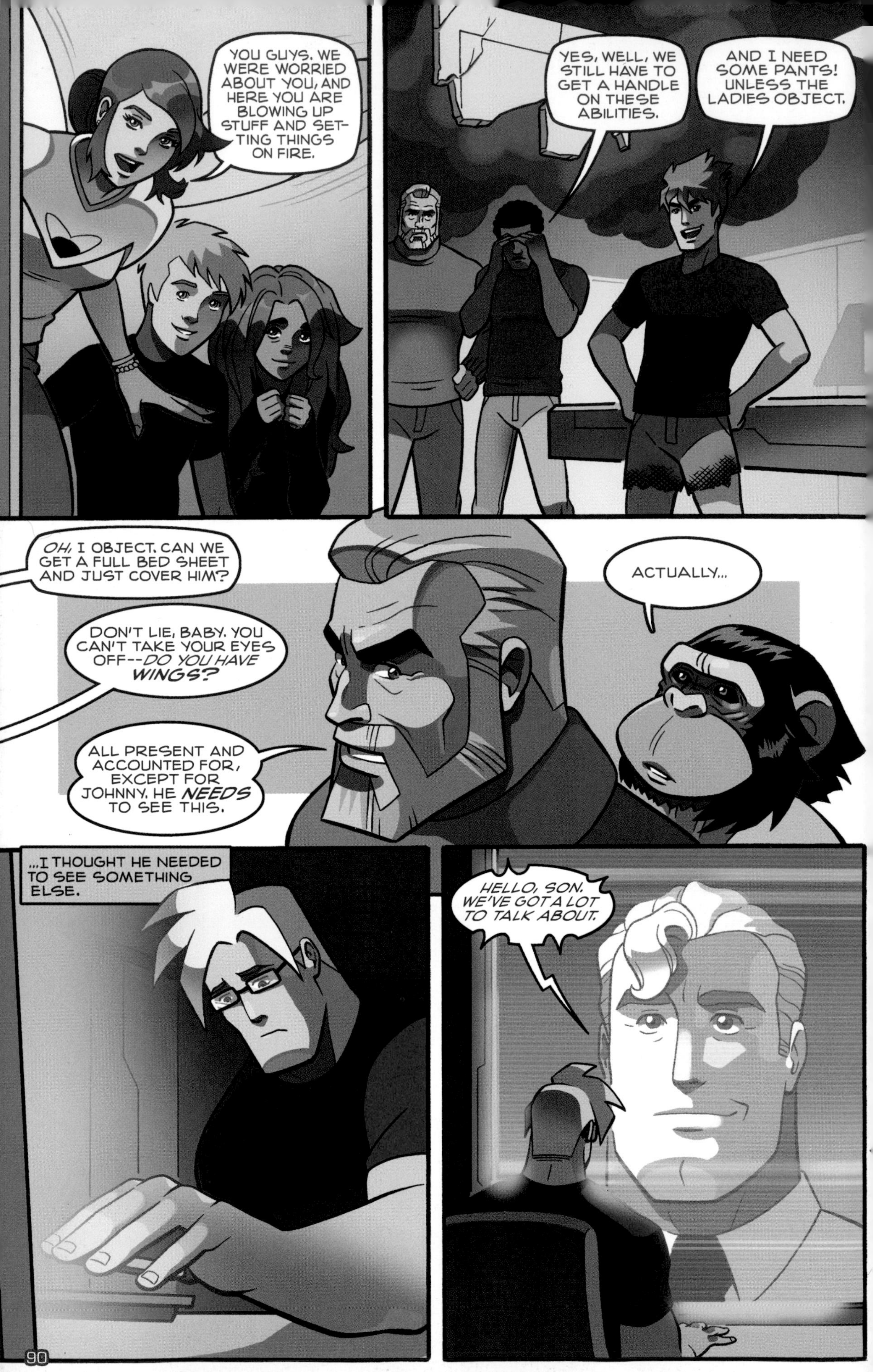
YOU GUYS. WE WERE WORRIED ABOUT YOU, AND HERE YOU ARE BLOWING UP STUFF AND SETTING THINGS ON FIRE.
YES, WELL, WE STILL HAVE TO GET A HANDLE ON THESE ABILITIES.
AND I NEED SOME PANTS! UNLESS THE LADIES OBJECT.
OH, I OBJECT. CAN WE GET A FULL BED SHEET AND JUST COVER HIM?
DON'T LIE, BABY. YOU CAN'T TAKE YOUR EYES OFF--DO YOU HAVE WINGS?
ACTUALLY...
ALL PRESENT AND ACCOUNTED FOR, EXCEPT FOR JOHNNY. HE NEEDS TO SEE THIS.
...I THOUGHT HE NEEDED TO SEE SOMETHING ELSE.
HELLO, SON. WE'VE GOT A LOT TO TALK ABOUT.

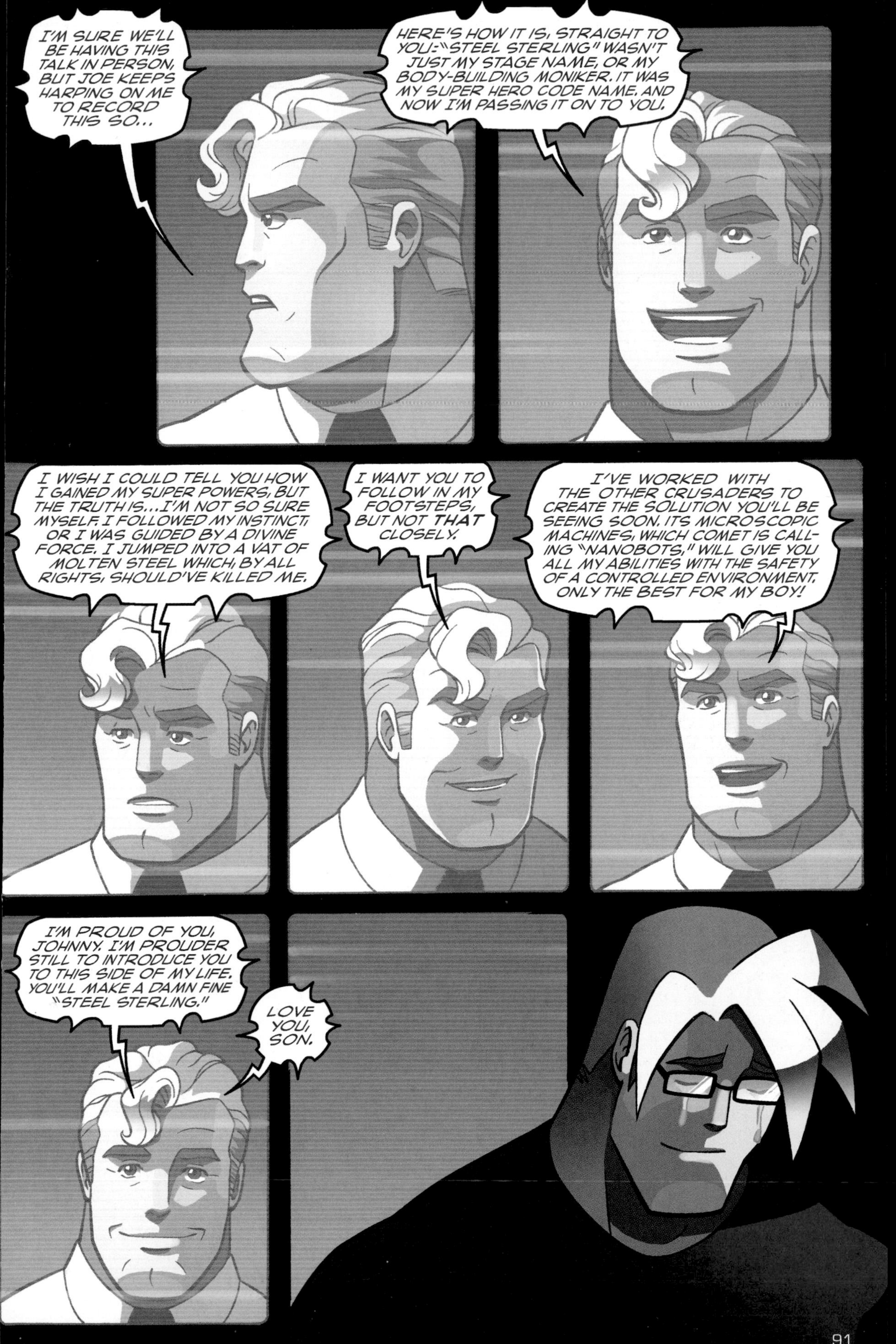
I'M SURE WE'LL BE HAVING THIS TALK IN PERSON, BUT JOE KEEPS HARPING ON ME TO RECORD THIS SO...
HERE'S HOW IT IS, STRAIGHT TO YOU: "STEEL STERLING" WASN'T JUST MY STAGE NAME, OR MY BODY-BUILDING MONIKER. IT WAS MY SUPER HERO CODE NAME. AND NOW I'M PASSING IT ON TO YOU.
I WISH I COULD TELL YOU HOW I GAINED MY SUPER POWERS, BUT THE TRUTH IS... I'M NOT SO SURE MYSELF. I FOLLOWED MY INSTINCT, OR I WAS GUIDED BY A DIVINE FORCE. I JUMPED INTO A VAT OF MOLTEN STEEL WHICH, BY ALL RIGHTS, SHOULD'VE KILLED ME.
I WANT YOU TO FOLLOW IN MY FOOTSTEPS, BUT NOT **THAT** CLOSELY.
I'VE WORKED WITH THE OTHER CRUSADERS TO CREATE THE SOLUTION YOU'LL BE SEEING SOON. ITS MICROSCOPIC MACHINES, WHICH COMET IS CALLING "NANOBOTS," WILL GIVE YOU ALL MY ABILITIES WITH THE SAFETY OF A CONTROLLED ENVIRONMENT. ONLY THE BEST FOR MY BOY!
I'M PROUD OF YOU, JOHNNY. I'M PROUDER STILL TO INTRODUCE YOU TO THIS SIDE OF MY LIFE. YOU'LL MAKE A DAMN FINE "STEEL STERLING."
LOVE YOU, SON.

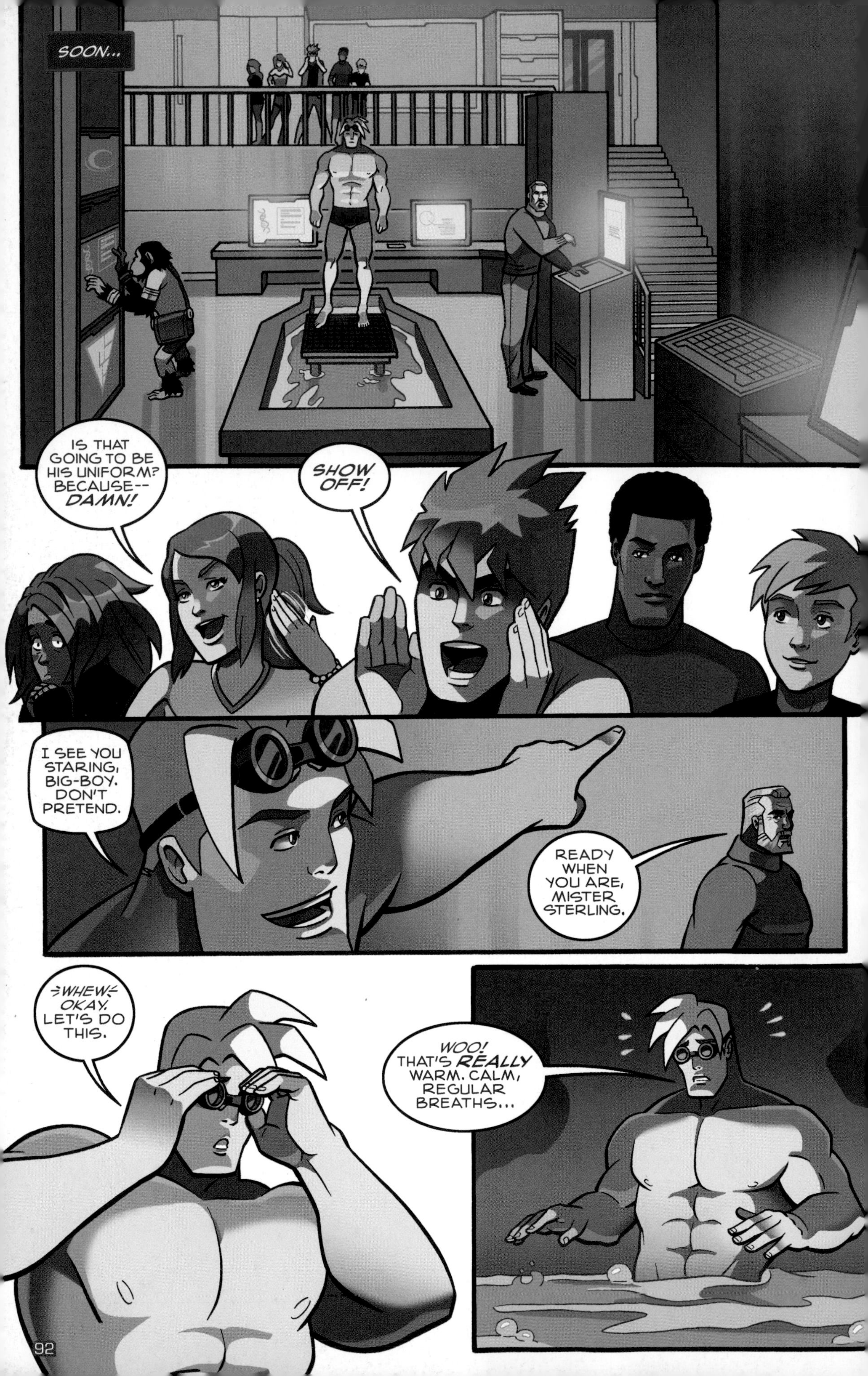
SOON...
IS THAT GOING TO BE HIS UNIFORM? BECAUSE-- DAMN!
SHOW OFF!
I SEE YOU STARING, BIG-BOY. DON'T PRETEND.
READY WHEN YOU ARE, MISTER STERLING.
WHEW OKAY. LET'S DO THIS.
WOO! THAT'S REALLY WARM. CALM, REGULAR BREATHS...

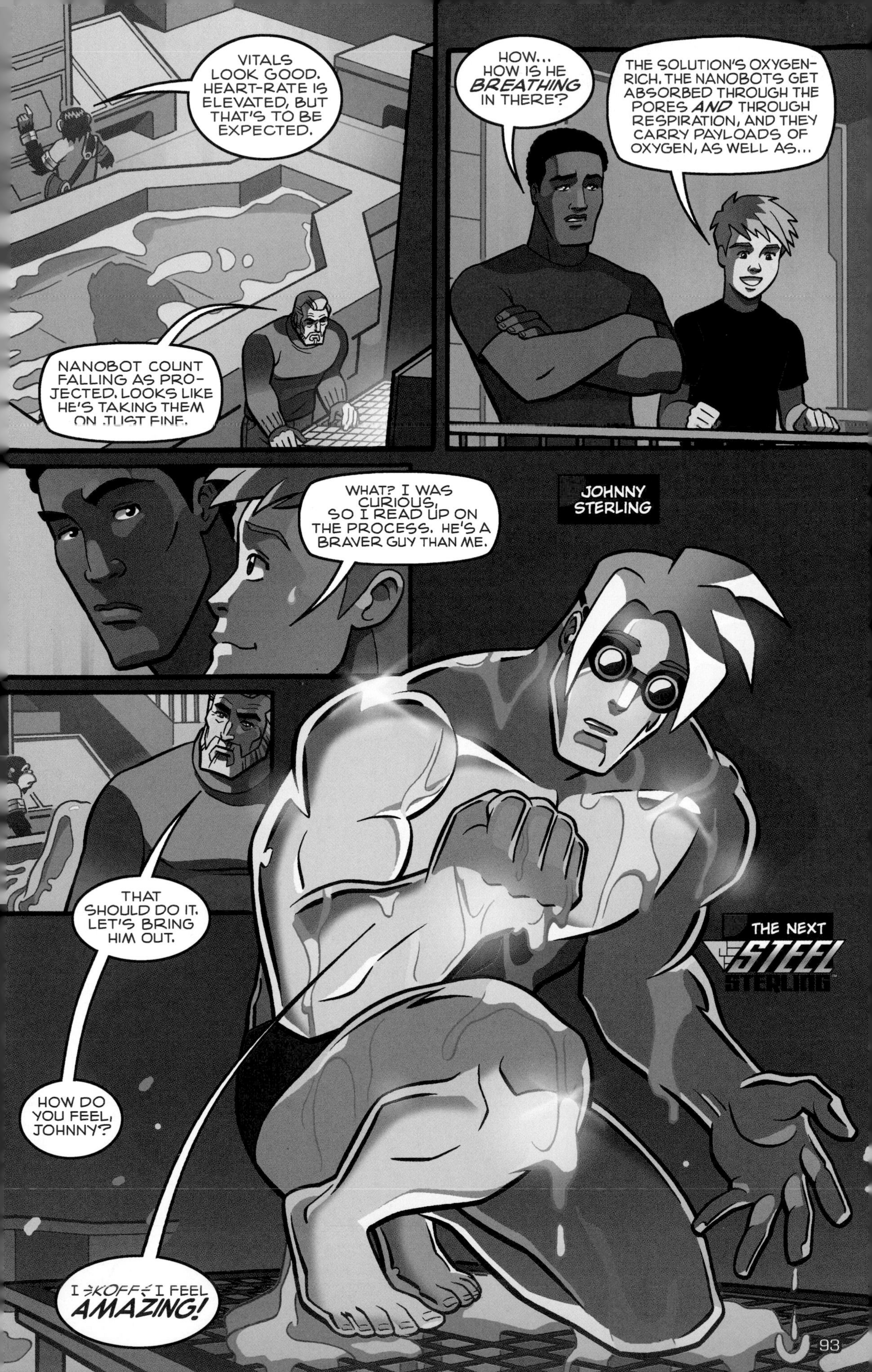
VITALS LOOK GOOD. HEART-RATE IS ELEVATED, BUT THAT'S TO BE EXPECTED.
NANOBOT COUNT FALLING AS PRO-JECTED. LOOKS LIKE HE'S TAKING THEM ON JUST FINE.
HOW... HOW IS HE BREATHING IN THERE?
THE SOLUTION'S OXYGEN-RICH. THE NANOBOTS GET ABSORBED THROUGH THE PORES AND THROUGH RESPIRATION, AND THEY CARRY PAYLOADS OF OXYGEN, AS WELL AS...
WHAT? I WAS CURIOUS, SO I READ UP ON THE PROCESS. HE'S A BRAVER GUY THAN ME.
JOHNNY STERLING
THAT SHOULD DO IT. LET'S BRING HIM OUT.
THE NEXT STEEL STERLING
HOW DO YOU FEEL, JOHNNY?
I ≯KOFF≮ I FEEL AMAZING!

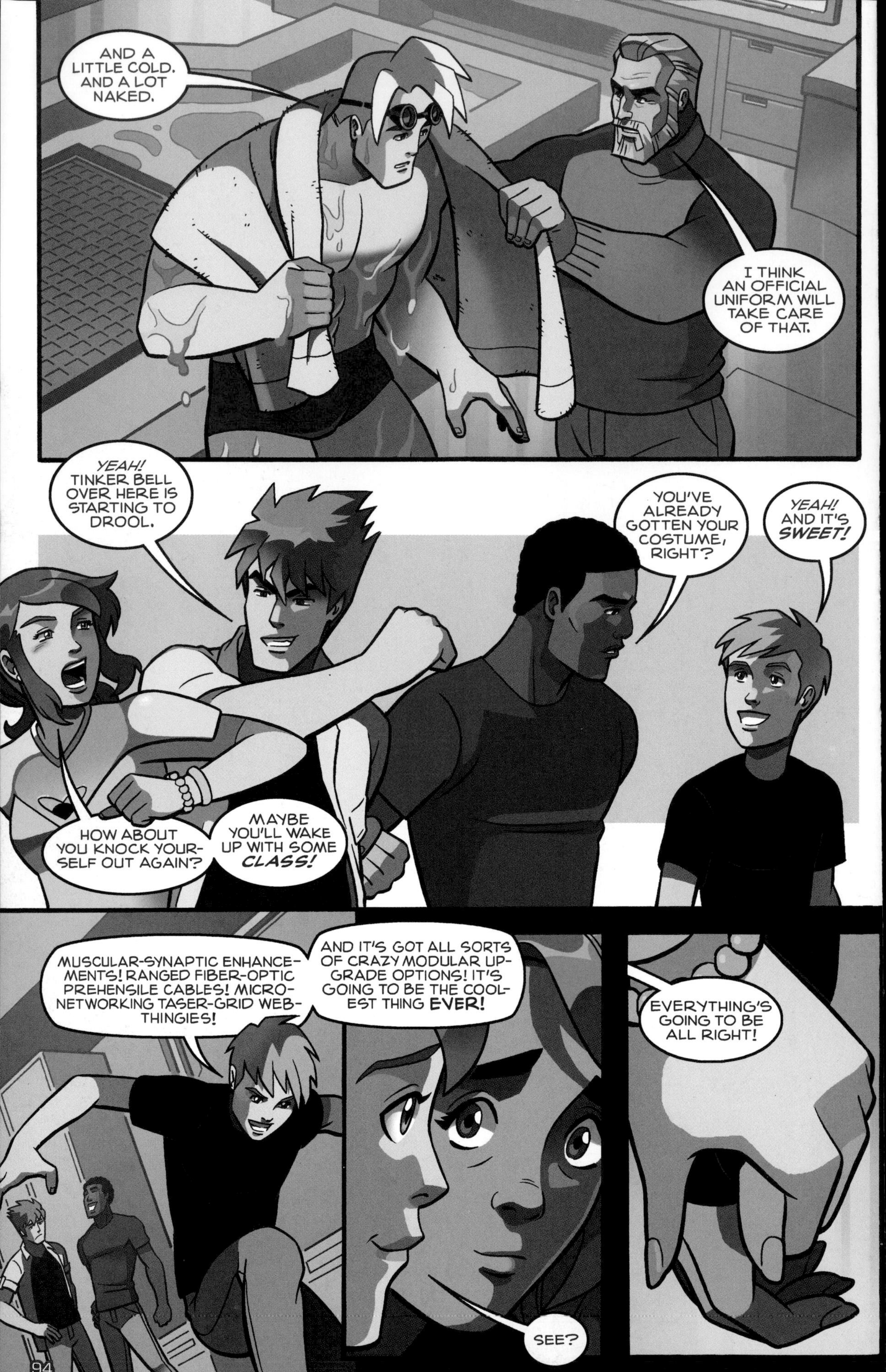
AND A LITTLE COLD. AND A LOT NAKED.
I THINK AN OFFICIAL UNIFORM WILL TAKE CARE OF THAT.
YEAH! TINKER BELL OVER HERE IS STARTING TO DROOL.
HOW ABOUT YOU KNOCK YOURSELF OUT AGAIN?
MAYBE YOU'LL WAKE UP WITH SOME ***CLASS!***
YOU'VE ALREADY GOTTEN YOUR COSTUME, RIGHT?
YEAH! AND IT'S ***SWEET!***
MUSCULAR-SYNAPTIC ENHANCEMENTS! RANGED FIBER-OPTIC PREHENSILE CABLES! MICRO-NETWORKING TASER-GRID WEB-THINGIES!
AND IT'S GOT ALL SORTS OF CRAZY MODULAR UPGRADE OPTIONS! IT'S GOING TO BE THE COOLEST THING **EVER!**
SEE?
EVERYTHING'S GOING TO BE ALL RIGHT!

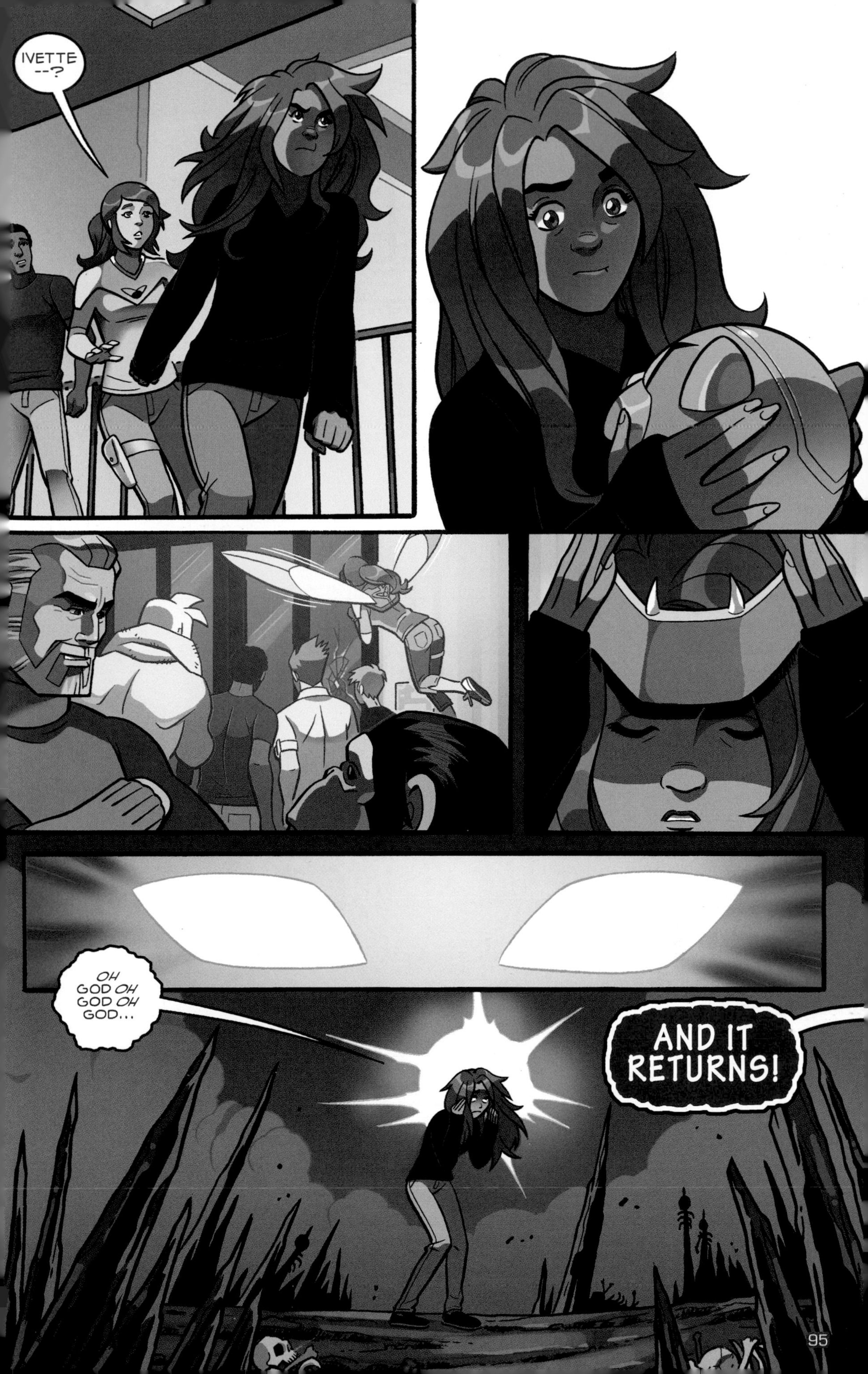
IVETTE --?
OH GOD OH GOD OH GOD...
AND IT RETURNS!

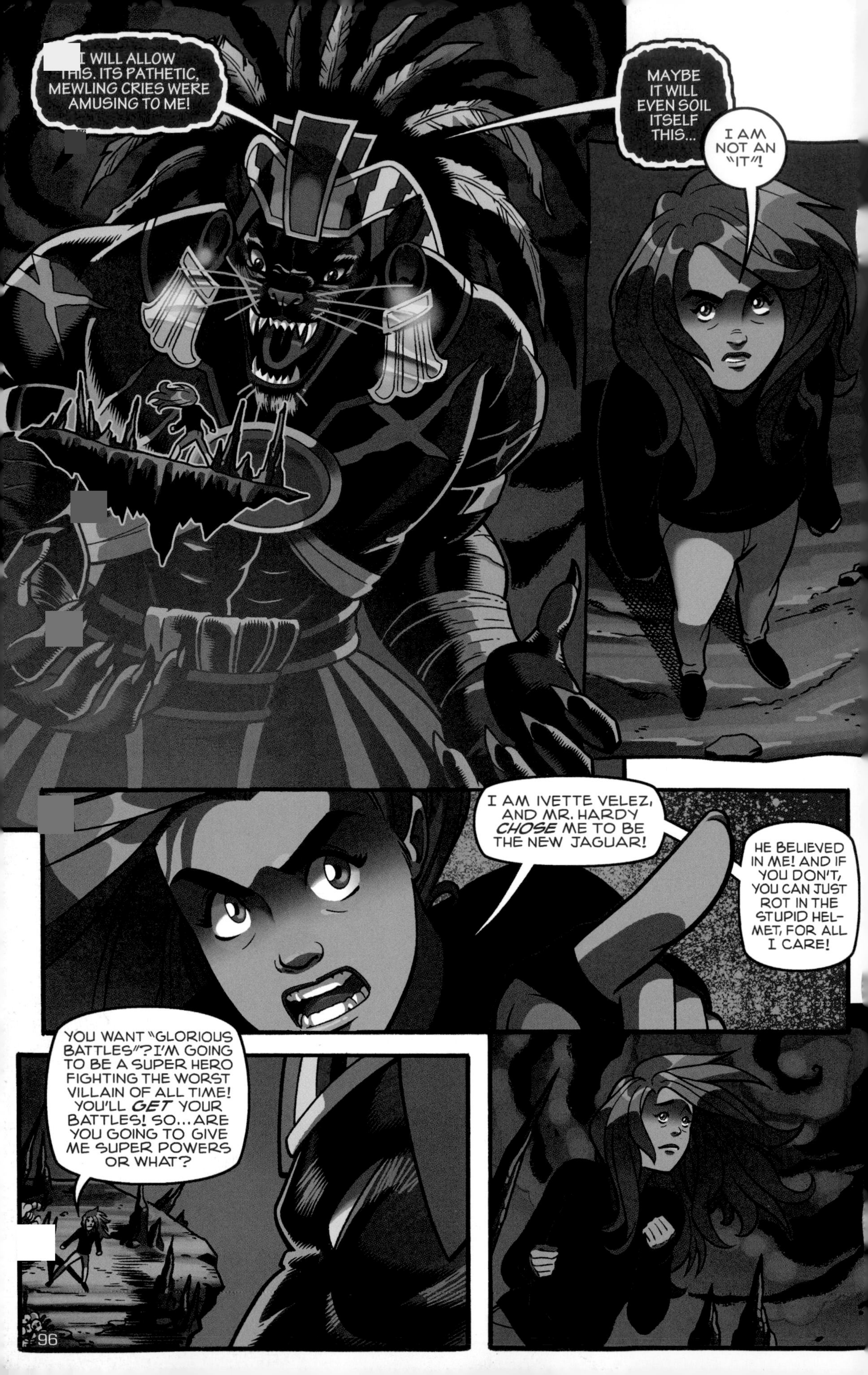
I WILL ALLOW THIS. ITS PATHETIC, MEWLING CRIES WERE AMUSING TO ME!
MAYBE IT WILL EVEN SOIL ITSELF THIS...
I AM NOT AN "IT"!
I AM IVETTE VELEZ, AND MR. HARDY *CHOSE* ME TO BE THE NEW JAGUAR!
HE BELIEVED IN ME! AND IF YOU DON'T, YOU CAN JUST ROT IN THE STUPID HEL-MET, FOR ALL I CARE!
YOU WANT "GLORIOUS BATTLES"? I'M GOING TO BE A SUPER HERO FIGHTING THE WORST VILLAIN OF ALL TIME! YOU'LL *GET* YOUR BATTLES! SO... ARE YOU GOING TO GIVE ME SUPER POWERS OR WHAT?

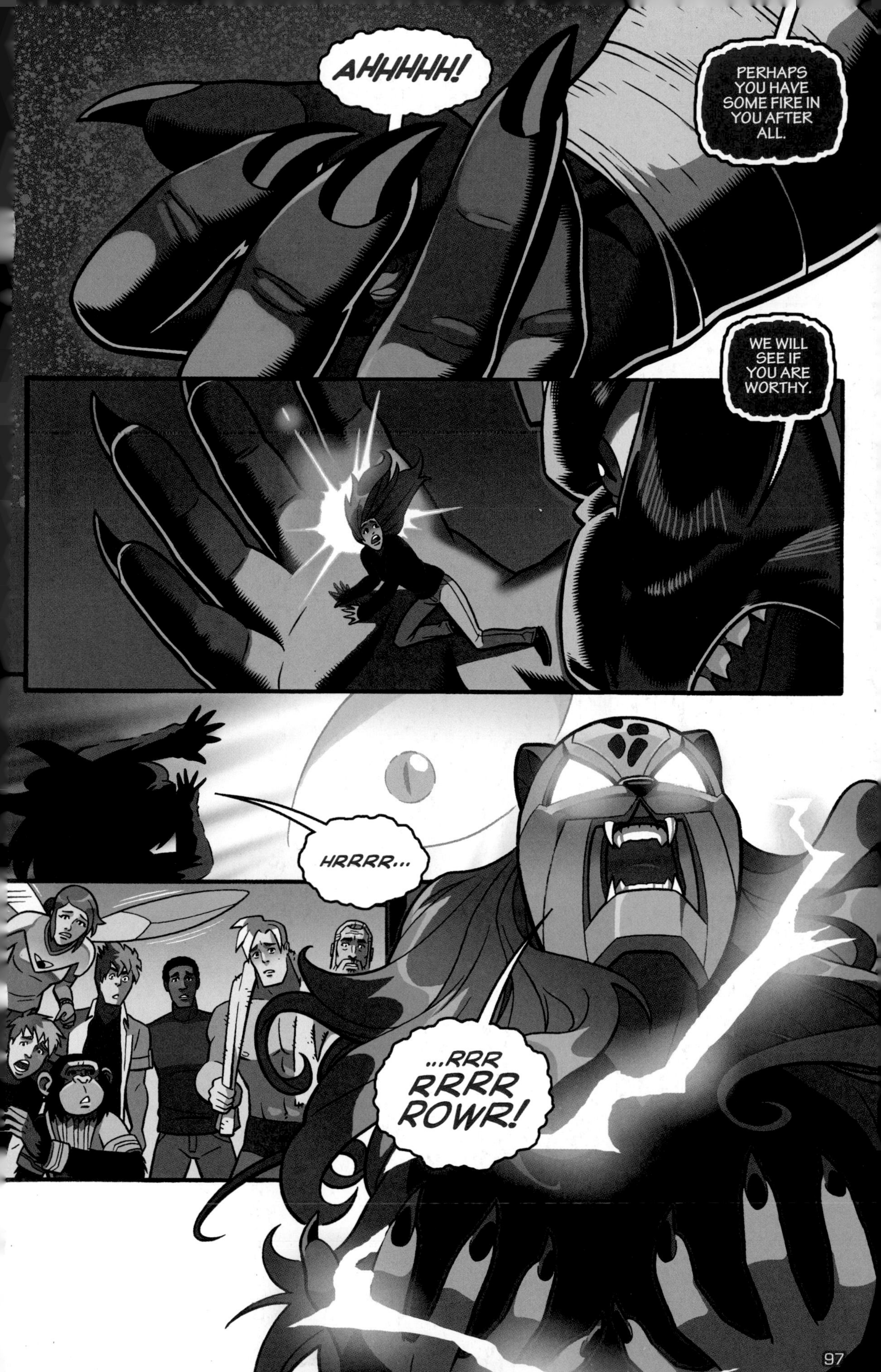
AHHHHH!
PERHAPS YOU HAVE SOME FIRE IN YOU AFTER ALL.
WE WILL SEE IF YOU ARE WORTHY.
HRRRR...
...RRR RRRR ROWR!

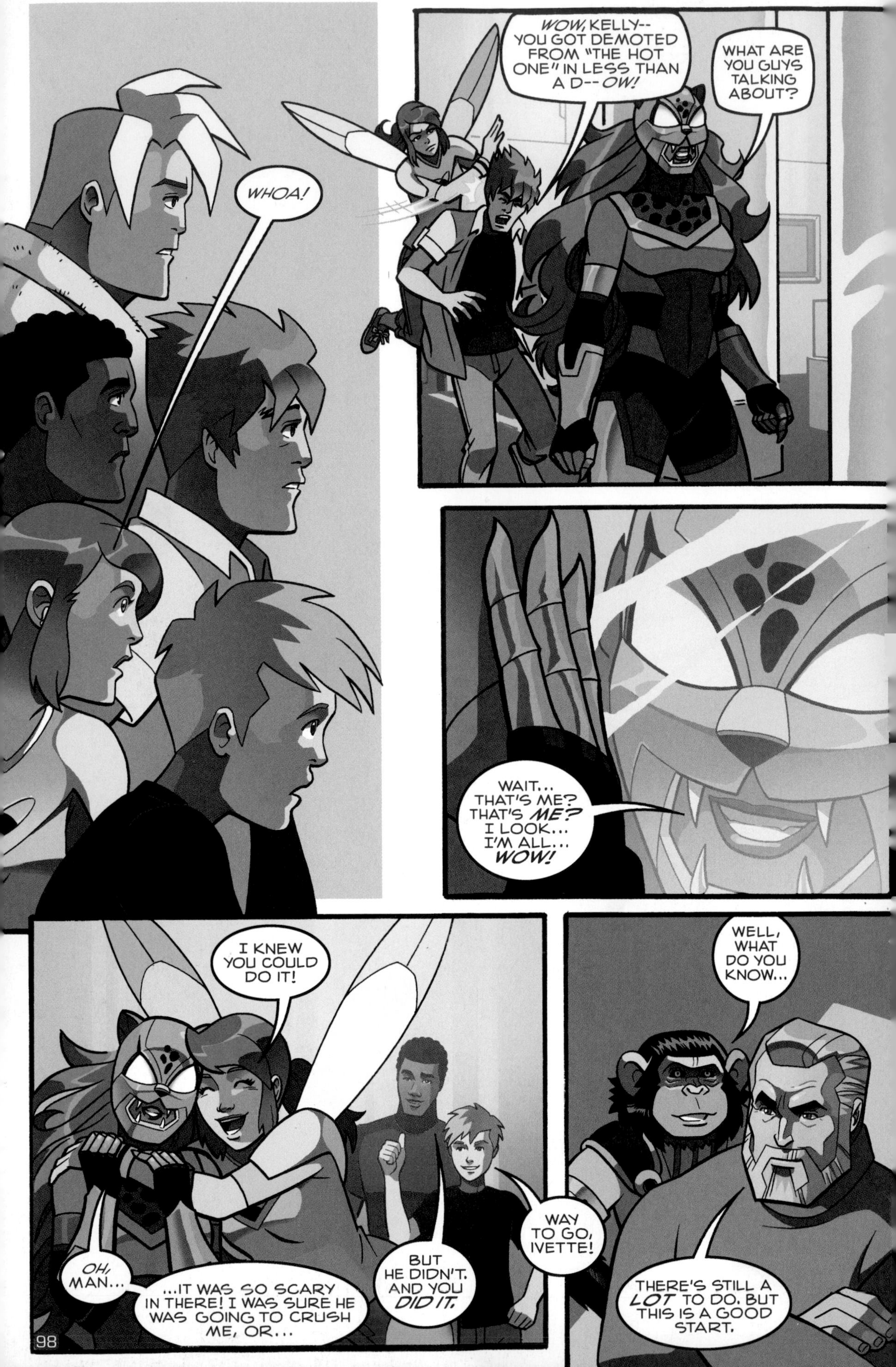
WHOA!
WOW, KELLY-- YOU GOT DEMOTED FROM "THE HOT ONE" IN LESS THAN A D--OW!
WHAT ARE YOU GUYS TALKING ABOUT?
WAIT... THAT'S ME? THAT'S ME? I LOOK... I'M ALL... WOW!
I KNEW YOU COULD DO IT!
OH, MAN...
...IT WAS SO SCARY IN THERE! I WAS SURE HE WAS GOING TO CRUSH ME, OR...
BUT HE DIDN'T. AND YOU DID IT.
WAY TO GO, IVETTE!
WELL, WHAT DO YOU KNOW...
THERE'S STILL A LOT TO DO. BUT THIS IS A GOOD START.

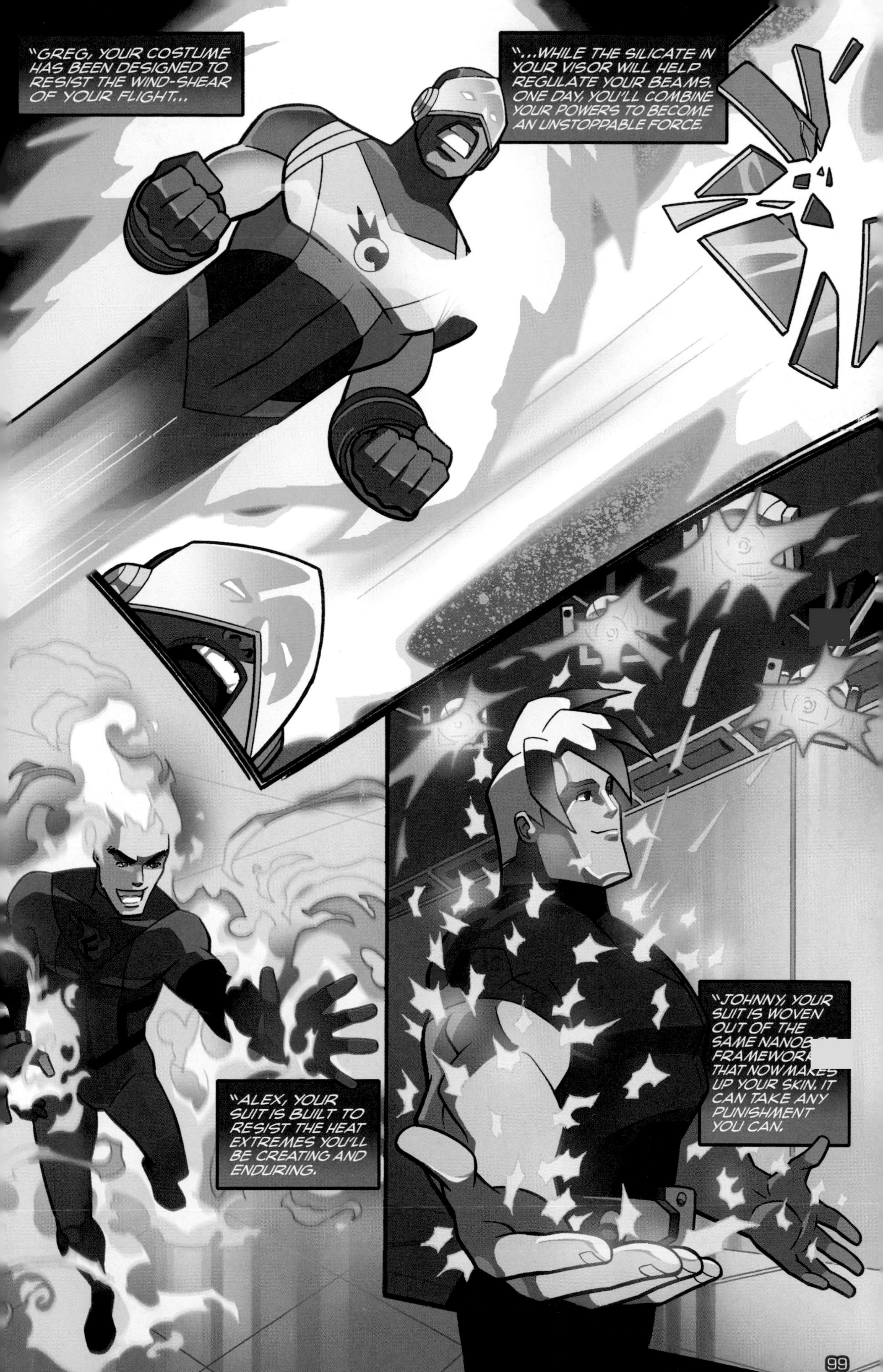
"GREG, YOUR COSTUME HAS BEEN DESIGNED TO RESIST THE WIND-SHEAR OF YOUR FLIGHT...
"...WHILE THE SILICATE IN YOUR VISOR WILL HELP REGULATE YOUR BEAMS. ONE DAY, YOU'LL COMBINE YOUR POWERS TO BECOME AN UNSTOPPABLE FORCE.
"ALEX, YOUR SUIT IS BUILT TO RESIST THE HEAT EXTREMES YOU'LL BE CREATING AND ENDURING.
"JOHNNY, YOUR SUIT IS WOVEN OUT OF THE SAME NANOB
FRAMEWOR
THAT NOW MAKES UP YOUR SKIN. IT CAN TAKE ANY PUNISHMENT YOU CAN.

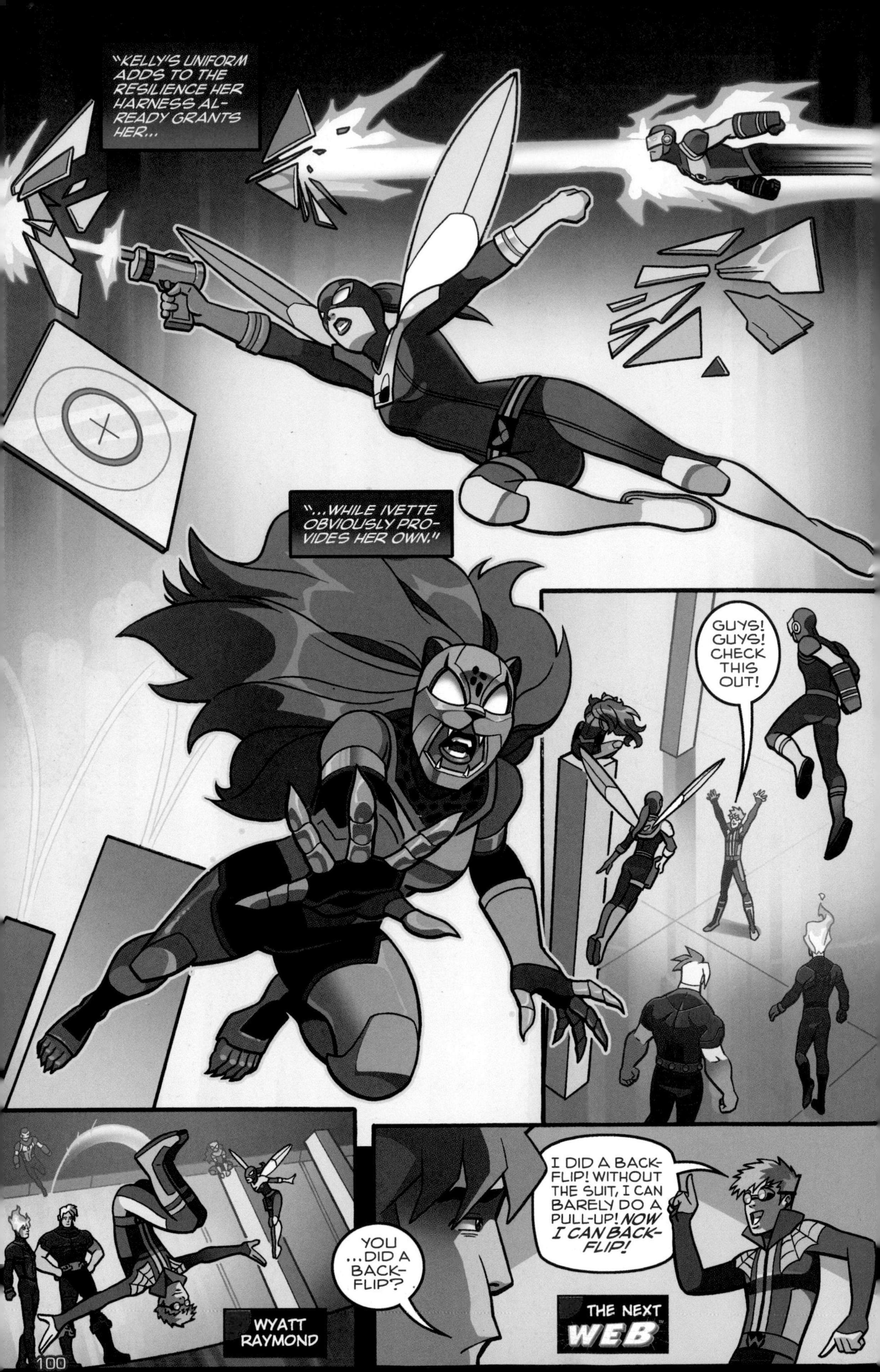
"KELLY'S UNIFORM ADDS TO THE RESILIENCE HER HARNESS AL-READY GRANTS HER...
"...WHILE IVETTE OBVIOUSLY PRO-VIDES HER OWN."
GUYS! GUYS! CHECK THIS OUT!
WYATT RAYMOND
YOU ...DID A BACK-FLIP?
I DID A BACK-FLIP! WITHOUT THE SUIT, I CAN BARELY DO A PULL-UP! NOW I CAN BACK-FLIP!
THE NEXT WEB

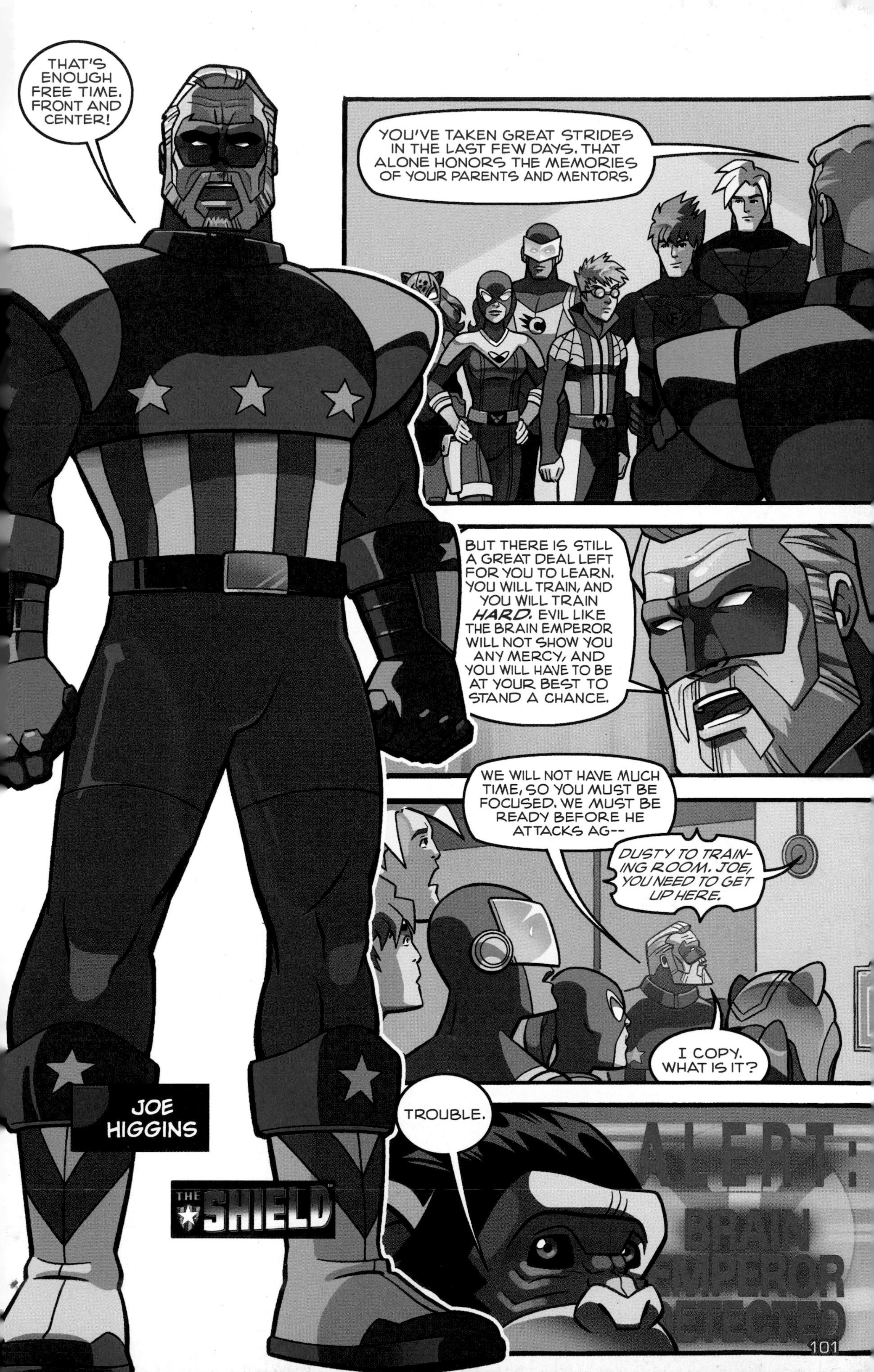
THAT'S ENOUGH FREE TIME. FRONT AND CENTER!
YOU'VE TAKEN GREAT STRIDES IN THE LAST FEW DAYS. THAT ALONE HONORS THE MEMORIES OF YOUR PARENTS AND MENTORS.
BUT THERE IS STILL A GREAT DEAL LEFT FOR YOU TO LEARN. YOU WILL TRAIN, AND YOU WILL TRAIN HARD. EVIL LIKE THE BRAIN EMPEROR WILL NOT SHOW YOU ANY MERCY, AND YOU WILL HAVE TO BE AT YOUR BEST TO STAND A CHANCE.
WE WILL NOT HAVE MUCH TIME, SO YOU MUST BE FOCUSED. WE MUST BE READY BEFORE HE ATTACKS AG--
DUSTY TO TRAINING ROOM. JOE, YOU NEED TO GET UP HERE.
I COPY. WHAT IS IT?
JOE HIGGINS
THE SHIELD
TROUBLE.
ALERT: BRAIN EMPEROR DETECTED

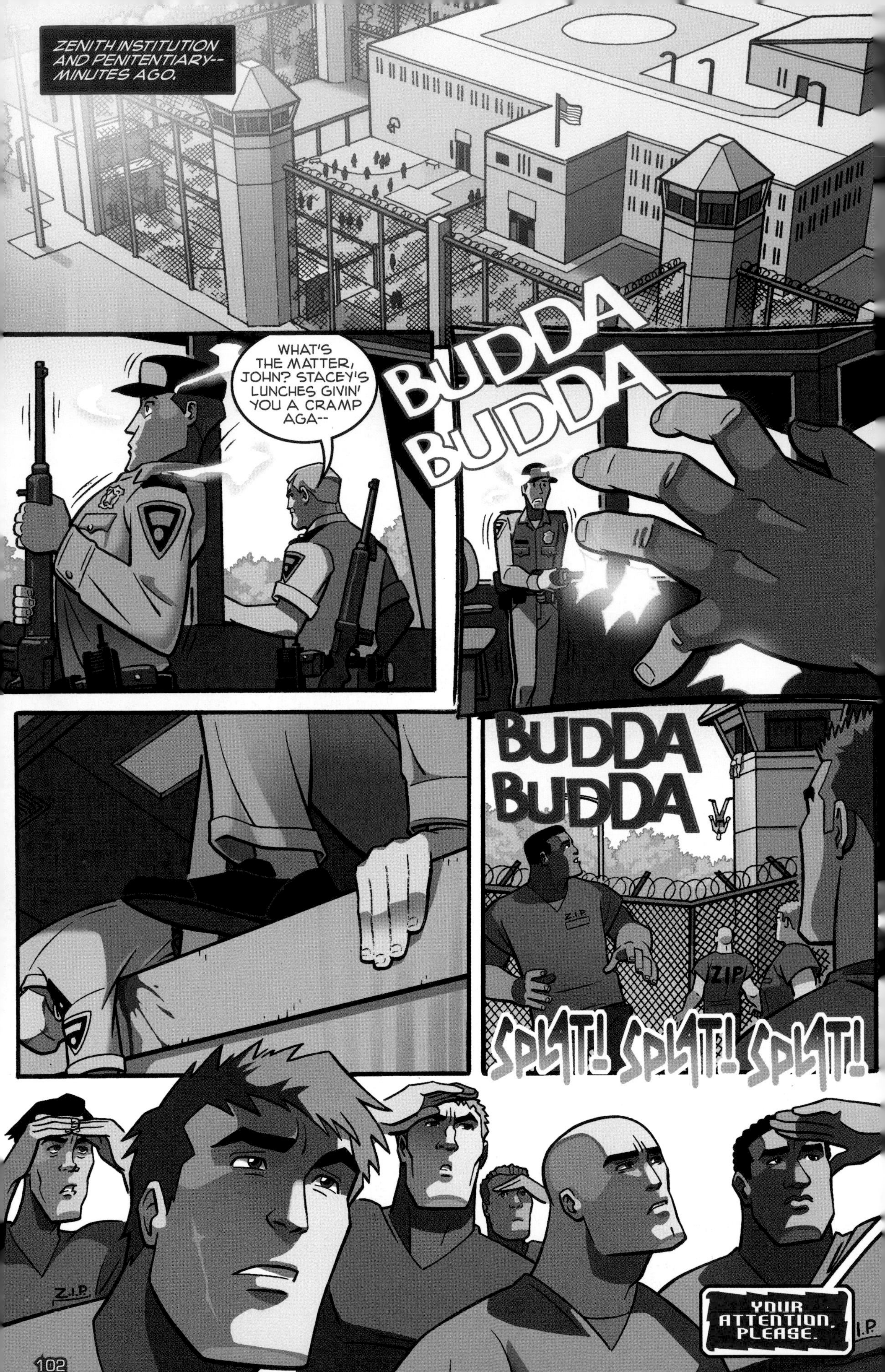

ZENITH INSTITUTION AND PENITENTIARY-- MINUTES AGO.
WHAT'S THE MATTER, JOHN? STACEY'S LUNCHES GIVIN' YOU A CRAMP AGA--
BUDDA BUDDA
BUDDA BUDDA
SPLAT! SPLAT! SPLAT!
YOUR ATTENTION, PLEASE.

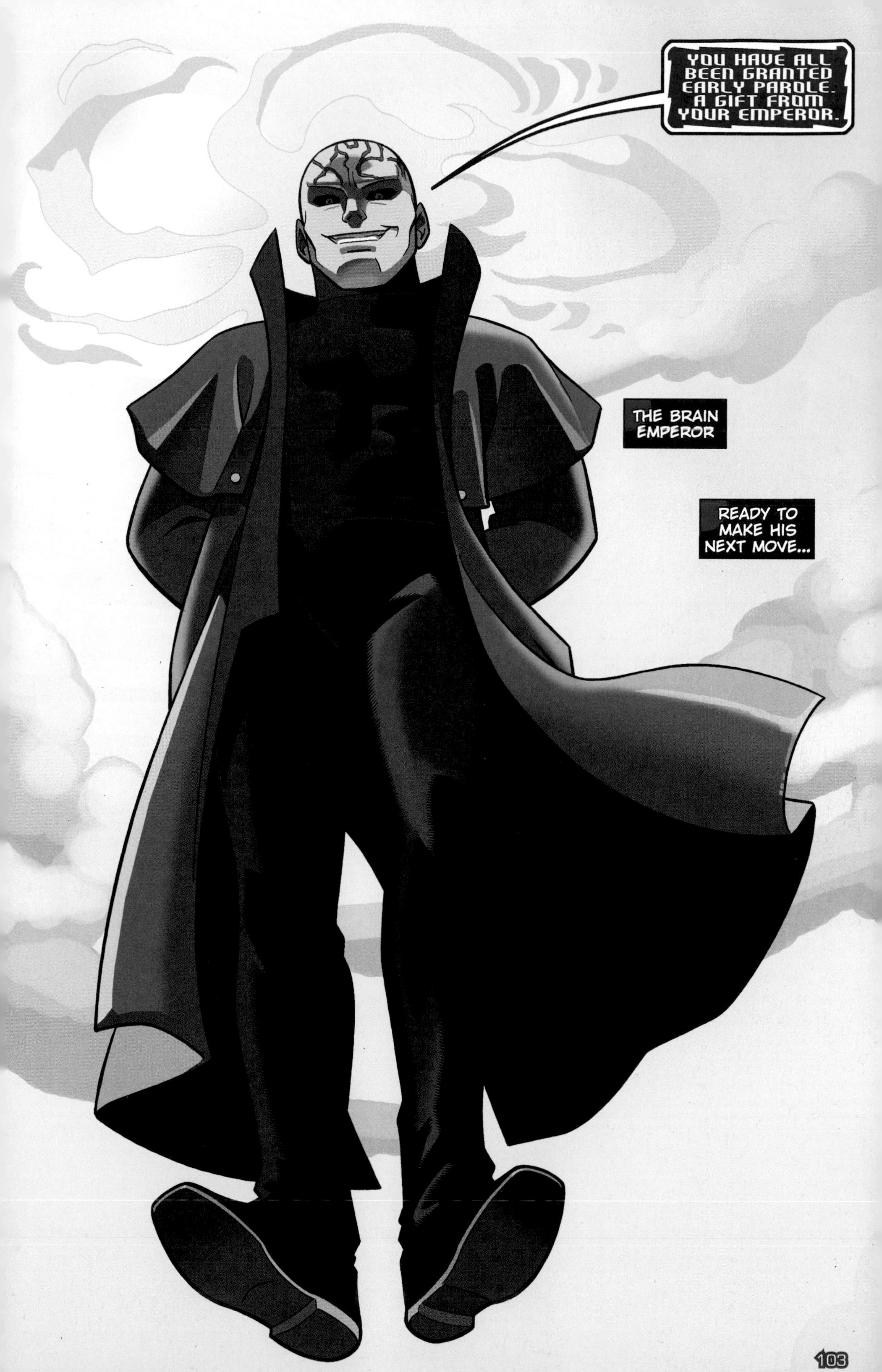
YOU HAVE ALL BEEN GRANTED EARLY PAROLE. A GIFT FROM YOUR EMPEROR.
THE BRAIN EMPEROR
READY TO MAKE HIS NEXT MOVE...

CHAPTER 5

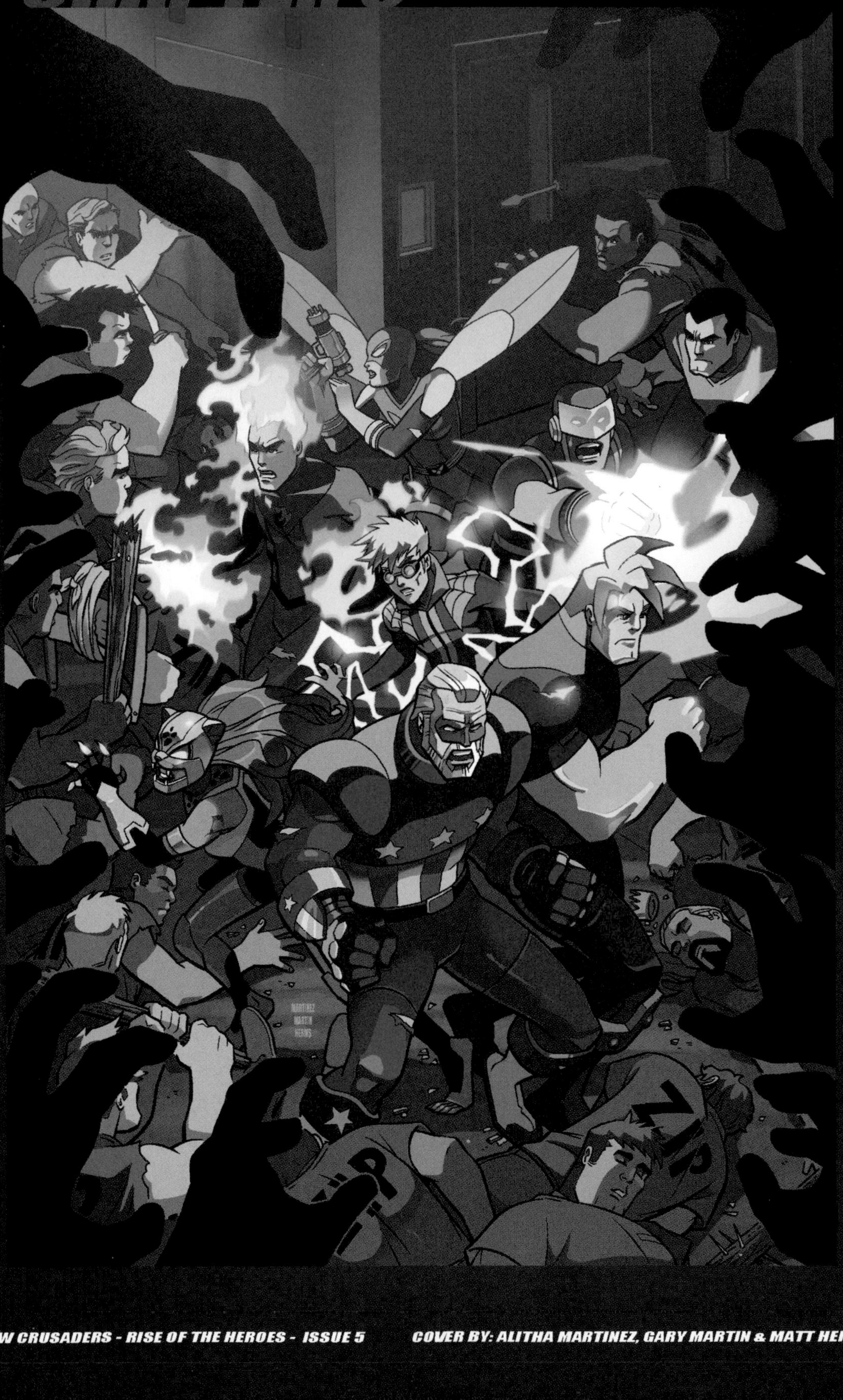
MARTINEZ
MARTIN
HERMS

NEW CRUSADERS - RISE OF THE HEROES - ISSUE 5 COVER BY: ALITHA MARTINEZ, GARY MARTIN & MATT HERMS

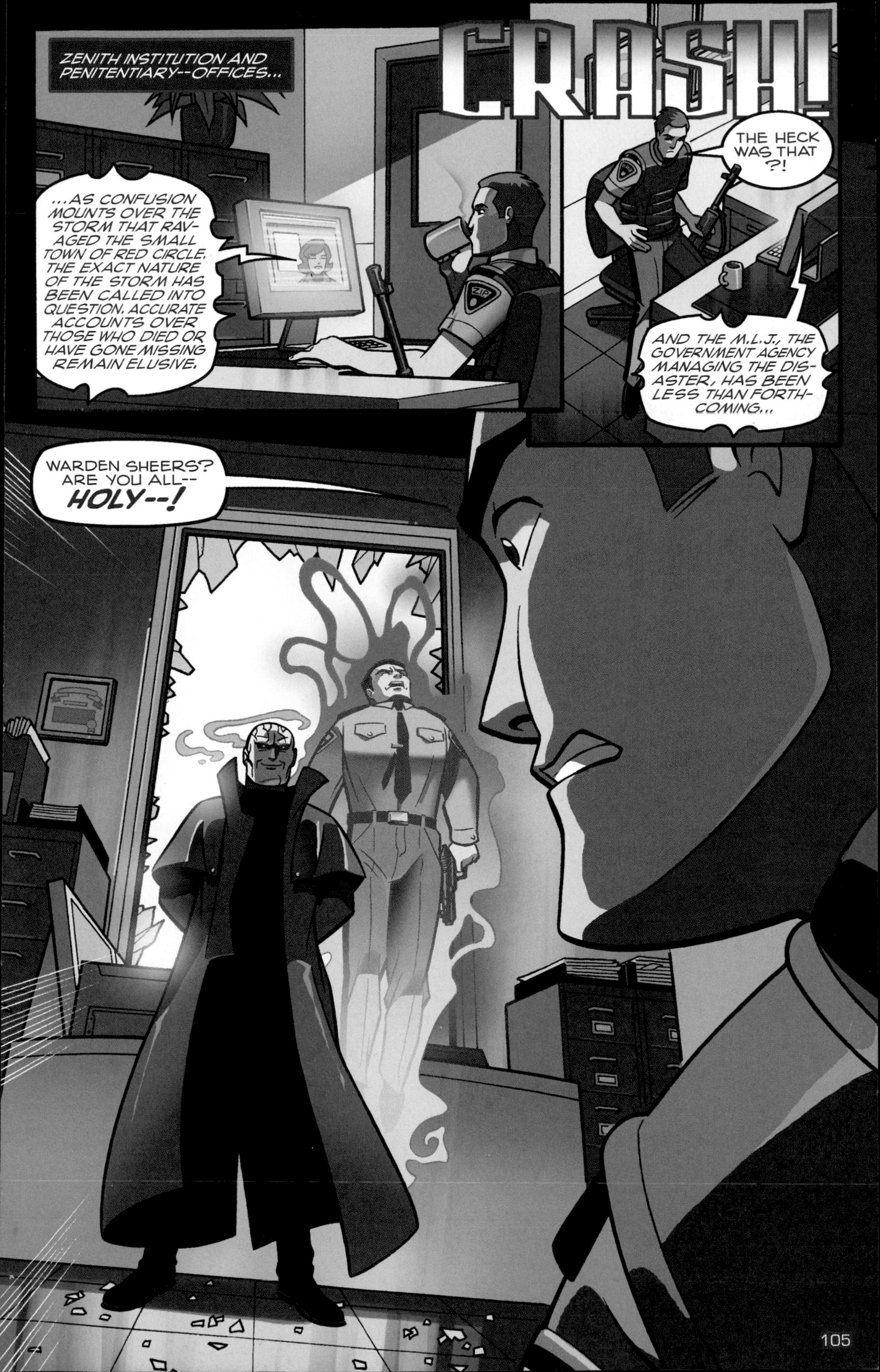
ZENITH INSTITUTION AND PENITENTIARY--OFFICES...
...AS CONFUSION MOUNTS OVER THE STORM THAT RAV-AGED THE SMALL TOWN OF RED CIRCLE, THE EXACT NATURE OF THE STORM HAS BEEN CALLED INTO QUESTION. ACCURATE ACCOUNTS OVER THOSE WHO DIED OR HAVE GONE MISSING REMAIN ELUSIVE.
ZIP
CRASH!
THE HECK WAS THAT ?!
AND THE M.L.J., THE GOVERNMENT AGENCY MANAGING THE DIS-ASTER, HAS BEEN LESS THAN FORTH-COMING...
WARDEN SHEERS? ARE YOU ALL-- HOLY--!

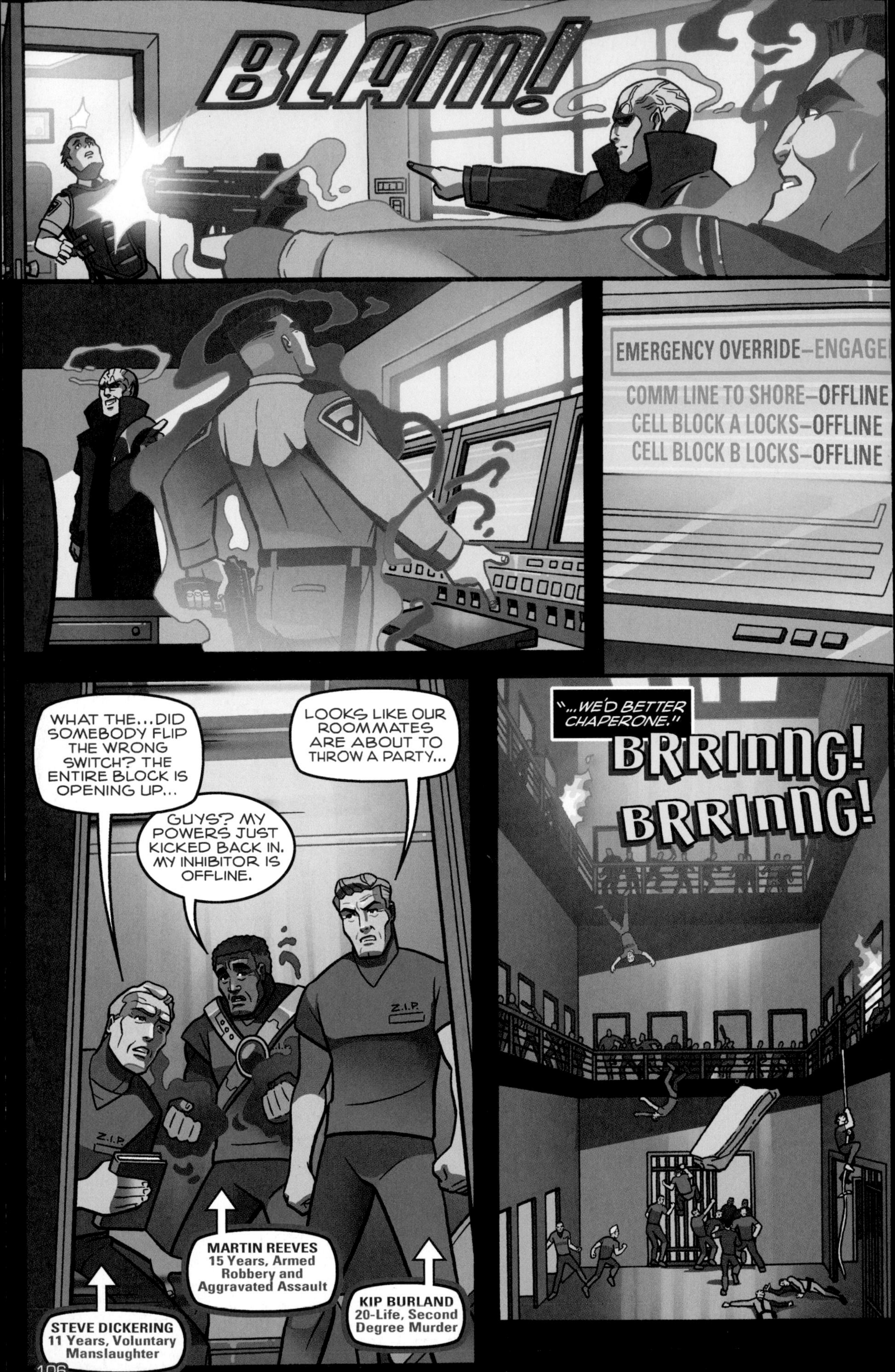

BLAM!
EMERGENCY OVERRIDE–ENGAGE
COMM LINE TO SHORE–OFFLINE
CELL BLOCK A LOCKS–OFFLINE
CELL BLOCK B LOCKS–OFFLINE
WHAT THE...DID SOMEBODY FLIP THE WRONG SWITCH? THE ENTIRE BLOCK IS OPENING UP...
LOOKS LIKE OUR ROOMMATES ARE ABOUT TO THROW A PARTY...
GUYS? MY POWERS JUST KICKED BACK IN. MY INHIBITOR IS OFFLINE.
Z.I.P.
Z.I.P.
MARTIN REEVES 15 Years, Armed Robbery and Aggravated Assault
KIP BURLAND 20-Life, Second Degree Murder
STEVE DICKERING 11 Years, Voluntary Manslaughter
"...WE'D BETTER CHAPERONE."
BRRINNG!
BRRINNG!

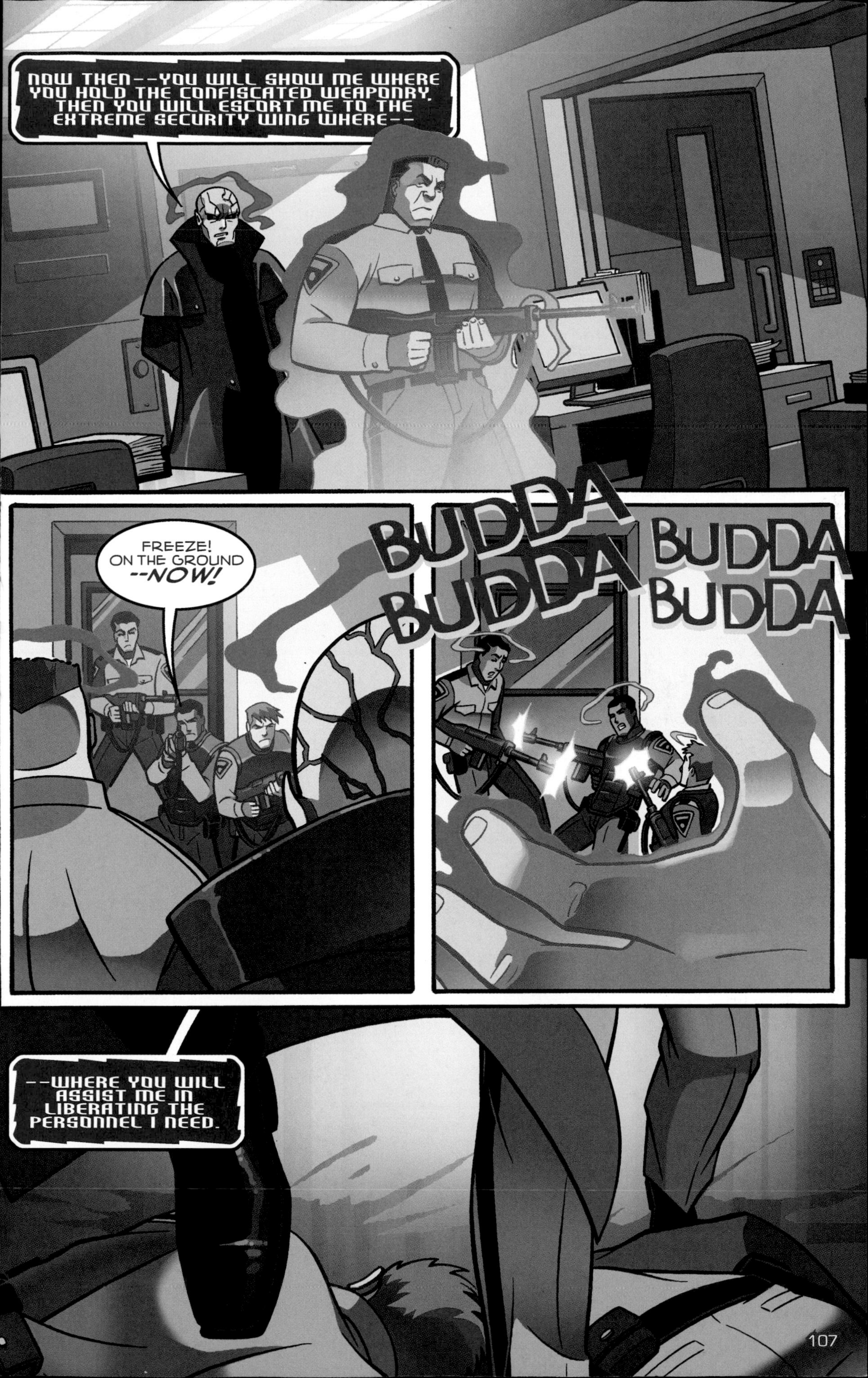
NOW THEN--YOU WILL SHOW ME WHERE YOU HOLD THE CONFISCATED WEAPONRY, THEN YOU WILL ESCORT ME TO THE EXTREME SECURITY WING WHERE--
FREEZE! ON THE GROUND --NOW!
BUDDA BUDDA BUDDA BUDDA
--WHERE YOU WILL ASSIST ME IN LIBERATING THE PERSONNEL I NEED.

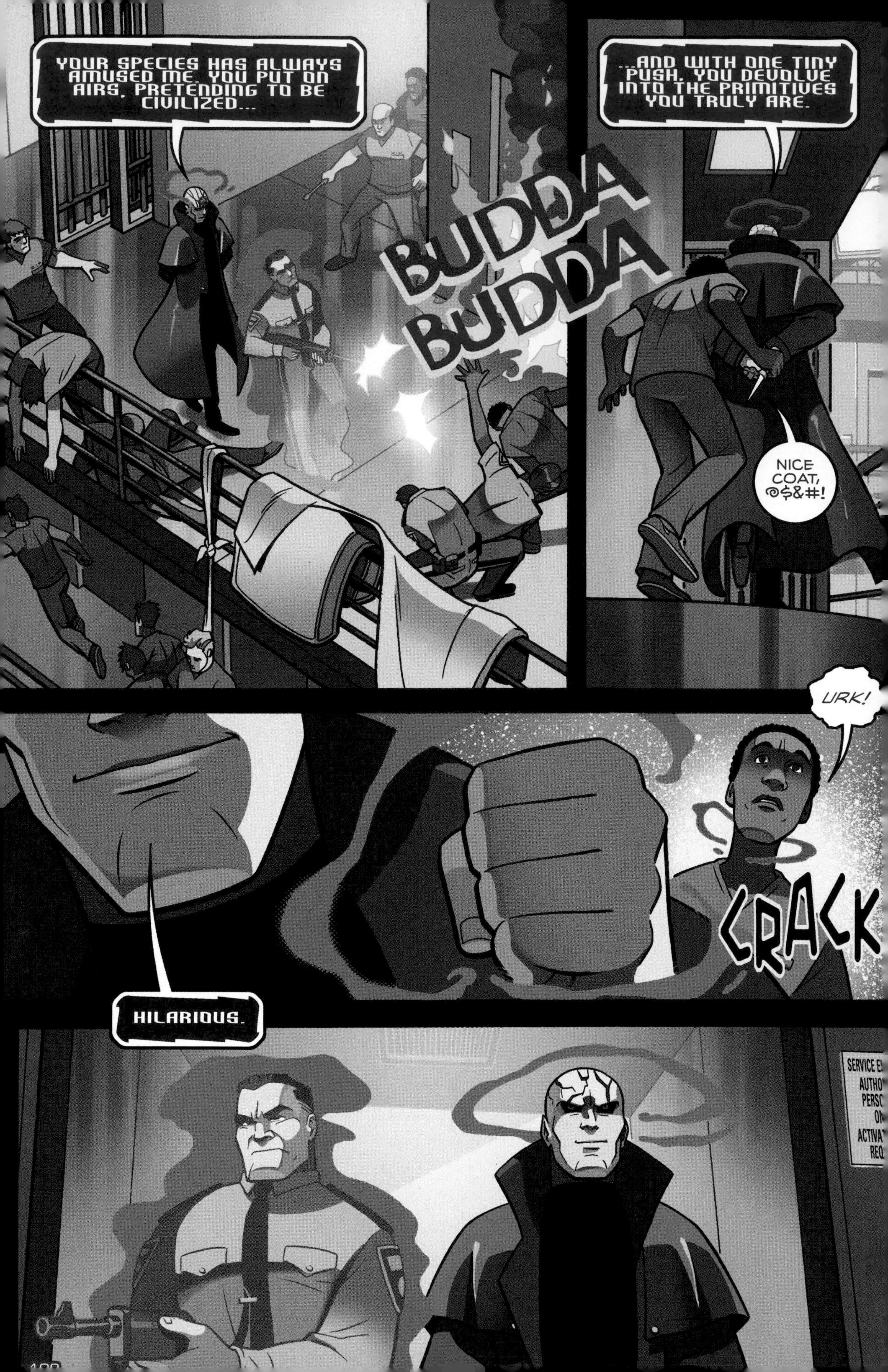
YOUR SPECIES HAS ALWAYS AMUSED ME. YOU PUT ON AIRS, PRETENDING TO BE CIVILIZED...
BUDDA BUDDA
...AND WITH ONE TINY PUSH, YOU DEVOLVE INTO THE PRIMITIVES YOU TRULY ARE.
NICE COAT, @$&#!
URK!
CRACK
HILARIOUS.
SERVICE

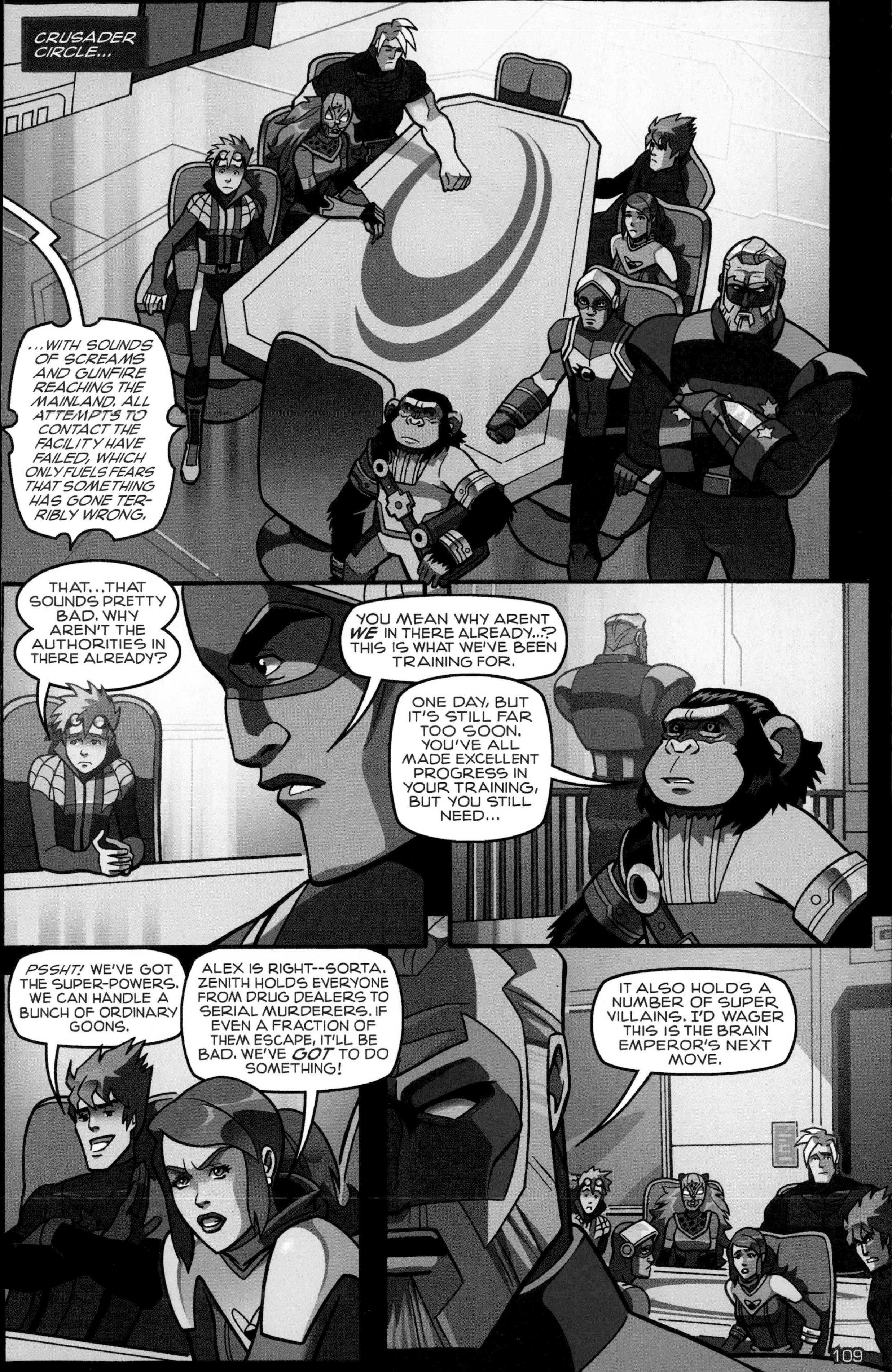

CRUSADER CIRCLE...
...WITH SOUNDS OF SCREAMS AND GUNFIRE REACHING THE MAINLAND, ALL ATTEMPTS TO CONTACT THE FACILITY HAVE FAILED, WHICH ONLY FUELS FEARS THAT SOMETHING HAS GONE TER-RIBLY WRONG.
THAT...THAT SOUNDS PRETTY BAD. WHY AREN'T THE AUTHORITIES IN THERE ALREADY?
YOU MEAN WHY ARENT *WE* IN THERE ALREADY...? THIS IS WHAT WE'VE BEEN TRAINING FOR.
ONE DAY, BUT IT'S STILL FAR TOO SOON. YOU'VE ALL MADE EXCELLENT PROGRESS IN YOUR TRAINING, BUT YOU STILL NEED...
PSSHT! WE'VE GOT THE SUPER-POWERS. WE CAN HANDLE A BUNCH OF ORDINARY GOONS.
ALEX IS RIGHT--SORTA. ZENITH HOLDS EVERYONE FROM DRUG DEALERS TO SERIAL MURDERERS. IF EVEN A FRACTION OF THEM ESCAPE, IT'LL BE BAD. WE'VE *GOT* TO DO SOMETHING!
IT ALSO HOLDS A NUMBER OF SUPER VILLAINS. I'D WAGER THIS IS THE BRAIN EMPEROR'S NEXT MOVE.

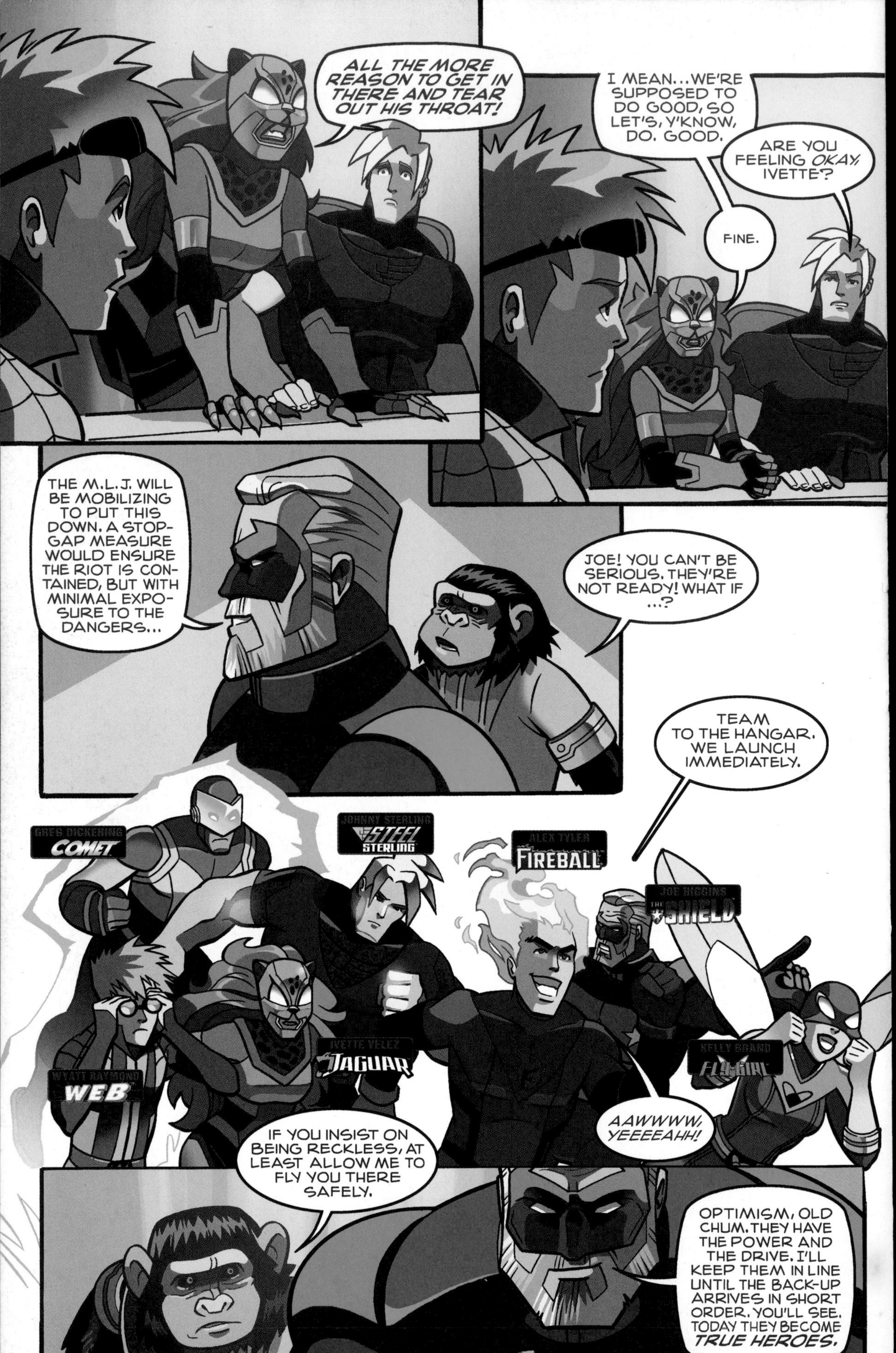
ALL THE MORE REASON TO GET IN THERE AND TEAR OUT HIS THROAT!
I MEAN... WE'RE SUPPOSED TO DO GOOD, SO LET'S, Y'KNOW, DO. GOOD.
ARE YOU FEELING OKAY, IVETTE?
FINE.
THE M.L.J. WILL BE MOBILIZING TO PUT THIS DOWN. A STOP-GAP MEASURE WOULD ENSURE THE RIOT IS CONTAINED, BUT WITH MINIMAL EXPOSURE TO THE DANGERS...
JOE! YOU CAN'T BE SERIOUS. THEY'RE NOT READY! WHAT IF ...?
TEAM TO THE HANGAR. WE LAUNCH IMMEDIATELY.
GREG DICKERING
COMET
JOHNNY STERLING
STEEL STERLING
ALEX TYLER
FIREBALL
JOE HIGGINS
THE SHIELD
IVETTE VELEZ
JAGUAR
WYATT RAYMOND
WEB
KELLY BRAND
FLY-GIRL
AAWWWW, YEEEEAHH!
IF YOU INSIST ON BEING RECKLESS, AT LEAST ALLOW ME TO FLY YOU THERE SAFELY.
OPTIMISM, OLD CHUM. THEY HAVE THE POWER AND THE DRIVE. I'LL KEEP THEM IN LINE UNTIL THE BACK-UP ARRIVES IN SHORT ORDER. YOU'LL SEE. TODAY THEY BECOME TRUE HEROES.

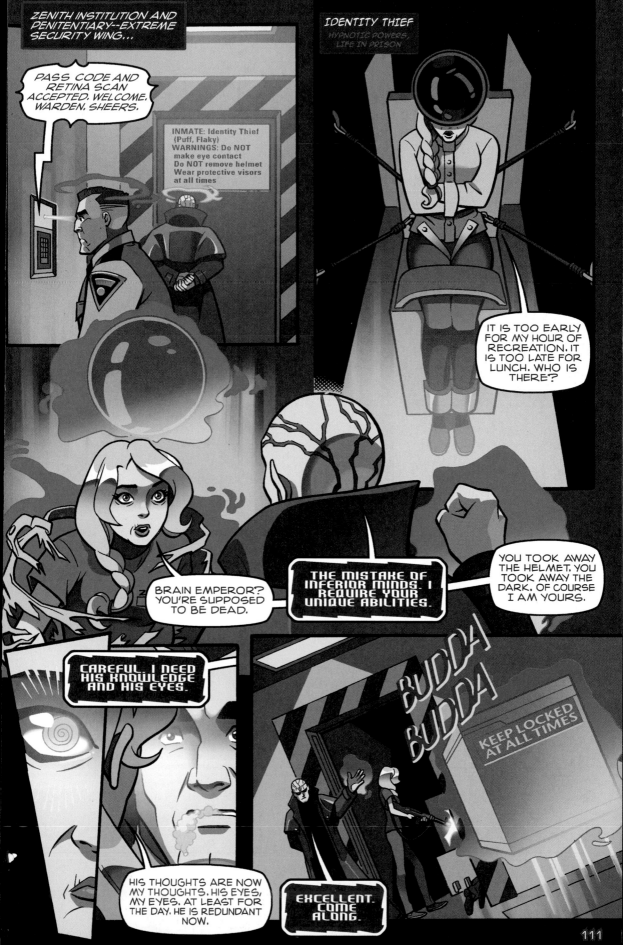

ZENITH INSTITUTION AND PENITENTIARY--EXTREME SECURITY WING...

PASS CODE AND RETINA SCAN ACCEPTED. WELCOME, WARDEN, SHEERS.

INMATE: Identity Thief (Puff, Flaky)
WARNINGS: Do NOT make eye contact
Do NOT remove helmet
Wear protective visors at all times

IDENTITY THIEF
HYPNOTIC POWERS, LIFE IN PRISON

IT IS TOO EARLY FOR MY HOUR OF RECREATION. IT IS TOO LATE FOR LUNCH. WHO IS THERE?

BRAIN EMPEROR? YOU'RE SUPPOSED TO BE DEAD.

THE MISTAKE OF INFERIOR MINDS. I REQUIRE YOUR UNIQUE ABILITIES.

YOU TOOK AWAY THE HELMET. YOU TOOK AWAY THE DARK. OF COURSE I AM YOURS.

CAREFUL. I NEED HIS KNOWLEDGE AND HIS EYES.

BUDDA! BUDDA BUDDA!

KEEP LOCKED AT ALL TIMES

HIS THOUGHTS ARE NOW MY THOUGHTS. HIS EYES, MY EYES. AT LEAST FOR THE DAY. HE IS REDUNDANT NOW.

EXCELLENT. COME ALONG.

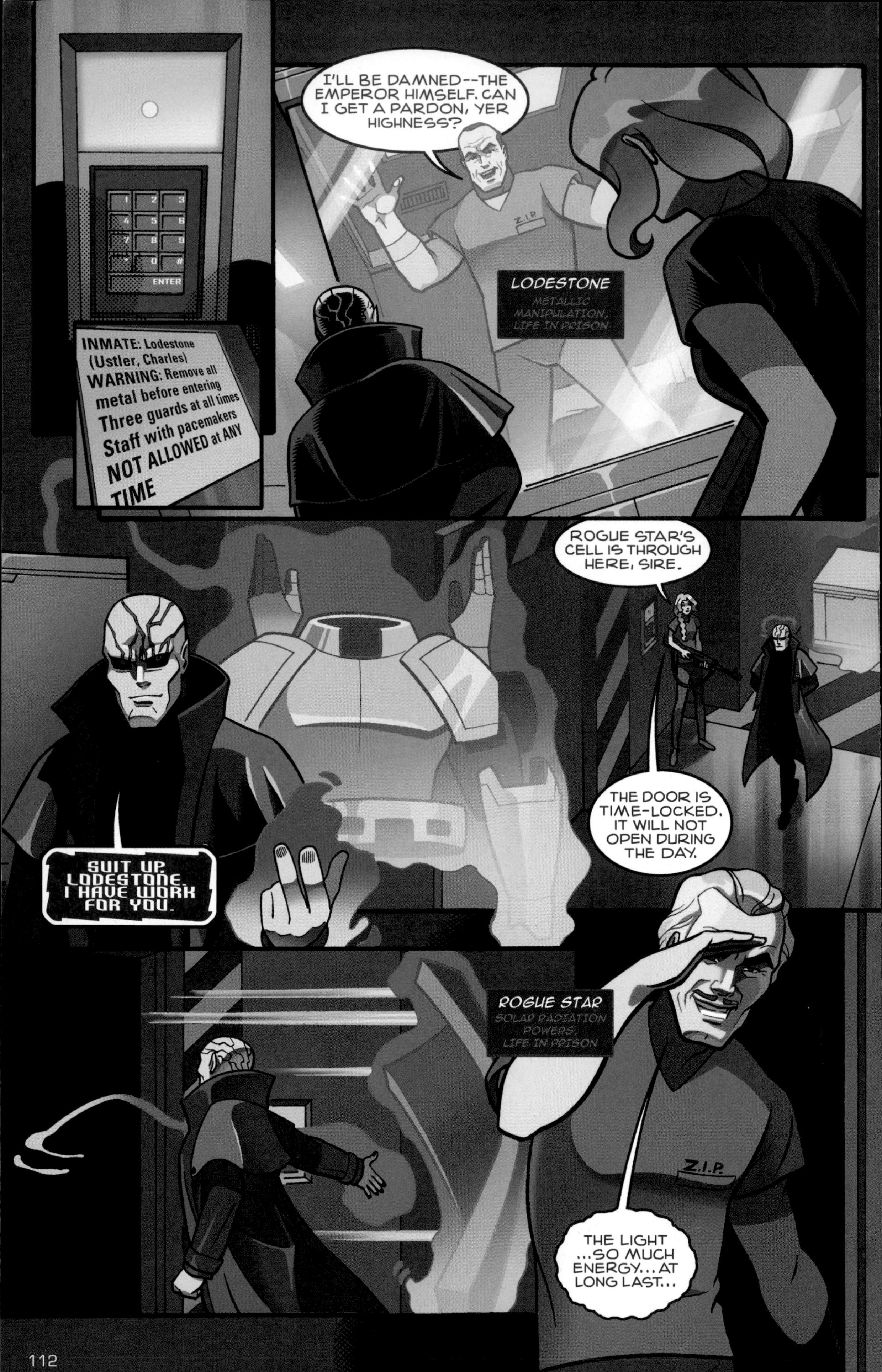

1 2 3
4 5 6
7 8 9
* 0 #
ENTER
INMATE: Lodestone (Ustler, Charles) WARNING: Remove all metal before entering Three guards at all times Staff with pacemakers NOT ALLOWED at ANY TIME
I'LL BE DAMNED--THE EMPEROR HIMSELF. CAN I GET A PARDON, YER HIGHNESS?
Z.I.P.
LODESTONE
METALLIC MANIPULATION, LIFE IN PRISON
ROGUE STAR'S CELL IS THROUGH HERE, SIRE.
THE DOOR IS TIME-LOCKED. IT WILL NOT OPEN DURING THE DAY.
SUIT UP, LODESTONE. I HAVE WORK FOR YOU.
ROGUE STAR
SOLAR RADIATION POWERS, LIFE IN PRISON
Z.I.P.
THE LIGHT ...SO MUCH ENERGY... AT LONG LAST...

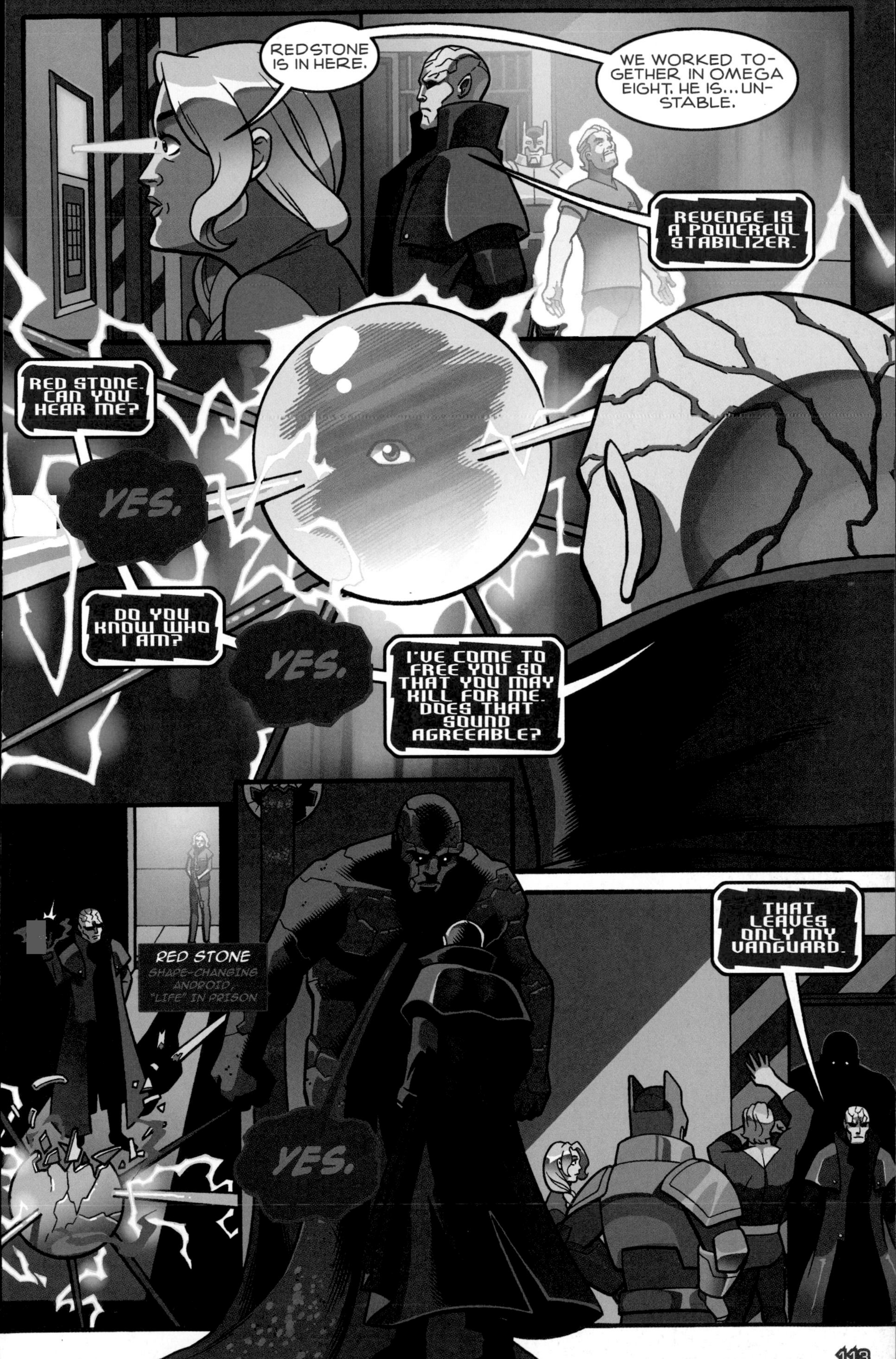

REDSTONE IS IN HERE.
WE WORKED TOGETHER IN OMEGA EIGHT. HE IS... UNSTABLE.
REVENGE IS A POWERFUL STABILIZER.
RED STONE. CAN YOU HEAR ME?
YES.
DO YOU KNOW WHO I AM?
YES.
I'VE COME TO FREE YOU SO THAT YOU MAY KILL FOR ME. DOES THAT SOUND AGREEABLE?
RED STONE
SHAPE-CHANGING ANDROID, "LIFE" IN PRISON
YES.
THAT LEAVES ONLY MY VANGUARD.

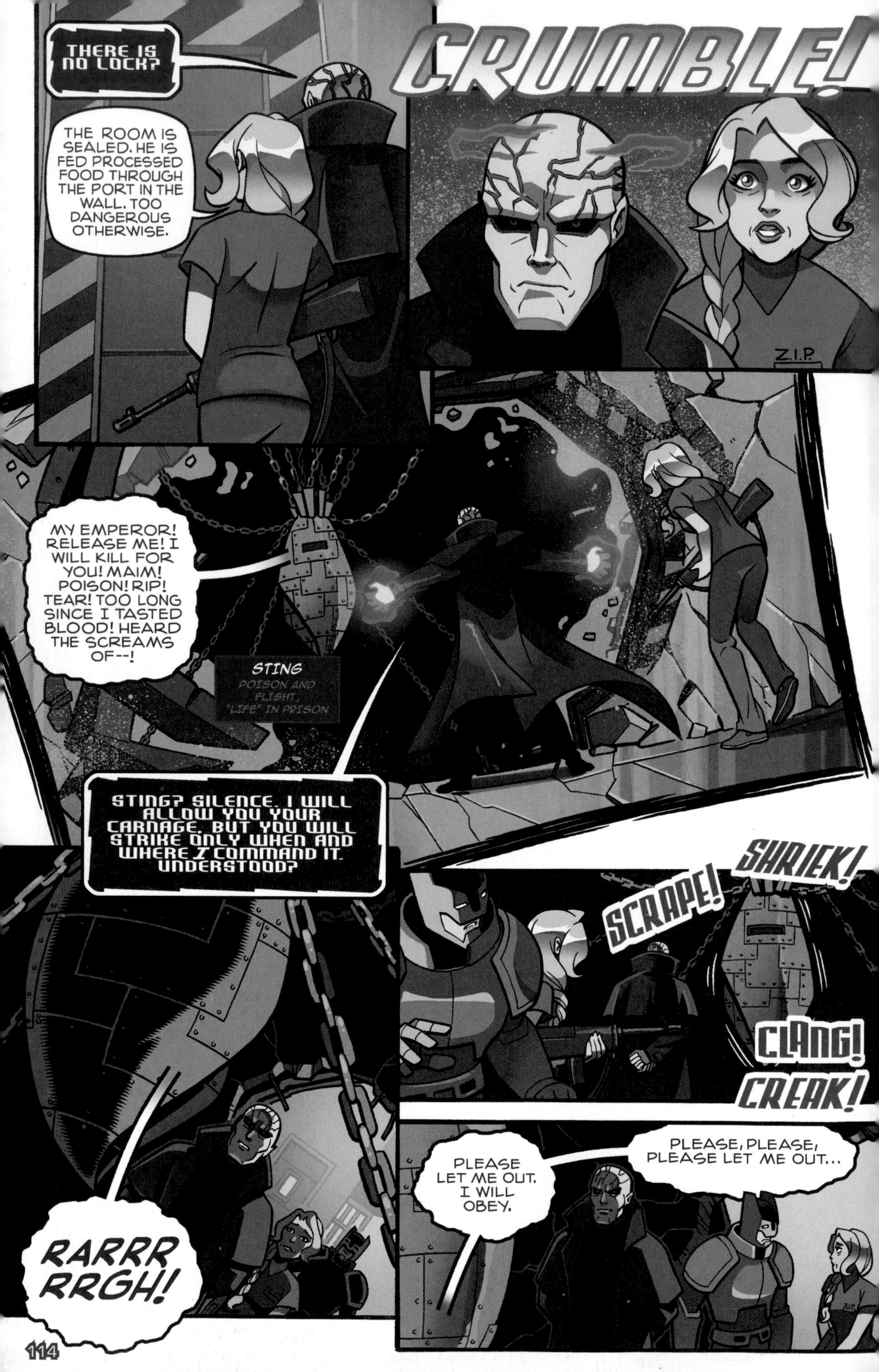
THERE IS NO LOCK?
THE ROOM IS SEALED. HE IS FED PROCESSED FOOD THROUGH THE PORT IN THE WALL. TOO DANGEROUS OTHERWISE.
CRUMBLE!
Z.I.P.
MY EMPEROR! RELEASE ME! I WILL KILL FOR YOU! MAIM! POISON! RIP! TEAR! TOO LONG SINCE I TASTED BLOOD! HEARD THE SCREAMS OF--!
STING
POISON AND FLIGHT, "LIFE" IN PRISON
STING? SILENCE. I WILL ALLOW YOU YOUR CARNAGE. BUT YOU WILL STRIKE ONLY WHEN AND WHERE I COMMAND IT. UNDERSTOOD?
SHRIEK!
SCRAPE!
CLANG!
CREAK!
RARRR RRGH!
PLEASE LET ME OUT. I WILL OBEY.
PLEASE, PLEASE, PLEASE LET ME OUT...

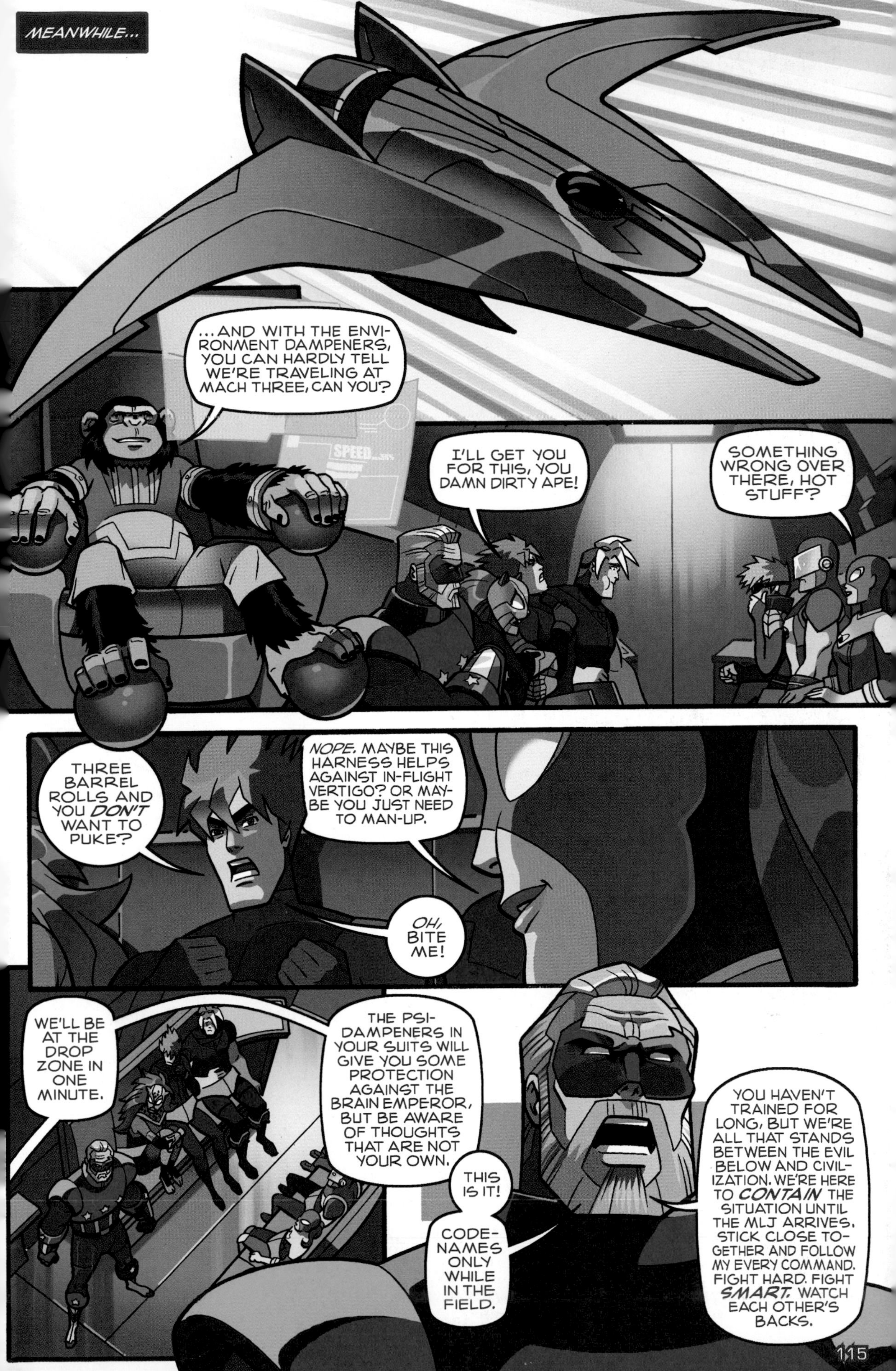
MEANWHILE...
...AND WITH THE ENVIRONMENT DAMPENERS, YOU CAN HARDLY TELL WE'RE TRAVELING AT MACH THREE, CAN YOU?
SPEED
I'LL GET YOU FOR THIS, YOU DAMN DIRTY APE!
SOMETHING WRONG OVER THERE, HOT STUFF?
THREE BARREL ROLLS AND YOU *DON'T* WANT TO PUKE?
NOPE. MAYBE THIS HARNESS HELPS AGAINST IN-FLIGHT VERTIGO? OR MAYBE YOU JUST NEED TO MAN-UP.
OH, BITE ME!
WE'LL BE AT THE DROP ZONE IN ONE MINUTE.
THE PSI-DAMPENERS IN YOUR SUITS WILL GIVE YOU SOME PROTECTION AGAINST THE BRAIN EMPEROR, BUT BE AWARE OF THOUGHTS THAT ARE NOT YOUR OWN.
THIS IS IT!
CODE-NAMES ONLY WHILE IN THE FIELD.
YOU HAVEN'T TRAINED FOR LONG, BUT WE'RE ALL THAT STANDS BETWEEN THE EVIL BELOW AND CIVILIZATION. WE'RE HERE TO *CONTAIN* THE SITUATION UNTIL THE MLJ ARRIVES. STICK CLOSE TOGETHER AND FOLLOW MY EVERY COMMAND. FIGHT HARD. FIGHT *SMART.* WATCH EACH OTHER'S BACKS.

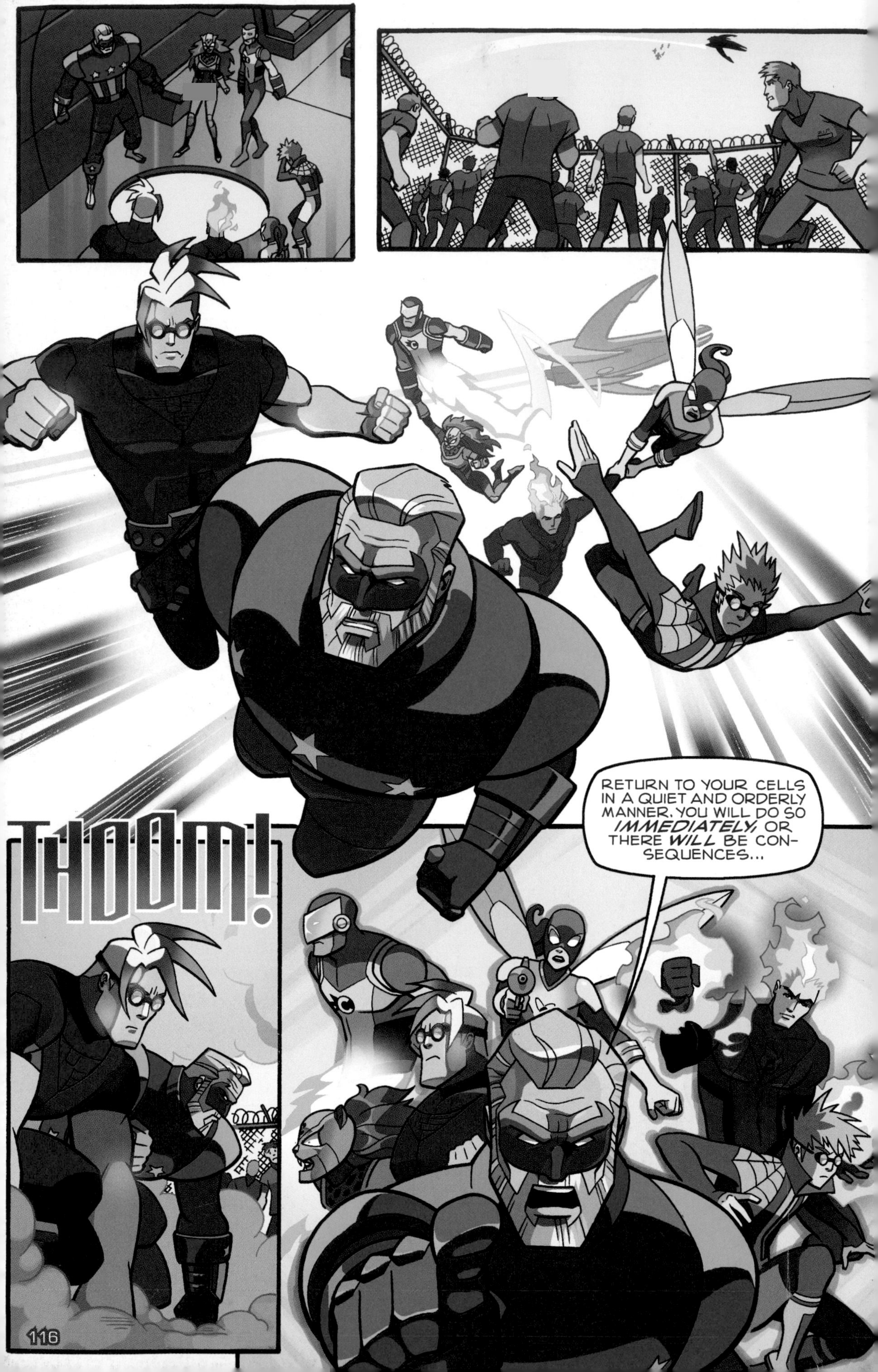

THOOM!
RETURN TO YOUR CELLS IN A QUIET AND ORDERLY MANNER. YOU WILL DO SO IMMEDIATELY, OR THERE WILL BE CONSEQUENCES...

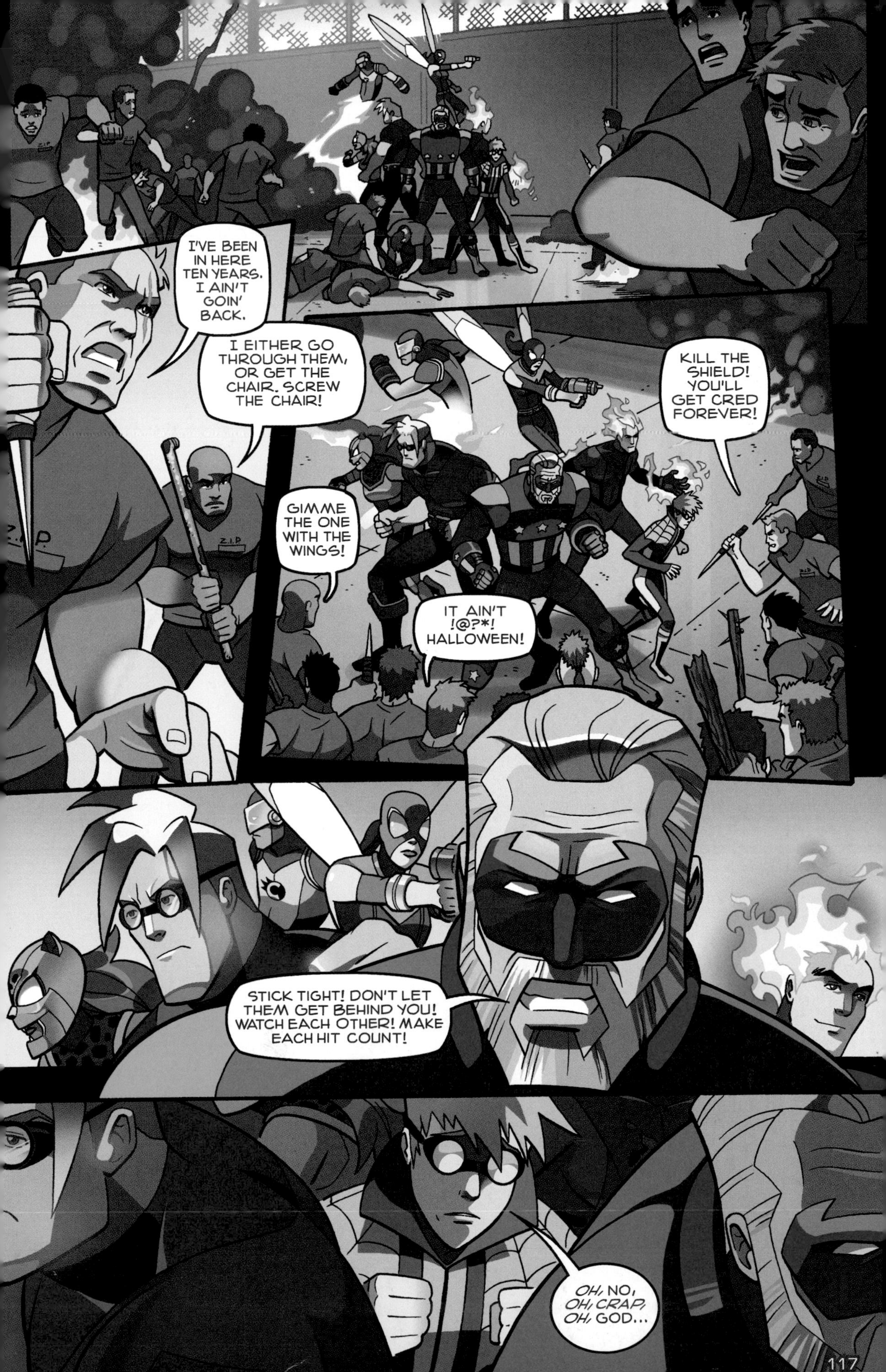
I'VE BEEN IN HERE TEN YEARS. I AIN'T GOIN' BACK.
I EITHER GO THROUGH THEM, OR GET THE CHAIR. SCREW THE CHAIR!
KILL THE SHIELD! YOU'LL GET CRED FOREVER!
GIMME THE ONE WITH THE WINGS!
IT AIN'T !@?*! HALLOWEEN!
STICK TIGHT! DON'T LET THEM GET BEHIND YOU! WATCH EACH OTHER! MAKE EACH HIT COUNT!
OH, NO, OH, CRAP, OH, GOD...

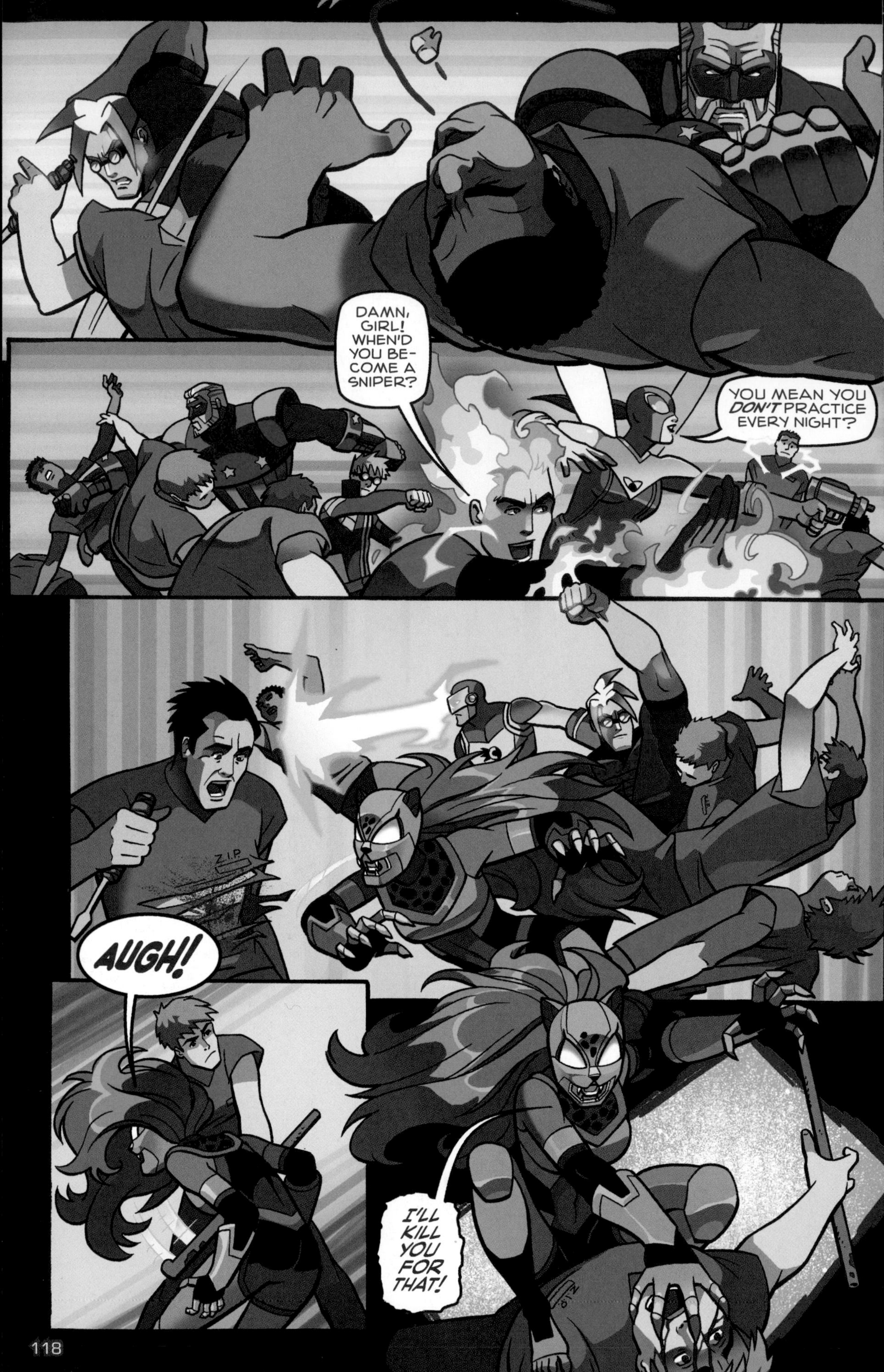
DAMN, GIRL! WHEN'D YOU BE-COME A SNIPER?
YOU MEAN YOU *DON'T* PRACTICE EVERY NIGHT?
Z.I.P.
AUGH!
I'LL KILL YOU FOR THAT!

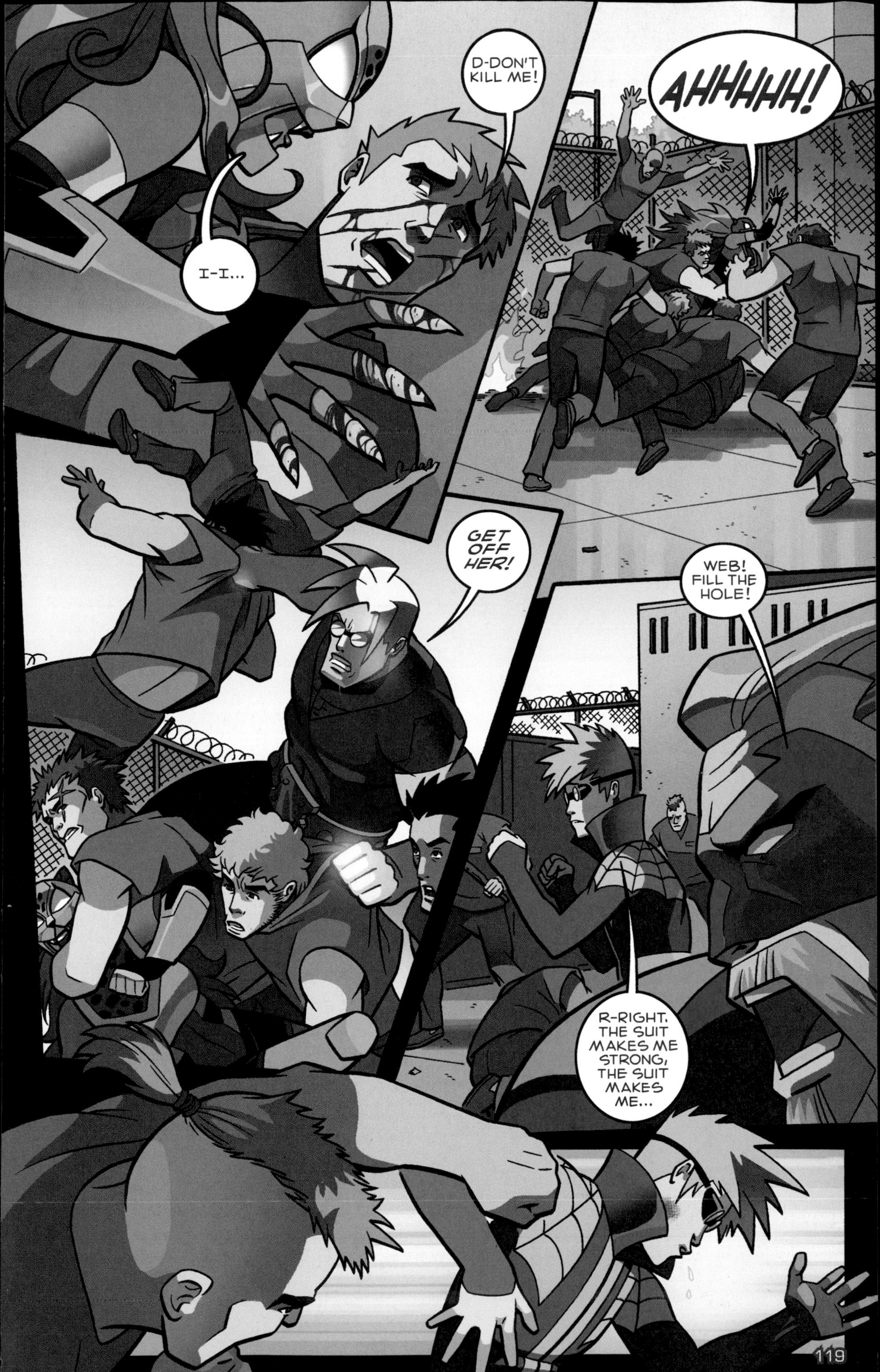
D-DON'T KILL ME!
I-I...
AHHHHH!
GET OFF HER!
WEB! FILL THE HOLE!
R-RIGHT. THE SUIT MAKES ME STRONG, THE SUIT MAKES ME...

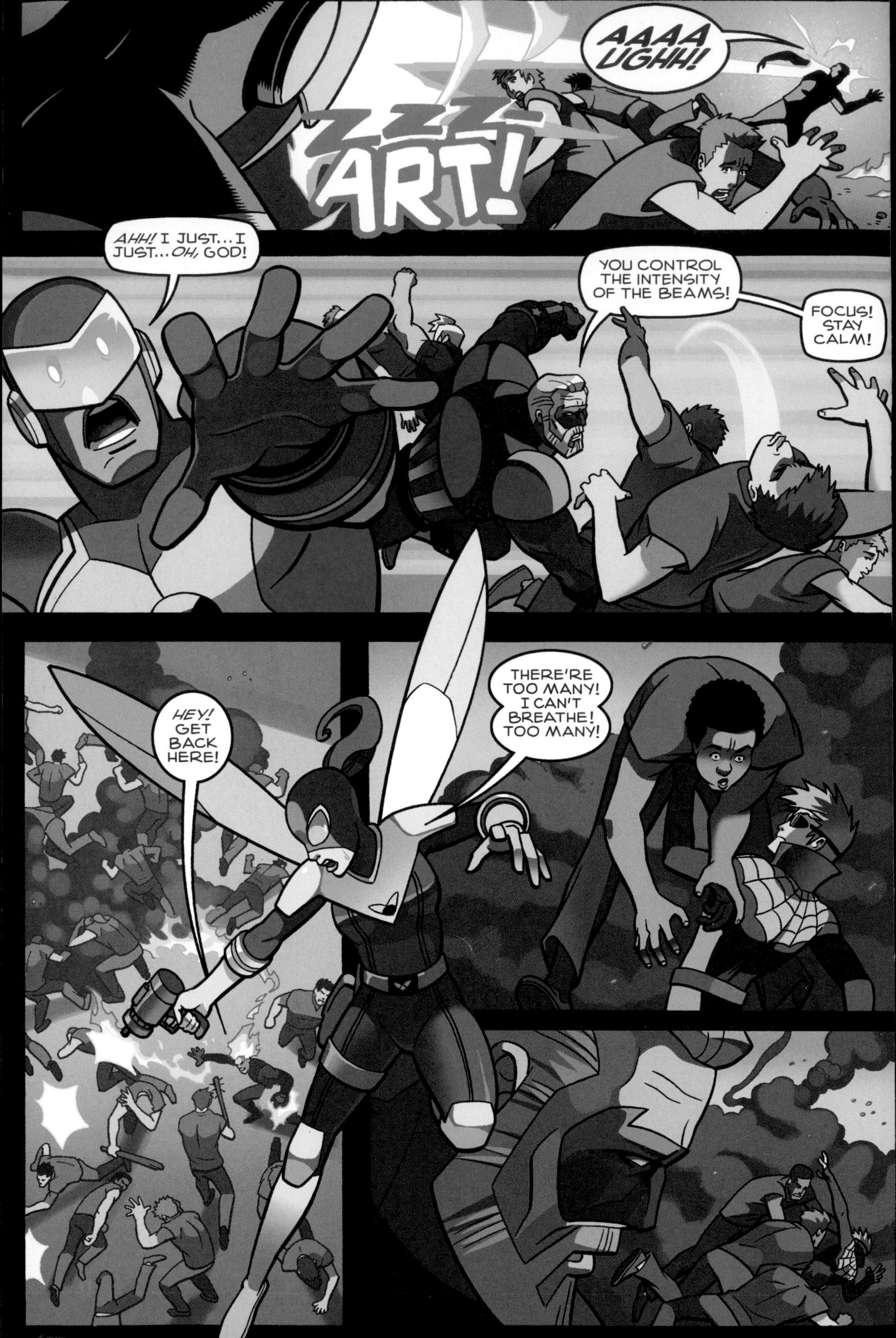
AAAA UGHH!
ZZZ-ART!
AHH! I JUST... I JUST... OH, GOD!
YOU CONTROL THE INTENSITY OF THE BEAMS!
FOCUS! STAY CALM!
HEY! GET BACK HERE!
THERE'RE TOO MANY! I CAN'T BREATHE! TOO MANY!

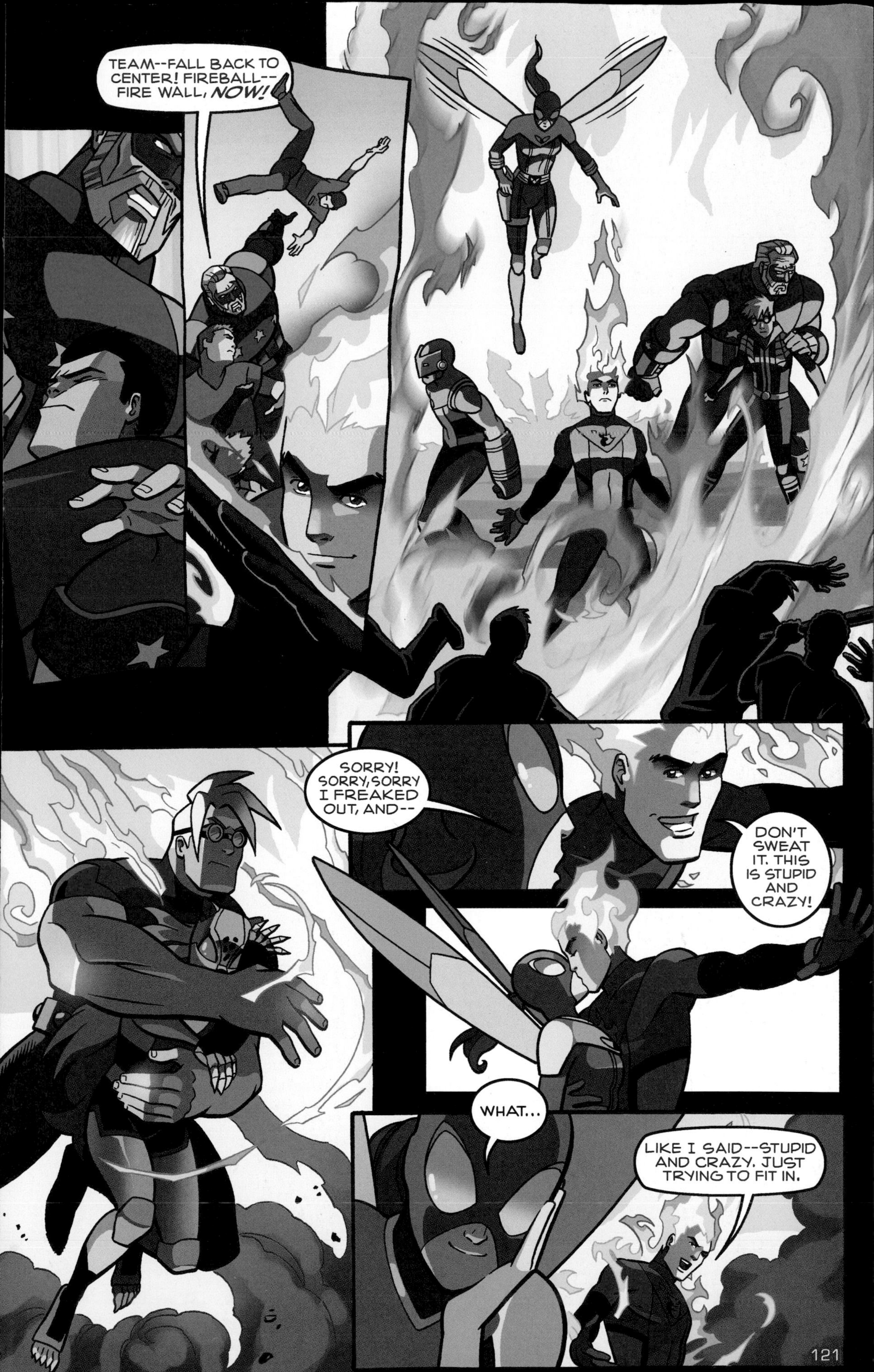
TEAM--FALL BACK TO CENTER! FIREBALL-- FIRE WALL, *NOW!*
SORRY! SORRY, SORRY I FREAKED OUT, AND--
DON'T SWEAT IT. THIS IS STUPID AND CRAZY!
WHAT...
LIKE I SAID--STUPID AND CRAZY. JUST TRYING TO FIT IN.

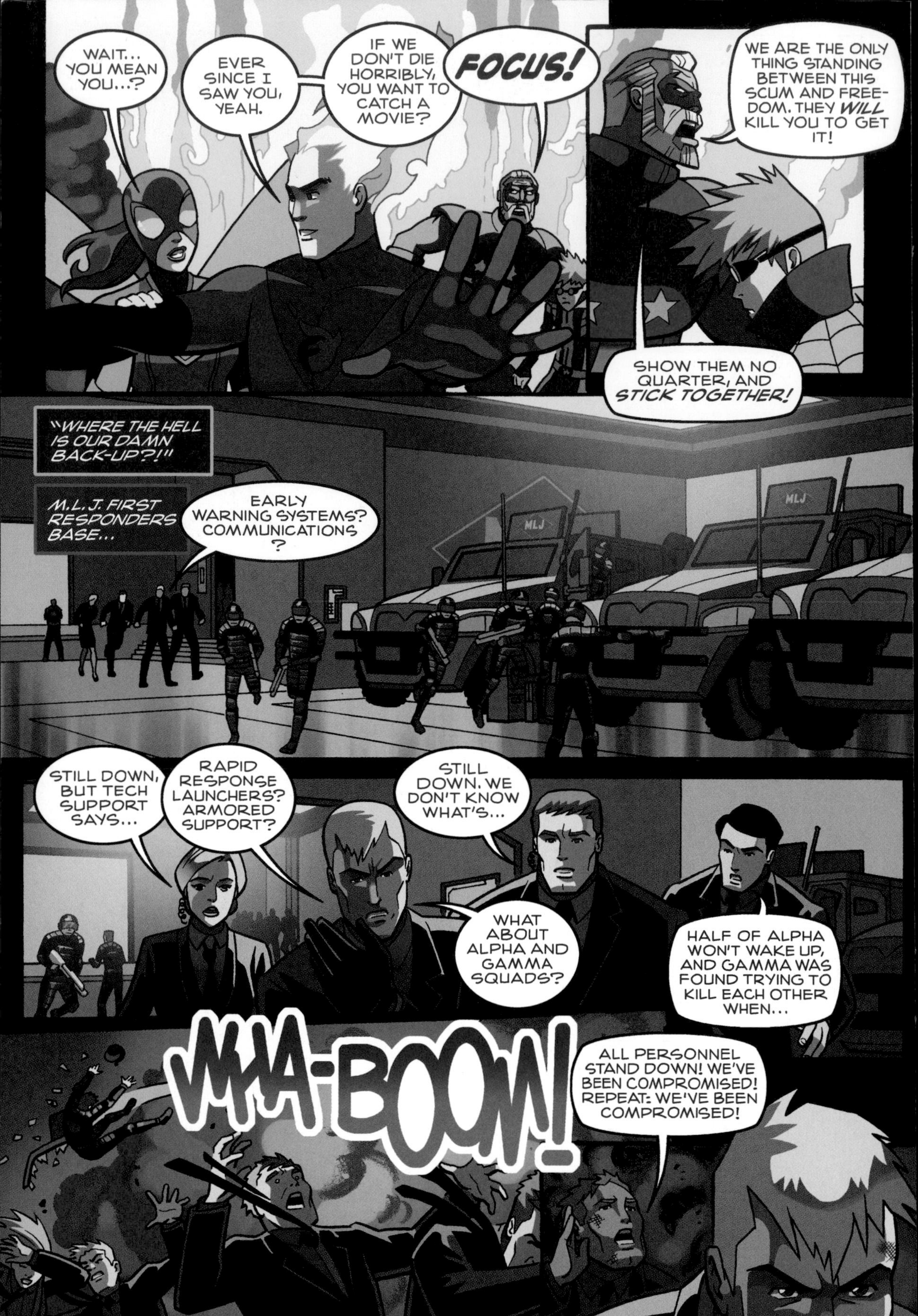
WAIT... YOU MEAN YOU...?
EVER SINCE I SAW YOU, YEAH.
IF WE DON'T DIE HORRIBLY, YOU WANT TO CATCH A MOVIE?
FOCUS!
WE ARE THE ONLY THING STANDING BETWEEN THIS SCUM AND FREE-DOM. THEY WILL KILL YOU TO GET IT!
SHOW THEM NO QUARTER, AND STICK TOGETHER!
"WHERE THE HELL IS OUR DAMN BACK-UP?!"
M.L.J. FIRST RESPONDERS BASE...
EARLY WARNING SYSTEMS? COMMUNICATIONS?
STILL DOWN, BUT TECH SUPPORT SAYS...
RAPID RESPONSE LAUNCHERS? ARMORED SUPPORT?
STILL DOWN. WE DON'T KNOW WHAT'S...
WHAT ABOUT ALPHA AND GAMMA SQUADS?
HALF OF ALPHA WON'T WAKE UP, AND GAMMA WAS FOUND TRYING TO KILL EACH OTHER WHEN...
WHA-BOOM!
ALL PERSONNEL STAND DOWN! WE'VE BEEN COMPROMISED! REPEAT: WE'VE BEEN COMPROMISED!
BRAIN EMPEROR...

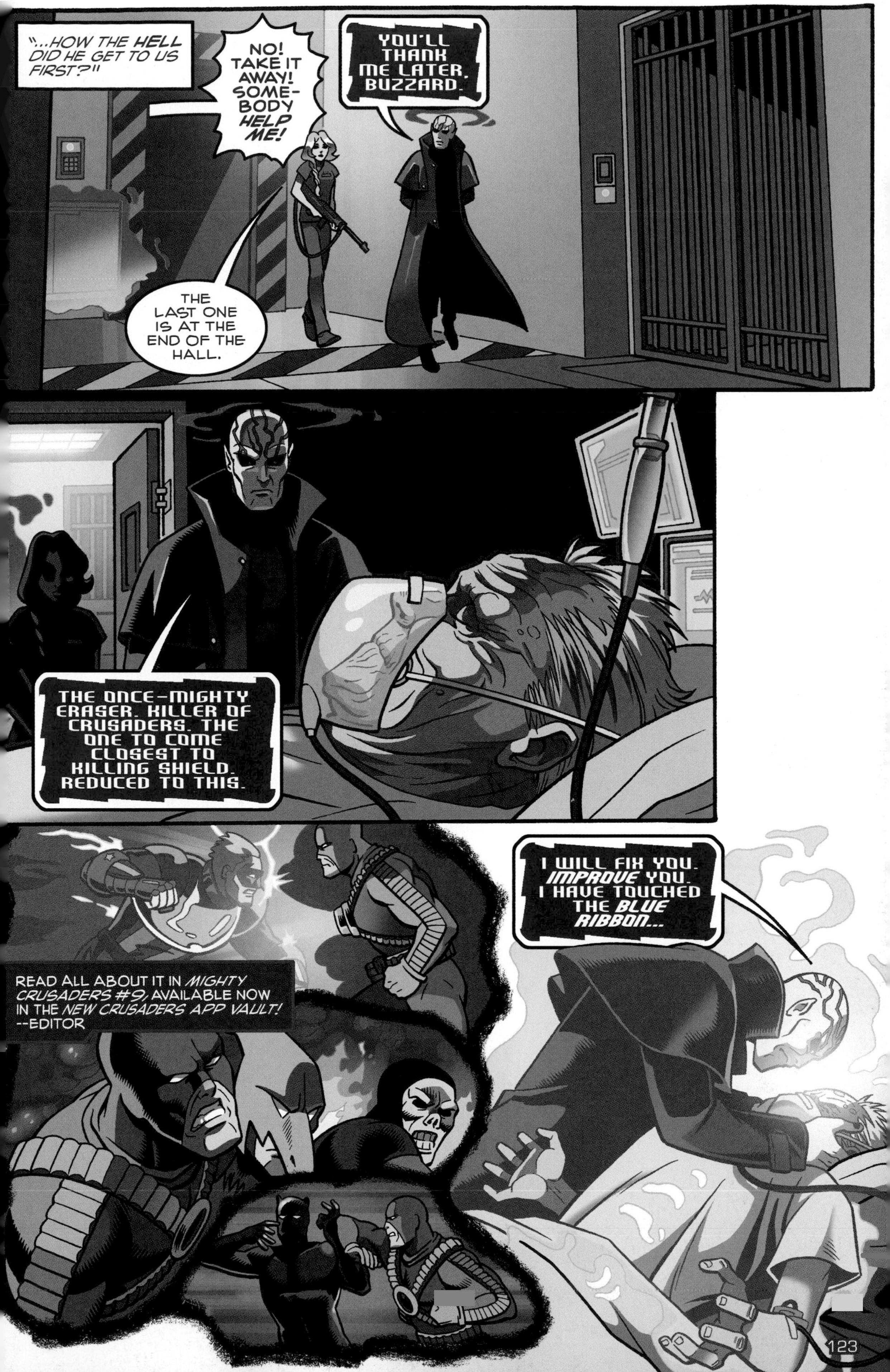
"...HOW THE HELL DID HE GET TO US FIRST?"
NO! TAKE IT AWAY! SOME-BODY HELP ME!
YOU'LL THANK ME LATER, BUZZARD.
THE LAST ONE IS AT THE END OF THE HALL.
THE ONCE-MIGHTY ERASER. KILLER OF CRUSADERS. THE ONE TO COME CLOSEST TO KILLING SHIELD. REDUCED TO THIS.
I WILL FIX YOU. IMPROVE YOU. I HAVE TOUCHED THE BLUE RIBBON...
READ ALL ABOUT IT IN MIGHTY CRUSADERS #9, AVAILABLE NOW IN THE NEW CRUSADERS APP VAULT! --EDITOR

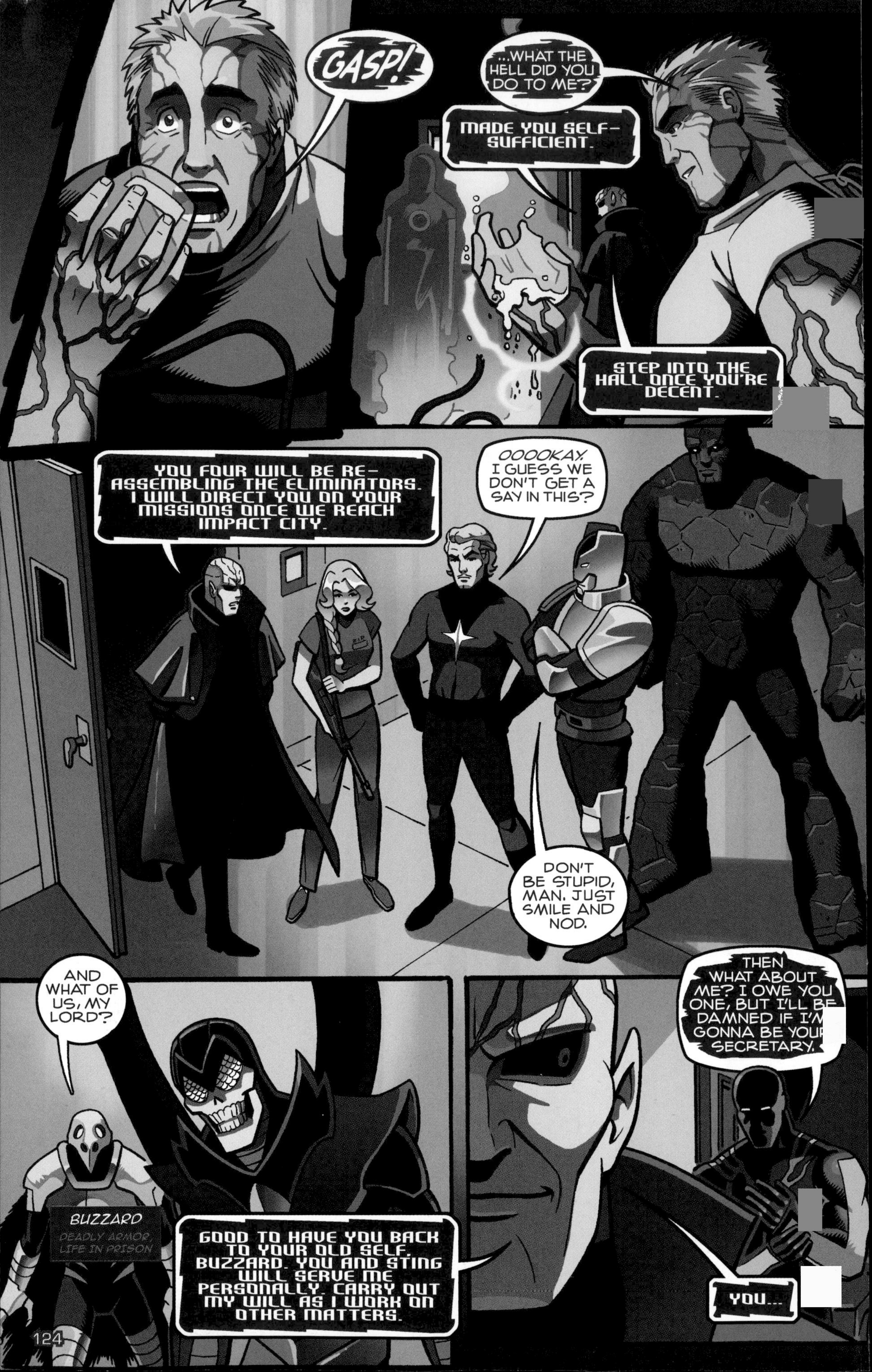
GASP!
...WHAT THE HELL DID YOU DO TO ME?
MADE YOU SELF-SUFFICIENT.
STEP INTO THE HALL ONCE YOU'RE DECENT.
YOU FOUR WILL BE RE-ASSEMBLING THE ELIMINATORS. I WILL DIRECT YOU ON YOUR MISSIONS ONCE WE REACH IMPACT CITY.
OOOOKAY. I GUESS WE DON'T GET A SAY IN THIS?
DON'T BE STUPID, MAN. JUST SMILE AND NOD.
AND WHAT OF US, MY LORD?
BUZZARD
DEADLY ARMOR
LIFE IN PRISON
GOOD TO HAVE YOU BACK TO YOUR OLD SELF, BUZZARD. YOU AND STING WILL SERVE ME PERSONALLY. CARRY OUT MY WILL AS I WORK ON OTHER MATTERS.
THEN WHAT ABOUT ME? I OWE YOU ONE, BUT I'LL BE DAMNED IF I'M GONNA BE YOUR SECRETARY.
YOU...

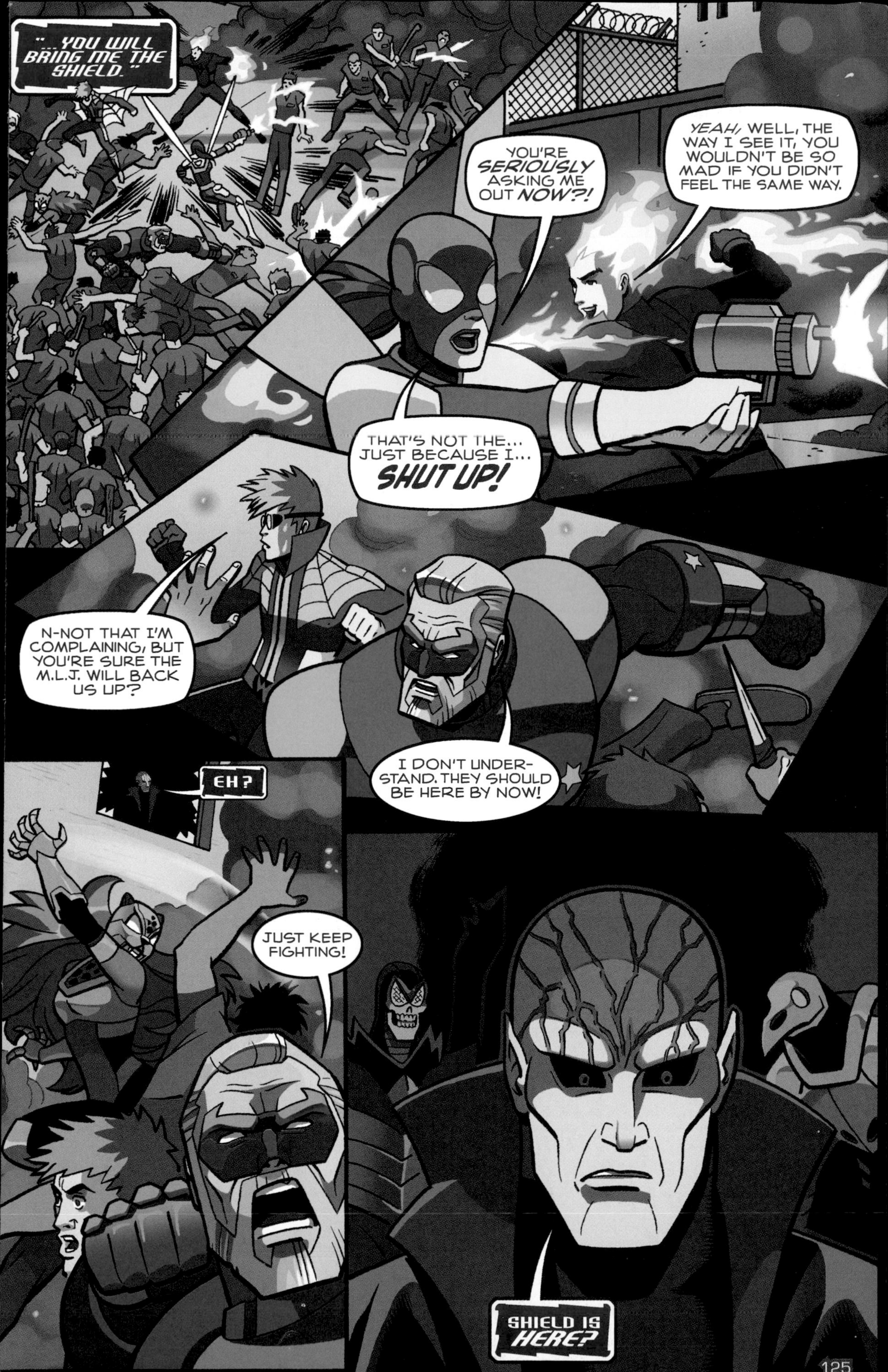
"...YOU WILL BRING ME THE SHIELD."
YOU'RE SERIOUSLY ASKING ME OUT NOW?!
YEAH, WELL, THE WAY I SEE IT, YOU WOULDN'T BE SO MAD IF YOU DIDN'T FEEL THE SAME WAY.
THAT'S NOT THE... JUST BECAUSE I... SHUT UP!
N-NOT THAT I'M COMPLAINING, BUT YOU'RE SURE THE M.L.J. WILL BACK US UP?
I DON'T UNDER-STAND. THEY SHOULD BE HERE BY NOW!
EH?
JUST KEEP FIGHTING!
SHIELD IS HERE?

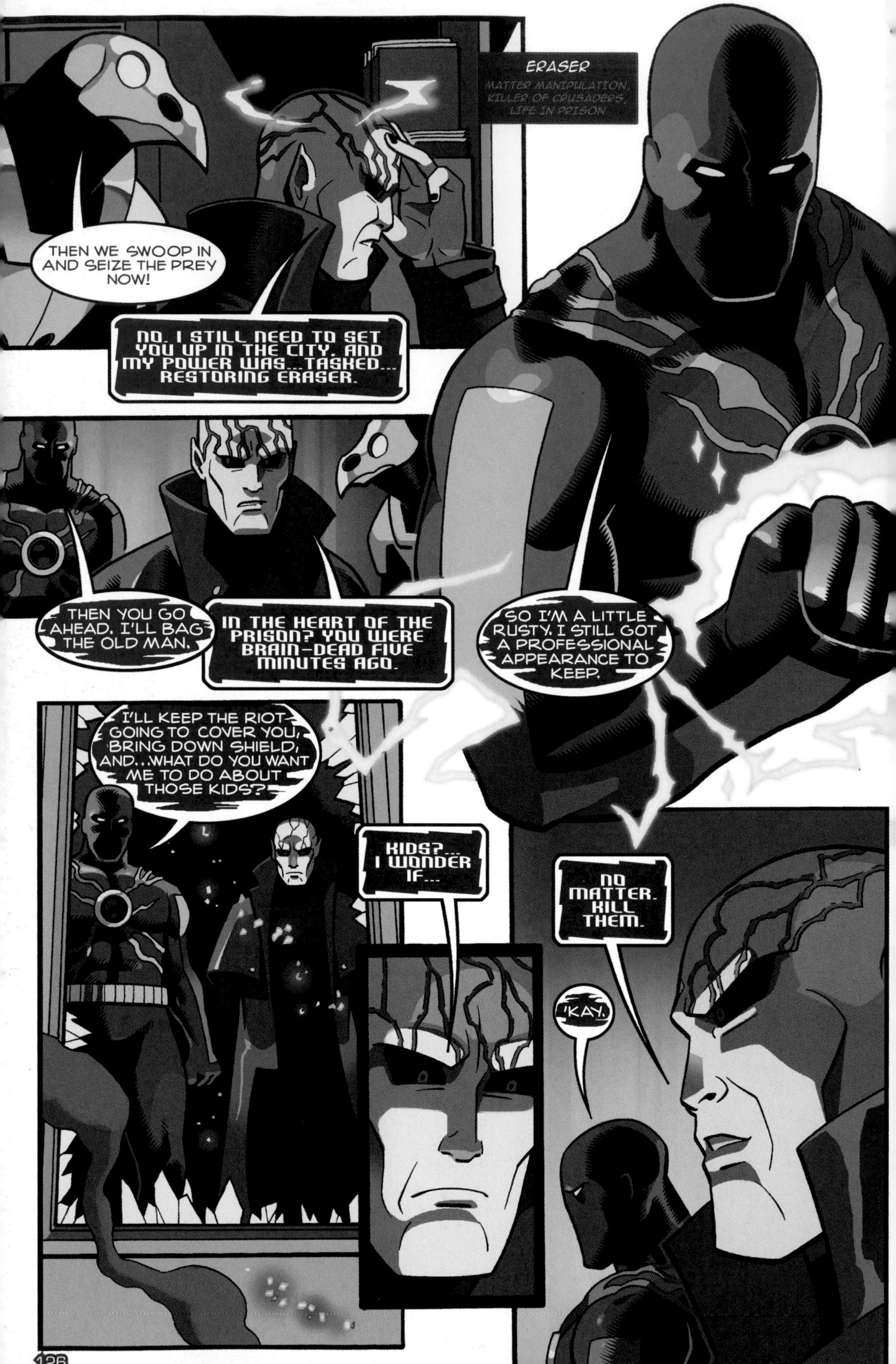
ERASER
MATTER MANIPULATION, KILLER OF CRUSADERS, LIFE IN PRISON
THEN WE SWOOP IN AND SEIZE THE PREY NOW!
NO. I STILL NEED TO SET YOU UP IN THE CITY. AND MY POWER WAS...TASKED... RESTORING ERASER.
THEN YOU GO AHEAD. I'LL BAG THE OLD MAN.
IN THE HEART OF THE PRISON? YOU WERE BRAIN-DEAD FIVE MINUTES AGO.
SO I'M A LITTLE RUSTY. I STILL GOT A PROFESSIONAL APPEARANCE TO KEEP.
I'LL KEEP THE RIOT GOING TO COVER YOU, BRING DOWN SHIELD, AND...WHAT DO YOU WANT ME TO DO ABOUT THOSE KIDS?
KIDS?... I WONDER IF...
NO MATTER. KILL THEM.
'KAY.

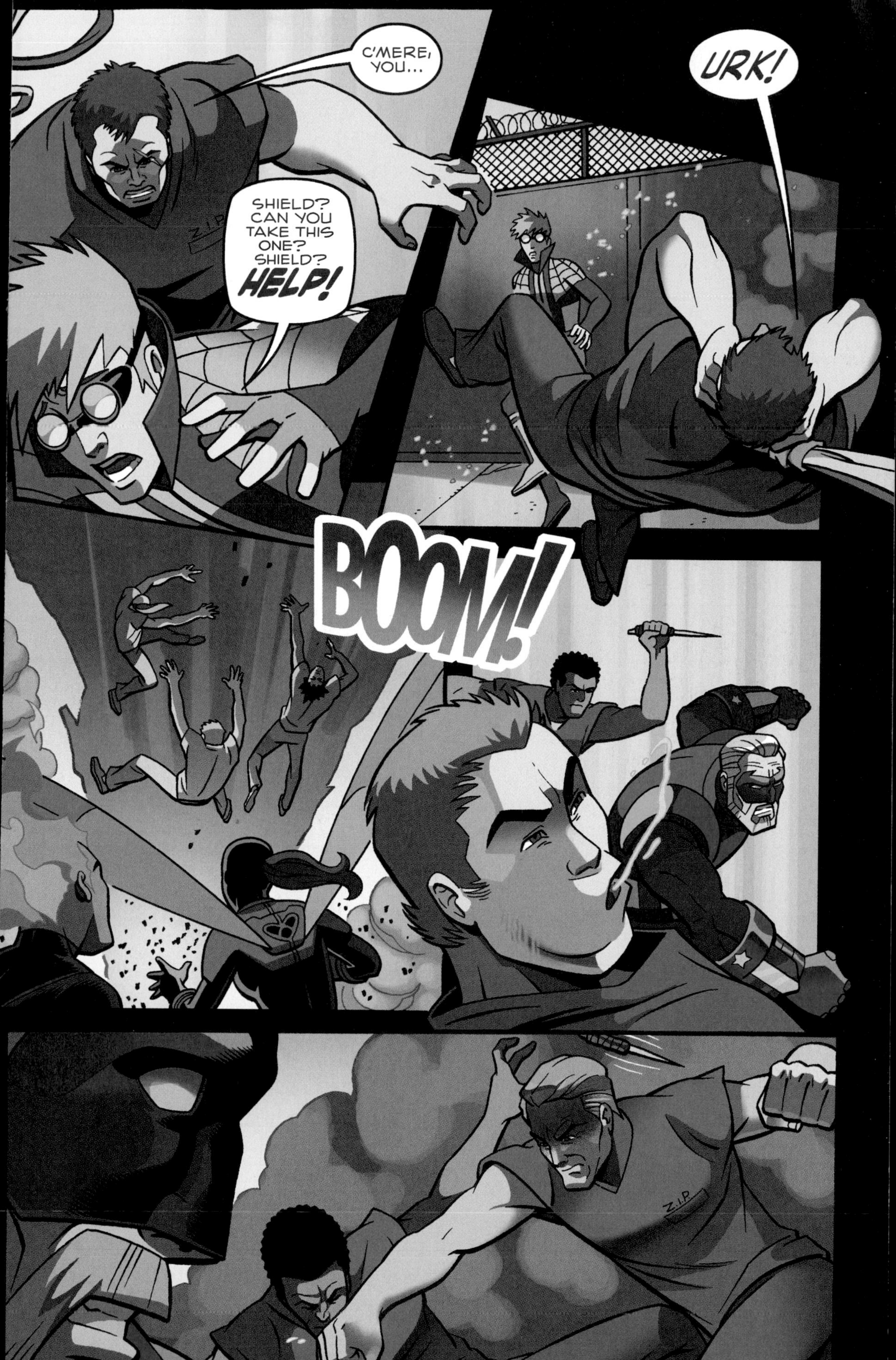

C'MERE, YOU...
SHIELD? CAN YOU TAKE THIS ONE? SHIELD? HELP!
URK!
BOOM!
Z.I.P.

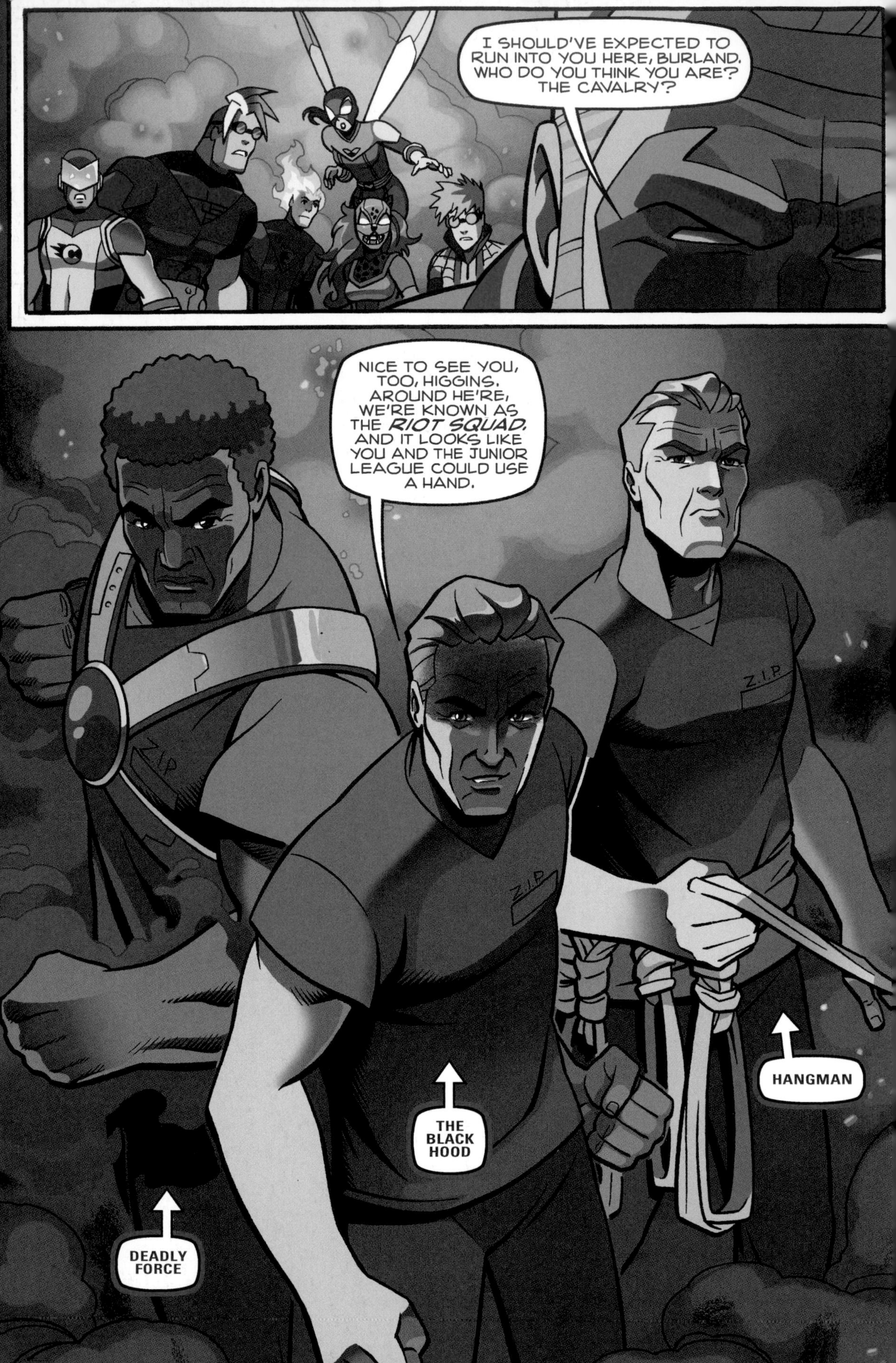
I SHOULD'VE EXPECTED TO RUN INTO YOU HERE, BURLAND. WHO DO YOU THINK YOU ARE? THE CAVALRY?
NICE TO SEE YOU, TOO, HIGGINS. AROUND HE'RE, WE'RE KNOWN AS THE *RIOT SQUAD,* AND IT LOOKS LIKE YOU AND THE JUNIOR LEAGUE COULD USE A HAND.
HANGMAN
THE BLACK HOOD
DEADLY FORCE

CHAPTER 6

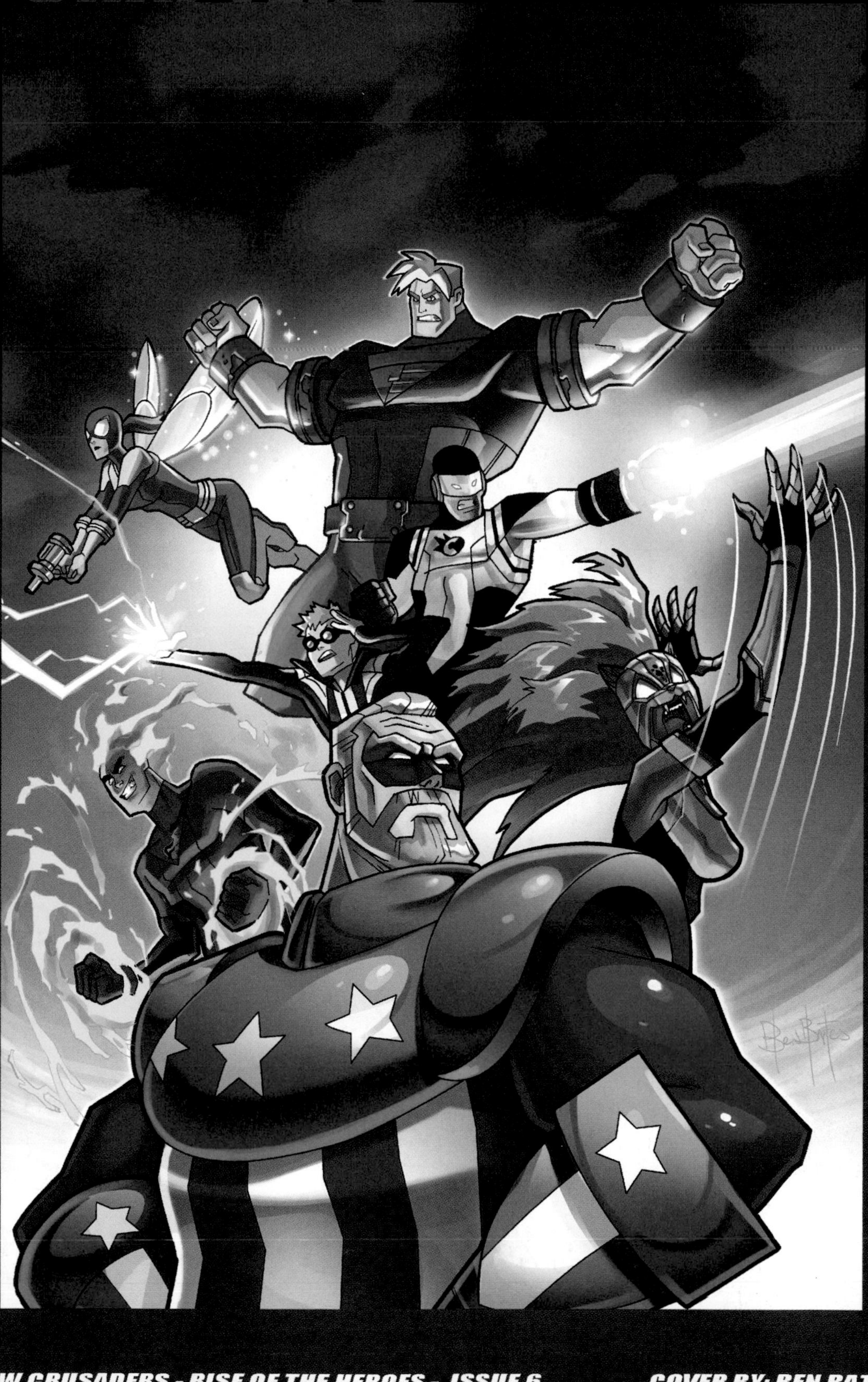
Ben Bates

NEW CRUSADERS - RISE OF THE HEROES - ISSUE 6 COVER BY: BEN BATES

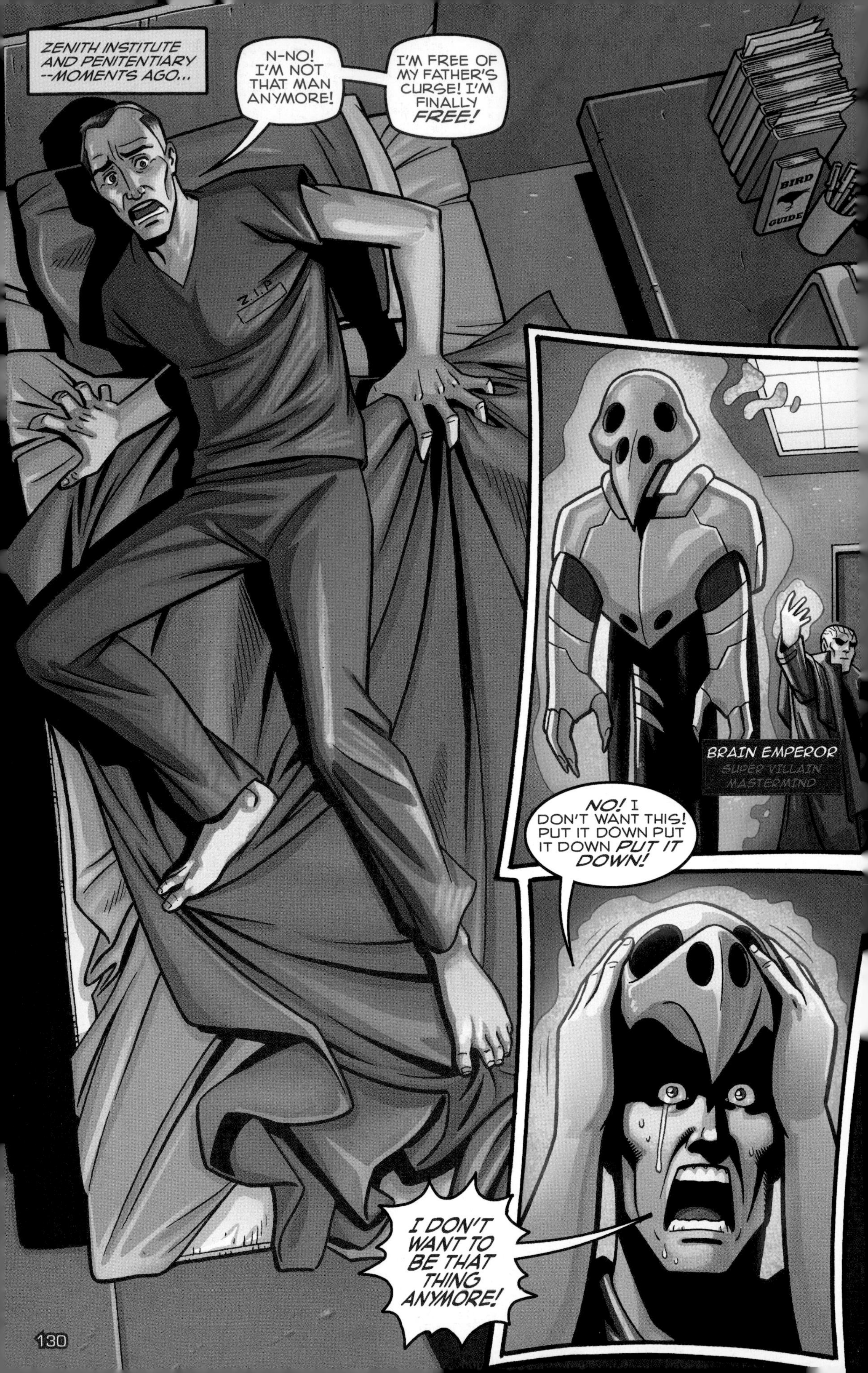

ZENITH INSTITUTE AND PENITENTIARY --MOMENTS AGO...
N-NO! I'M NOT THAT MAN ANYMORE!
I'M FREE OF MY FATHER'S CURSE! I'M FINALLY FREE!
BIRD GUIDE
Z.I.P.
BRAIN EMPEROR
SUPER VILLAIN MASTERMIND
NO! I DON'T WANT THIS! PUT IT DOWN PUT IT DOWN PUT IT DOWN!
I DON'T WANT TO BE THAT THING ANYMORE!

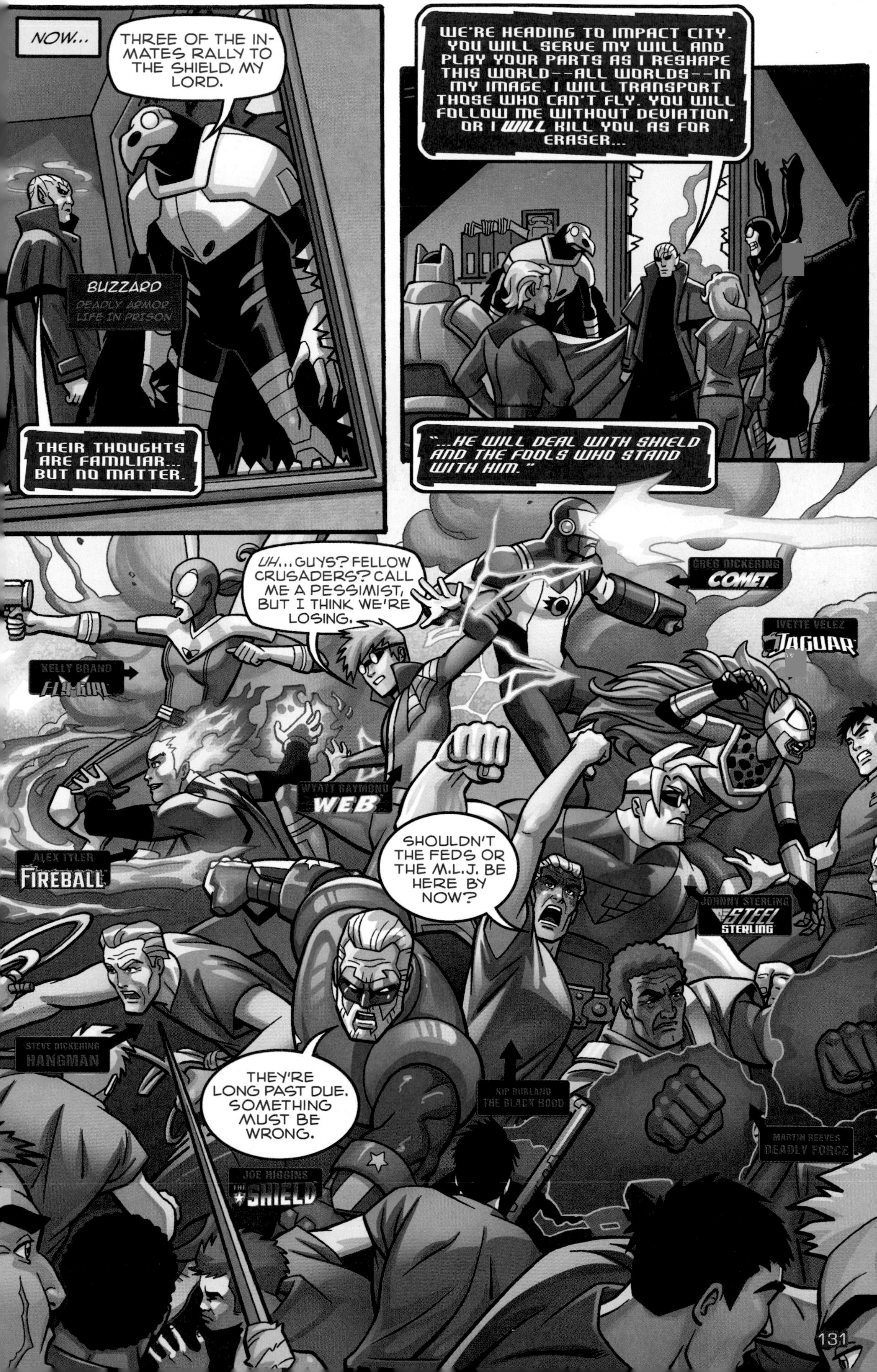

NOW...
THREE OF THE INMATES RALLY TO THE SHIELD, MY LORD.
BUZZARD
DEADLY ARMOR, LIFE IN PRISON
THEIR THOUGHTS ARE FAMILIAR... BUT NO MATTER.
WE'RE HEADING TO IMPACT CITY. YOU WILL SERVE MY WILL AND PLAY YOUR PARTS AS I RESHAPE THIS WORLD--ALL WORLDS--IN MY IMAGE. I WILL TRANSPORT THOSE WHO CAN'T FLY. YOU WILL FOLLOW ME WITHOUT DEVIATION, OR I WILL KILL YOU. AS FOR ERASER...
"...HE WILL DEAL WITH SHIELD AND THE FOOLS WHO STAND WITH HIM."
UH... GUYS? FELLOW CRUSADERS? CALL ME A PESSIMIST, BUT I THINK WE'RE LOSING.
GREG DICKERING
COMET
IVETTE VELEZ
JAGUAR
KELLY BRAND
FLY-GIRL
WYATT RAYMOND
WEB
ALEX TYLER
FIREBALL
SHOULDN'T THE FEDS OR THE M.L.J. BE HERE BY NOW?
JOHNNY STERLING
STEEL STERLING
STEVE DICKERING
HANGMAN
THEY'RE LONG PAST DUE. SOMETHING MUST BE WRONG.
KIP BURLAND
THE BLACK HOOD
MARTIN REEVES
DEADLY FORCE
JOE HIGGINS
THE SHIELD

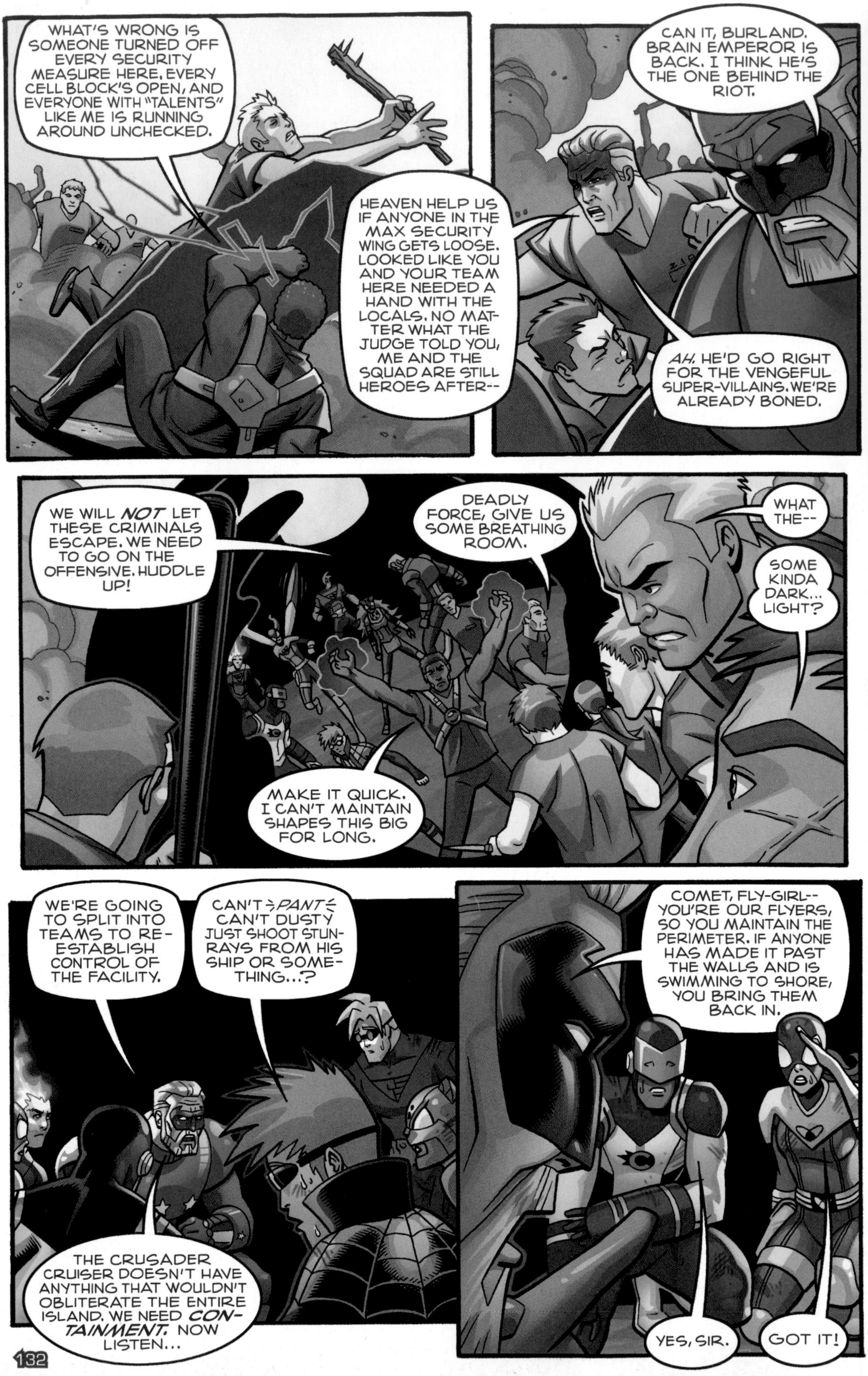
WHAT'S WRONG IS SOMEONE TURNED OFF EVERY SECURITY MEASURE HERE. EVERY CELL BLOCK'S OPEN, AND EVERYONE WITH "TALENTS" LIKE ME IS RUNNING AROUND UNCHECKED.
HEAVEN HELP US IF ANYONE IN THE MAX SECURITY WING GETS LOOSE. LOOKED LIKE YOU AND YOUR TEAM HERE NEEDED A HAND WITH THE LOCALS. NO MATTER WHAT THE JUDGE TOLD YOU, ME AND THE SQUAD ARE STILL HEROES AFTER--
CAN IT, BURLAND. BRAIN EMPEROR IS BACK. I THINK HE'S THE ONE BEHIND THE RIOT.
AH. HE'D GO RIGHT FOR THE VENGEFUL SUPER-VILLAINS. WE'RE ALREADY BONED.
WE WILL *NOT* LET THESE CRIMINALS ESCAPE. WE NEED TO GO ON THE OFFENSIVE. HUDDLE UP!
DEADLY FORCE, GIVE US SOME BREATHING ROOM.
MAKE IT QUICK. I CAN'T MAINTAIN SHAPES THIS BIG FOR LONG.
WHAT THE--
SOME KINDA DARK... LIGHT?
WE'RE GOING TO SPLIT INTO TEAMS TO RE-ESTABLISH CONTROL OF THE FACILITY.
CAN'T ⋾*PANT*⋲ CAN'T DUSTY JUST SHOOT STUN-RAYS FROM HIS SHIP OR SOMETHING...?
THE CRUSADER CRUISER DOESN'T HAVE ANYTHING THAT WOULDN'T OBLITERATE THE ENTIRE ISLAND. WE NEED *CONTAINMENT.* NOW LISTEN...
COMET, FLY-GIRL-- YOU'RE OUR FLYERS, SO YOU MAINTAIN THE PERIMETER. IF ANYONE HAS MADE IT PAST THE WALLS AND IS SWIMMING TO SHORE, YOU BRING THEM BACK IN.
YES, SIR.
GOT IT!

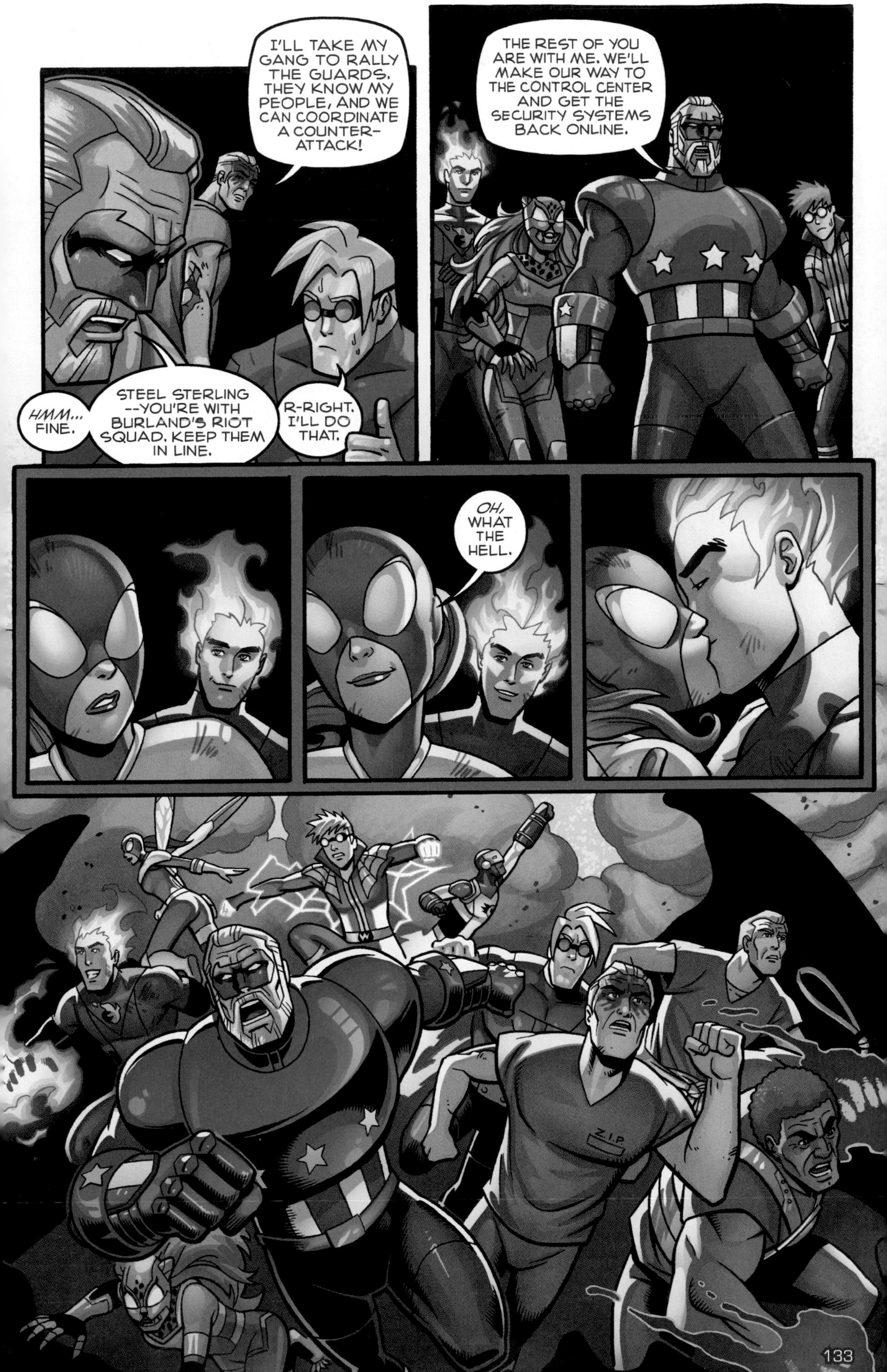
I'LL TAKE MY GANG TO RALLY THE GUARDS. THEY KNOW MY PEOPLE, AND WE CAN COORDINATE A COUNTER-ATTACK!
HMM... FINE.
STEEL STERLING --YOU'RE WITH BURLAND'S RIOT SQUAD. KEEP THEM IN LINE.
R-RIGHT. I'LL DO THAT.
THE REST OF YOU ARE WITH ME. WE'LL MAKE OUR WAY TO THE CONTROL CENTER AND GET THE SECURITY SYSTEMS BACK ONLINE.
OH, WHAT THE HELL.
Z.I.P.

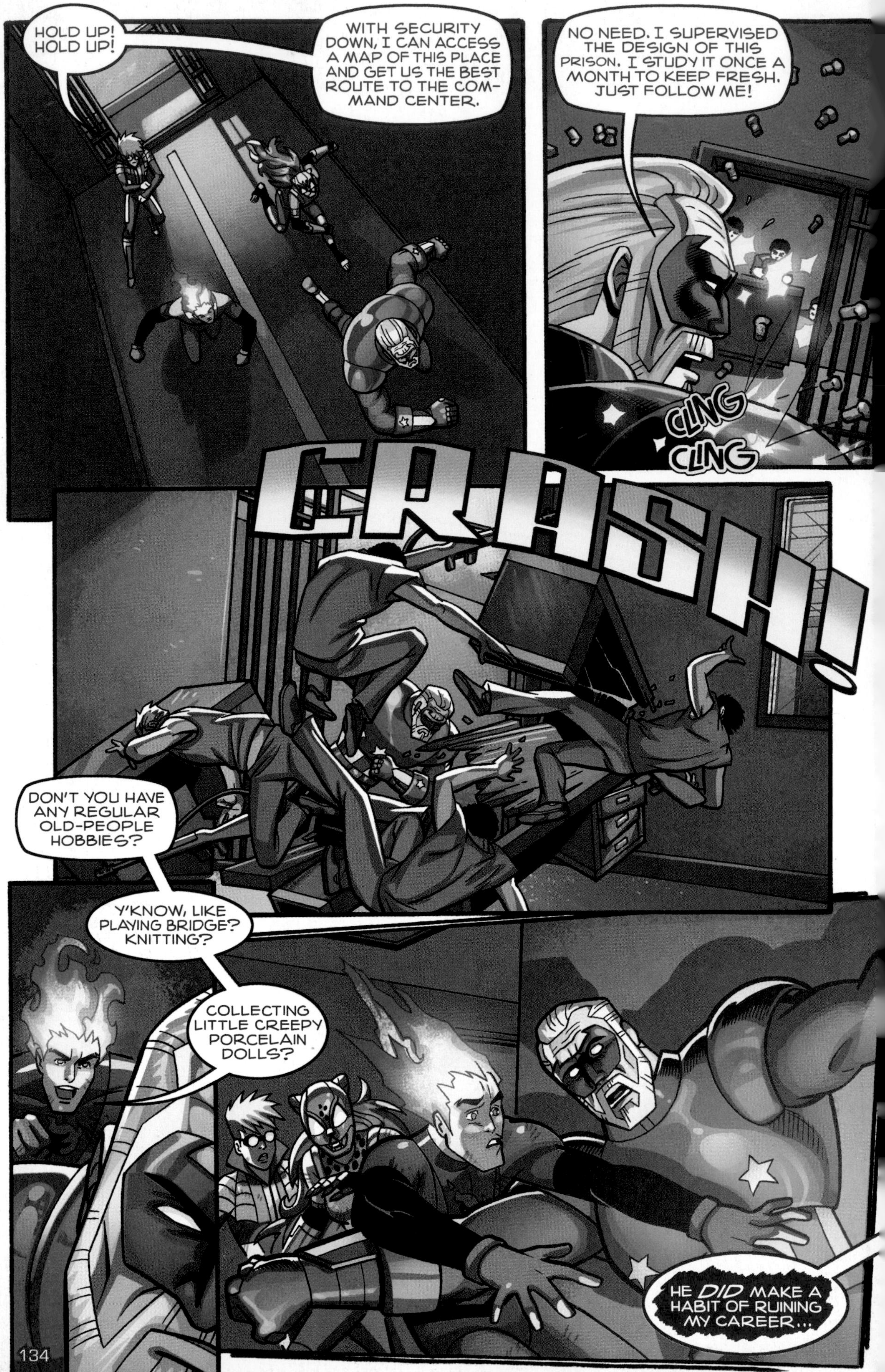

HOLD UP! HOLD UP!
WITH SECURITY DOWN, I CAN ACCESS A MAP OF THIS PLACE AND GET US THE BEST ROUTE TO THE COMMAND CENTER.
NO NEED. I SUPERVISED THE DESIGN OF THIS PRISON. I STUDY IT ONCE A MONTH TO KEEP FRESH. JUST FOLLOW ME!
CLING
CLING
CRASH!
DON'T YOU HAVE ANY REGULAR OLD-PEOPLE HOBBIES?
Y'KNOW, LIKE PLAYING BRIDGE? KNITTING?
COLLECTING LITTLE CREEPY PORCELAIN DOLLS?
HE *DID* MAKE A HABIT OF RUINING MY CAREER...

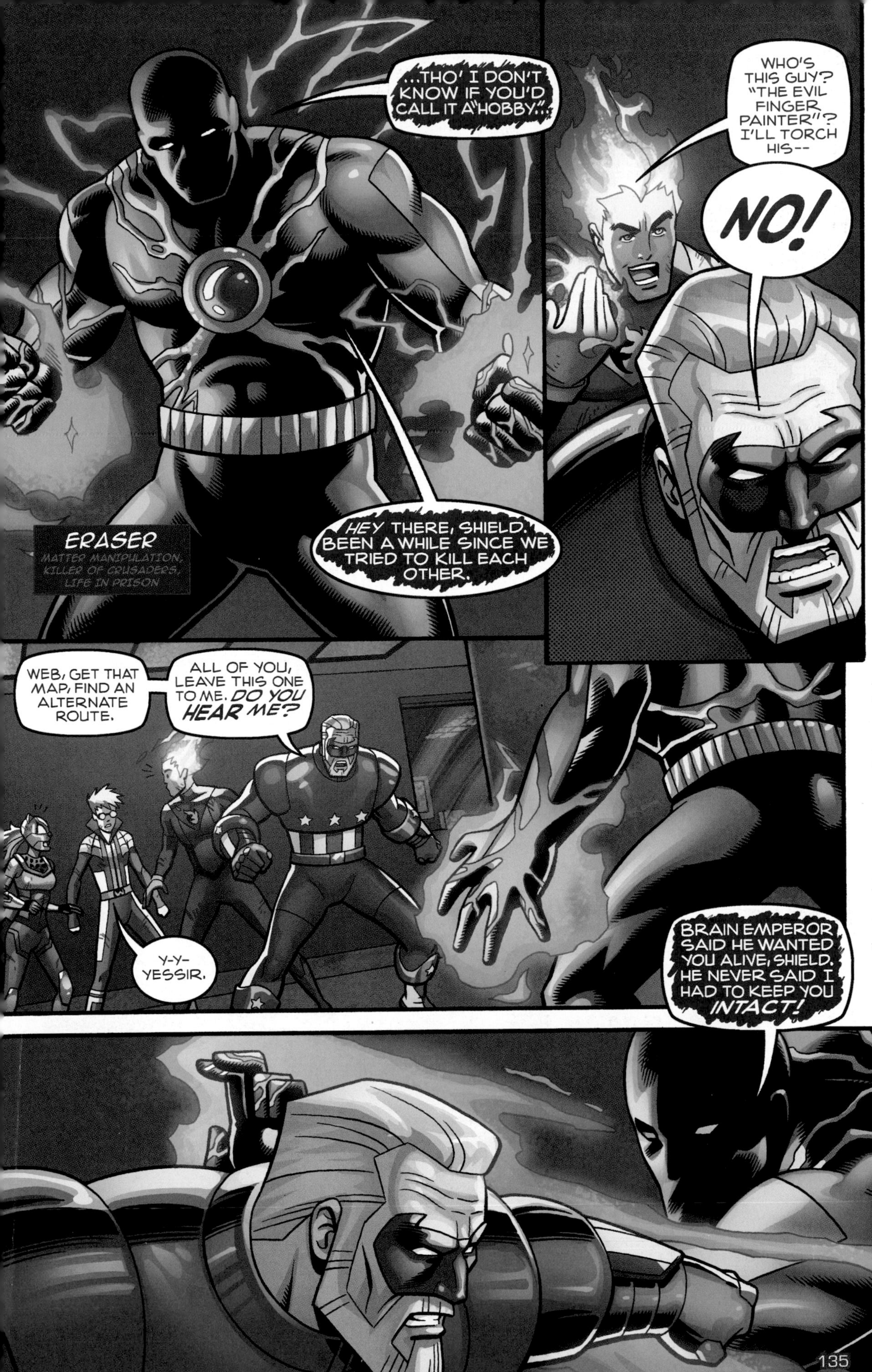
...THO' I DON'T KNOW IF YOU'D CALL IT A "HOBBY."...
ERASER
MATTER MANIPULATION, KILLER OF CRUSADERS, LIFE IN PRISON
HEY THERE, SHIELD. BEEN A WHILE SINCE WE TRIED TO KILL EACH OTHER.
WHO'S THIS GUY? "THE EVIL FINGER PAINTER"? I'LL TORCH HIS--
NO!
WEB, GET THAT MAP, FIND AN ALTERNATE ROUTE.
ALL OF YOU, LEAVE THIS ONE TO ME. DO YOU HEAR ME?
Y-Y-YESSIR.
BRAIN EMPEROR SAID HE WANTED YOU ALIVE, SHIELD. HE NEVER SAID I HAD TO KEEP YOU INTACT!

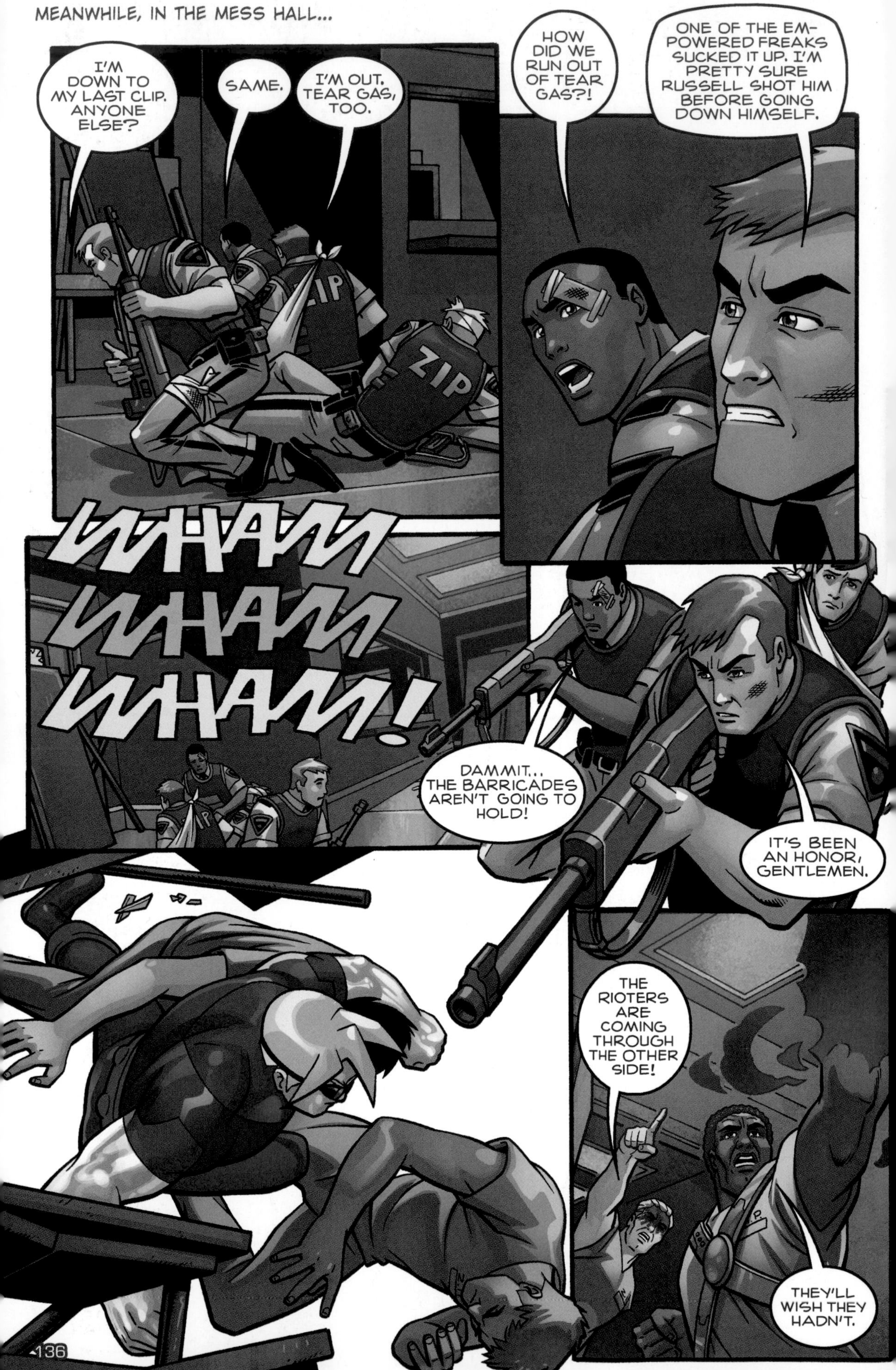
MEANWHILE, IN THE MESS HALL...
I'M DOWN TO MY LAST CLIP. ANYONE ELSE?
SAME.
I'M OUT. TEAR GAS, TOO.
ZIP
ZIP
HOW DID WE RUN OUT OF TEAR GAS?!
ONE OF THE EMPOWERED FREAKS SUCKED IT UP. I'M PRETTY SURE RUSSELL SHOT HIM BEFORE GOING DOWN HIMSELF.
WHAM WHAM WHAM!
DAMMIT... THE BARRICADES AREN'T GOING TO HOLD!
IT'S BEEN AN HONOR, GENTLEMEN.
THE RIOTERS ARE COMING THROUGH THE OTHER SIDE!
THEY'LL WISH THEY HADN'T.

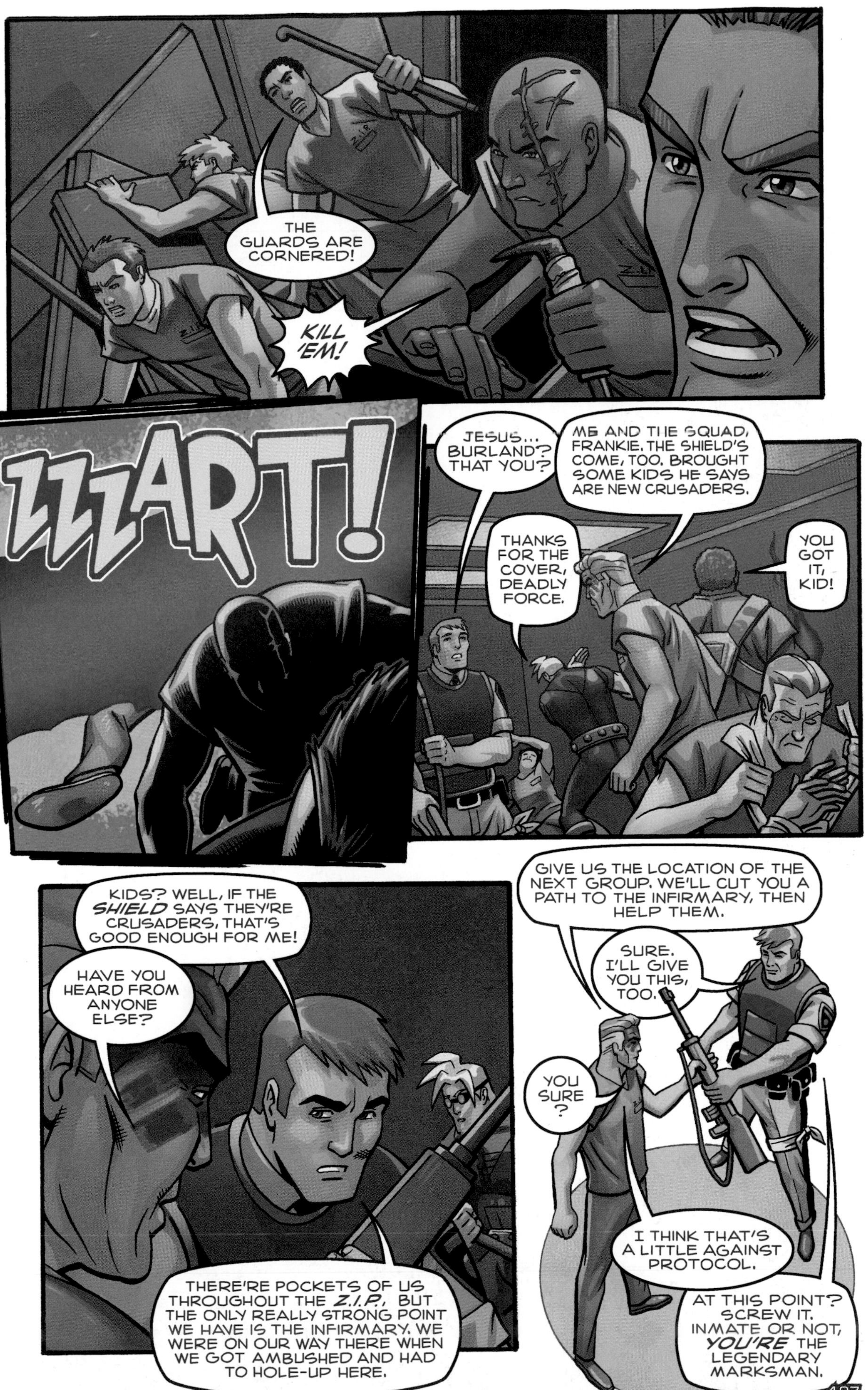
THE GUARDS ARE CORNERED!
KILL 'EM!
ZZZART!
JESUS... BURLAND? THAT YOU?
ME AND THE SQUAD, FRANKIE. THE SHIELD'S COME, TOO. BROUGHT SOME KIDS HE SAYS ARE NEW CRUSADERS.
THANKS FOR THE COVER, DEADLY FORCE.
YOU GOT IT, KID!
KIDS? WELL, IF THE SHIELD SAYS THEY'RE CRUSADERS, THAT'S GOOD ENOUGH FOR ME!
HAVE YOU HEARD FROM ANYONE ELSE?
THERE'RE POCKETS OF US THROUGHOUT THE Z.I.P., BUT THE ONLY REALLY STRONG POINT WE HAVE IS THE INFIRMARY. WE WERE ON OUR WAY THERE WHEN WE GOT AMBUSHED AND HAD TO HOLE-UP HERE.
GIVE US THE LOCATION OF THE NEXT GROUP. WE'LL CUT YOU A PATH TO THE INFIRMARY, THEN HELP THEM.
SURE. I'LL GIVE YOU THIS, TOO.
YOU SURE?
I THINK THAT'S A LITTLE AGAINST PROTOCOL.
AT THIS POINT? SCREW IT. INMATE OR NOT, YOU'RE THE LEGENDARY MARKSMAN.

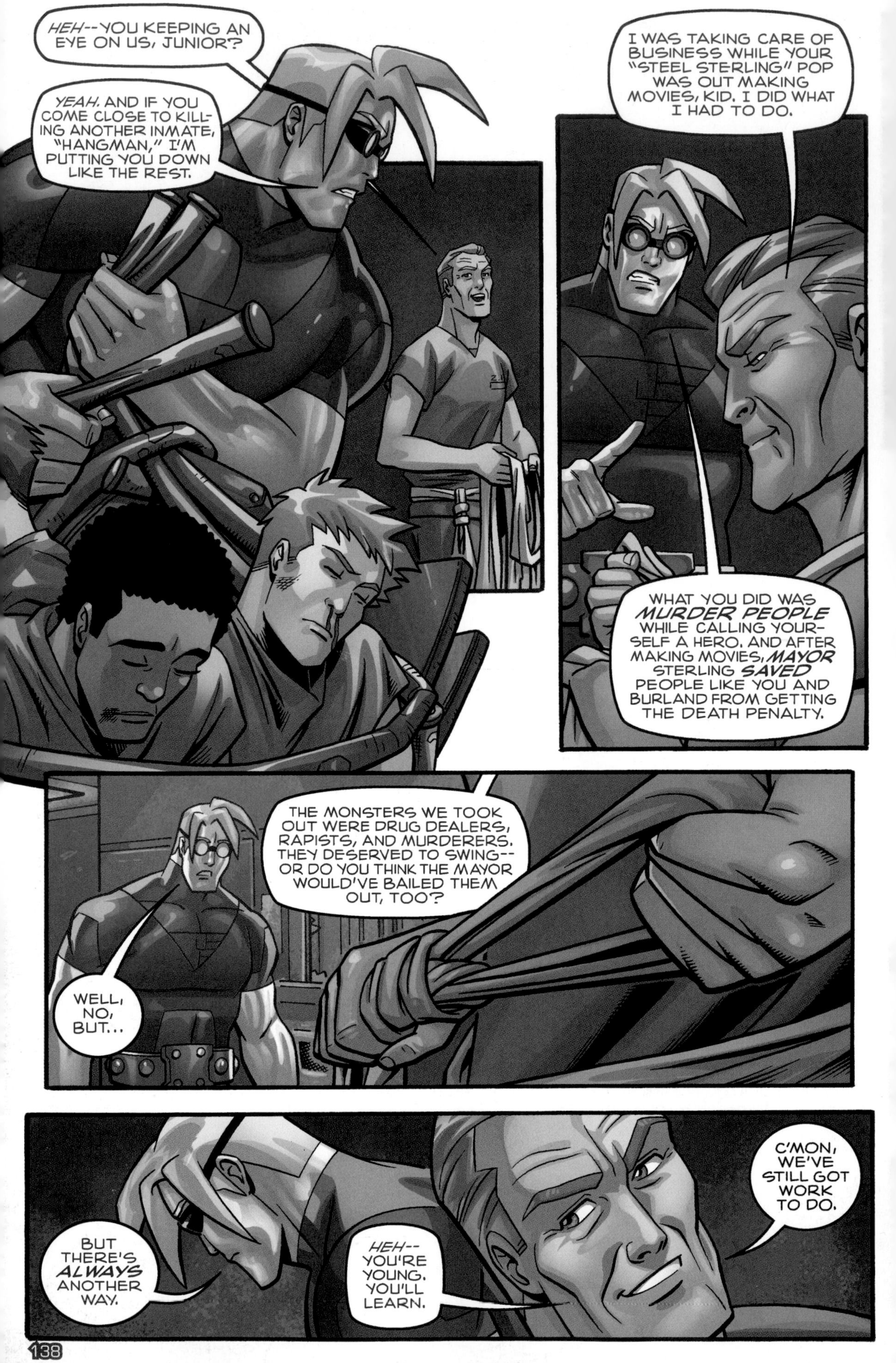
HEH--YOU KEEPING AN EYE ON US, JUNIOR?
YEAH. AND IF YOU COME CLOSE TO KILLING ANOTHER INMATE, "HANGMAN," I'M PUTTING YOU DOWN LIKE THE REST.
I WAS TAKING CARE OF BUSINESS WHILE YOUR "STEEL STERLING" POP WAS OUT MAKING MOVIES, KID. I DID WHAT I HAD TO DO.
WHAT YOU DID WAS MURDER PEOPLE WHILE CALLING YOURSELF A HERO. AND AFTER MAKING MOVIES, MAYOR STERLING SAVED PEOPLE LIKE YOU AND BURLAND FROM GETTING THE DEATH PENALTY.
THE MONSTERS WE TOOK OUT WERE DRUG DEALERS, RAPISTS, AND MURDERERS. THEY DESERVED TO SWING--OR DO YOU THINK THE MAYOR WOULD'VE BAILED THEM OUT, TOO?
WELL, NO, BUT...
BUT THERE'S ALWAYS ANOTHER WAY.
HEH--YOU'RE YOUNG. YOU'LL LEARN.
C'MON, WE'VE STILL GOT WORK TO DO.

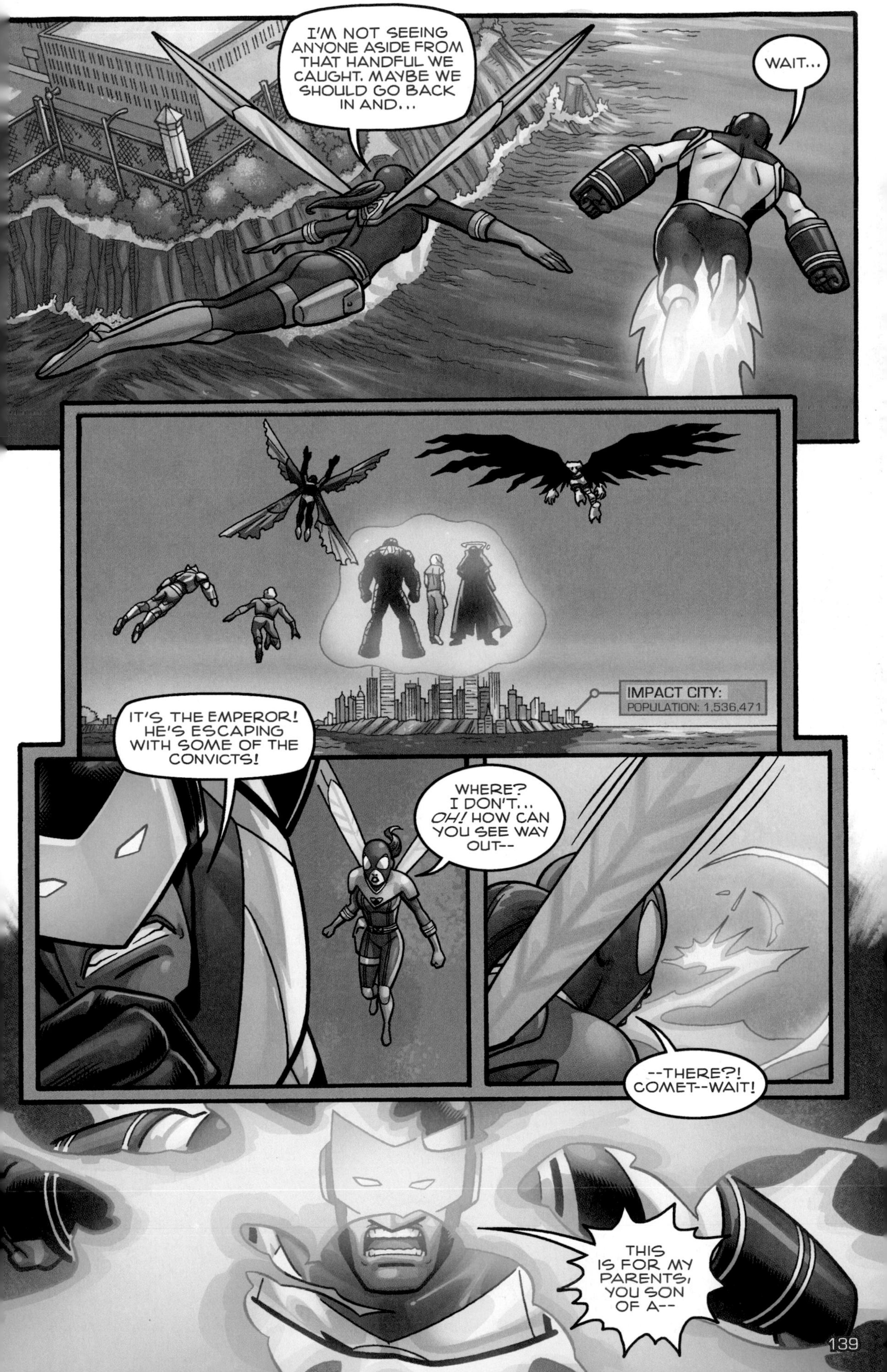
I'M NOT SEEING ANYONE ASIDE FROM THAT HANDFUL WE CAUGHT. MAYBE WE SHOULD GO BACK IN AND...
WAIT...
IMPACT CITY:
POPULATION: 1,536,471
IT'S THE EMPEROR! HE'S ESCAPING WITH SOME OF THE CONVICTS!
WHERE? I DON'T... *OH!* HOW CAN YOU SEE WAY OUT--
--THERE?! COMET--WAIT!
THIS IS FOR MY PARENTS, YOU SON OF A--

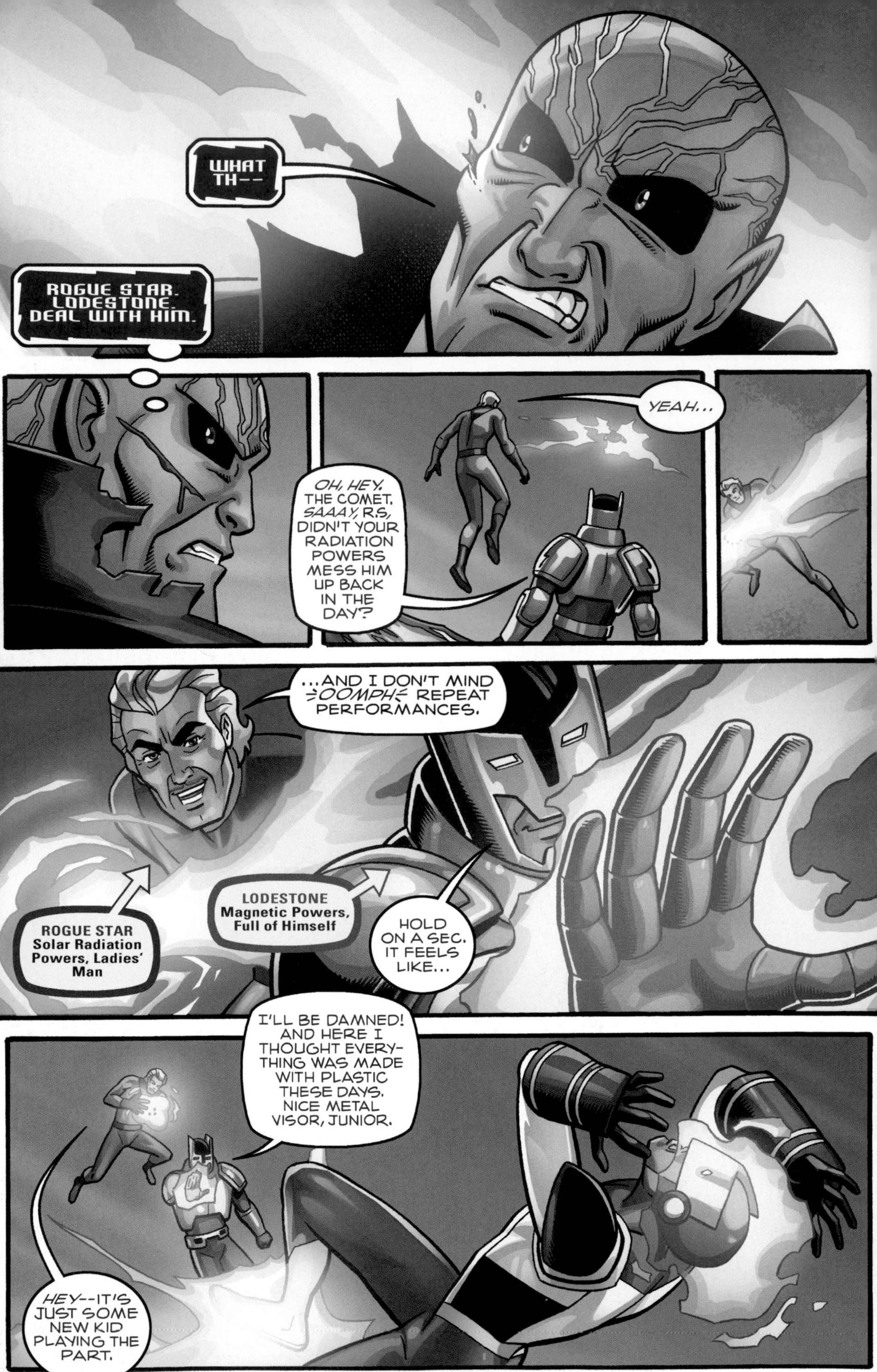
WHAT TH--
ROGUE STAR. LODESTONE. DEAL WITH HIM.
YEAH...
OH, HEY. THE COMET. SAAAY, R.S, DIDN'T YOUR RADIATION POWERS MESS HIM UP BACK IN THE DAY?
...AND I DON'T MIND OOMPH REPEAT PERFORMANCES.
ROGUE STAR Solar Radiation Powers, Ladies' Man
LODESTONE Magnetic Powers, Full of Himself
HOLD ON A SEC. IT FEELS LIKE...
I'LL BE DAMNED! AND HERE I THOUGHT EVERY-THING WAS MADE WITH PLASTIC THESE DAYS. NICE METAL VISOR, JUNIOR.
HEY--IT'S JUST SOME NEW KID PLAYING THE PART.

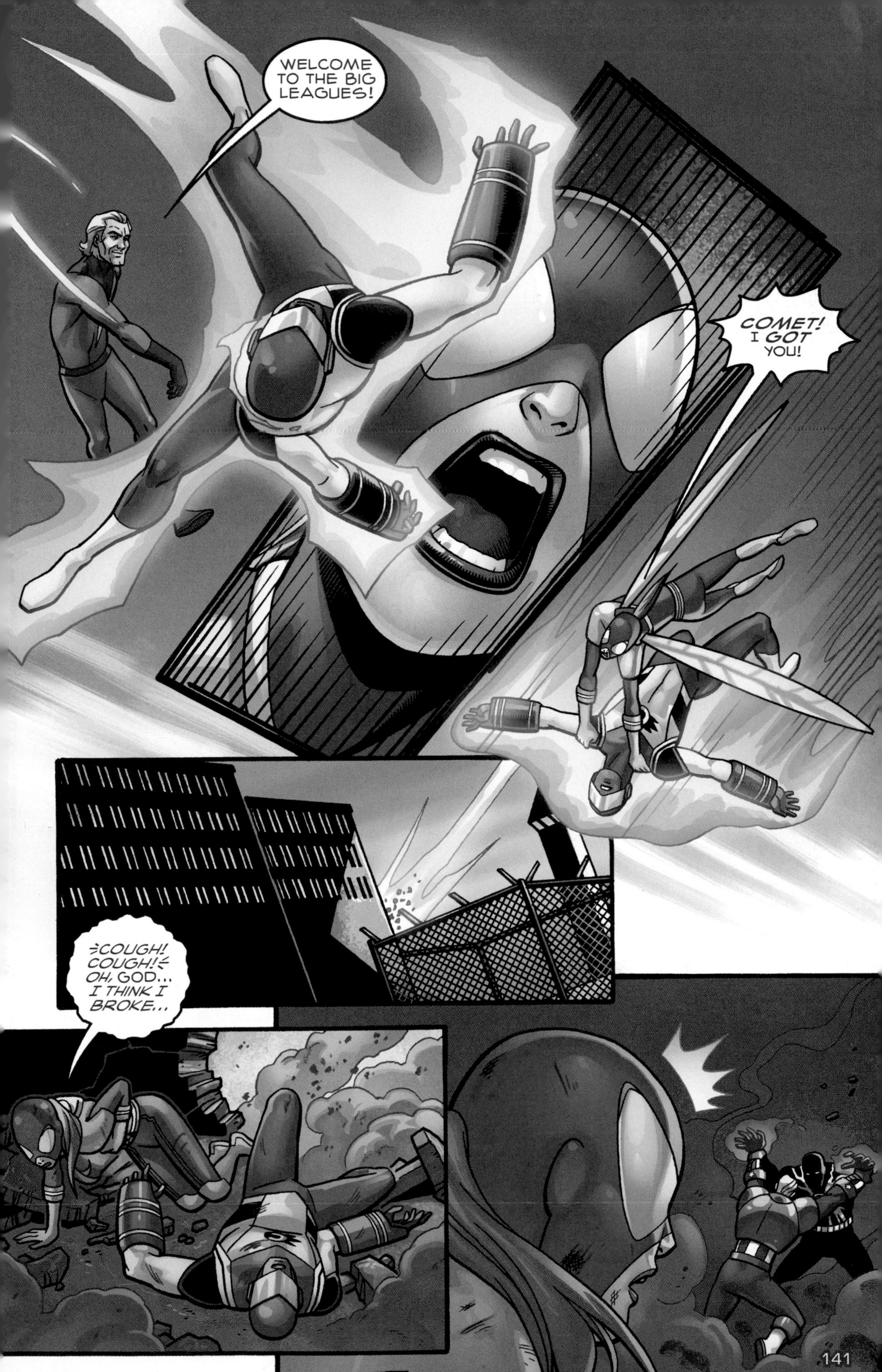
WELCOME TO THE BIG LEAGUES!
COMET! I GOT YOU!
≈COUGH! COUGH!≈ OH, GOD... I THINK I BROKE...

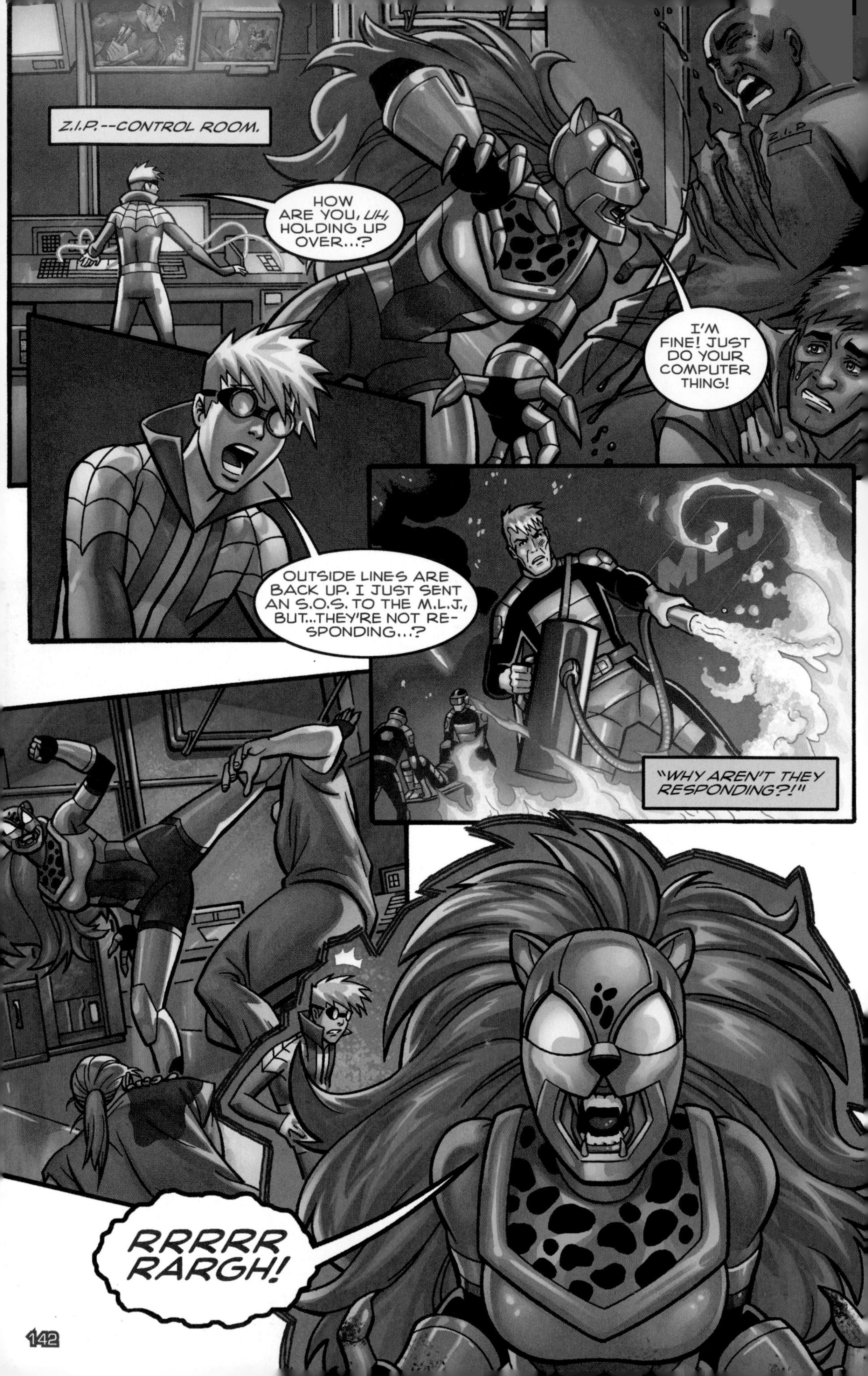
Z.I.P.--CONTROL ROOM.
HOW ARE YOU, UH, HOLDING UP OVER...?
I'M FINE! JUST DO YOUR COMPUTER THING!
OUTSIDE LINES ARE BACK UP. I JUST SENT AN S.O.S. TO THE M.L.J., BUT...THEY'RE NOT RESPONDING...?
"WHY AREN'T THEY RESPONDING?!"
RRRRR RARGH!

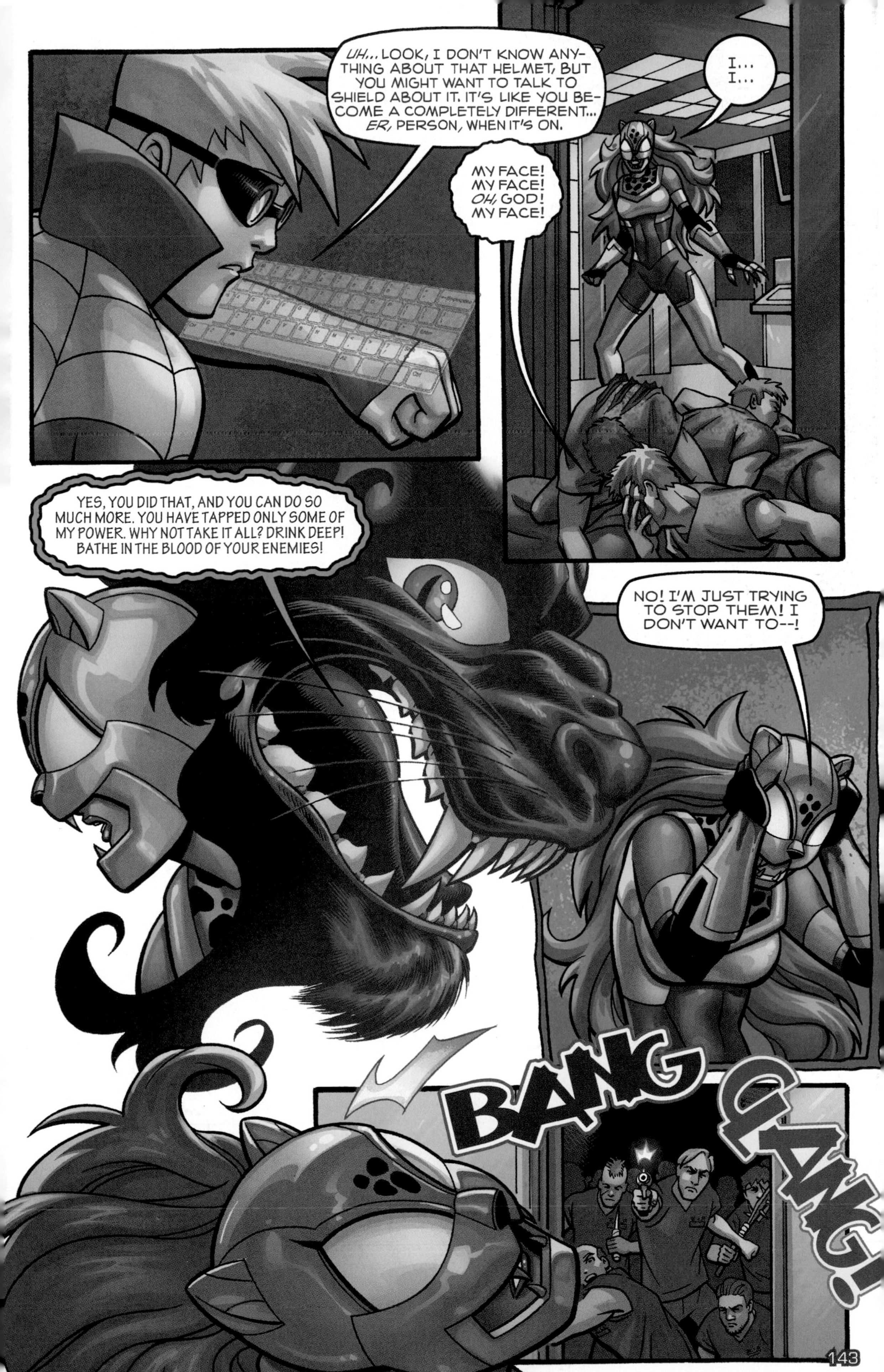

UH... LOOK, I DON'T KNOW ANYTHING ABOUT THAT HELMET, BUT YOU MIGHT WANT TO TALK TO SHIELD ABOUT IT. IT'S LIKE YOU BECOME A COMPLETELY DIFFERENT... ER, PERSON, WHEN IT'S ON.
I... I...
MY FACE! MY FACE! OH, GOD! MY FACE!
YES, YOU DID THAT, AND YOU CAN DO SO MUCH MORE. YOU HAVE TAPPED ONLY SOME OF MY POWER. WHY NOT TAKE IT ALL? DRINK DEEP! BATHE IN THE BLOOD OF YOUR ENEMIES!
NO! I'M JUST TRYING TO STOP THEM! I DON'T WANT TO--!
BANG
BANG!

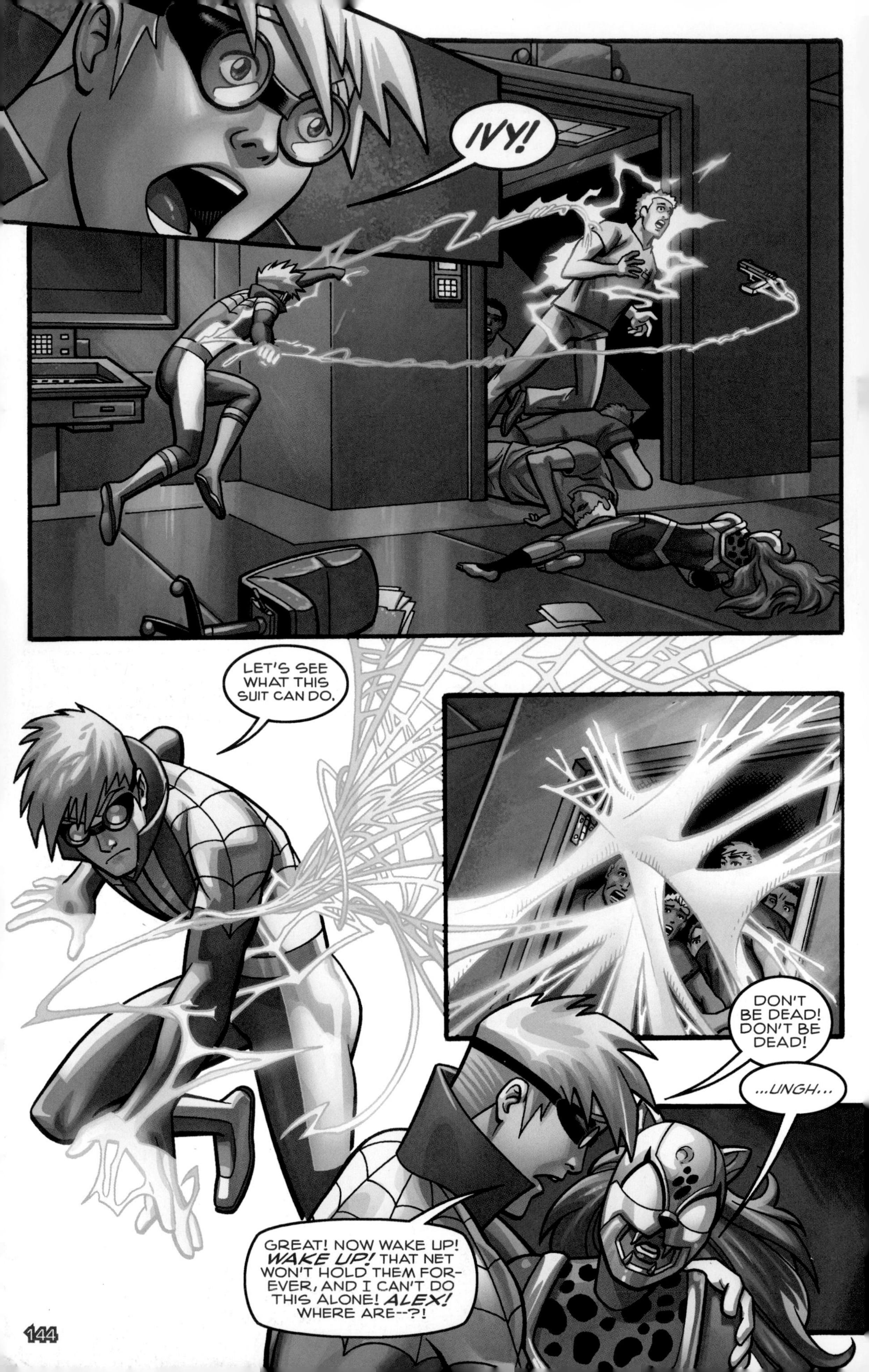

IVY!
LET'S SEE WHAT THIS SUIT CAN DO.
DON'T BE DEAD! DON'T BE DEAD!
...UNGH...
GREAT! NOW WAKE UP! WAKE UP! THAT NET WON'T HOLD THEM FOR-EVER, AND I CAN'T DO THIS ALONE! ALEX! WHERE ARE--?!

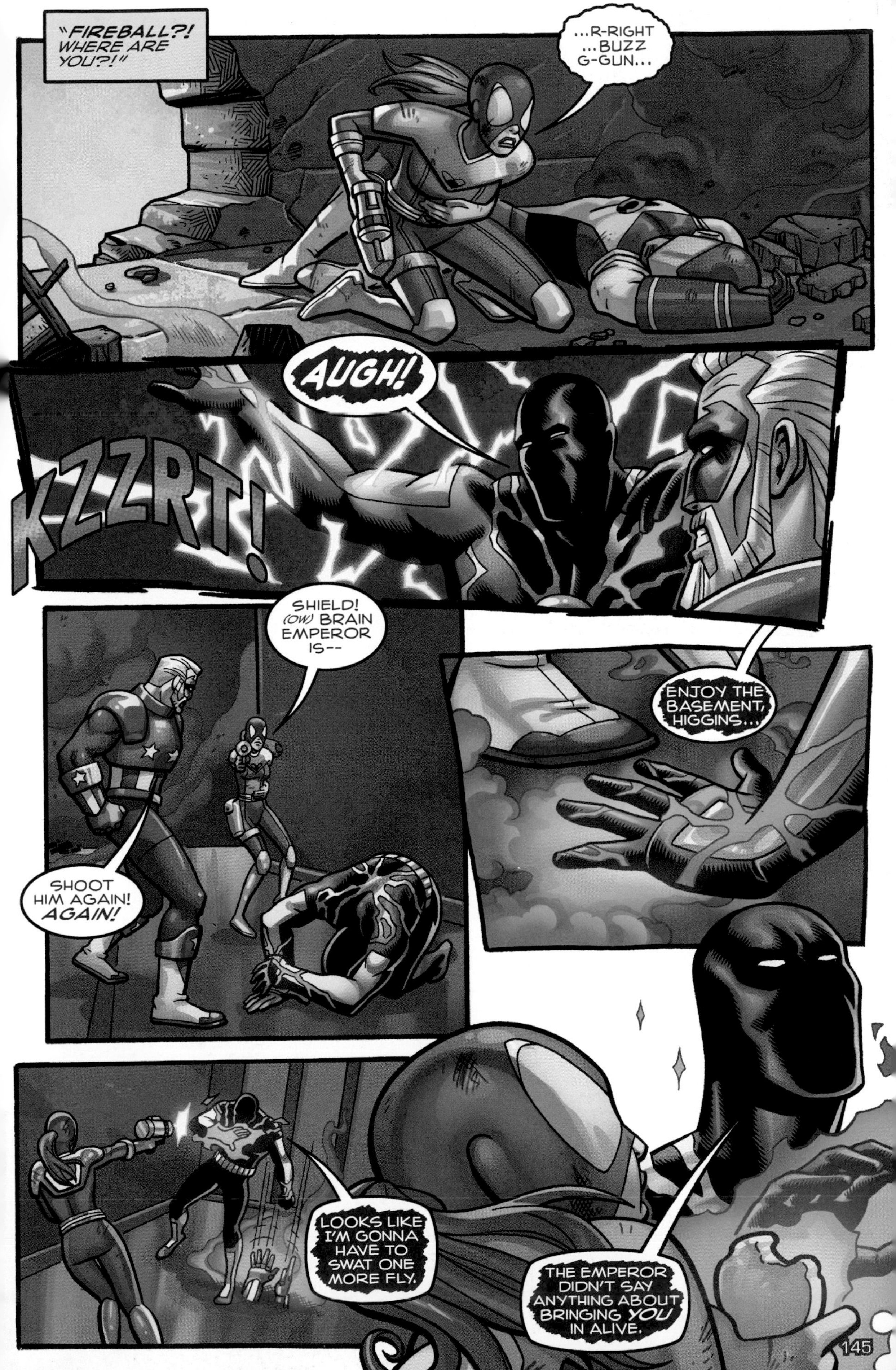
"FIREBALL?! WHERE ARE YOU?!"
...R-RIGHT ...BUZZ G-GUN...
AUGH!
KZZRT!
SHIELD! (OW) BRAIN EMPEROR IS--
ENJOY THE BASEMENT, HIGGINS...
SHOOT HIM AGAIN! AGAIN!
LOOKS LIKE I'M GONNA HAVE TO SWAT ONE MORE FLY.
THE EMPEROR DIDN'T SAY ANYTHING ABOUT BRINGING YOU IN ALIVE.

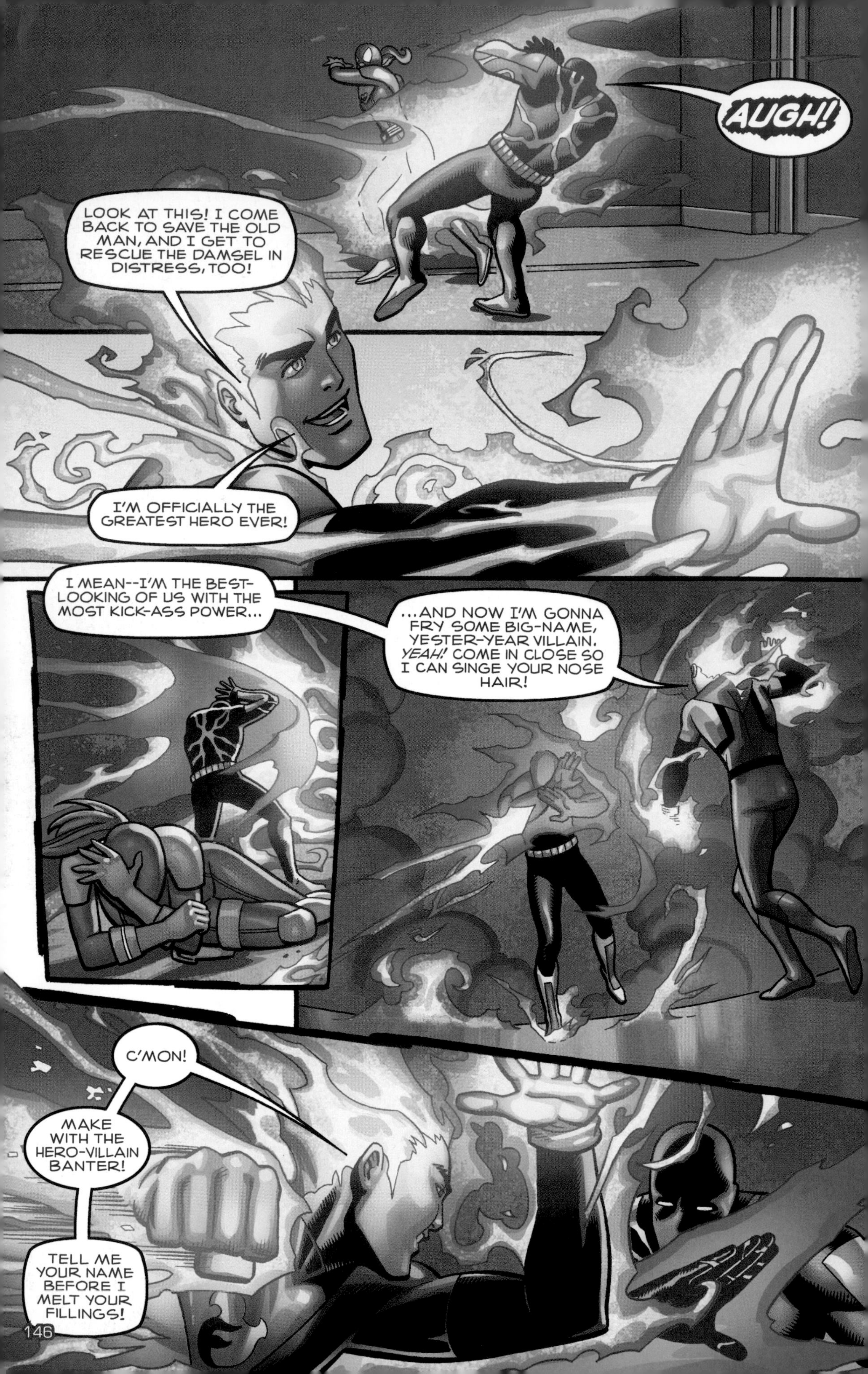
AUGH!
LOOK AT THIS! I COME BACK TO SAVE THE OLD MAN, AND I GET TO RESCUE THE DAMSEL IN DISTRESS, TOO!
I'M OFFICIALLY THE GREATEST HERO EVER!
I MEAN--I'M THE BEST-LOOKING OF US WITH THE MOST KICK-ASS POWER...
...AND NOW I'M GONNA FRY SOME BIG-NAME, YESTER-YEAR VILLAIN. YEAH! COME IN CLOSE SO I CAN SINGE YOUR NOSE HAIR!
C'MON!
MAKE WITH THE HERO-VILLAIN BANTER!
TELL ME YOUR NAME BEFORE I MELT YOUR FILLINGS!

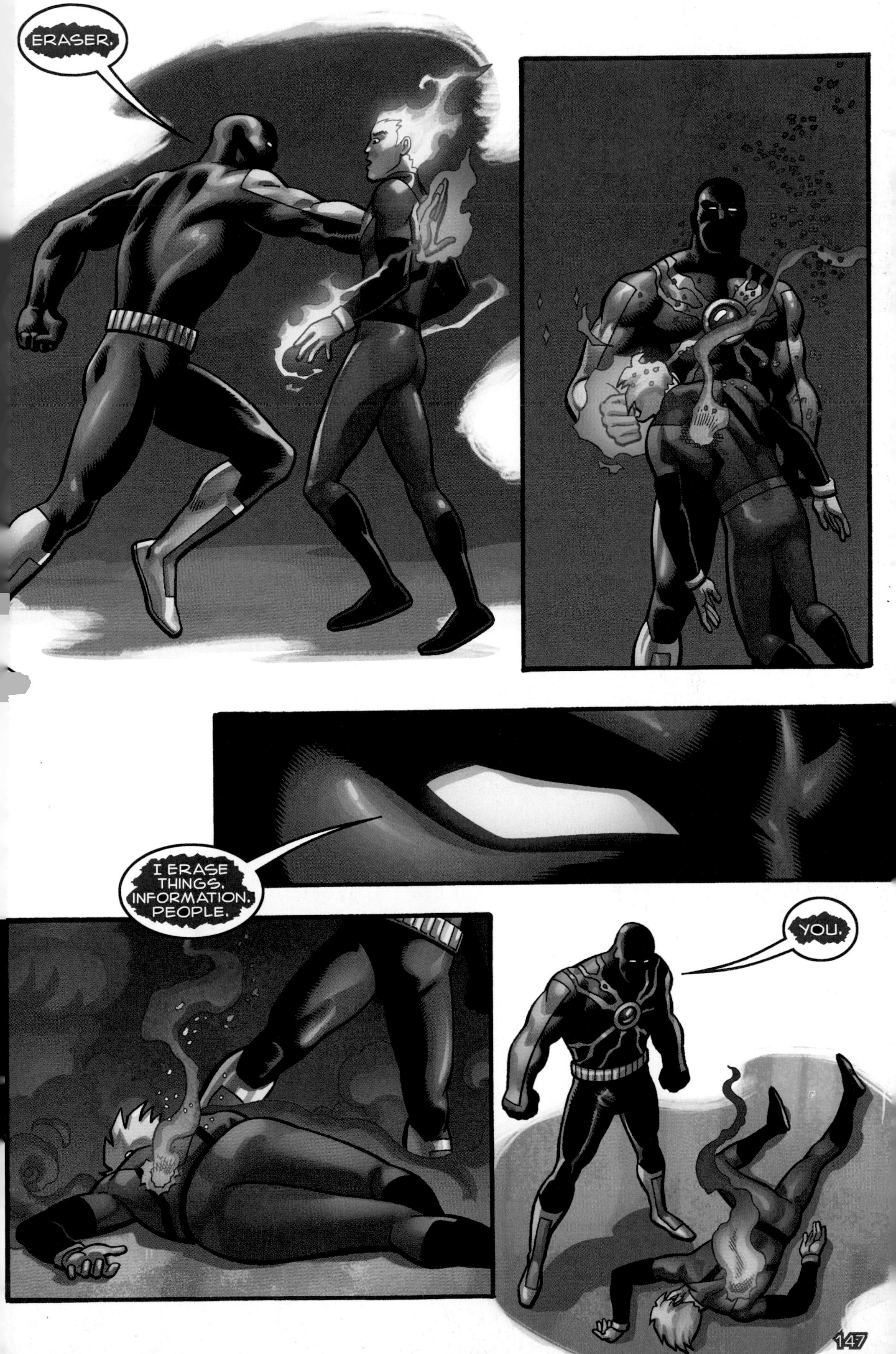
ERASER.
I ERASE THINGS. INFORMATION. PEOPLE.
YOU.

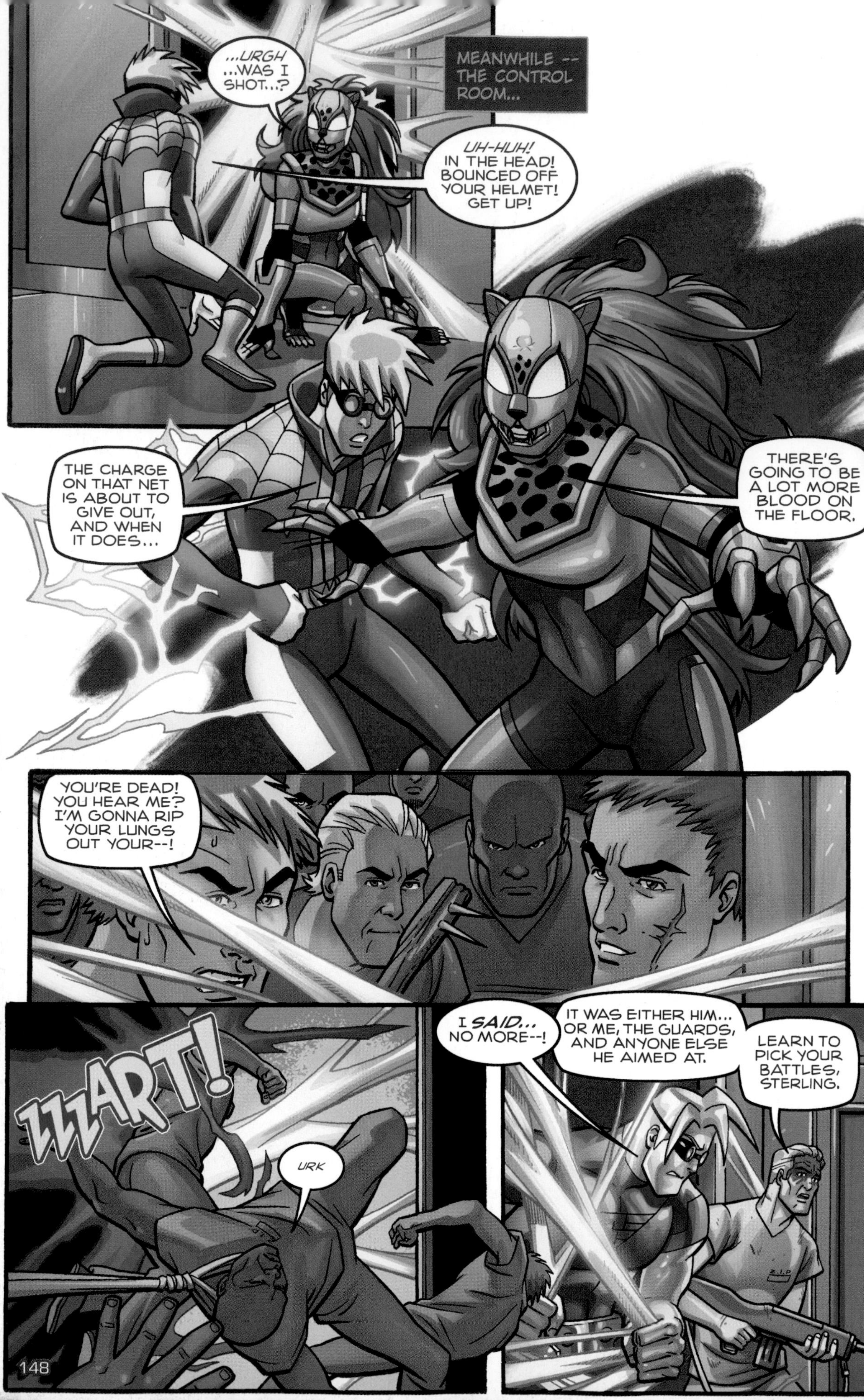

...URGH ...WAS I SHOT...?
MEANWHILE -- THE CONTROL ROOM...
UH-HUH! IN THE HEAD! BOUNCED OFF YOUR HELMET! GET UP!
THE CHARGE ON THAT NET IS ABOUT TO GIVE OUT, AND WHEN IT DOES...
THERE'S GOING TO BE A LOT MORE BLOOD ON THE FLOOR.
YOU'RE DEAD! YOU HEAR ME? I'M GONNA RIP YOUR LUNGS OUT YOUR--!
ZZZART!
URK
I SAID... NO MORE--!
IT WAS EITHER HIM... OR ME, THE GUARDS, AND ANYONE ELSE HE AIMED AT.
LEARN TO PICK YOUR BATTLES, STERLING.

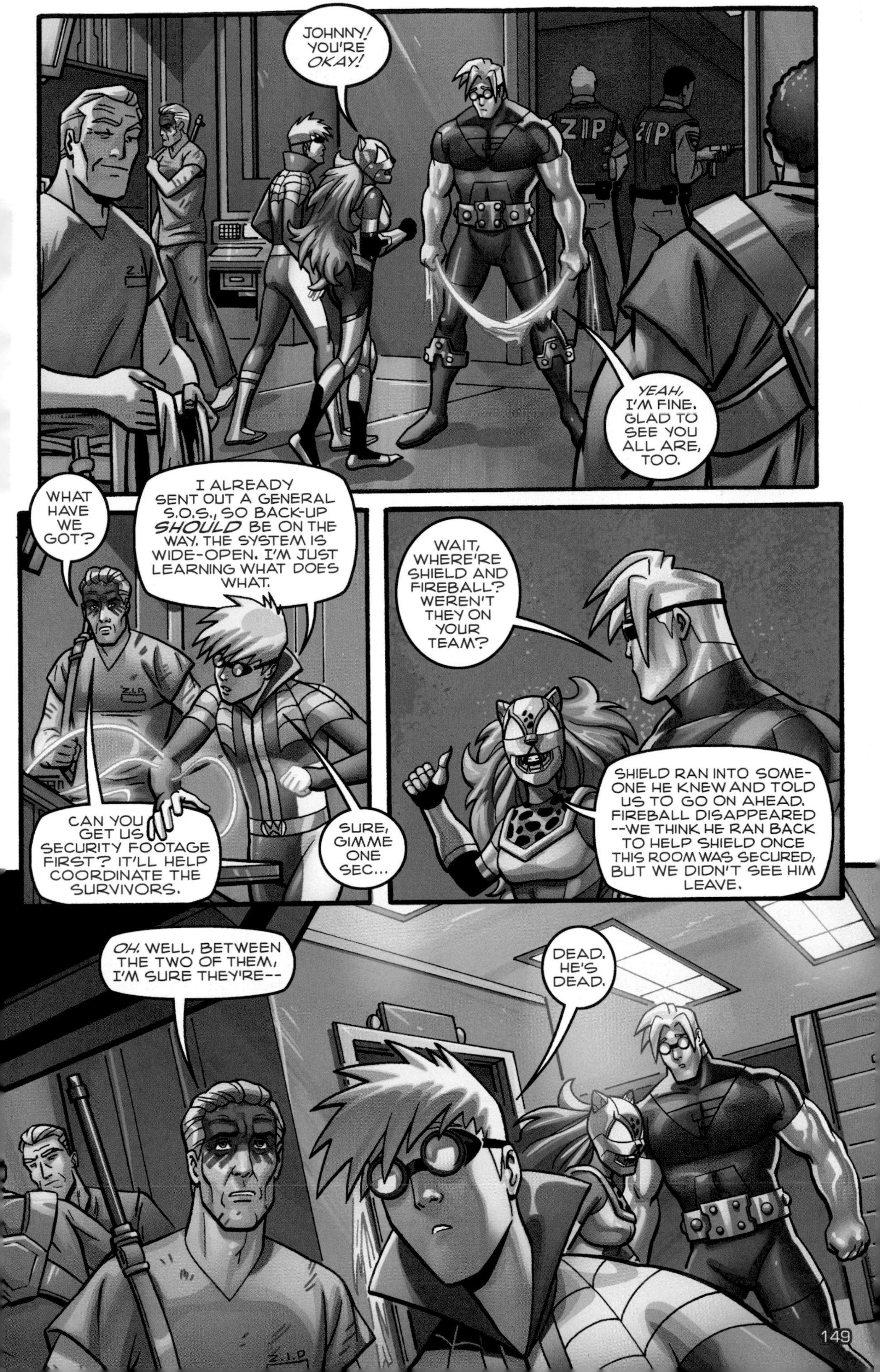
JOHNNY! YOU'RE OKAY!
YEAH, I'M FINE. GLAD TO SEE YOU ALL ARE, TOO.
WHAT HAVE WE GOT?
I ALREADY SENT OUT A GENERAL S.O.S., SO BACK-UP SHOULD BE ON THE WAY. THE SYSTEM IS WIDE-OPEN. I'M JUST LEARNING WHAT DOES WHAT.
CAN YOU GET US SECURITY FOOTAGE FIRST? IT'LL HELP COORDINATE THE SURVIVORS.
SURE, GIMME ONE SEC...
WAIT, WHERE'RE SHIELD AND FIREBALL? WEREN'T THEY ON YOUR TEAM?
SHIELD RAN INTO SOMEONE HE KNEW AND TOLD US TO GO ON AHEAD. FIREBALL DISAPPEARED --WE THINK HE RAN BACK TO HELP SHIELD ONCE THIS ROOM WAS SECURED, BUT WE DIDN'T SEE HIM LEAVE.
OH. WELL, BETWEEN THE TWO OF THEM, I'M SURE THEY'RE--
DEAD. HE'S DEAD.

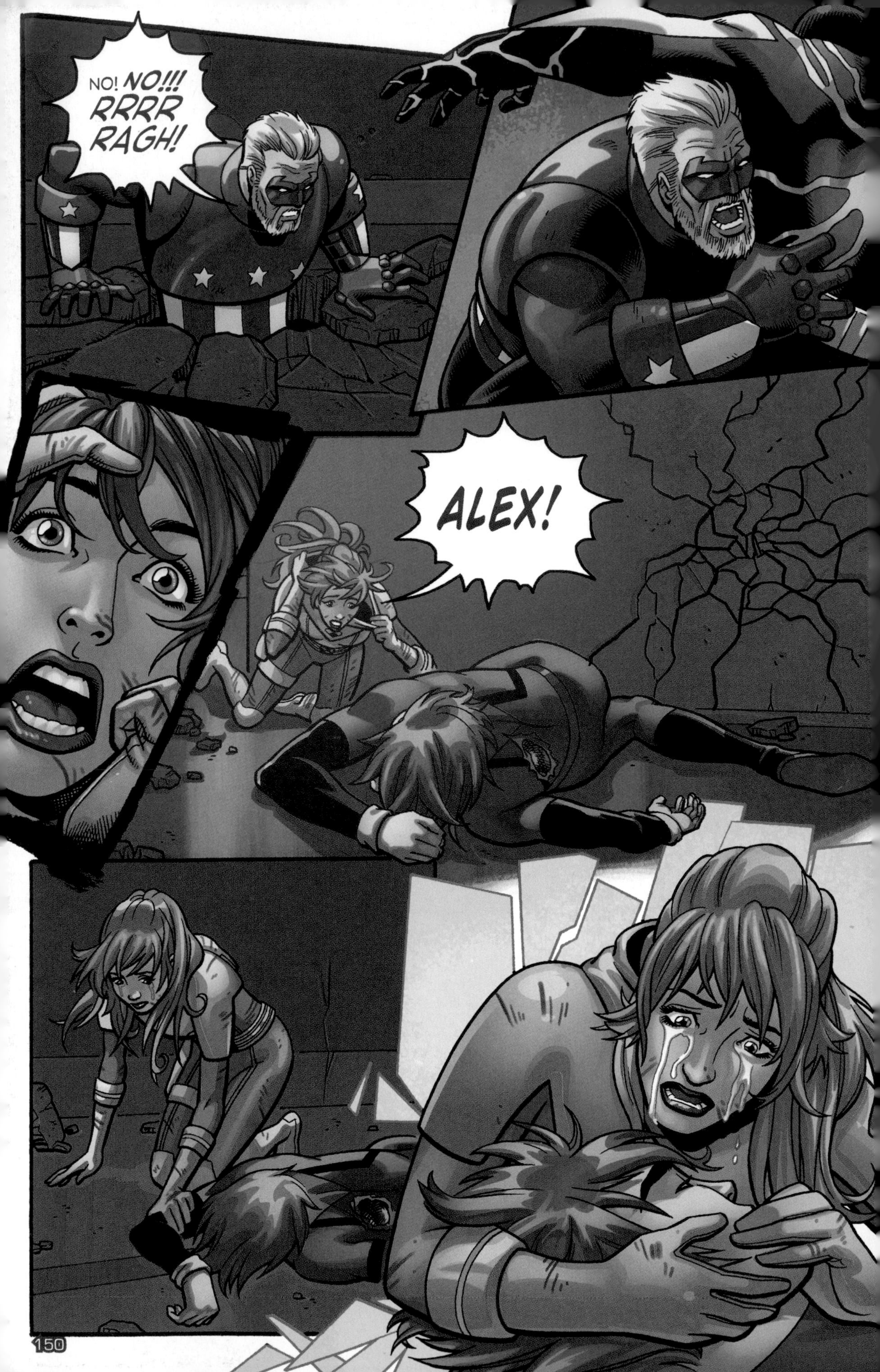

NO! NO!!! RRRR RAGH!
ALEX!

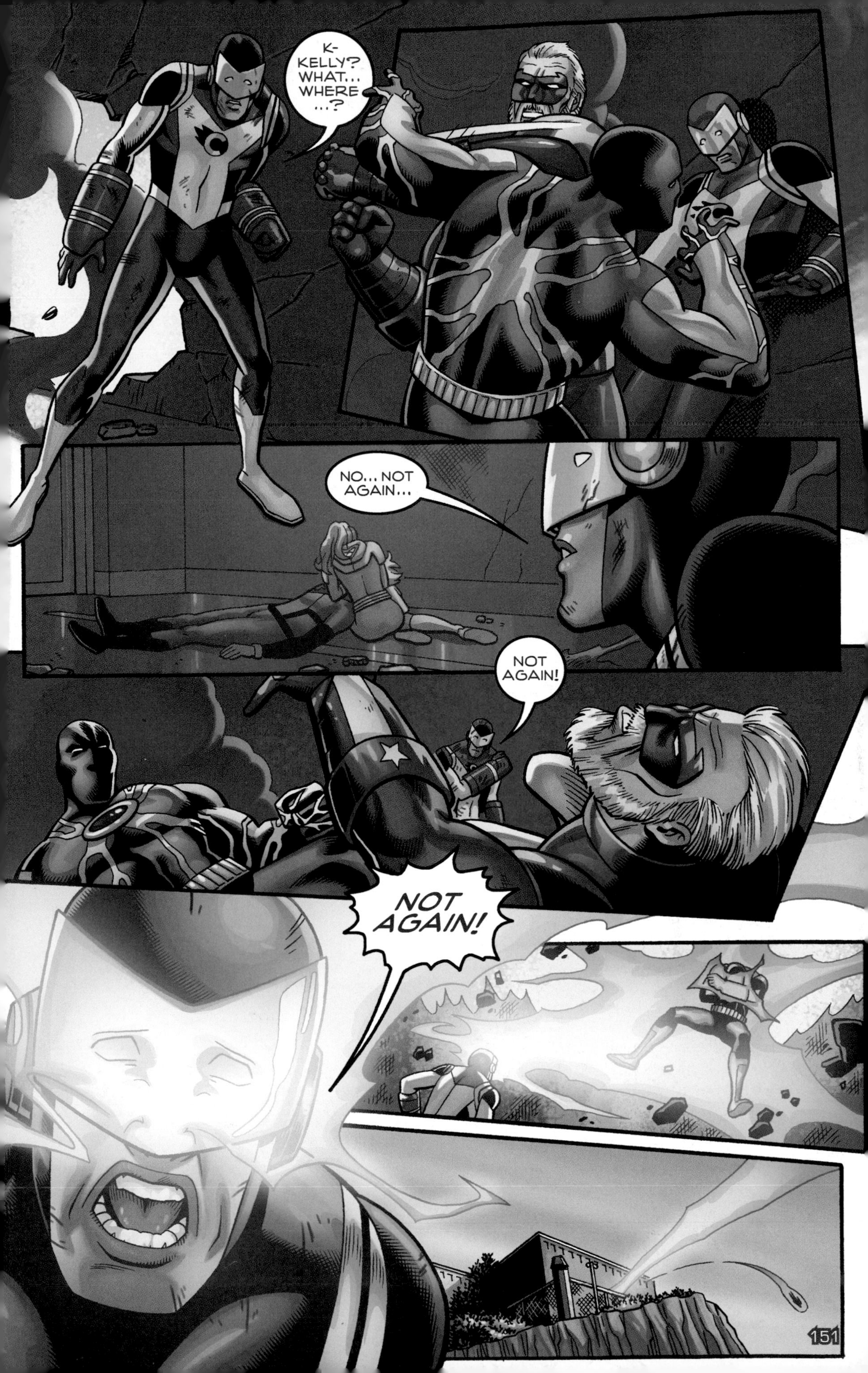
K-KELLY? WHAT... WHERE ...?
NO... NOT AGAIN...
NOT AGAIN!
NOT AGAIN!

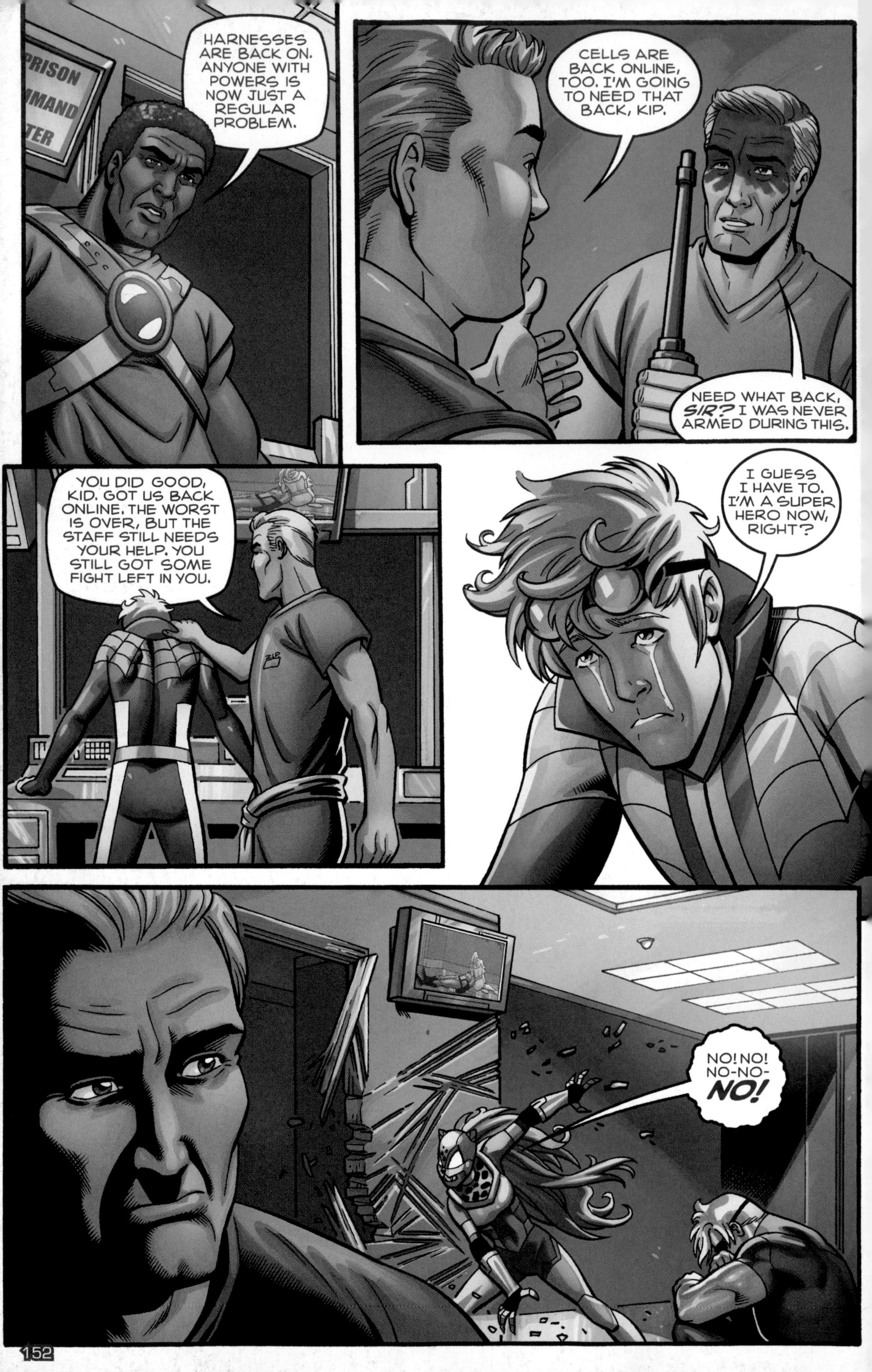
PRISON
MMAND
TER
HARNESSES ARE BACK ON. ANYONE WITH POWERS IS NOW JUST A REGULAR PROBLEM.
CELLS ARE BACK ONLINE, TOO. I'M GOING TO NEED THAT BACK, KIP.
NEED WHAT BACK, SIR? I WAS NEVER ARMED DURING THIS.
YOU DID GOOD, KID. GOT US BACK ONLINE. THE WORST IS OVER, BUT THE STAFF STILL NEEDS YOUR HELP. YOU STILL GOT SOME FIGHT LEFT IN YOU.
I GUESS I HAVE TO. I'M A SUPER HERO NOW, RIGHT?
NO! NO! NO-NO-NO!

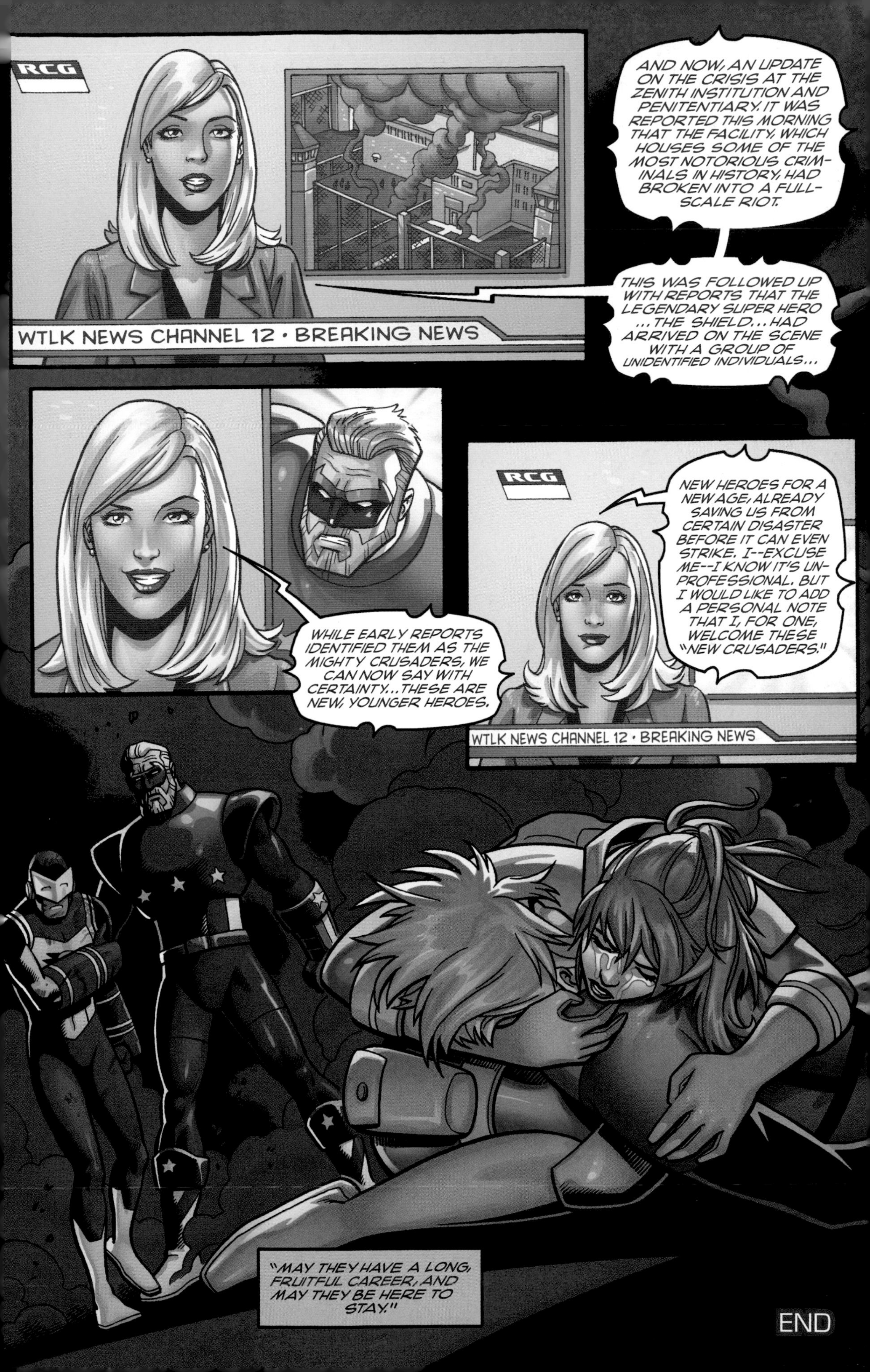
RCG
AND NOW, AN UPDATE ON THE CRISIS AT THE ZENITH INSTITUTION AND PENITENTIARY. IT WAS REPORTED THIS MORNING THAT THE FACILITY, WHICH HOUSES SOME OF THE MOST NOTORIOUS CRIMINALS IN HISTORY, HAD BROKEN INTO A FULL-SCALE RIOT.
WTLK NEWS CHANNEL 12 • BREAKING NEWS
THIS WAS FOLLOWED UP WITH REPORTS THAT THE LEGENDARY SUPER HERO ...THE SHIELD...HAD ARRIVED ON THE SCENE WITH A GROUP OF UNIDENTIFIED INDIVIDUALS...
WHILE EARLY REPORTS IDENTIFIED THEM AS THE MIGHTY CRUSADERS, WE CAN NOW SAY WITH CERTAINTY...THESE ARE NEW, YOUNGER HEROES.
RCG
NEW HEROES FOR A NEW AGE, ALREADY SAVING US FROM CERTAIN DISASTER BEFORE IT CAN EVEN STRIKE. I--EXCUSE ME--I KNOW IT'S UNPROFESSIONAL, BUT I WOULD LIKE TO ADD A PERSONAL NOTE THAT I, FOR ONE, WELCOME THESE "NEW CRUSADERS."
WTLK NEWS CHANNEL 12 • BREAKING NEWS
"MAY THEY HAVE A LONG, FRUITFUL CAREER, AND MAY THEY BE HERE TO STAY."
END

ISSUE 1 VARIANT COVERS

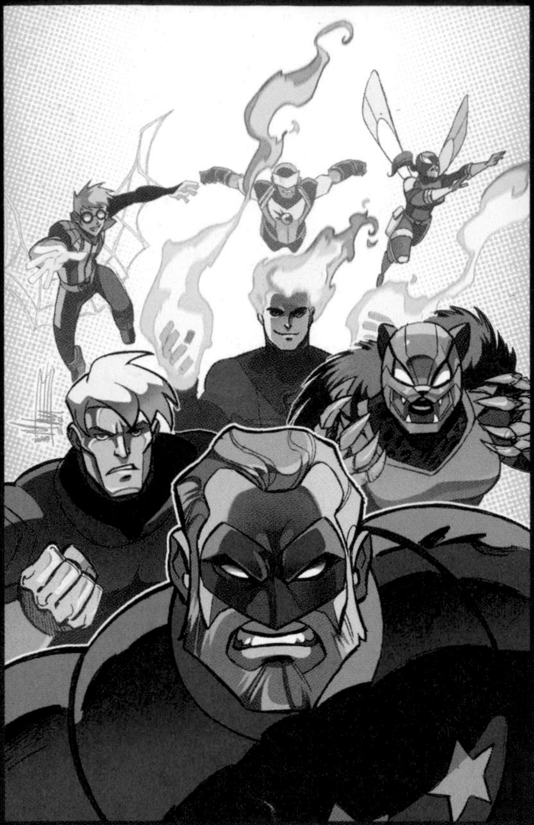

COVER BY: MIKE NORTON & MATT HERMS

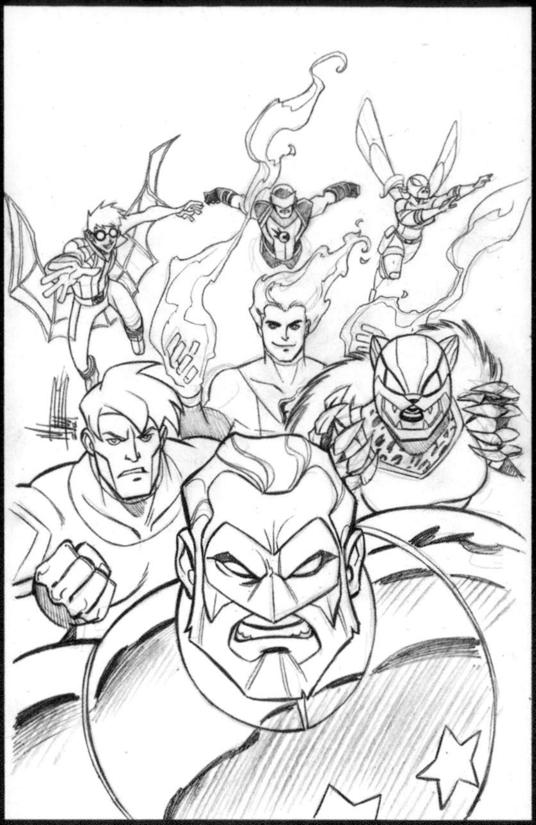

SKETCH VARIANT COVER BY: MIKE NORTON

DUSTY'S FILES

— THE PITCH —

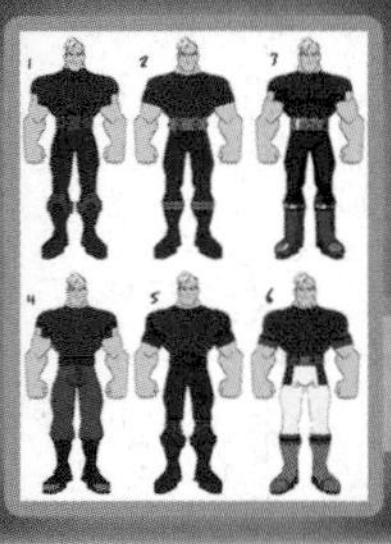

The road to NEW CRUSADERS was a long one, dating way back to 2005. Then-editor, now-President Mike Pellerito put a pitch together to bring back the Red Circle heroes in a new and interesting way. When the idea came up again in the summer of 2011, Mike worked with editor Paul Kaminski to take elements of that initial idea and combine them with a "Steel Sterling" pitch Paul was working on. "Super heroes for everyone" was the battle cry, and from there the series was formed.

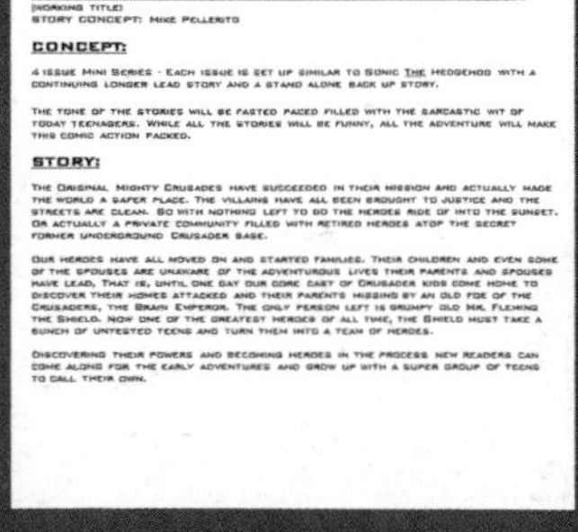

MLJ HEROES (MIGHTY LEGENDS OF JUSTICE)
(WORKING TITLE)
STORY CONCEPT: MIKE PELLERITO

CONCEPT:

4 ISSUE MINI SERIES - EACH ISSUE IS SET UP SIMILAR TO SONIC THE HEDGEHOG WITH A CONTINUING LONGER LEAD STORY AND A STAND ALONE BACK UP STORY.

THE TONE OF THE STORIES WILL BE FASTED PACED FILLED WITH THE SARCASTIC WIT OF TODAY TEENAGERS. WHILE ALL THE STORIES WILL BE FUNNY, ALL THE ADVENTURE WILL MAKE THIS COMIC ACTION PACKED.

STORY:

THE ORIGINAL MIGHTY CRUSADES HAVE SUCCEEDED IN THEIR MISSION AND ACTUALLY MADE THE WORLD A SAFER PLACE. THE VILLAINS HAVE ALL BEEN BROUGHT TO JUSTICE AND THE STREETS ARE CLEAN. SO WITH NOTHING LEFT TO DO THE HEROES RIDE OF INTO THE SUNSET. OR ACTUALLY A PRIVATE COMMUNITY FILLED WITH RETIRED HEROES ATOP THE SECRET FORMER UNDERGROUND CRUSADER BASE.

OUR HEROES HAVE ALL MOVED ON AND STARTED FAMILIES. THEIR CHILDREN AND EVEN SOME OF THE SPOUSES ARE UNAWARE OF THE ADVENTUROUS LIVES THEIR PARENTS AND SPOUSES HAVE LEAD, THAT IS, UNTIL ONE DAY OUR CORE CAST OF CRUSADER KIDS COME HOME TO DISCOVER THEIR HOMES ATTACKED AND THEIR PARENTS MISSING BY AN OLD FOE OF THE CRUSADERS, THE BRAIN EMPEROR. THE ONLY PERSON LEFT IS GRUMPY OLD MR. FLEMING THE SHIELD. NOW ONE OF THE GREATEST HEROES OF ALL TIME, THE SHIELD MUST TAKE A BUNCH OF UNTESTED TEENS AND TURN THEM INTO A TEAM OF HEROES.

DISCOVERING THEIR POWERS AND BECOMING HEROES IN THE PROCESS NEW READERS CAN COME ALONG FOR THE EARLY ADVENTURES AND GROW UP WITH A SUPER GROUP OF TEENS TO CALL THEIR OWN.

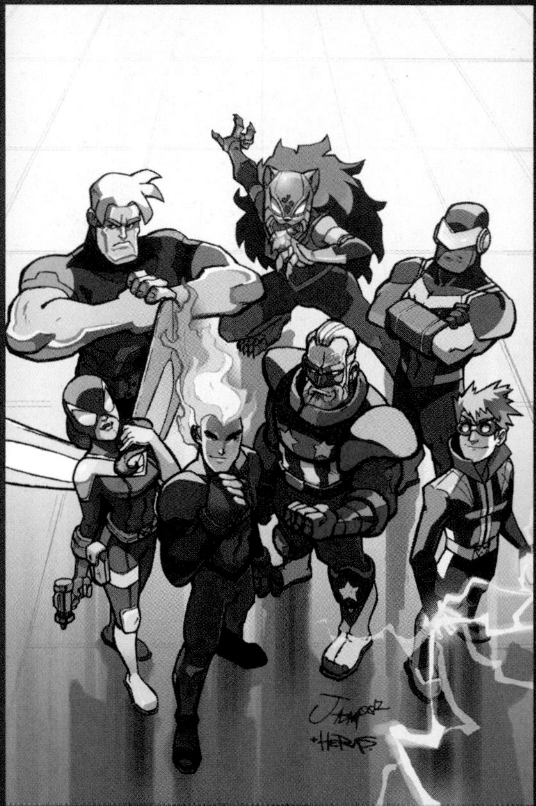

VARIANT COVER BY: RYAN JAMPOLE & MATT HERMS

ISSUE 2 VARIANT COVER

BY: CHRISCROSS AND THOMAS MASON

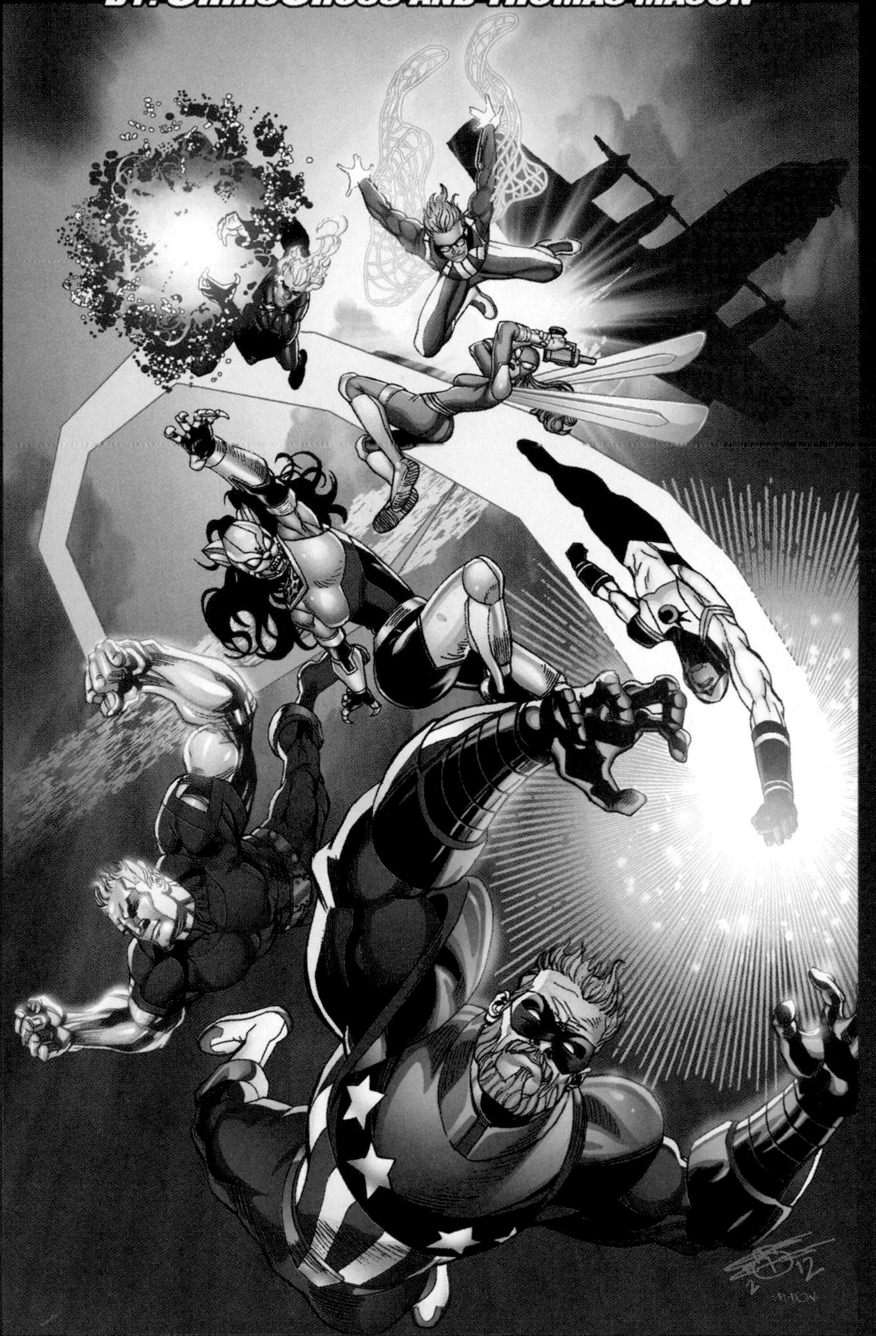

DUSTY'S FILES
— THE CAST —

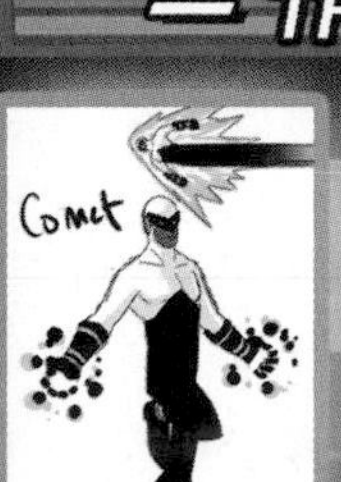
Comet

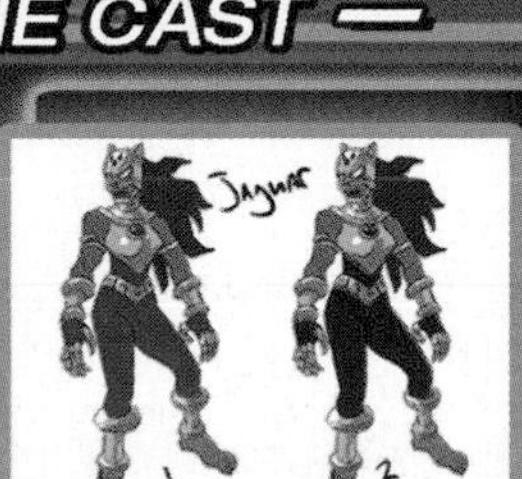
Jaguar
1
2

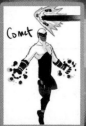

Joe Higgins, the Original Shield, was chosen early on to lead this new team, and from there everyone picked some of their favorites from the previous CRUSADERS incarnations. Initial series artist Ben Bates worked with the Brain Trust to redesign the classic Crusaders costumes for a new era, and from there the team took shape.

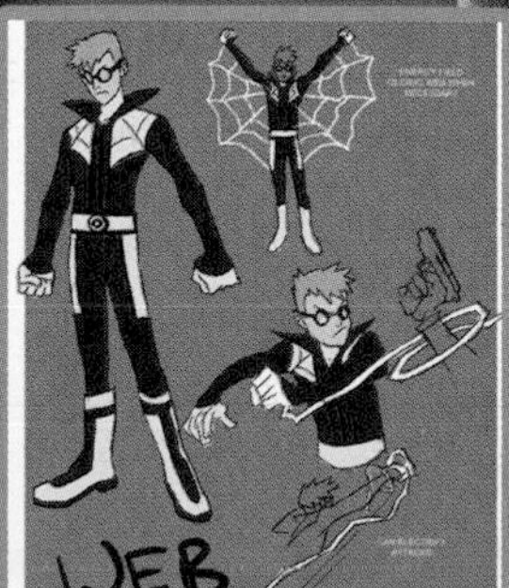
WEB

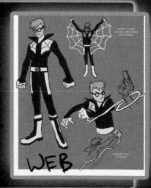

ISSUE 3 VARIANT COVER

BY: SANFORD GREENE

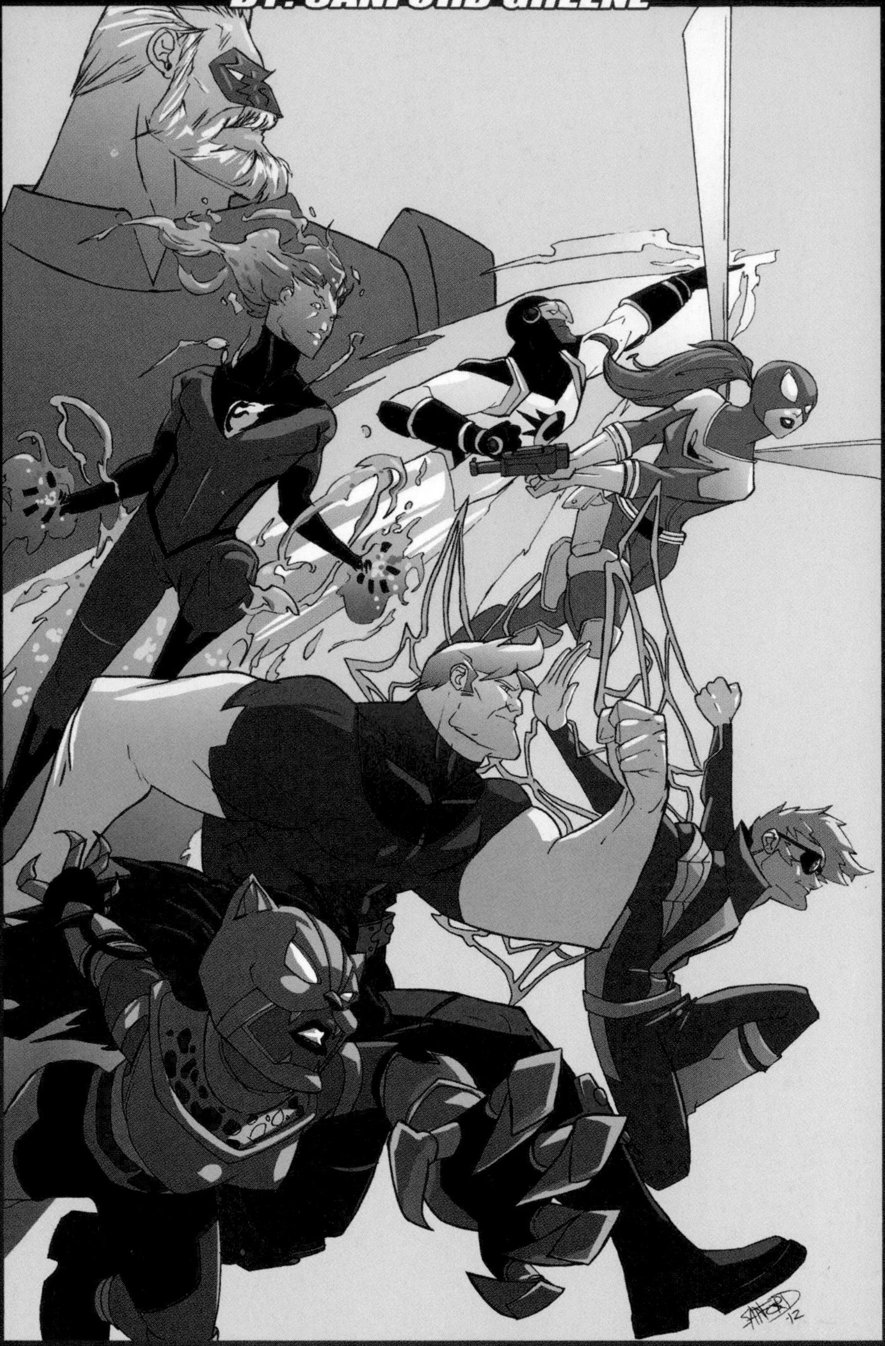

DUSTY'S FILES — THE BRAINTRUST —

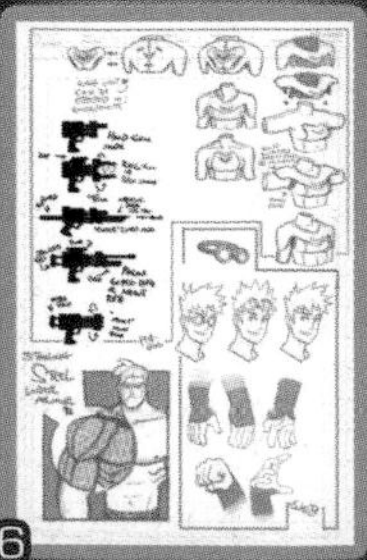

Writer Ian Flynn was brought on right after the basic premise got the green light, and together with Ben Bates took the types of storytelling they were doing in the SONIC THE HEDGEHOG™ and MEGA MAN™ comics and applied that to super heroes. Once the cast and the look was nailed down, the "braintrust" at Archie worked with Ian to plot out the first several issues of the comic, with some threads that are so large they are only peripherally included in RISE OF THE HEROES.

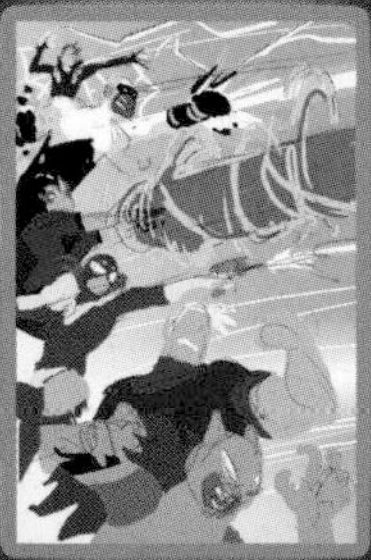

ISSUE 4 VARIANT COVER

BY: RICH BUCKLER & THOMAS MASON

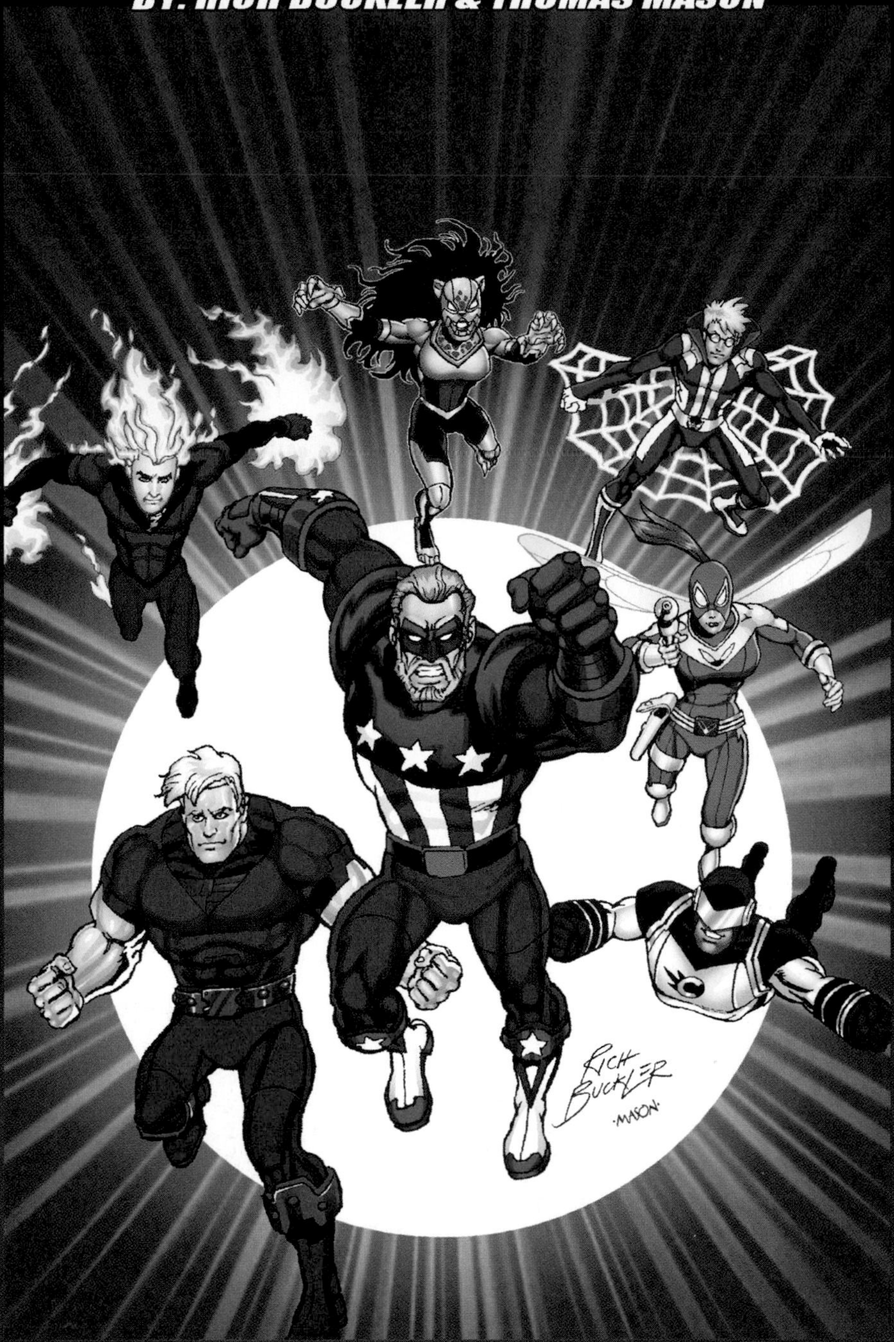
RICH BUCKLER
MASON

DUSTY'S FILES — THE LEGACY —

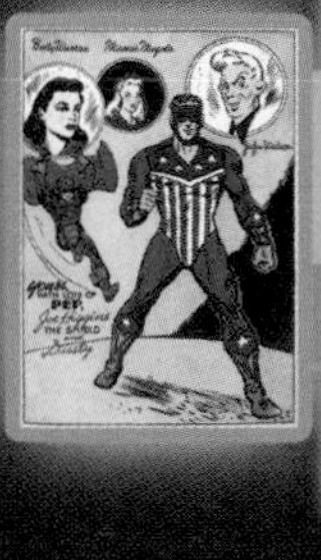

The approach was to keep the original heroes as they were – that was the main surviving element from Mike's 2005 pitch. The heroes were the same heroes from the '40s, '50s and beyond – but back issues from those eras were hard to come by, so the New Crusaders App was created to allow readers both new and old access to the entire backlog of the Red Circle universe. Veteran readers will definitely pick up on nuances and nods, but the story is about the new characters – the teens thrust into this crazy world of super heroes and villains. Their journey is the reader's journey.

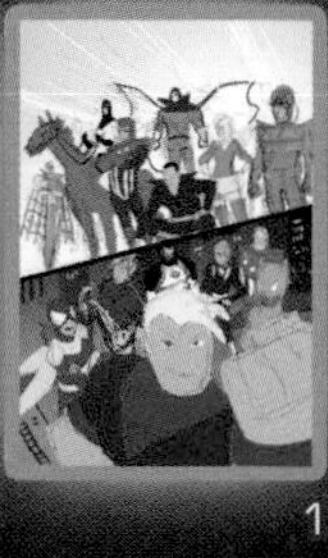

ISSUE 5 VARIANT COVER

BY: FRANCESCO FRANCAVILLA

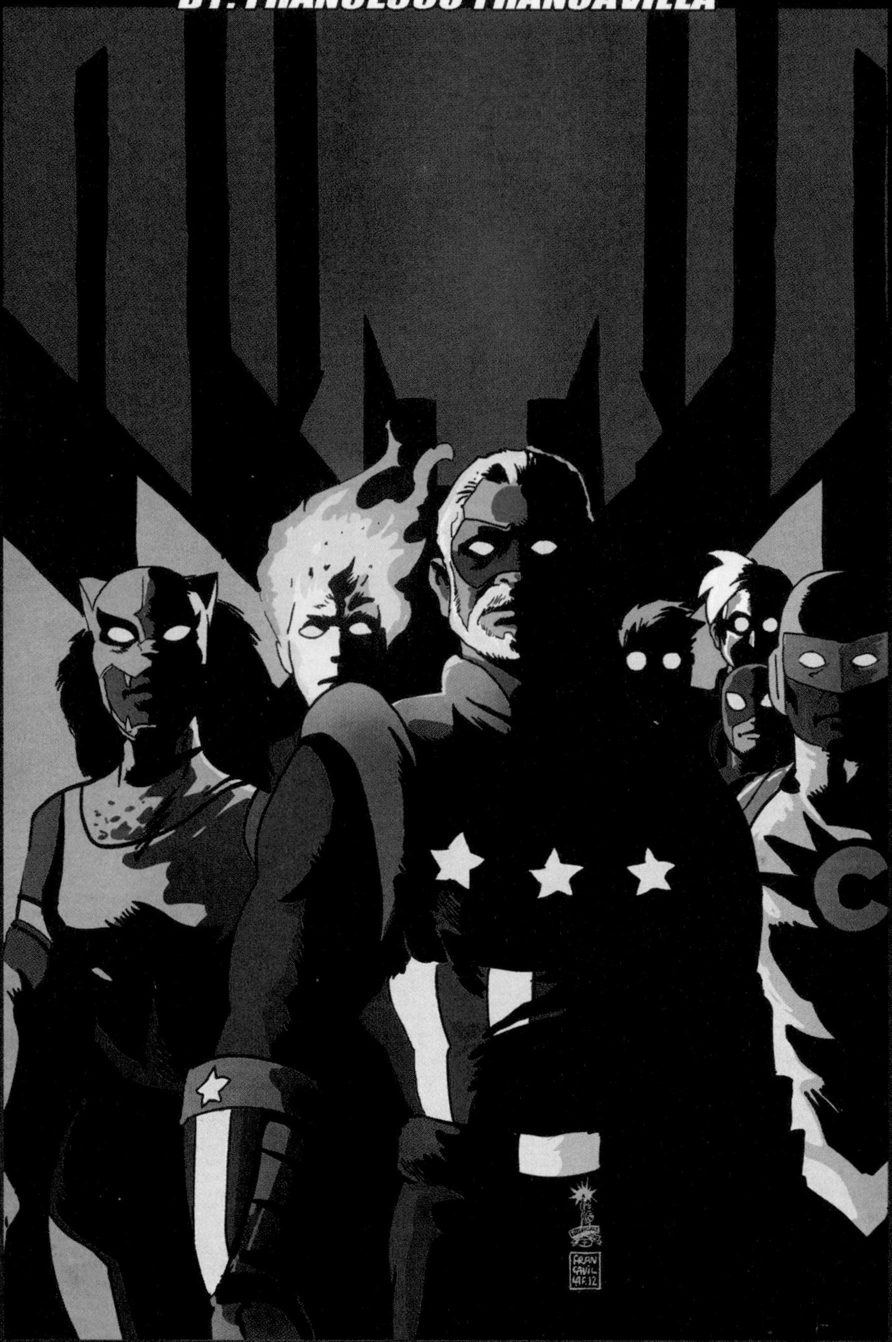

DUSTY'S FILES — THE VILLAINS —

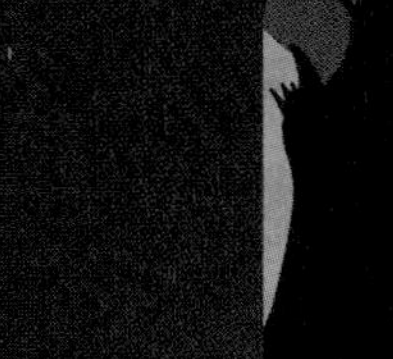

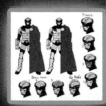

At the top of the villain pantheon is the Brain Emperor, who is the driving evil force for the series, in addition to the New Crusaders' personal lives and conflicts. Brain Emperor is the same character from the previous Red Circle incarnations, but with an updated look courtesy of artist Ben Bates. Some of Ben's earlier ideas had a more regal look, but the look that appears in the comic is very much a story element and has to do with where this guy went when he was vanquished so many years ago.

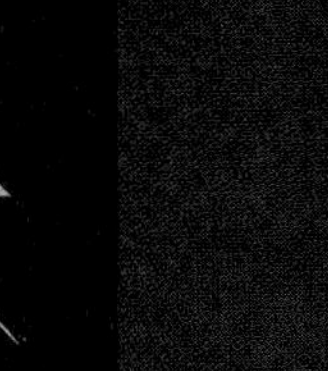

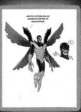

ISSUE 6 VARIANT COVER

BY: FIONA STAPLES

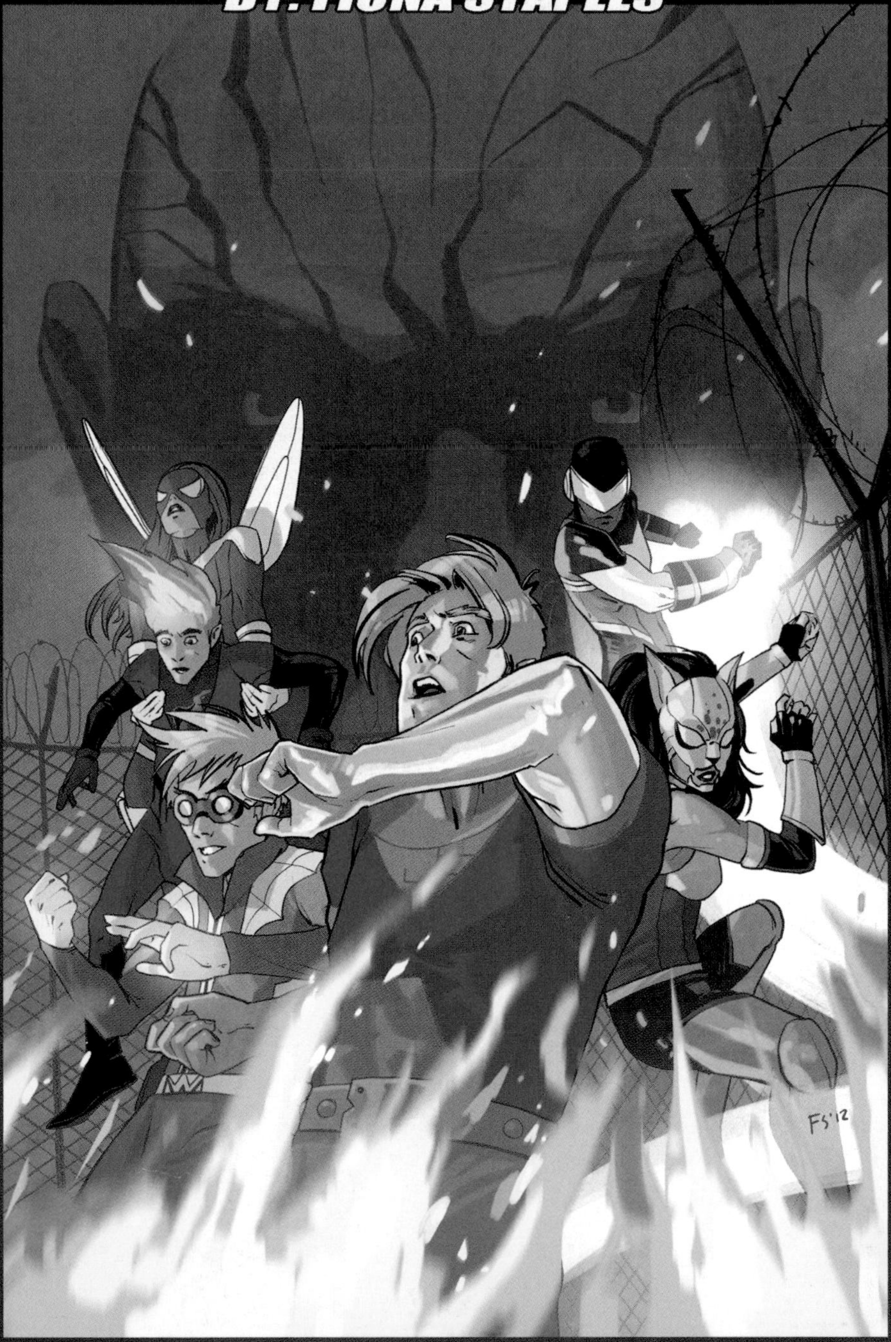
FS'12

DUSTY'S FILES — THE FUTURE —

NEW CRUSADERS: DARK TOMORROW picks up exactly where RISE OF THE HEROES left off, with the kids still reeling from the traumatic prison riot that left Fireball dead. DARK TOMORROW will take our kids back to normal high school, where they begin to juggle their super hero identities with the normal trials of high school life. We will also finally learn the answers to the burning questions surrounding the disappearance of Mr. Justice, and just what the deal is with this "blue ribbon." Get ready for a wild ride from here on out!

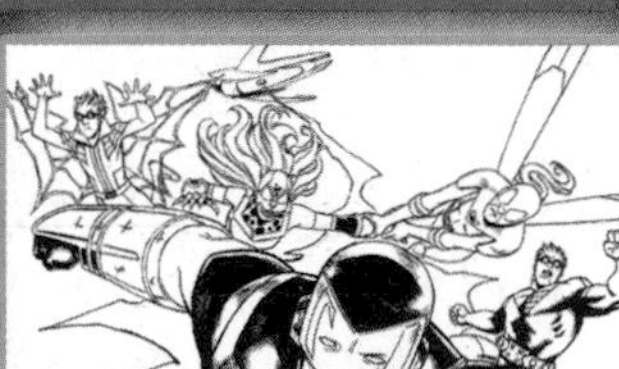

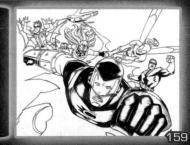

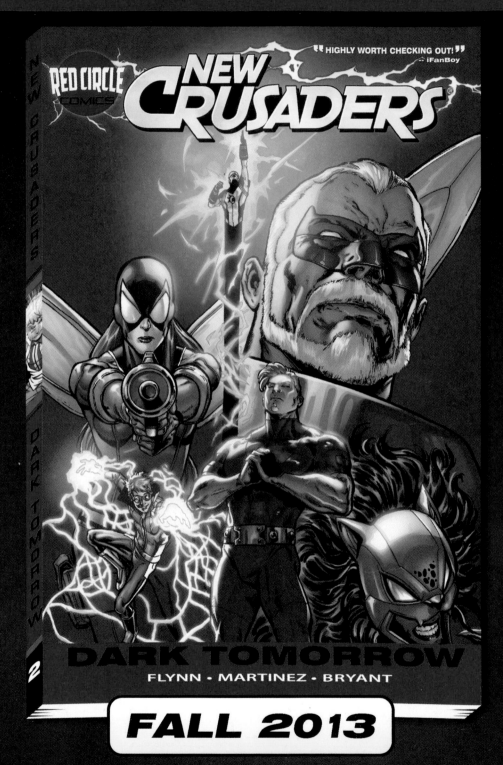